Here's what they're saying . . . .

". . .The treatment is logical, methodical and yet easy to read.
. . .This is a book that I can recommend without reservation. . .
. . .joins my list of best books."

PERSONAL COMPUTER WORLD

". . .No knowledge is assumed on the part of the reader—unless
such knowledge has been previously put forth. . ."

ELEMENTARY ELECTRONICS

". . .an engineering tool of value. . ."

POWERCONVERSION INTERNATIONAL

". . .For beginners in the field, a cover-to-cover reading would be
well worthwhile. . .

". . .The conversational style liberally sprinkled with charts,
photographs and diagrams leads to a pleasantly educating
experience. . ."

INTERFACE AGE

FROM CHIPS TO SYSTEMS:

An Introduction to Microprocessors

FROM CHIPS TO SYSTEMS:

An Introduction to Microprocessors

Rodnay Zaks

Berkeley • Paris • Düsseldorf • London

Cover Design by Daniel Le Noury
Technical illustration and design by J. Trujillo Smith

Library of Congress Card Number: 81-51126
ISBN 0-89588-063-6
First Edition 1981
Printed in the United States of America
10 9 8 7 6

Contents

CHAPTER 1   1

FUNDAMENTAL CONCEPTS

CHAPTER 2   37

INTERNAL OPERATION OF A MICROPROCESSOR

CHAPTER 8   393

MICROPROCESSOR PROGRAMMING

CHAPTER 9   415

ASSEMBLY AND HIGH-LEVEL PROGRAMMING

CHAPTER 10   475

SYSTEM DEVELOPMENT

CHAPTER **11**   505
THE FUTURE

APPENDICES   513

Preface

This book is an updated version of *Microprocessors: From Chips To Systems*, originally published in 1977. It has been completely revised and re-illustrated. It follows the same organization as the original edition and the main changes are in the descriptions of new components. The design techniques and implementation philosophies are unchanged from the earlier editions and will probably remain valid for many years to come because microprocessor design is now standardized.

Comments from the readers of previous editions were an important consideration during the revision process. Any new comments on this updated edition are welcomed by the author.

Introduction

This book is written for everyone who wants to understand how a microprocessor operates and how a complete system is assembled from chips. In particular, it is an important resource for students, scientists, and engineers, as well as the nontechnical reader. Surprisingly, no preliminary knowledge of computer or microprocessor technology is needed to understand this book. The concepts are carefully defined, each in turn, and the text is presented in a simple and progressive way.

The information presented is applicable to *any microprocessor* although many specific examples are given. You are introduced to concepts and design principles common to all microprocessors. You are given the standard rules of design and shown how they apply to various microprocessors. You are shown both the differences between various microprocessors, and the advantages and disadvantages of specific microprocessors.

This book is organized to introduce you quickly and effectively to the inner workings of a microprocessor. It will help you understand how a microprocessor works, even if you have had no prior experience with electronics.

Chapter 1 provides the basic definitions necessary to understand microprocessors and introduces many basic concepts.

Chapter 2 takes you inside a microprocessor. At first glance this chapter may appear very technical, but once you understand all the definitions presented in Chapter 1, you will find this internal journey both easy and enjoyable. By the end of Chapter 2, you will be familiar with the operation of a standard microprocessor. You will know how instructions are executed and how the automatic sequencing of instructions is accomplished.

Chapter 3 then examines the other components that make up a complete system, from the memory chips to the input/output chips.

Once you become familiar with the various types of chips used in a microprocessor system, you will probably want to know about the advantages and disadvantages of the various microprocessors available today. *Chapter 4* provides this information.

Chapter 5 teaches you how to put together a system easily and rapidly.

You are shown how to connect the basic chips including the memory and input/output, wire by wire. Various design strategies are discussed and evaluated according to specific standards of efficiency and economy. By the end of this chapter you will know how to assemble a system.

Chapter 6 then examines the main application areas for microprocessors, ranging from computer systems to consumer applications. It explains that most microprocessors use a common system organization, which greatly simplifies the hardware design.

Once you have assembled a system, you still have two tasks to complete: connecting the system to the outside world and programming it. Chapters 7 (Interfacing Techniques), 8 (Microprocessor Programming), and 9 (Assembly and High-Level Programming) address these issues.

Chapter 7 presents the techniques necessary for connecting the main input/output devices and peripherals, from keyboard to floppy disk. *Chapter 8* teaches the basic definitions and techniques for programming microprocessors. *Chapter 9* examines the resources available in assembly language, and surveys high-level languages.

Finally, *Chapter 10* looks at the tools available for efficiently developing a system, from a development system to in-circuit emulation. In conclusion, *Chapter 11* forecasts future developments.

Sequential reading of this book is recommended, but not necessary. We recommend that you read every chapter even though you may be familiar with much of its content.

Microprocessor technology has become an essential component of the industrial world today. It is the author's contention that it is possible to learn about microprocessors in a short time. This book represents a step in that direction.

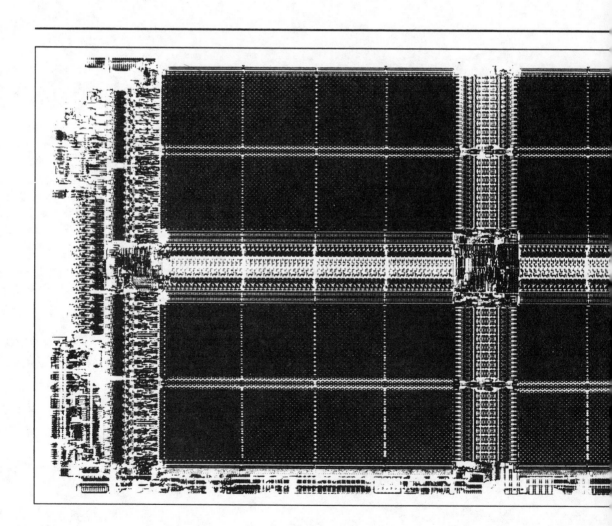

CHAPTER 1

FUNDAMENTAL CONCEPTS

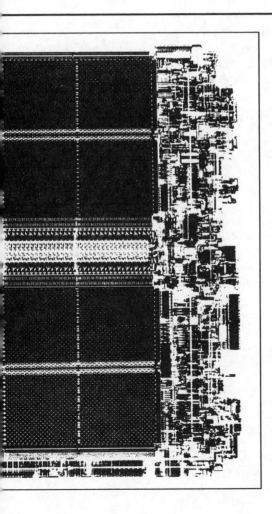

INTRODUCTION

In this chapter we will discuss the principles of operation of a computer system, along with the basic definitions relating to microprocessors and microcomputers. We will also review the history and manufacturing process of microprocessors in order to facilitate the evaluation of existing products and the understanding of future ones.

After reading this chapter, you will be familiar with the terms used in describing microprocessors and microcomputers. We will then proceed to the actual operation of a microprocessor in Chapter 2.

All the concepts and terms introduced in this chapter are fundamental and should be well understood.

BASIC DEFINITIONS

In order to describe precisely the systems and components that will be presented in this book, specific words and abbreviations will be used. Every effort has been made to define these words before they are used. You will learn the language of microprocessors as we proceed.

Here are some initial definitions. Others will be presented throughout the chapter.

An *integrated circuit* (IC) is a device that integrates a circuit of several electronic components in a single package. The number of logical components, typically transistors, may range in number from 2 to more than 100,000.

Large-scale integration (LSI) designates the new technology that integrates thousands of transistors on a single integrated circuit (IC).

A *chip* is the small rectangular piece of silicon on which most integrated circuits are implemented (see Figure 1.1). By extension, "chip" is often used to refer to the package containing the chip (see Figure 1.2).

A *microprocessor* is an LSI component that implements most of the functions of a traditional processor on a single chip.

A *microcomputer* is a computer whose central processing unit (CPU) has been implemented with a microprocessor. Typically, a microcomputer uses one or more boards to implement all the functions of a complete computer. However, simplified computers can be implemented on a single chip and are called *single-chip microcomputers*.

A *microprocessor system* refers to the electronic boards required to implement a functional computer. Generally, this does not include the cabinet, power supply, and peripherals.

A *microcomputer system* refers to the complete set of devices required to use and operate the computer, including the peripherals such as terminal, printer, and disks.

The *binary number system* is used to represent all information in the computer, whether program or data. Each character, number, or entity is encoded internally as a group of 0s and 1s. Each 0 or 1 is called a binary digit or *bit*. A group of eight bits is called a *byte*.

ORGANIZATION OF A COMPUTER

Microprocessors are used, along with other LSI components, to implement computers. The microprocessor implements most of the functions of the *processing unit*, while the other components provide the memory, input/output, and other required functions. The logical

Figure 1.1: A Chip

organization of a computer system is described in this section and each of the functions is explained.

All general-purpose computers have the same basic logical organization with five fundamental units, as shown in Figure 1.3. Each unit will now be described.

The *central processing unit* or *processor* is shown at the center of the illustration and includes two units: the *control unit* (CU) and the *arithmetic and logical unit* (ALU). The arithmetic and logical unit performs arithmetic and logical operations on the data passing through it. Typical arithmetic functions include addition and subtraction. Typical logical operations include logical AND, logical OR, and shift operations.

The main function of the control unit is to fetch, decode, and execute

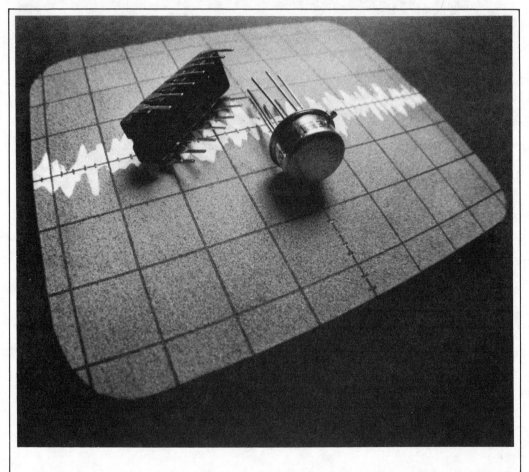

Figure 1.2: The LSI Package (left) and SSI "Can" (right)

the successive instructions of a *program* stored in the memory. The control unit sequences the operation of the entire system. In particular, it generates and manages the control signals necessary to synchronize operations, as well as the flow of program instructions and data within and outside the ALU. The CU controls the flow of information on the *address* and *data buses*, and interprets and manages the signals presented on the *control bus*. A *bus* is a means of transmitting signals; buses are described in the next section. The three standard buses used to interconnect a microprocessor system are the data bus, the address bus, and the control bus.

The control unit is generally connected to the ALU that it controls. Recall that this combination (CU and ALU) is known as the *central processing unit* (CPU). Thus, a microprocessor is basically a CPU on a chip.

In the designing of a computer, the CPU is not necessarily implemented as a *single* component. The CU can be separate from the ALU. For instance, *bit-slices* implement the ALU section of a traditional

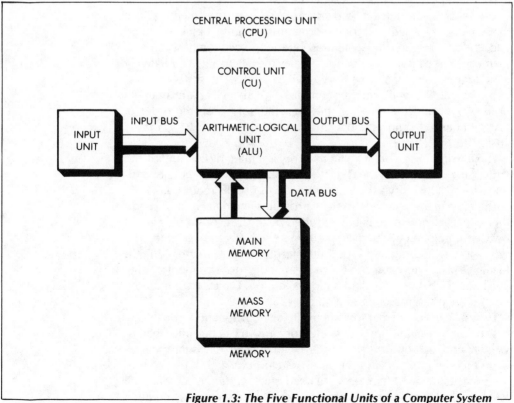

Figure 1.3: The Five Functional Units of a Computer System

computer exclusive of the control section. Chapter 5 provides more information on this topic.

The memory module, shown beneath the CPU in Figure 1.3, is used to store information. Functionally, the memory may contain two types of information: *programs* and *data*. A program is a sequence of instructions that has been coded into binary form so that it can reside in an electronic memory. Programs and data are used in different ways.

The *program* specifies the sequence of steps executed by the computer. Under the supervision of the control unit, each of the successive instructions of the program is fetched and deposited into a special register of the control unit, where it is decoded and executed. For example, a typical instruction might add the contents of two registers and then deposit the results back into a third register. This process is explained in Chapter 2.

The *data* contained in memory are processed by the ALU. Data may have a variety of formats. Typically, data are numbers or characters represented in the binary system.

The term *memory* usually designates several types of memory, and two types are nearly always used: *main memory* and *mass memory*. The main memory is used to store the programs currently being executed and the data required or generated by their execution. This type of memory must be fast (in order not to delay the CPU), and it is relatively expensive. Typical main memory devices are LSI integrated circuits and core. MOS (metal oxide semiconductor) LSI devices are generally used. A typical cycle time for the main memory is on the order of several hundred nanoseconds: 200 ns to 1 μs (1 ns = 10^{-9}s, 1 μs = 10^{-6}s).

The maximum size of the main memory is limited by cost and by the addressing capability of the CPU; therefore, a larger and more economical form of memory—the *mass memory*—is usually required.

The mass memory is used to store programs and data, or portions of them, that are not immediately required by the CPU or simply cannot be accommodated by the main memory. Accessing the mass memory slows down the computer, especially if frequent accesses are required. Ideally, a program is stored in the mass memory for permanent storage and loaded into the main memory for execution. Typical mass memory devices are disks, cassettes, and tapes.

Two logical types of memory are distinguished, depending on the access possibilities: random-access memory (RAM) can be either read or written, and read-only memory (ROM) can only be read once data has been entered into it. A ROM is non-volatile but may not be used for temporary storage: its contents are fixed once written. A standard LSI RAM is volatile and loses its contents when power is removed, creating the need for a permanent storage in the system, such as ROM or magnetic mass memory or both.

The two remaining modules in Figure 1.3 are the *input module* and the *output module*. These two modules are used to communicate with the outside world. The *input module*, which appears on the left of the illustration, supplies information to the ALU, or the memory. Typical input devices are a keyboard or a sensor, such as a temperature sensor, a presence detector, or a pressure sensor. The *output module* displays the data coming out of the ALU or executes commands. Typical output modules are a printer, a set of lights, or a control mechanism, such as a motor or a relay, also light-emitting diodes (LEDs) or liquid crystal display (LCDs), such as the ones used on digital watches and calculators.

THE BUSES

In the simplified diagram in Figure 1.3, all logical modules communicate with the central processing unit but not with each other. In practice, many interconnection designs may be used, generally through buses. Recall that a *bus* is a means of transmitting information, or signals, grouped by function. In the case of microprocessor systems, at least three standard buses are provided:

1. The *data bus* transmits data between units. Thus, an 8-bit microprocessor requires an 8-bit data bus in order to transmit 8 bits of data in parallel. Similarly, a 16-bit microprocessor requires a 16-bit data bus in order to transmit 16 bits of data in parallel. If the data bus is only eight bits wide, two successive transmissions will be required, thus slowing down the system. The data bus is bidirectional, i.e., it can transmit in both directions.

2. The *address bus* is used to select the origin or destination of signals transmitted on another bus or line. It carries addresses. Typically, the address bus selects a register within one of the system devices that is to be used as a source or destination of data. Traditionally, the standard address bus has 16 lines and can address 2^{16} (64K) locations (1K = 1024, or 2^{10}, in computer language).

3. The *control bus* synchronizes the activities of the system. It carries status and control information both to and from the microprocessor unit (MPU). For a control bus to be useful, at least 10 (but generally more) control lines are required.

Buses are implemented as actual communication lines. They may be laid down as a circuit on the chip itself (*internal* buses) or they may be cables (*external* buses). External buses may be expanded to facilitate the connection of special devices. An efficient bus design is crucial to the speed of the system. This point is explained in Chapter 2.

SUMMARY—COMPUTER ORGANIZATION

Each general-purpose computer system has five functional elements: the control unit (CU), the arithmetic and logical unit (ALU), the memory, and the input and output units (generally called I/O). These elements are interconnected by three buses: the data bus, the address bus, and the control bus.

A SIMPLE COMPUTER

To illustrate the principles of operation of a simple computing system, let us examine the operation of a pocket calculator (see Figure 1.4). Note that the grouping of functions in Figure 1.4 is slightly different from the grouping in Figure 1.3. In a pocket calculator, the calculator chip implements both the CPU and memory. Recall that the CPU provides the control and computing functions while the memory stores the program and data. The input/output control chip provides the

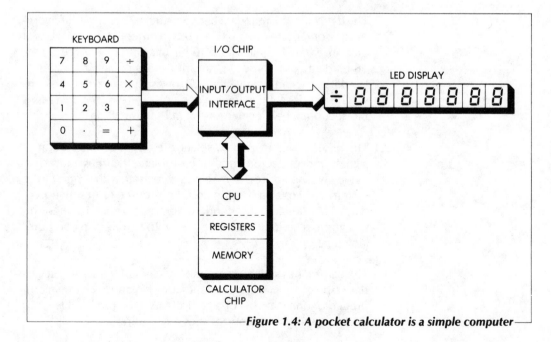

Figure 1.4: A pocket calculator is a simple computer

specialized interface required to sense or activate the input and output devices. The input module here is a hexadecimal (16-key) keyboard and the output module is an LED display with eight LEDs.

We will now consider a simple sequence illustrating the use of the components of a computing system: the input/output devices, the memory, and the CPU. This example will also introduce the concept of registers. Here is a typical sequence of events:

1. The user types in a number on the keyboard.

2. This number, a data item, is transmitted to the calculator chip via the I/O interface (see Figure 1.4), where it is stored in a special memory element called a *register*.

Typically, each CPU is equipped with several registers that it can access directly, using high speed buses. This set of registers is used to speed up operations on the information or data they contain. This is the fastest memory available to the processor.

In our example, this simple pocket calculator uses only three registers. Two registers are used to store the two data elements, or *operands*, on which an operation will be performed. Each data register can store a 6-digit decimal number in binary form along with its sign. The third register stores the operation to be performed, such as $+$, $-$, $\times$, or $\div$. Sometimes an additional register called "memory" is available for storing a number. The second data register is also used to store the result of the operation and is called the *accumulator*, as it accumulates the results of successive operations.

In this example, the *memory* (see Figure 1.4) contains only the program required to read the keyboard, and to convert the number into binary, perform the computations, and display the results. This program is stored in a (non-volatile) ROM on the chip.

3. Once the first number (up to six decimal digits) has been read from the keyboard, an operation is specified by hitting the appropriate key. The code for this operation is stored in the calculator's operator register until it can be executed. Let us assume that a $+$ is specified.

4. The second operand required for the addition is then typed in by the user, read and converted into binary form by the program, and stored in the second data register. The situation is shown in Figure 1.5.

5. Nothing happens until the user hits the operation key $=$. The user now hits $=$. This is sensed by the program and causes execution of the *arithmetic program* specified by the stored operator ($+$, in this case). The instructions of the addition program are executed as stored in the memory, the addition is performed, and the result is deposited in the

second data register, called the accumulator. This process is illustrated in Figure 1.6. Note that the previous number contained in the accumulator (12) is erased by the new total (18).

6. The result is sent from the accumulator to the LED display unit where it is displayed to the user. The result remains in the internal accumulator until it is cleared by turning the unit off or until a new operation is executed. Most calculators also provide a C (clear) key that can be used to clear any register.

SUMMARY—A SIMPLE COMPUTER

This example has shown how data is read in, and how a simple program is executed. It has also illustrated the role of the functional elements of a small computer. A new concept was introduced: the *register*. Registers are part of the *memory hierarchy* in a computer system. We will now examine the operation of the memory in more detail.

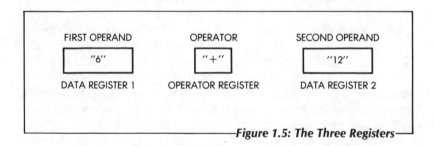

Figure 1.5: The Three Registers

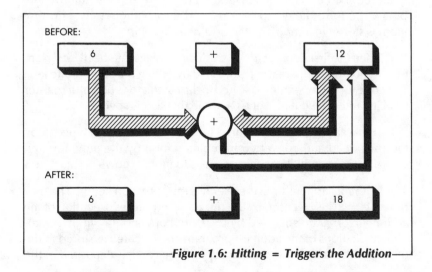

Figure 1.6: Hitting = Triggers the Addition

THE MEMORY

We will begin by clarifying the concepts of *memory hierarchy* and the actual *access mechanism* to information that has been stored in the memory.

MEMORY HIERARCHY

Two levels of memory have already been described: the main memory and the mass memory. A third level—the *internal registers* of the CPU—was introduced in the calculator example. Let us now examine each of these levels:

1. *Internal registers* are part of the ALU. They provide the fastest level of data memory available to the system. Typically, the contents of internal registers can be accessed by the ALU in less than 100 ns (versus 500 ns or more for the main memory). Usually there are few (from 8 to 64) internal registers.

2. *Main memory*, usually called "the memory" of a system, is implemented in one or more components, depending on its size. A typical size ranges from 4K to 64K bytes. Memory is now normally implemented in MOS/LSI technology. A limited amount of memory can even reside directly on the microprocessor chip itself, along with some input/output facilities. The device is then called a *microcomputer-on-a-chip*, as it incorporates all the logical elements of a computer on a single chip. "Standard" microprocessors require an external memory. Typical access time is 200-1000 ns.

3. *Mass memory* is used to provide low-cost, high-capacity storage. Special storage devices are used to store large quantities of data on inexpensive supports such as magnetic tape, cassette, and disk. Such storage media will typically store hundreds or thousands of K bytes (kilobytes) but are relatively slow when accessed frequently.

MEMORY ACCESS

A memory is logically organized in *words*. A *word* is a logical unit of information consisting of a number of bits (say 4, 8, 12, or 16 bits; recall that a bit is a binary digit that takes the value 0 or 1). An 8-bit microprocessor requires eight bits of data. The normal word size for an 8-bit microprocessor is therefore eight bits, i.e., the memory of an 8-bit microprocessor is logically structured in 8-bit words.

Eight bits are called a *byte*; four bits are called a *nibble*. The word size of an 8-bit microprocessor is thus a byte. Similarly, for a 16-bit processor the word size is normally two bytes.

The logical organization of a memory module is shown in Figure 1.7. We will now study it in more detail. The *width* of a memory is the number of bits that can be accessed simultaneously, i.e., its word-size (in this example, one byte). Bits are normally numbered from 0 to n. In the case of an 8-bit microprocessor (which is used as our "standard microprocessor" throughout most of the text), the position of a bit within the memory will, therefore, be referenced by a digit from 0 to 7. Each digit from 0 to 7 represents the *binary position* of the bit in the word.

In the binary system, the rightmost digit (bit 0) represents 2^0; the next bit on the left, bit 1, represents 2^1, and so on. This is why bit positions are usually labeled from 0 to 7 rather than from 1 to 8, and also why they are labeled from right to left rather than from left to right.

The "height", or size, of a memory is the number of words it contains. The position of a word within the memory is called its *address*. The first word of the memory has address 0, the next word has address 1, and so on. For reasons of efficiency in decoding, the size of the memory is normally a power of two, e.g., 256, 512, 1K, 2K, or 4K words.

In order to read the contents of a word in the memory, it is necessary to specify its address. Each memory module is therefore connected to the address bus. A typical address bus includes 16 lines so that it may specify up to 2^{16} (64K) locations. If the actual memory size is smaller than 64K, fewer address lines may be used.

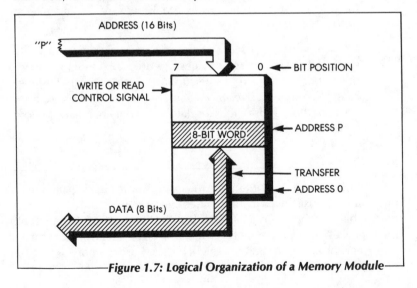

Figure 1.7: Logical Organization of a Memory Module

In order to reference one word in the memory, a bit pattern specifying the address of the desired word in the memory is sent on the address bus. The bits coming from the address bus are gated to a decoder within the chip. The *decoder* selects the word at the specified address within the memory. In response to a control signal, such as WRITE for a WRITE operation, a word is written from the data bus into the memory. In the case of a read operation, a word is read from the memory to the data bus. After a certain *access time* the data becomes available on the eight output pins of the memory chip. (Words are eight bits wide in our example). These eight pins are connected to the data bus.

A logical question here might be: why are there only 8 bits of data coming out of a memory that is receiving 16 bits of address? This is an important point to clarify. There is no direct relationship between the number of bits coming out of the memory as data and the number of address bits coming in. The address bits specify a *position* within the memory and are used to *select* one-word locations through special decoders. The data word corresponding to the selected position can be of arbitrary length, from one to p bits. As an example, a small memory chip might include only 64 words × 8 bits. In this case, the address bus required to select a word in this memory would require only six lines ($2^6 = 64$). However, for each of the specified 64 addresses that might come in on this reduced address bus, there would still be 8 bits of data leaving the memory during a read operation. If the memory should be large, say 64K locations, 16 bits of *address* would be required, even though there would be only 8 bits of *data* on the data bus.

Let us review the sequence for a WRITE operation. An address is specified on the address bus and the data is placed on the data bus. An order, WRITE, is sent to the memory through the control bus, and the memory writes the data presented on the data bus (8 bits in our example) at the specified memory location. The time required to write data in the memory is called the *memory cycle time*. It is normally longer than the access time by about 20 to 50 percent.

Many microprocessor programs used for control applications require fewer than 4K words for program and data. Addressing 4K words requires only 12 bits. Four lines of the address bus are therefore not required for memory addressing. These remaining lines may be used for selecting other devices connected to the system buses, such as input/output devices. The address bus is not used exclusively to address the memory and can be used to address any device, or, more precisely, any register within any device that is connected to the system buses. A *register* is broadly defined here as any addressable memory location in any device.

Note: several words of caution should be included here. First, about the meaning of K: a 4K memory is a memory containing 4K *words*. A 4K memory-chip, on the other hand, is a chip containing 4K *bits*, not 4K *words*. When referring to a component (a chip), K refers to bits; when referring to a memory system, K traditionally refers to words (8-bit words or 16-bit words, for example, depending on the processor). Remember that K refers to the number of logical elements of the device.

Second, an instruction stored in the memory does not necessarily occupy a single word, but may occupy one or more words, depending on the instruction itself. For an instruction set that uses one to three bytes, instructions will require 8, 16, or 24 bits of memory. To read a 2-byte instruction from the memory into the control unit of the microprocessor, two successive read operations from the memory are required (assuming an 8-bit data bus).

Third, two bit positions within a word play a special role in microprocessor systems. The rightmost bit of a word, usually labeled bit 0, is called the *least-significant bit*, or LSB, as it carries the smallest weight in the binary representation of data. The leftmost bit, usually labeled bit 7, is the *most-significant bit*, MSB. The LSB and the MSB play a special role in view of testing limitations inherent to many microprocessors. Most 8-bit microprocessors can directly test only the value of the leftmost bit (the MSB) of the data contained in their accumulator. This bit happens to be the *sign bit* in the *two's complement* notation generally used to represent numbers.

Bit 0, the LSB, is the second most convenient bit to use as it can be tested within the ALU after a single right-shift operation. For this reason, status information from input or output devices usually appears in either bit position 7 of a register or in bit position 0.

The techniques and various components used to implement the main memory are described in Chapter 3.

SUMMARY—MEMORY

We have just described and illustrated all the functional elements of a system. We will now introduce additional definitions and, in the process, review some terms that have already been introduced. Then, having learned the basic vocabulary of the microprocessor "language", we will go on to see how a microprocessor is manufactured and to learn how microprocessors came into existence.

BASIC MICROPROCESSOR DEFINITIONS

The following important definitions are organized into three categories: hardware, firmware and software, large-scale integration, and the microprocessor. (*Note*: In addition to this section, there is a list of acronyms presented in Appendix F of this book).

HARDWARE, FIRMWARE AND SOFTWARE

The *hardware* refers to the physical components of a system. The *software* refers to the programs. The *firmware* refers to the micro-programs. By extension, the term firmware is also frequently applied to any program residing in read-only memory, i.e., a program that cannot be changed (a combination of hardware and software).

A *microprogram* is a sequencing program for the control unit of any processor. Typically, a microprogram interprets the external *instruction set* of a "machine." (The term *machine* refers to any computer).

The *instruction set* is the list of instructions available to the programmer that can be used to give direct orders to the machine, such as: "Add Register 1 to Register 2." The instruction sets of a few typical microprocessors are presented in the Appendix.

A microprogram is not a program for a microprocessor. A microprocessor program is simply called a *program*. There is no significant difference between a *microprocessor program* and a *minicomputer program*, except that a microprocessor program is usually more difficult to write and may control different components than are controlled by a minicomputer program. Programming techniques for a microcomputer and a minicomputer are essentially similar except that more hardware knowledge is sometimes required in the case of microprocessors because of their reduced instruction set.

Remember that a microprogram is fundamentally different from a normal, user-written program. Typically, in a monolithic microprocessor (a microprocessor on a single chip), the microprogram performs the sequencing of the control unit and executes the desired instruction set. However, some manufacturers use the term *microprogram* to refer to any program executing on a microcomputer or stored in ROM.

LARGE-SCALE INTEGRATION

LSI (large-scale integration) technology appeared in the late sixties and refers to the technology used to implement 1000 or more transistors on a single chip. A typical microprocessor implements over 3000 transistors on a single chip. The fabrication process is described later in this chapter.

Since the birth of the transistor around 1946-47, component densities per square millimeter have continually increased. First, the integrated circuit (IC) appeared, then SSI technology (small-scale integration), then MSI technology (medium-scale integration), then the LSI technology (large-scale integration) that is used today. Technology is now rapidly progressing toward VLSI (very-large-scale integration), and soon toward SLSI (super-large-scale integration).

Although there are no strict borders between SSI, MSI, LSI, and VLSI, an approximate classification is the following:

SSI = 1 to 10 transistors per chip

MSI = 10 to 100-500 transistors

LSI = 100-500 transistors to 10,000-20,000 transistors

VLSI = 10,000-20,000 transistors to 50,000-100,000 transistors

SLSI = Over 100,000 transistors.

THE MICROPROCESSOR

With these new terms, a microprocessor can now be defined more precisely: a *microprocessor* is an LSI component that implements the functions of an arithmetic and logical unit plus its associated control unit on a single chip.

In practice, most "monolithic" microprocessors require at least two and sometimes three components in order to implement these functions. For example, in order to implement the functions of a CPU, the Intel 8080 requires not only the 8080 MPU, but also (at the least) the 8224 clock circuit plus its crystal, and the 8228 "system controller."

A picture of an actual microprocessor is shown in Figure 1.8. The lid has been removed in order to expose the *chip* underneath. The *chip* is a rectangular piece of silicon (or *die*) on which the circuit is implemented. The chip is bonded to the *package*, in this case a DIP (dual in-line package). The pins of the package can be directly inserted in the holes on a board or some other medium. Typical microprocessors have a maximum of 40 to 48 pins. This is not due to a physical limitation of packages but rather to an economic limitation: industrial incoming testers are generally limited to 40-pin DIPs. An incoming tester may cost $500,000 or more and is not frequently replaced.

The small white rectangles appearing on both sides of the chip inside the exposed portion of the package are the *pads*. These pads are connected to the pins via an internal printed circuit inside the package. Thin gold wires are bonded to the pads belonging to the package and to the pads on the outside of the chip itself. The chip is thus electrically connected to the pins of the DIP via the gold wire, the pads, and finally the printed circuit.

MANUFACTURING A MICROPROCESSOR

MOS technology (MOS stands for metal oxide semiconductor) is the technology used to create transistors and other components on the surface of the small piece of silicon called the chip. It is the technology currently used to achieve the densities that characterize LSI microprocessors.

The fabrication of a transistor on a chip will illustrate the manufacturing process. Then, major technologies will be surveyed. A basic understanding of these technologies helps in evaluating the characteristics of the devices.

Let us first examine the process by which a chip is created.

MAKING A CHIP

In order to make an MOS circuit, a single crystal of silicon must first be grown. This crystal is then sliced in a specific direction into very thin circular slices called *wafers*. Several dozen chips can be created from a

Figure 1.8: A Microprocessor: Chip, DIP, Package and Pins

single wafer. These chips will be microprocessor chips, memory chips, or other modules. *Dice* (a die is an uncut "chip" during the manufacturing process) are created on the wafer by a photolithographic process analogous to the commercial printing of photographs. Electrically positive and negative areas are created in the silicon by injecting impurities (this is called *doping*) through a process of masking and diffusion. Once complete dice have been created on a wafer, the wafer is tested at special test points created on the edges and in the center of the wafer. If the tests are successful, the wafer will then be scribed and broken into individual *chips*. Each chip is mounted on a package, connected through gold wires to the pads of the package, and then subjected to further visual, electrical, and environmental tests. After that, the package is sealed, and it undergoes final tests. Sealed packages that successfully pass the production tests are then sold.

Fabrication of a PMOS Transistor

PMOS refers to p-channel technology. (Other types of MOS technologies are described later). Figure 1.9 shows a typical PMOS transistor using n-type silicon that has been doped with p-type impurities in order to create the source and drain of the transistor. Areas to be doped are defined by a mask. The doping agents are boron and phosphorus. The traditional process used to define these areas is the photolithographic process in which the mask is printed on the silicon. A new process uses electron beams. Impurities (boron or phosphorus) are injected into the exposed area of the silicon, generally by thermal diffusion. An ion-implantation process is also used for more precise gate alignment,

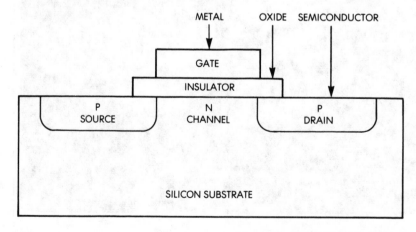

Figure 1.9: P-Channel Transistor

thus reducing the parasitic capacitance and improving switching speed. This last process, however, is more expensive as it cannot be used to operate in batch mode and requires an accelerator.

At the center of Figure 1.9 is the *gate* of the transistor. It has been implemented by depositing a layer of metal. Depending on whether silicon or aluminum is used, the device is called a *silicon-gate* or *aluminum-gate* transistor. The gate is isolated from the substrate by a layer of silicon dioxide that has been grown on top of the silicon. The transistor is switched on or off by applying a bias between the source and the gate. Let us examine what happens.

A negative bias with respect to the source is now applied to the gate. The presence of negative charges in the gate causes positive charges (holes) to appear in the *channel* between the source and drain. There will then be a conduction channel between the source and the drain, and the transistor will be turned on. This is a p-channel transistor or PMOS transistor. The structure of an n-channel transistor is essentially similar, but the polarities are reversed, as is shown in Figure 1.10.

We will now describe the actual fabrication in more detail. The silicon wafer is manufactured by cutting a monocrystal of silicon in the appropriate direction, for example, direction 111 of the lattice (see Figure 1.11). A thick layer of oxide (5000 to 6000 Å, where $1 Å = 10^{-10}$m) is then deposited on the silicon. (See Figure 1.12.) A first mask is used to define the p-zones within the silicon. The p-zones will be the source and drain areas of transistors. A photosensitive emulsion is deposited on top of the silicon oxide and a mask is used to imprint the areas to be doped. The oxide facing the areas to be doped is then removed by

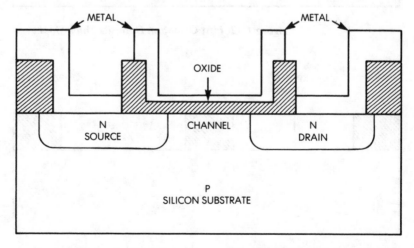

Figure 1.10: N-Channel Transistor

chemical etching (see Figure 1.13). Doping can then be performed on the exposed areas: p-type impurities are introduced in the silicon, usually by a thermal diffusion process (see Figure 1.14). A thick layer of oxide is again grown on top of the silicon (perhaps 10,000 to 15,000 Å; see Figure 1.15). A new mask is used to define the areas that will later be metallized. The oxide is removed at these locations (see Figure 1.16). A thin layer of oxide (1000 to 1500 Å; see Figure 1.17) is then grown during the last, or *gate*, oxidation.

Figure 1.11: The Silicon Substrate

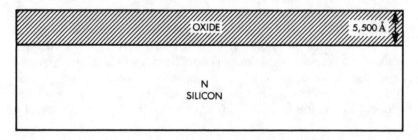

Figure 1.12: First Oxidation Deposits Thick SiO_2 Layer

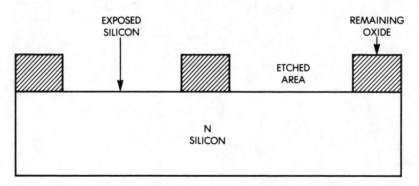

Figure 1.13: Etching Removes Oxide

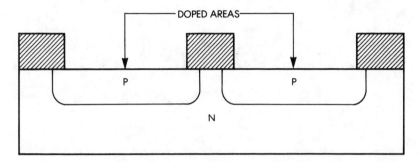

Figure 1.14: Doping is Performed by Thermal Diffusion

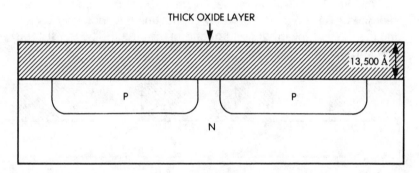

Figure 1.15: Second, Thick Oxidation

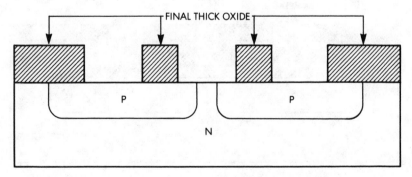

Figure 1.16: Second Oxide Removal

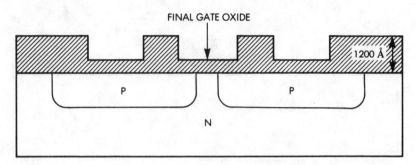

FINAL GATE OXIDE

1200 Å

P   P

N

Figure 1.17: Gate Oxidation

A third and final oxide-removal phase is performed that exposes the source and drain areas that are to be connected to the rest of the circuit after the metallization phase (see Figure 1.18).

In the final metallization phase (Figure 1.19), aluminum is typically deposited over the exposed areas, connecting the source, the gate, and the drain to the other components of the circuit. The transistor is now finished.

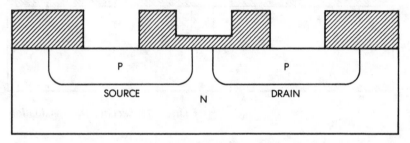

P   P

SOURCE   DRAIN

N

Figure 1.18: Third Oxide Removal Exposes Source and Drain

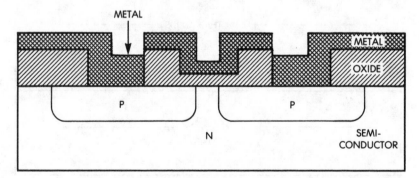

METAL

METAL

OXIDE

P   P

N   SEMI-
CONDUCTOR

Figure 1.19: Final Metallization (A1) Results in Finished Transistor

TECHNOLOGIES

We will now discuss six main technologies used to manufacture MSI and LSI devices:

1. PMOS Technology.   We have just described the fabrication of a p-channel transistor. P-channel transistors use the mobility of positive charges called *holes* to conduct electricity. PMOS is a relatively old MOS technology that is well understood and economical. It was used extensively for manufacturing all of the first microprocessors. PMOS technology gives excellent density (up to 20,000 transistors or more per chip). However, it is relatively slow when compared with newer technologies such as NMOS. An attractive feature of PMOS to manufacturers is that it is a well-understood process and therefore allows a very complex device to be created with a high probability of success.

2. NMOS Technology.   NMOS is intrinsically faster than PMOS as it uses electrons rather than holes as charge-carriers. It gives an excellent density and is generally regarded as the best compromise for implementing fast and complex microprocessors today. Being a newer technology, however, it is not as well developed as PMOS, and it is not used by all manufacturers. A typical NMOS microprocessor achieves execution speeds on the order of 1 microsecond per instruction. It is typically at least twice as fast as an equivalent PMOS microprocessor.

3. CMOS (Complementary MOS) Technology.   CMOS uses a combination of p-channel and n-channel transistors. The characteristics of CMOS technology therefore lie somewhere between those of the NMOS and PMOS technologies. CMOS is faster than PMOS but it is somewhat slower than NMOS and achieves a good density. However, because it uses two transistors rather than one, CMOS offers less integration than NMOS.

Essential advantages of CMOS are that it has very low power consumption, will operate between 2V and 12V, and has an excellent noise immunity (40%, which is almost ideal). CMOS technology was specifically created for avionics and aerospace applications. It is now mainly used in systems that require portability or very low power consumption. The RCA Cosmac and the Intersil 6100 are two commercial microprocessors using this technology. The structure of a CMOS circuit appears in the illustrations in Figures 1.20 and 1.21.

4. Bipolar Technologies.   Bipolar technology is one of the fastest technologies available today. Within the various bipolar technologies, the main technology is low-power-Schottky TTL (LPSTTL). It is used for

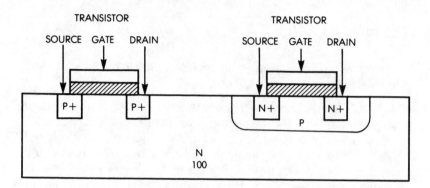

Figure 1.20: CMOS Requires Two Transistors

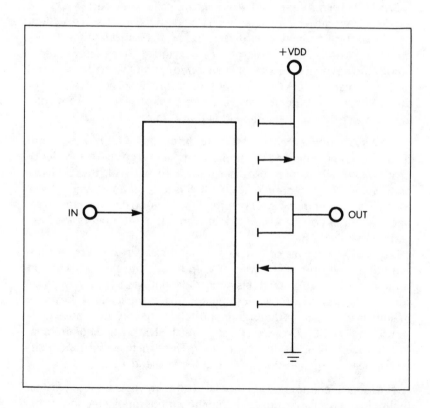

Figure 1.21: Basic CMOS Circuit Uses Two Transistors

the implementation of fast bit-slice devices. LPSTTL results in instruction speeds of 70 to 100 ns per instruction versus approximately 1 μs (microsecond) for a monolithic microprocessor. The three main disadvantages of bipolar technology are:

1. significant power consumption

2. high power dissipation

3. low density.

It is, therefore, not yet possible to implement a complete monolithic microprocessor on a single chip. Bipolar technology is generally used for MSI densities so that only slices of a traditional CPU can be implemented on a single chip. These are the new bit-slice devices (described in Chapter 4). The essential characteristic of bipolar technology is its high speed. Figure 1.22 shows the implementation of a bipolar transistor.

Within the field of bipolar technologies, ECL (emitter-coupled logic) holds a good potential for reaching very high speeds. Another bipolar technology that deserves special mention is I²L or "Integrated Injection Logic," which was developed as a result of the pocket calculator and digital watch markets. It is characterized bv bipolar speed (at least in theory) and low power consumption (critical for such portable applications). I²L is now being used in the consumer market, but it has not yet achieved the speed characteristic of bipolar devices. I²L technology has been used in particular for the implementation of bit-slice devices.

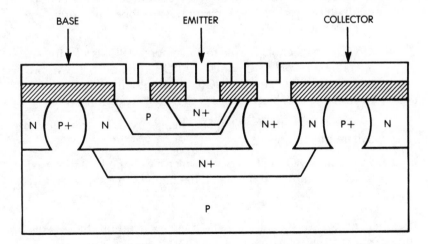

Figure 1.22: A Bipolar Transistor

However, these devices cannot yet compete with the speeds of their TTL equivalents. Another advantage claimed for I²L is the high theoretical integration that can be achieved. Once high integration and high speed become a reality, I²L could be an important technology for portable microprocessors.

5. CCD Technology. Charge-coupled devices (CCDs) provide a new form of very high density memory. It is already possible to implement a 64K-bit memory chip using CCD technology. The principle of operation is the following. Regular squares of aluminum are deposited onto silicon oxide. Each of these squares is used as a capacitor and stores a charge. Because of this simple geometry, a large number of squares can be realized on a single chip. Like all capacitors, however, these elementary cells leak, and each charge must be refreshed. Charges are refreshed through a circular shift of charges from one aluminum square to the next. This memory is, therefore, a *circulating memory*. It has been called a drum-type memory because of the analogy with a rotating magnetic drum. If the price of CCD memories continues to decrease, CCD memories could become competitive with floppy disks.

6. Other Technologies. Several other technologies exist that have been used by some manufacturers in special cases. These include:

— *Bubble memories*, which now achieve very large densities for memories. However, bubble memories are still expensive and relatively slow. In the future they could represent a serious competition for disk-type memories. (Bubble memories are non-volatile.)

— *MNOS*, the technology used to implement EAROMs (electrically alterable read-only memories). EAROMs and other ROMs are described in Chapter 3. MNOS (metal nitride oxide semiconductor) must not be confused with NMOS (N-channel MOS).

— *DMOS* (Double-diffused MOS), which is used for high density dynamic memories.

— *VMOS*, an NMOS technology in which a V-shaped notch is used to achieve improved density. It has been used for high density dynamic RAMs.

New technologies are continually being introduced but these technologies are usually refinements of the main technologies that we have already described.

SUMMARY—TECHNOLOGIES

NMOS is generally used for standard microprocessors. PMOS is used in some industrial and military applications to achieve very high densities. CMOS is used in applications that require portability. Bipolar is used for very high-speed devices but limits the complexity of the device.

A BRIEF HISTORY OF MICROPROCESSORS

Now that we understand the microprocessor from a technical standpoint, let's discuss its history.

The emergence of microprocessors was not due to foresight, astute design, or advanced planning. It was accidental. The first microprocessors introduced on the market were accidents of the technology, and often rejects. This fact is fundamental to the understanding of early microprocessor products. Because of the disorderly and unplanned introduction of microprocessors, initial design errors and inadequacies have been propagated in the name of compatibility. Many of the "features" that equip today's microprocessors are the result of this fact. Let us, therefore, briefly retrace the history of microprocessors.

The emergence of working transistors can be traced to the late 1940s, after the war. Only ten years later, the first working model for an integrated circuit was developed by Jack St. Clair Kilby from Texas Instruments. At about the same time, the planar process was developed by Jean Hoerni and Robert Noyce at Fairchild (1959). Integrated circuits were first produced in quantity around 1961. The integration of circuitry then advanced rapidly. Small scale integration (SSI), with a complete gate on a single chip, appeared in 1964. (A gate, which incorporates several transistors, implements logical functions such as AND, OR, and NOT.) In 1968, medium scale integration (MSI) appeared, offering a complete register on a single chip.

Commercial LSI (large-scale integration) appeared in 1971 in the forms of the first 1K-bit memory, the UART, and the first microprocessor. The first "general-purpose" microprocessor (the Intel 4004) was introduced in late 1971.

The search for higher integration resulted initially from government contracts, in particular from NASA and other military programs. In these programs cost was not an essential factor— miniaturization was. In the early 1970s, research contracts from NASA and the government diminished rapidly, prompting manufacturers to seek other sources of funding. It was also at this time that manufacturers of integrated circuits found a market for their products in the general public. For the first time it became possible to sell LSI to the public in the form of the early desk calculators, followed by the pocket calculators. The production and sale of hundreds of thousands of units became a reality. Figure 1.23 displays a chart showing the evolution of LSI.

By early 1971 only two standardized LSI products, the first 1K-bit dynamic RAM and the UART (Universal Asynchronous Receiver-Transmitter) had been developed. At that time no one could imagine what the next standard product would be. It was then that the micro-processor was accidentally introduced, with the results that we now know. Here is what happened.

The introduction in 1971 of the Intel 4004, a 4-bit PMOS micro-processor, resulted from a contract with a Japanese desk calculator

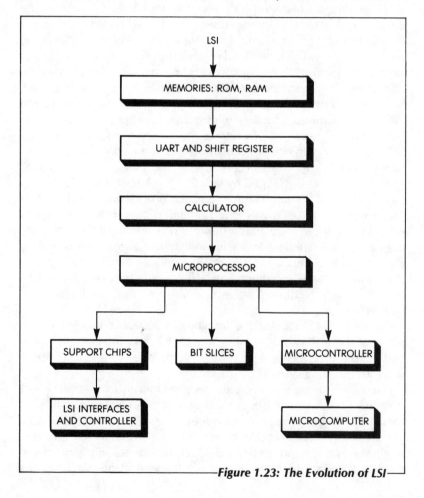

Figure 1.23: The Evolution of LSI

manufacturer. The early purchasers of the 4004 had to agree not to develop a desk calculator with the chip for at least one year. This "general-purpose microprocessor" was, in fact, designed as a calculator. Thus, it was not powerful and was inadequate for general-purpose computing. High sales were not expected; however, they occurred.

The next significant event was in 1972 when Intel introduced the 8008, the first general-purpose 8-bit microprocessor. Display Terminals Corporation, now known as Datapoint, then a CRT display manufacturer, requested bids for the production of a monolithic processor capable of controlling a CRT. Two companies, Texas Instruments and Intel, vied for and obtained the development contracts. After months of effort, Texas Instruments withdrew. Intel continued the development and came up with a component that could satisfy all but one of Datapoint's functional requirements: it was too slow. At about the same time, a price war had started over the prices of bipolar components, resulting in significantly lower prices for bipolar devices.

For these reasons, Datapoint decided to implement its CRT controller in bipolar technology. Intel, then a very young company, was left with a chip whose development had been paid for, but for which there was no obvious market. Since Intel produced memory products, the 8008 was introduced on the market on the assumption that it would sell memory chips. Apparently, all design efforts were halted and the design team were assigned to other tasks. That was to be the end of microprocessors at Intel.

To the surprise of its manufacturer (and of its competitors) sales of the microprocessor progressed rapidly. This manufacturer had stumbled by accident onto the next standard LSI product, the microprocessor. Intel quickly realized the potential of this new device, reassembled a design team, and a year later introduced the successor of the 8008, the 8080. Simultaneously, Intel's competitors set to work on their version of what an 8080 should have been had it been designed correctly for its market. Within two years, all the main "standard" 8-bit microprocessors had been introduced, most of them inspired by the early design of the 8080. Motorola introduced the 6800 (nearly one year after the 8080), Rockwell the PPS-8, Signetics the 2650, etc.

In a third generation of microprocessor design, the successors to the 8080 and the 6800 were introduced. The Z80 from Zilog, the 8085 from Intel, the 6809 from Motorola, and the first 1-chip microcomputers appeared: the F8 from Fairchild and Mostek, the 8048 from Intel, the TMS 1000, and the 9940 from Texas Instruments. (A comparative evaluation of the various microprocessors is presented in Chapter 4.)

Now that we have retraced the birth of the first microprocessors, let us examine briefly the people and the industry that invented and developed them.

SILICON VALLEY

The semiconductor industry began at Bell Telephone laboratories in New Jersey but was soon transplanted to the intellectually fertile region of the Santa Clara Valley south of San Francisco, now dubbed "Silicon Valley." Many of the companies populating Silicon Valley today are familiarly viewed as the offspring of Fairchild. As an example of the process that populated Silicon Valley, let us follow the story of Intel.

In 1955, William Shockley (who had won the Nobel Prize for his part in developing the transistor) left Bell Laboratories to create his own research company, Shockley Semiconductor Laboratories, which later became the unsuccessful commercial venture called Shockley Transistor. Two years later, a small group of scientists left Shockley's company to start a venture of their own and, backed by Fairchild Camera and Instrument Company, they formed Fairchild Semiconductor in the area that was to become known as Silicon Valley. Two of those scientists, Robert Noyce and Gordon Moore, left Fairchild in 1968 to create still another company in Sunnyvale, which they named Intel (for *Inte*grated *E*lectronics).

Three years later, in 1971, Intel introduced the first microprocessor with the success known today. It is interesting to note that in 1974, two of the leading designers of the 8080, the most popular early 8-bit microprocessor, left Intel to create yet another company, Zilog. Zilog then introduced a successor to the 8080, the Z80, which competes directly with Intel's 8080. Leading designers of Zilog products have already separated from that company in order to create their own company in Silicon Valley.

This mechanism of company creation has been typical of the electronics field and in particular of the integrated circuit field. As a result, many of the leading microprocessors on the market today have strikingly similar features (and design inadequacies).

ADVANTAGES OF MICROPROCESSORS

We have now presented the basic definitions, explained the main organization of a system, described the manufacturing process, and briefly studied the history of microprocessors. As a conclusion to this chapter, now that we have defined the required terms, let us examine the main advantages claimed by microprocessors.

Microprocessors are displacing traditional electronics in nearly every area involving programs or automatic control. The three essential advantages of microprocessors are that they require fewer components, represent a low-cost solution, and offer the flexibility of programming.

1. Fewer Components.   The small number of components required by a microprocessor system results in several advantages:

— reduced physical volume and system miniaturization, often resulting in portability

— reduced power consumption

— reduced power dissipation

— increased reliability because of a smaller number of components.

2. Lower Cost.   The above characteristics result in a substantially lower cost. A typical general-purpose microprocessor today sells for around $10, and can go as low as $1 to $2 if purchased in large quantities (say 10,000).

3. Programmability.   Programming concepts and techniques are described in Chapter 8. The essential advantages of programming are that it simplifies the design, reduces the development time, and allows easy changes. In short, a keyboard takes the place of a soldering iron, and powerful programming development tools are used instead of inefficient and complex hardware debugging aids. (*Debugging* is the process of identifying and removing errors.) In addition, programming allows the use of standardized hardware modules. This means that a standard microprocessor-based module can be programmed for a variety of tasks. Substituting one program for another may involve no hardware changes or may simply require substituting memory chips containing the new program. The product can thus be developed rapidly, tested in the field, and then refined progressively, without the need for hardware redesign (except in the case of correcting design errors). In addition, new functions can be invented and later implemented without requiring substantial hardware modifications. The hardware portion of the system can then be mass-produced and standardized, resulting in a very low cost.

The cost of generating software is not small, but it is usually distributed over a large number of units. Typical microprocessor applications involve at least 100 units so that the cost of software development can be spread over a large number of systems. It is only in cases where there is a definite need for microminiaturization (medical and military applications), or where programming time is essentially free, that the cost of programming a microprocessor for a small number of systems is justified.

From a conceptual point of view, the use of programs is analogous to an ''intelligence'' function being included on the system. Many microprocessor-based devices are thus qualified as *intelligent* devices. Devices that were previously hardwired have been replaced by a microprocessor system equipped with a powerful program, resulting in an ''intelligent'' device behavior.

When designing an automatic or a control device, four main choices are possible: hardwired logic, a minicomputer, a system using custom chips, or a microprocessor-based device. (These options are compared in Figure 1.24 and a simplified decision chart is shown in Figure 1.25.) However, as densities increase, minicomputers are becoming microcomputers, so that microprocessor devices should at least be considered in all cases.

	HARDWARE LOGIC	MINICOMPUTER	CUSTOM-CHIP	MICRO-PROCESSOR
DESIGN	COMPLEX	SIMPLEST	MOST COMPLEX	SIMPLE
POSSIBILITY OF EVOLUTION	COMPLEX	EXCELLENT	NONE	EXCELLENT
DEVELOPMENT TIME	POOR	FASTEST	WORST	FAST
COST (LOW VOLUME HIGH COMPLEXITY)	HIGH	LOW	VERY HIGH	LOW TO MEDIUM
COST (HIGH VOLUME HIGH COMPLEXITY)	HIGH	HIGH	LOW	LOW
PERFORMANCE	BEST POTENTIAL	AVERAGE TO GOOD	LOW TO AVERAGE	LOW TO AVERAGE
SIZE REDUCTION	POOR	WORST	BEST	EXCELLENT
RELIABILITY	FAIR TO GOOD (IF JAN PARTS)	GOOD	QUESTIONABLE	GOOD
COMPLEXITY POTENTIAL	POOR	EXCELLENT	FAIR	EXCELLENT
EASE OF APPLICATION	WORST	BEST	GOOD	GOOD

Figure 1.24: The Four Options—A Comparison

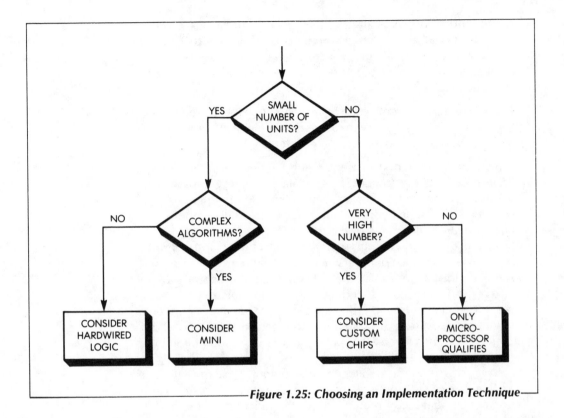

Figure 1.25: Choosing an Implementation Technique

SUMMARY

A *microprocessor* is a single-chip LSI implementation of a traditional central processing unit. It may incorporate not only the CPU, but also the memory and some of the input/output functions of a traditional computer. It is then called a *microcomputer-on-a-chip*. The cost of a microprocessor is low (typically selling for less than $10) and it continually decreases while integration progresses. Execution speed is approximately 1 μs for a typical instruction.

The microprocessor incorporates at least two of the standard units of any computer system: the *arithmetic logical unit*, which performs computations, and the *control unit*, which synchronizes the operation of the system.

The microprocessor creates three buses:

1. *The data bus*: typically an 8-bit bidirectional bus along which the data exchanged by the elements of the system transit.

2. *The address bus*: typically a 16-bit monodirectional bus, propagating from the microprocessor towards the devices that it can address. The address propagated by the address bus selects a register within one of the devices connected to the system, or it selects a chip.

3. *The control bus*: a collection of lines to or from the microprocessor and other devices, with signals that implement the synchronization and control of the entire system.

A microprocessor requires *memory* and *input/output* facilities. Typically memory is implemented by specialized memory chips, while input/output is implemented by specialized input/output peripherals connected to the system by special interface devices. All components of the system are connected to the buses.

The system's memory contains *programs*, collections of instructions that specify the sequence of orders given to the system. The memory also contains the *data* on which the ALU operates. A program is a sequence of instructions corresponding to the algorithmic solution of a problem. The set of instructions that the computer can directly understand (generally expressed in binary) is the *machine language*. *Programming* is the art of translating an algorithm into a programming language.

We have shown how the architecture of a computer system relates to the architecture of a microprocessor system. The microprocessor is an LSI component that incorporates most of the functions of the traditional ALU in one or more components. We have introduced the other specialized components, such as ROM and RAM, that are normally used in the design of a microprocessor-based system. We will examine these components in detail in later chapters.

In Chapter 2 we will learn how a microprocessor operates internally, then work our way out of the microprocessor. We will study the internal architecture of a typical microprocessor chip, and see how it manipulates information along its internal buses, and how it uses its *registers*. We will see how it *fetches*, *decodes* and *executes* instructions sequentially, or out of sequence. The mechanism of executing instructions in a program will then be clear. We will then examine the other components, beyond the microprocessor, which provide the required memory and input/output facilities. This will be the topic of Chapter 3. Let us proceed to Chapter 2 and into the heart of the microprocessor.

EXERCISES

1-1: Define LSI, chip, microcomputer, CPU, ALU, CU, and I/O.

1-2: What is a bit? What is a byte?

1-3: How many bytes are in a word?

1-4: What is the difference between ROM and RAM?

1-5: Can the memory store both programs and data?

1-6: What is a bus? Define the data bus, the address bus, the control bus.

1-7: Explain how two numbers are multiplied by a pocket calculator using two chips: a calculator chip and an I/O chip.

1-8: Why are bit positions labeled from 0 to 7 rather than from 1 to 8?

1-9: What is the address of the nth word of the memory?

1-10: What is the advantage of registers?

1-11: Why is the number of registers in the CPU usually small?

1-12: Why is mass memory required?

1-13: Can a 12-bit address bus be used to access 16-bit data?

1-14: What is the maximum number of words that can be accessed with an 8-bit address bus?

1-15: Why do bits 0 and 7 usually play a special role in a microprocessor system?

1-16: Is it possible to access 64K words of 64 bits with a 17-bit address bus?

1-17: How many memory cycles are required to write a 3-byte instruction into an 8-bit wide memory?

1-18: What is the access time of a memory? Is it longer than the cycle time?

1-19: Define hardware, firmware, and software.

1-20: What is a microprogram?

1-21: Explain the difference between NMOS and PMOS.

1-22: Why did the first microprocessors use PMOS?

1-23: Is bipolar a slow or fast technology?

1-24: How fast are microprocessor instructions?

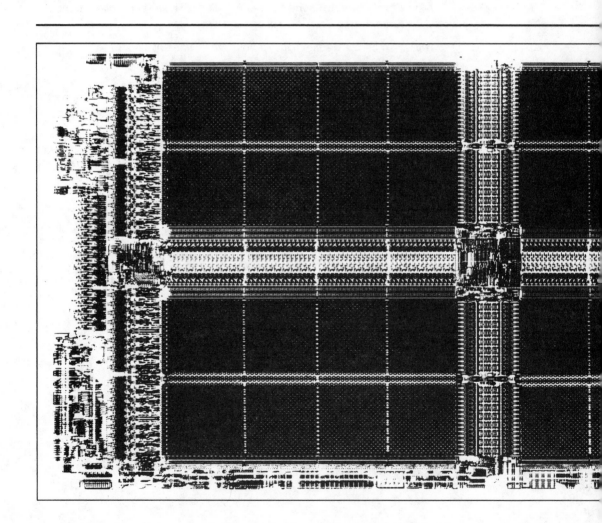

CHAPTER 2

INTERNAL OPERATION OF A MICROPROCESSOR

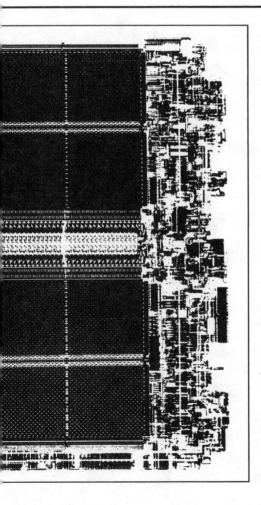

OBJECTIVE

This chapter describes the actual architecture and operation of a typical microprocessor. To this effect, we will present the major architectural trade-offs available to the microprocessor designer. We will establish that nearly all monolithic microprocessors have, essentially, a common internal architecture. They are *single-bus, accumulator-based* processors. We will examine the architecture and follow the detailed sequencing of an actual device, the Intel 8080. We will follow the execution of instructions as they proceed from the memory into the internal *instruction register* to be decoded and executed. We will also follow data as it is transferred and manipulated between the memory and the internal registers. Finally, we will look at the uses and operation of the various buses of the system.

THE CONSTRAINTS OF LSI

Let us first examine the design constraints. Most of the constraints in designing microprocessors are inherent to Large-Scale Integration. The constraints are best illustrated by using an actual example. Figure 2.1 shows the photomicrograph of an early microprocessor—the 8080 from Intel. This photomicrograph illustrates the characteristics and limitations of a typical microprocessor device. An understanding of these limitations will reveal why most manufacturers have, in fact, standardized their architectures along similar lines.

Examining Figure 2.1, we notice several distinct areas that stand out on the photograph. For example, in the upper-right quadrant of the photograph, we see several adjacent rectangles with highly geometrical patterns; in fact, we can count eight identical rectangles in this area from top to bottom. These are *8-bit registers*. Those areas on the chip with highly geometrical patterns are memory areas; they are either ROM or RAM.

The implementation of memory on a chip, rather than other functions, makes efficient use of the chip area available. The geometrical, repetitive pattern of a memory area results in very high density. Such a pattern is often computer-generated so that both high density and ease in design are achieved. In fact, the implementation of memory on a chip is so easily accomplished, compared to the implementation of other functions, that early designers of microprocessors made a number of design errors. For example, early microprocessors had an oversupply of internal registers.

Internal registers are implemented by a *RAM bank*, i.e., a set of read/write registers in a RAM. A small RAM requires only a very small area. It was thus tempting to fill a blank area with a RAM. As a result, early microprocessors were equipped with a large number of internal registers. At first this might seem to be an advantage; however, addressing multiple registers typically involves longer instructions and therefore a slower execution time.

In principle, multiple register banks might have given early microprocessors the potential for handling *interrupts* quickly. However, these early microprocessors were missing other facilities that are needed to take advantage of this design characteristic. In particular, the *program counter* and the *status word* or *status register* must be duplicated for the efficient handling of interrupts through multiple register banks.

Figure 2.1: 8080 Photomicrograph

This requires, in turn, special connections on the internal buses. Such errors, however, have been corrected, but only recently.

It is likely then that many chip designers, having completed an initial design, took a second look at the chip and saw blank areas where no circuitry had been implemented. This tempted them to add additional 4- or 8-bit registers, which could easily be implemented on a small area of the chip. However, designers subsequently learned that a large number of internal registers is not necessarily advantageous unless coupled with other system facilities.

The maximum area of a chip is limited by the technology. Chip sizes today are roughly 150 mils by 150 mils. The size of the chip cannot be doubled without increasing production problems exponentially and, therefore, increasing the cost exponentially. For this reason, the basic problem is that of implementing all of the functions necessary for a complete microprocessor in a limited area. As we shall see in Chapter 11, increasing the size of the area of a chip is one of the important concerns of the industry today.

Looking again at Figure 2.1, note that areas on the chip that have an irregular appearance contain *random logic*. Random-logic circuits must generally be drawn by hand and are subject to reliability problems such as *pattern-sensitivity*. (It is not possible to predict in advance all possible bit combinations that might appear in the geometry of the chip or to predict which particular combinations might turn a bit on unintentionally.) Although designers continually try to minimize the area occupied by the random logic, this function does not use the chip as efficiently as memory.

In Figure 2.1, there are many lines that connect the elements of the chip, particularly around the edges. These are the internal communication lines or *internal buses* of the microprocessor. These lines occupy a relatively large area of the chip. This area is an *inactive* area of the chip; it cannot be used to implement logical functions. One of the important concerns of designers is to minimize this area in order to provide more functional complexity per unit of chip area. Newer microprocessors use the chip area more efficiently; photomicrographs taken of them verify this claim.

Finally, the white rectangles on the outside of the chip in Figure 2.1 are the *pads* that serve as contact points with the outside world. Gold wires are bonded to the pads and connect them to the pads of the package, establishing the connection between the chip and its package.

These basic observations illustrate the limitations imposed by LSI technology on the internal architecture of the microprocessor chip.

Let us now look more closely at the internal buses that connect the elements of the chip and are used to transfer data.

BUSES

A *bus* is a set of communication lines grouped by function. For each function, there are typically two kinds of buses: internal and external. In this chapter we will be looking mostly at internal buses, i.e., the buses implemented on the chip to interconnect all of its logical elements.

For the person who interconnects a system, however, the essential buses are the external buses. We will examine them briefly first. There are three standard system buses in any microprocessor system. These buses are:

1. *The data bus*. The data bus transmits data back and forth between the various chips of the system. For example, it will carry data from an input chip to the microprocessor and back from the microprocessor to the memory. In our standard microprocessor, the data bus is an 8-bit, *bidirectional* bus (i.e., it can be used in both directions). The data bus is nearly always a *tri-state* bus (3-level logic), so that it can be used in conjunction with a DMA (direct memory access). (The DMA is studied in Chapter 3.)

2. *The address bus*. The address bus originates from the microprocessor and carries addresses to all the devices that are connected to the data bus. In our standard microprocessor, the address bus is a 16-bit bus that allows the transmission of up to 64K (2^{16}) external addresses. An address carried by the address bus normally selects a device (usually a chip) or a location (usually a register) within a device. (The use of the address bus is explained in detail in Chapter 5.) The address bus is always used in conjunction with the data bus to specify the source or destination of the data transmitted on the data bus. The address bus originates from a specialized microprocessor register, the *program counter* (PC). This connection will be detailed later in this chapter.

3. *The control bus*. The control bus carries synchronization signals between the microprocessor and all the devices connected to the buses. Typical signals traveling on the control bus are read, write, interrupt, reset, and acknowledgments of various types.

Each of the three buses created by the microprocessor proper can carry up to one TTL load; the typical capacitance is 100 to 130 pico-farads (approximately 5 to 7 LSI packages). In most systems, with the exception of the smaller ones, it is necessary to add *bus drivers* on the data bus, the address bus, and sometimes the control bus in order to connect a sufficient number of external devices.

The data bus is the bus that defines the architecture of a system. It is the only bus that is consistently shown in an illustration of a micro-processor system. The address bus is sometimes shown; the control bus rarely appears.

A processor is said to have a single-, dual-, or triple-bus architecture according to the number of data buses that it uses for accessing the registers. The following sections will describe and evaluate these archi-tectures. As a result of this evaluation, it should become clear why most standard microprocessors have selected the same basic bus architec-ture.

SINGLE-BUS ARCHITECTURE

A usual way to differentiate between the various internal processor architectures is to count the number of buses used to communicate between the registers and the arithmetic and logical unit (ALU). The simplest architecture is the single-bus architecture, which is illustrated in Figure 2.2. In a single-bus system, data are brought from a register to the ALU through the single bus that appears at the top of the illustra-tion. The bus connects to both the left and the right input of the ALU. The results of an operation performed by the ALU are deposited on the same bus, to be gated back to the registers. This single bus is *multiplexed* in time.

A typical instruction to be executed by the microprocessor is: R0 = R0 + R1. This instruction means: "ADD the contents of R0 and R1 and store the result in R0." This instruction can also be read as: "R0 receives the result of R0 + R1." To perform this operation, register R0 is read from R0 onto the bus, carried via the single bus to the left input of the ALU, and stored in the accumulator register there (Figure 2.3). R1 is then selected, its contents are read onto the bus, then sent to the right input of the ALU (Figure 2.4). At this point, the right input of the ALU is conditioned by R1, and the left input of the ALU is conditioned by the accumulator register containing the previous value of R0. The opera-tion can now be performed. The addition is performed by the ALU, and the result appears on the ALU output (Figure 2.5). The result is gated on the single bus and sent back to R0. In practice, this means that the *input latch* of R0 must be *enabled* so that data can be written into it. Execution of the instruction is now complete. The result of the addition is in R0.

Note that the contents of R1 have not been modified by this operation. This illustrates a general principle: *the contents of a register or of a read/write memory location are not modified by a read operation.*

The accumulator register on the left input of the ALU is a buffer register required to *memorize* the contents of R0 so that the single bus can be used again for another transfer. This simple internal organization, as shown in Figure 2.2, however, is not adequate. A problem remains.

The Critical Race Problem

The simple organization shown in Figure 2.2 is not sufficient and will result in a timing problem. The problem occurs when the result is deposited by the ALU onto the single bus. The result does not just propagate in the direction of R0 but all along the bus. In this simple system, it reconditions the right input of the ALU, changing the result coming out of it a fraction of a microsecond later. There is no guarantee that the correct, initial value of the result will be written in R0. This is a *critical race*. The output of the ALU must be isolated from its input.

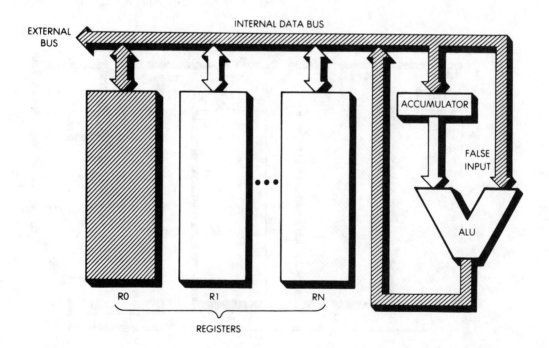

Figure 2.2: Single-Bus Architecture

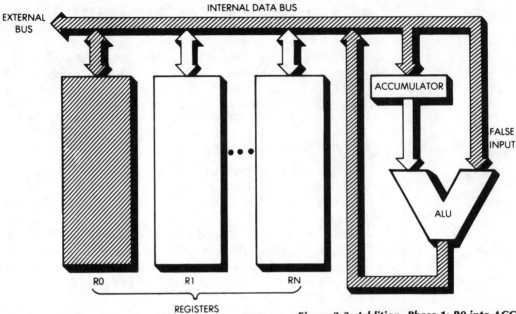

Figure 2.3: Addition, Phase 1: R0 into ACC

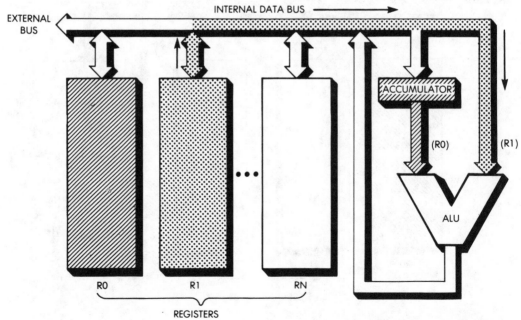

Figure 2.4: Addition, Phase 2: R1 into ALU

There are several solutions to this problem. The simplest way to isolate the input of the ALU from the output is to use a *buffer register*. A buffer register is a register that loses its contents when read. It is used to *latch,* i.e., hold information temporarily. The buffer register could be placed either on the output or on the right input of the ALU. It is usually placed on the input. In the case of Figure 2.6, it would be placed on the *right* input. The buffering of the system is now sufficient for a correct operation. We will see later in this chapter that if the left register is to be used as an accumulator (permitting the use of 1-byte-long instructions), then the accumulator will also require a buffer. The resulting organization is shown in Figure 2.7.

Advantages and Disadvantages of a Single-Bus System _____

The primary *advantage* of a single-bus system is that its architecture requires the least bus area: a single-bus architecture saves space on a chip. As space is a critical consideration for the implementation of a complete microprocessor, most microprocessor chips today use a single-bus architecture. High-performance designs such as bit-slices are not limited by this consideration and normally provide at least three separate buses.

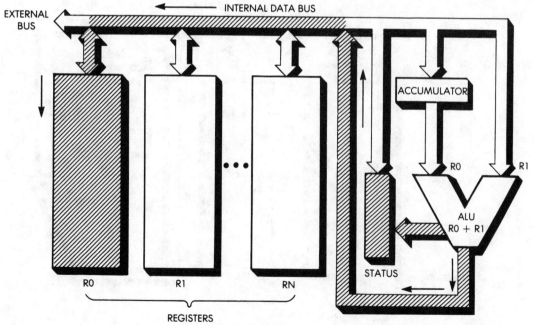

Figure 2.5: Addition, Phase 3: Result Is Generated and Stored in R0

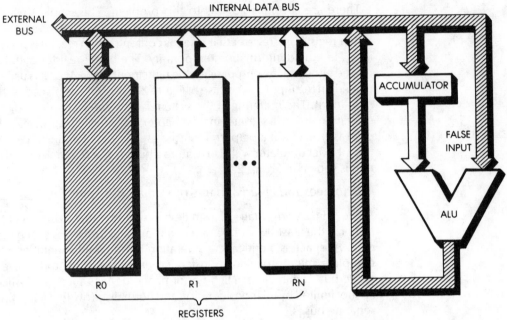

Figure 2.6: The Critical Race Problem

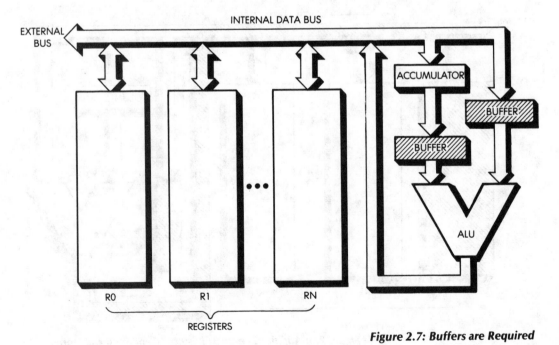

Figure 2.7: Buffers are Required

The primary *disadvantage* of a single-bus system is its slow operation. With a single-bus system, three transfers are necessary: (1) from register R1, (2) from register R0, and (3) back from the ALU to the result register. The bus is multiplexed, i.e., used for several purposes over a period of time. To improve the execution speed of a processor, the use of multiple buses is desirable. A double-bus and a triple-bus architecture are described in the next section.

DOUBLE- AND TRIPLE-BUS ARCHITECTURE

A *double-bus* system uses two buses. An example is shown in Figure 2.8, where a single input bus or source bus (S-bus) connects to both inputs of the ALU and a separate result bus (D-bus) connects the ALU to the registers. Many National Semiconductor products employ this architecture in order to improve speed. Examine the right part of Figure 2.9, for example, and count the buses.

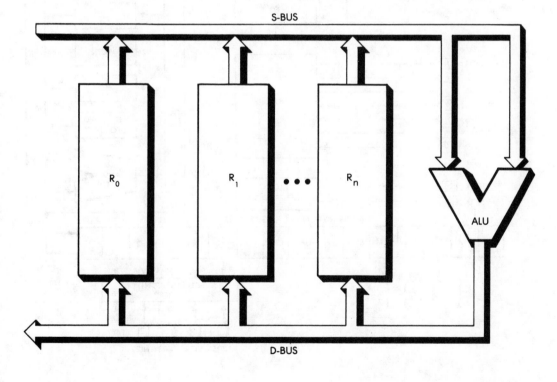

Figure 2.8: Double-Bus Architecture

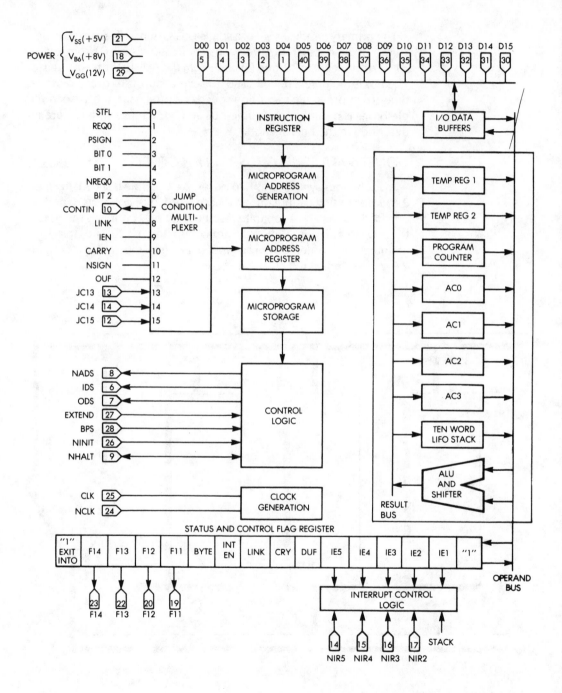

Figure 2.9: The Pace Microprocessor (National Semiconductor)

The architecture of a *triple-bus* system provides maximum performance. It is shown in Figure 2.10. Two input-buses named A-bus and B-bus are provided. The A-bus is connected to the right input of the ALU, and the B-bus is connected to the left input of the ALU. Both inputs of the ALU can now be selected *simultaneously*. In addition, they do not need to be buffered, although buffers might be provided for other reasons. Also, results can be gated on the D-bus independently of the two source-buses. If the result must be written back to one of the source registers, a buffering is required. This buffering must be provided on the D-bus or directly within the registers, as is usually the case.

STANDARD MICROPROCESSOR ARCHITECTURE

A majority of all microprocessor chips on the market today implement the same "standard" architecture: a single-bus architecture that

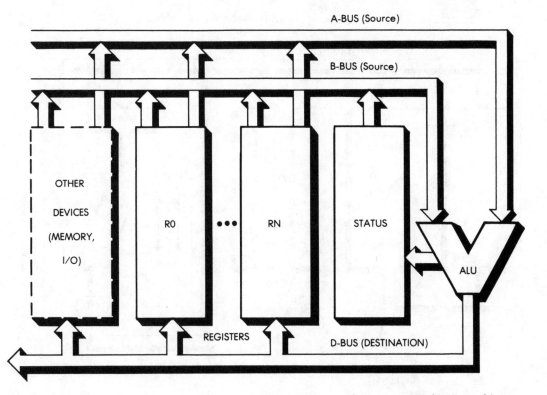

Figure 2.10: Triple-Bus Architecture

makes efficient use of the chip area. A detailed illustration of this standard design appears in Figure 2.11. Moving from right to left, let us examine the elements of this standard microprocessor.

The *control box* represents the *control unit* that synchronizes the operation of the entire system. Its role will be clarified later on in this chapter.

As discussed previously, the *ALU* performs arithmetic and logical operations. One of the inputs of the ALU (in this case the left input) is equipped with a special register, the accumulator. Multiple accumulators may also be provided. Virtually all microprocessors use an accumulator-based, single-bus architecture. The accumulator may be referenced both as input and output within the same instruction, as shown in Figure 2.12. A disadvantage of this architecture is that it introduces a buffering level and therefore it introduces a delay when accessing the left input of the ALU.

The ALU also provides *shift* and *rotate* facilities. A shift operation moves the contents of a word by one or more positions to the left or to

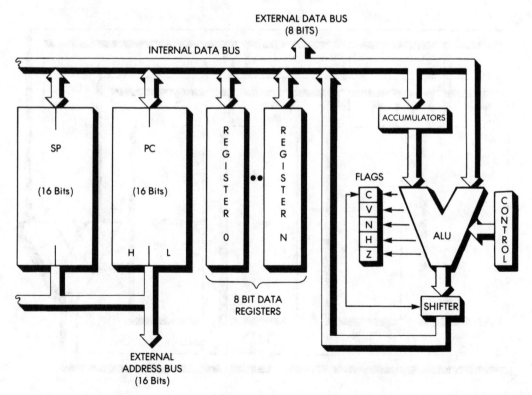

Figure 2.11: "Standard" Microprocessor Architecture (8 Bits)

the right. This process is illustrated in Figure 2.13 (upper drawing), where each bit has been moved one position to the left.

At this point you may be asking: which bit comes in on the right? And what happens to the bit that "falls off" on the left?

In a regular shift, the bit coming in on the right is a 0. The bit falling off the left side is captured in a bit of the special status register, i.e., the carry bit, where it is stored and can later be tested. If, on the other hand, the leftmost bit is sent back to the right input of the accumulator, a *rotate* operation results. This operation is illustrated in Figure 2.13 (lower drawing). In a rotate operation each bit is shifted left by one position. The bit coming in on the right of the register is the old value of the carry bit. At the end of the shift the leftmost bit, which falls off, sets the new value of the carry bit. Mathematically, this is called a *9-bit rotation*. Details of this operation may vary for each microprocessor.

Efficient implementation of arithmetic operations requires various shifts and rotate operations, including a "sign-extend" facility, which repeats the value of the leftmost bit during a right-shift operation. Such facilities are missing on many early microprocessors. A *true (8-bit) rotation* would consist of writing back the leftmost bit directly into the rightmost position, but this capability is often not provided in early microprocessors.

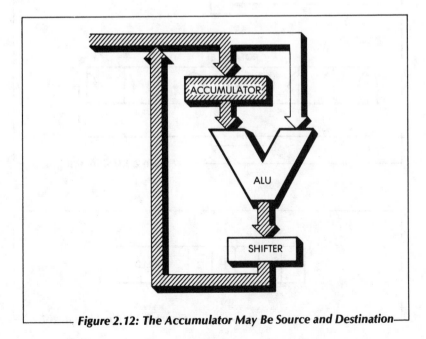

Figure 2.12: The Accumulator May Be Source and Destination

In order to provide these facilities, the ALU is equipped with a *shifter*. The shifter may be on the ALU output, as illustrated in Figure 2.11, or on the accumulator input.

The *flags* (or *status*) *register* appears to the left of the ALU. The flags register stores exceptional conditions occurring within the ALU. The contents of the flags register may then be tested by specialized instructions or read on the internal data bus. For example, depending on the value of one of these bits, a *conditional-branch* instruction may be used to cause the execution of a new program sequence.

STATUS BITS

Let us now examine the role of the status bits in the microprocessor. We will examine the flags register from left to right, as shown in Figure 2.14.

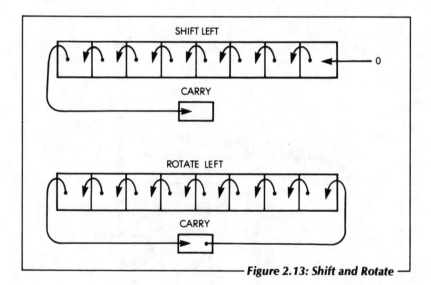

Figure 2.13: Shift and Rotate

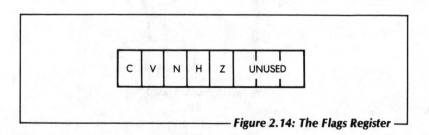

Figure 2.14: The Flags Register

C (Carry).   The carry bit C performs two different and independent functions. On a large processor these two functions would be performed by separate bits.

1. *The carry bit stores the arithmetic carry,* i.e., the ninth bit, which may be generated during an arithmetic operation. It is the overflow of the 8-bit result. However, the word "overflow" has a specific meaning that will be explained below. As an example, if the following two binary numbers are added:

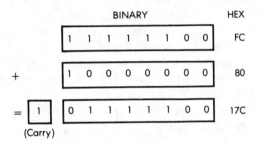

the result generates a carry (i.e., a ninth bit). The 1 generated by this addition is stored by the ALU in the C-bit, where it can be tested. Special instructions, such as "ADD with carry" can be used to automatically add the carry to the result of the next addition. A test can also be performed by the programmer, using a conditional-branch instruction, to determine whether or not some action should be undertaken.

2. *The carry is used as a spill-out* during the shift and rotate operations. When used as a spill-out, the carry behaves again as a ninth bit of the result, which justifies the merging of these two functions into the same bit. This merging facilitates and improves the speed of the arithmetic multiply and divide operations.

V (Overflow).   Overflow denotes that an arithmetic carry within a word has modified the value of the most significant bit. This results in a sign error when the two's-complement notation is used (this notation is explained in Chapter 8). Bit 7 in two's-complement (the most significant bit or MSB) indicates the sign of a number: 1 is negative, 0 is positive. Whenever 2 two's-complement numbers are added, the carry generated during an addition or subtraction might overflow into the sign bit. When this happens, it might change a negative number into a positive number. The overflow bit is used to indicate this occurrence.

Mathematically, the overflow is the exclusive OR of the carry bit (out of bit 7) and the carry generated from bit 6 into bit 7. The overflow will normally be used only when performing two's-complement arithmetic.

N (Negative), or S (Sign).   The N-bit is directly connected to bit position 7 of the result. Recall that in two's-complement notation, a 1 in bit position 7 indicates a negative number, hence the name of the status bit. Unfortunately, in most microprocessors it is generally not possible to test *any* given bit within a given register or even within the accumulator. Usually the only bit that can be directly tested within the accumulator is bit 7, which is effectively the N-flag of the status register. Whenever another bit of the accumulator must be tested, the programmer must perform a series of shifts. A shift places one of the accumulator's bits into the carry bit where it is then tested.

Thus, bit 7 in any byte can be readily tested (because of the availability of N within the status register) and is therefore the preferred position for storing status for any input/output latch or register. When performing arithmetic operations, the N-bit is used to determine if a number or result is positive or negative.

H or AC (Half-Carry).   This bit is used during *binary-coded decimal* (BCD) operations. (Binary-coded decimal is explained in detail in Chapter 8.) BCD is a notation often used in business applications requiring exact results without the round-off errors caused by the usual two's-complement notation. BCD uses a 4-bit code to represent each decimal digit. In order to provide data compaction, a standard 8-bit word will contain two BCD digits placed side by side. When performing arithmetic on bytes, an addition might generate a carry from bit 3 into bit 4, i.e., from the first BCD digit into the second BCD digit. This carry is normally undesirable and must be detected. The H-bit performs this role. The H-bit is the carry from bit 3 into bit 4. The disadvantages of BCD are that it is inefficient in its use of memory space and that it is somewhat slow in performing arithmetic calculations. Here is an example:

								BCD
	0	1	0	1	1	0	0	0	58
+	0	0	0	0	1	0	0	1	09
= 1	0	1	1	0	0	1	1	1	67

V

Adding the rightmost digits (8 and 9) has changed the value of the left one.

Z (Zero). The Z-bit is set to 1 whenever the result of an operation is 0. It is used by arithmetic instructions to determine whether or not a result is 0, and by logical operations such as COMPARE. The latter implements a logical XOR between the word being tested and the pattern to which it is being compared. Whenever the result of a comparison is successful, the Z-bit is set to 1.

The Z-bit is frequently tested by input and output instructions to determine whether or not the contents of any bit within a register have changed. This is done by simply XORing the value of the register with its previous value. If no bit has changed, the result is 0. If a bit has changed, the result of the XOR is not 0 and will be detected by the Z-bit.

P (Parity). The P-bit is not normally provided in most microprocessors, but it is provided in the older 8080. Parity is used to detect whether or not data has been transmitted correctly. The principle of parity is to count the number of 1s present in the eight bits. An even parity scheme completes the number of 1s of a 7-bit word by adding either a 0 or a 1 so that the total number is even. Conversely, an odd parity scheme sets the eighth bit so that the total number of 1s contained in the eight bits is odd.

The parity-bit is used to detect whether or not the parity count is correct. Assuming, for example, even parity, the parity bit will be set whenever the number of bits within the word is not even, indicating a *parity error.* Because parity is generally not used in microcomputer memories, but is used for external communications, a parity detection facility is not normally supplied within the microprocessor. Instead, it is usually implemented in the UART, a communication chip, which will be described in the next chapter. Data arriving at the MPU are assumed to be correct.

Other Status Bits. Other status bits can be provided within the flags register. In particular, an interrupt bit, which normally functions as an *interrupt-enable,* can be provided. Whenever the interrupt bit is set, outside interrupts will be accepted. Whenever an interrupt bit is not set (0), external interrupts will be inhibited; they are said to be *masked.* This process is described in detail in Chapter 3. Additional status information may also be incorporated in the flags register, thus facilitating the testing of other flip-flops that store internal events of the processor. That is why this register is also usually called *PSW* or *Program-Status-Word.* It stores the complete status information of the processor for the program it is executing.

SETTING FLAGS

Most of the instructions executed by the processor will modify some or all of the flags. It is always important to refer to the chart provided by the manufacturer, which lists the flag bits that will be modified by the instructions. This information is essential in understanding the way in which a program is being executed.

THE REGISTERS

Let us once again go back to Figure 2.11 and move toward the left side of the illustration where the registers of the microprocessor appear. Here we see the *general-purpose registers* and the *address registers*.

The General-Purpose Registers

General-purpose registers are fast memories provided so that the ALU can manipulate data at high speed. Because of restrictions placed on the number of bits that it is reasonable to provide within an instruction, the number of directly addressable registers is usually limited to eight or sixteen. Each of these registers is a set of eight flip-flops connected to the bidirectional internal data bus. These eight bits can be transferred simultaneously to or from the data bus. The implementation of these registers as MOS flip-flops provides the fastest level of memory available, and their contents can be accessed within tens of nanoseconds.

Internal registers are usually labeled from 0 to n. The specific role of these registers is not defined in advance; they are said to be "general-purpose." They may be used to contain any data generated by the program.

These general-purpose registers are normally used to store 8-bit data. On some microprocessors, it is possible to operate on *two* of these registers simultaneously. Such *register-pairs* facilitate the storage of 16-bit quantities, whether data or addresses.

The Address Registers

Address registers, also called *data-counters* or *pointers*, are 16-bit registers intended for the storage of addresses. They are *double registers*, i.e., two 8-bit registers. Their essential characteristic is that they are connected to the address bus; in fact, they are said to "create" the address bus. The address bus appears on the bottom left side of the illustration in Figure 2.11. Another representation of a group of address registers is shown in Figure 2.15.

Contents can only be loaded into these 16-bit registers via the data bus. Two 8-bit transfers along the data bus are necessary in order to transfer 16 bits. To differentiate between the lower and higher half of each register, the two halves are usually labeled as L (low) or H (high), denoting bits 0 through 7, and 8 through 15, respectively. All microprocessors contain at least the program counter. Most contain two or more address registers, as shown in Figure 2.15.

PC—Program Counter. The program counter contains the address of the next instruction to be executed. Its presence is indispensable and fundamental to program execution. The mechanism of program execution and the automatic sequencing implemented with the program counter is described in the next section. Briefly, execution of a program is normally sequential. To execute the next instruction from memory, it must be brought from the memory into the microprocessor. The contents of the PC are deposited on the address bus and propagated towards the memory. The memory then reads the contents of the location specified by this address and sends the corresponding byte back to the MPU. This is the instruction (assuming a 1-byte instruction length). An exception is a microprocessor such as the two-chip F8, which has no PC on the microprocessor chip. This system still uses a program counter; however, for technological reasons, it is implemented directly on the memory chip.

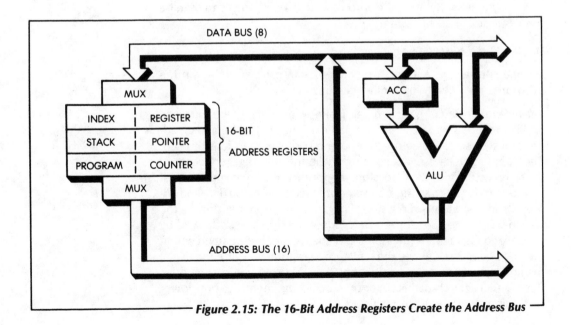

Figure 2.15: The 16-Bit Address Registers Create the Address Bus

SP—Stack Pointer.   The *stack* has not yet been introduced and will be described in the next section. It is indispensable for interrupts and subroutines. In most powerful general-purpose microprocessors, the stack is implemented in "software," i.e., within the memory. A stack pointer is then provided that contains the address of the top of the stack within the memory. To keep track of the top of the stack, a 16-bit register is dedicated to the pointer. This is the stack pointer.

IX—Index Register.   Indexing is a powerful memory-addressing facility that was not always provided in early microprocessors. (The various memory-addressing techniques are described in Chapter 9.) Indexing is used to access blocks of data in the memory using a single instruction. An index register will typically contain either a displacement that is automatically added to a base or a base that is added to a displacement.

Indexing is used to access any word within a block of instructions. The Motorola 6800 and the Signetics 2650 are examples of two early microprocessors that are equipped with an IX register. Note that the 8080 does not have an IX register; however, some of its general-purpose registers can be used in pairs to store a number used as an index. A comparison between the 8080 and the 6800 is presented in Chapter 4. Most recent microprocessors have at least one index register.

Some microprocessors such as the SC/MP from National provide general-purpose 16-bit registers that may also be used as general-purpose pointers. By using the auto-indexing facility they can then be used as index or stack pointers.

Specialized Registers _____

Some specialized register structures may also be available on the microprocessor chip. These may include:

The Scratch-pad.   A *scratch-pad* is simply a set of general-purpose internal registers. In fact, a scratch-pad is an internal RAM, and an address must be specified before the contents of the registers may be used. The name *scratch-pad* was given to these internal registers because they are essentially used to store temporary information in a fast memory. Normally a scratch-pad is connected to both the data and address buses. Scratch-pad registers differ from the usual registers by the way in which they are addressed. *Normal* registers are addressed by specialized instructions (the number of the register is contained within the instruction itself) while the *scratch-pad* registers require the use of memory-type addressing instructions (i.e., 2- or 3-byte instructions). Accessing a scratch-pad is faster than accessing memory, but slower than using general-purpose registers.

The Stack.   A *stack* is a "last-in first-out" (LIFO) structure. It is a *chronological* structure that accumulates events (or symbols) in the order in which they are deposited. The oldest symbol is located at the bottom of the stack and the newest is located at the top. A stack works in the same way as a stack of plates in a restaurant (see Figure 2.16). In such a stack, plates are piled up in a circular hole equipped with a spring at the bottom. New plates are deposited on top and a plate is always removed from the top (i.e., access to the stack is via the top). In other words, the last element in is the first element out: this is a LIFO structure.

As shown in Figure 2.17, a stack is manipulated by two instructions: PUSH and POP (or PULL). A PUSH operation deposits the contents of a register on the stack. A POP operation removes the top element of the stack and deposits it into a register (the accumulator). Stacks are necessary to provide interrupt and subroutine levels. They can be implemented in two essential ways—through hardware and through software.

A *hardware stack* is implemented directly on the MPU chip by a set of internal registers. N registers are dedicated to a stack operation. The advantage of a hardware stack is the high speed inherent to the use of internal registers, while the disadvantage is the limitation imposed on the depth of the stack. Whenever the n registers are full, the internal stack is full. So that the stack can continue to be used after it is full, all of the n registers must be copied into the memory. This process gives rise

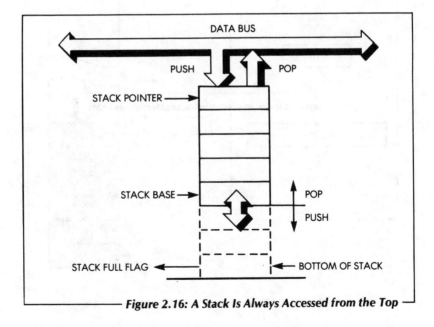

Figure 2.16: A Stack Is Always Accessed from the Top

to another problem. One must be able to tell when the stack is empty or full. Most of the manufacturers of early microprocessors simply forgot to incorporate this detail into their designs, and most of the processors did not provide a ''stack-full'' or a ''stack-empty'' flag. Unfortunately, in these early microprocessors one can be merrily pushing items into the stack only to have them fall through the last word, without giving any indication to the programmer that something might be wrong. Naturally, this is a programming error; the programmer should know better. In practice, a flag would solve this problem. Conversely, it is possible for the programmer to keep pulling elements out of a hardware stack forever. For this reason, it is advisable to have a ''stack-empty'' indicator.

The idea of a hardware stack was particularly attractive to manufacturers of early microprocessors because it was felt either that interrupts were not needed or that, in view of the slow execution speeds of these early microprocessors, interrupt levels did not need to be numerous. Also, it was convenient to use any ''blank'' area on the die to implement additional registers. We have already pointed out that registers provide the most efficient use of any chip area available. It was

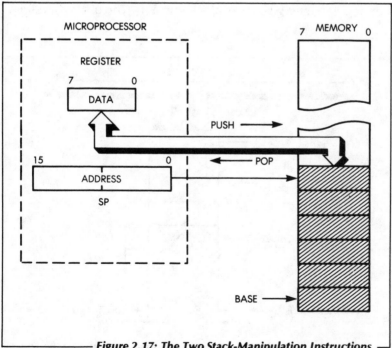

Figure 2.17: The Two Stack-Manipulation Instructions

therefore particularly tempting to provide large numbers of internal registers such as on-chip stack facilities. This is indeed the approach that was chosen in these early designs, but frequently with disappointing results.

The alternative to a hardware stack is a *software stack*. To provide for "unlimited" growth, the stack is implemented in the read/write memory of the system, i.e., in the RAM. The base of the stack is arbitrarily selected by the programmer. The top of the stack is contained and updated automatically within the SP register. Each time a PUSH operation is executed, the SP is incremented or decremented, depending on the convention used (i.e., depending on whether the memory "grows" or "shrinks" from bottom to top). Similarly, each time a POP is done, the stack pointer is immediately updated. In practice, the SP usually points to the word *above* the last element of the stack; that is, it points to the first available word of the stack. The goal is to provide the fastest possible PUSH operation. (This is important for interrupts or for capturing a block of characters). With this convention (pointing to the first available word on top of the stack), the stack pointer can be used directly, without having to wait for incrementation when saving a word quickly on the stack.

We will now describe a PUSH A and a POP A, where the contents of the accumulator will be transferred to or read from the top of the stack. In the PUSH operation illustrated in Figure 2.18, the contents of the accumulator are transferred to the top of the stack. The address of the first available word in the stack (2001) is contained in SP at the beginning. After the PUSH is executed, SP is automatically incremented to the value 2002 (see Figure 2.19) and points to the new "first-available location."

Conversely, POP A fetches the top element of the stack (see Figure 2.20) and loads it into the accumulator. The initial value of SP was 2002. It is automatically decremented to 2001 prior to the memory fetch. The final contents of the stack appear in Figure 2.21.

Still other implementations use combinations of hardware and software methods, but we will not describe them here since they are seldom implemented in microprocessors.

THE ADDRESS BUS

Our standard microprocessor now has two internal buses: a data bus and an address bus. The bidirectional data bus propagates to the outside via a tri-state buffer. The pins of the data bus are normally labeled D0 through D7. The address bus is created by the 16-bit address registers and propagates to the outside world via a 16-bit address buffer. The pins of the address bus are normally labeled A0 through A15.

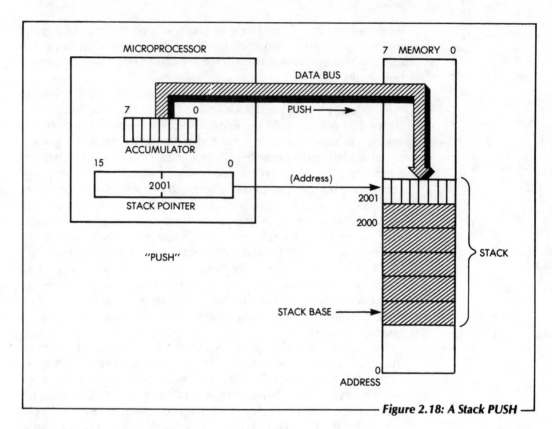

Figure 2.18: A Stack PUSH

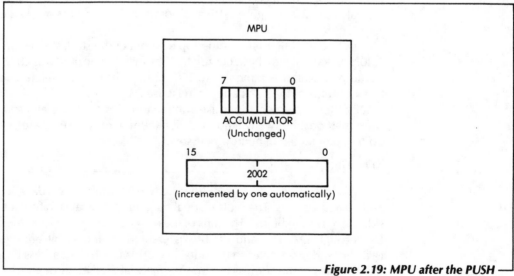

Figure 2.19: MPU after the PUSH

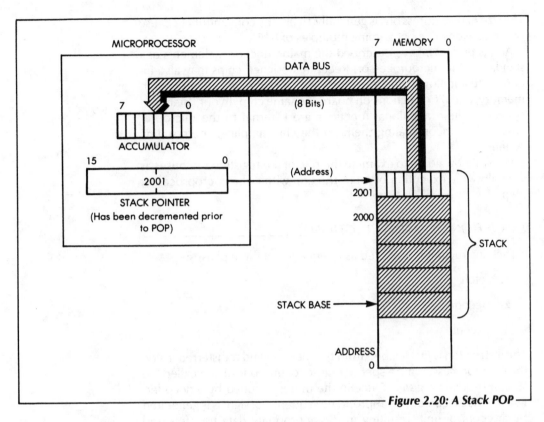

MICROPROCESSOR

DATA BUS

(8 Bits)

7   0

ACCUMULATOR

15   0

2001

STACK POINTER
(Has been decremented prior
to POP)

(Address)

7   MEMORY   0

2001

2000

STACK

STACK BASE

ADDRESS
0

Figure 2.20: A Stack POP

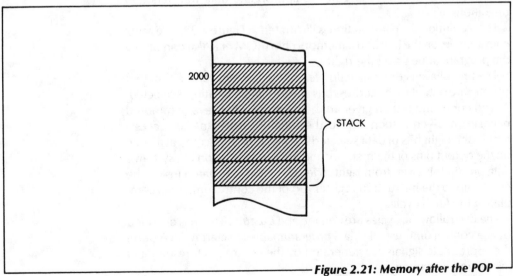

2000

STACK

Figure 2.21: Memory after the POP

The size of the address bus is generally 16 bits, by convention, because of the convenience of handling multiples of 8 bits.

At this point we have described the major functional elements of a standard 8-bit microprocessor. Recently designed chips may also incorporate additional functions, such as a clock circuit, a timer circuit, memory, and I/O functions on board the same chip. In our "standard system," these additional functions are external to the microprocessor chip. Incorporating them on the chip simplifies the resulting system.

We will now go on to examine the role of the registers and buses as we follow the execution of an instruction within the microprocessor chip.

EXECUTION OF AN INSTRUCTION

Each instruction is executed as a sequence of three phases:

1. fetch

2. decode

3. execute.

The instruction is first *fetched* from the memory and transferred inside the microprocessor into a special register of the control unit called the IR or *instruction register*. Once in the IR it is *decoded* by a decoder. Finally, it is *executed*. The appropriate sequence of signals is generated by the control unit, resulting in the appropriate data transfers and operations.

The execution of an instruction is illustrated in Figure 2.22. The MPU chip appears on the left, and a memory chip (ROM or RAM) containing the program appears on the right.

The first phase is the *instruction fetch*: the contents of the program counter are output to the address bus and a memory location is selected. A read command is then given to the memory. After several hundred nanoseconds—corresponding to the memory read-time (or access-time)—the eight bits of data selected by this address become available on the output pins of the memory and are propagated on the system's data bus (in this case, from right to left). The data are gated inside the MPU chip to the instruction register (IR) of the control unit, thus completing the fetch cycle.

The two following cycles are *decode* and *execute*. The IR is decoded by the control unit, usually via a *programmable logic-array* (PLA), and the appropriate signals are generated by the control unit, resulting in instruction execution.

An instruction is not necessarily eight bits long. In fact, it generally uses one, two, three, or four words, i.e., 8, 16, 24, or 32 bits. When an instruction has more than eight bits, the control unit must go back to the memory and read the following byte or bytes successively into the IR. The process will be explained later in this chapter.

The first word of the instruction always contains its *opcode*, i.e., the binary code that specifies the operation to be done. After decoding the opcode, the control unit "knows" whether or not it must go back to the memory to fetch additional bytes.

Having described the sequence of events in the execution of a single instruction, we will now solve the next problem, that of *automatic sequencing*, i.e., the sequential execution of instructions. A program is

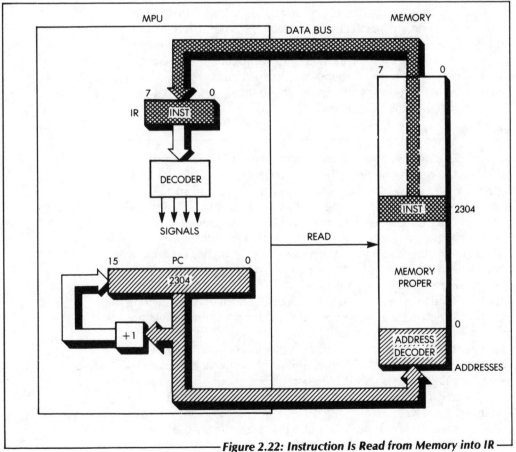

Figure 2.22: Instruction Is Read from Memory into IR

stored as a sequence of binary instructions residing at successive addresses. Once an instruction has been fetched and executed, the program counter (PC) must be updated so that the next instruction can be fetched and executed. The problem lies in updating the program counter. This problem is solved by adding an incrementer or a decrementer (depending on the convention used) to the PC. Thus, each time the PC is used (i.e., its contents are output) its value is automatically incremented (or decremented) and loaded back into the PC. The next time the PC is used, it will be pointing to the next byte in memory, i.e., to the next instruction or to the next byte of a given instruction, if the instruction uses two bytes or more. This incrementer is shown as $+1$ in Figure 2.22.

Program instructions are stored sequentially (one after another) in the memory. However, instructions are not always executed in sequence. In order to take different actions based on the results of tests or decisions, different parts of the program may be executed. In this case, the next instruction to be executed is specified by the current instruction. Such an instruction, which inhibits the automatic sequencing mechanism, is called a branch instruction. The programmer can specify a *branch* or *jump* to a specified memory address. Such an instruction will force a new value within the program counter. This alternative is studied in detail in the next section.

THE CONTROL UNIT

From a functional standpoint, the control unit (CU) is in charge of sequencing the operation of the entire microprocessor system (as illustrated in Figure 2.23). The CU generates synchronization signals and manages commands exchanged between the ALU, the I/O, and the memory. The CU decodes, fetches, and executes instructions.

The control unit communicates with the external world via input and output lines that make up the control bus. The control bus is normally managed by the control unit (see Figure 2.24). Typical signals on the control bus are shown in Figure 2.25.

Two main techniques are used to design a control unit: *hardwiring* and *microprogramming*. Most control units for microprocessors are implemented using a microprogramming technique. The sequencing of the control unit is accomplished by a specialized internal program called the microprogram. The microprogram defines the instruction set of the microprocessor and the way it is executed. The microprogram is stored in an internal ROM or PLA inside the chip and is normally invisible to the user.

Bit-slices are the only type of LSI chips that are normally user-microprogrammable (because control is external to the slices themselves).

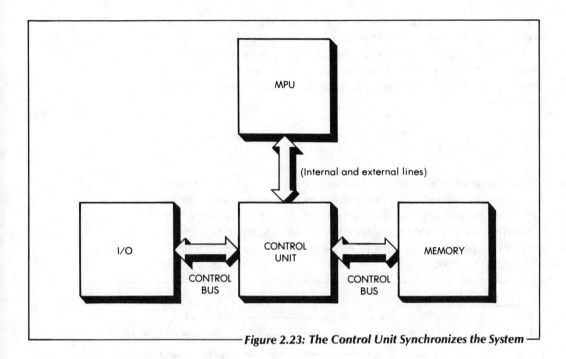

Figure 2.23: The Control Unit Synchronizes the System

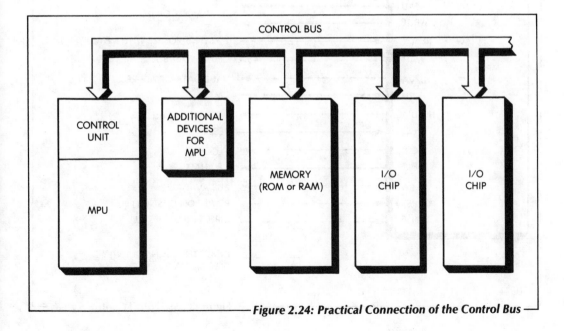

Figure 2.24: Practical Connection of the Control Bus

For all practical purposes, microprogrammed microprocessors are essentially hardwired, in that they cannot be modified by the user.

Having presented the main modules and the basic concepts, we will now study the execution of typical instructions in a real microprocessor, the 8080. The experience gained will be applicable to all microprocessors.

A CASE STUDY: THE 8080

The Intel 8080 was the first "standard" 8-bit microprocessor introduced on the market. More recent microprocessors operate in the same manner and offer additional features. Understanding how the 8080 operates will help in understanding how other standard microprocessors operate because the principles of operation are common to all microprocessors.

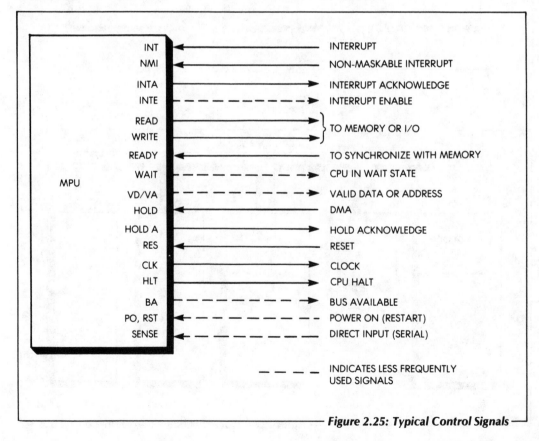

Figure 2.25: Typical Control Signals

The simplified internal architecture of the 8080 microprocessor is shown in Figure 2.26. *The 8080 is a single-bus, accumulator-based system.* The microprocessor is equipped with six general-purpose registers, labeled B, C, D, E, H and L, that appear on the right side of the illustration in Figure 2.26. The accumulator is normally abbreviated A. The other registers are therefore called B, C, D, E, and so on. To maintain compatibility with its predecessor, the early 8008, the 8080 has also been equipped with two special internal registers for communicating with the address bus. These are the H and L registers (where H stands for high and L stands for low, referring to bit positions 15-8 and 7-0). The 8080 is also equipped with two more registers, labeled W and Z in Figure 2.27, which are required and used exclusively by the control unit. These are completely invisible to the user and thus will be ignored at this point.

The 8080 is equipped with the usual two 16-bit registers (which appear at the bottom of the illustration in Figure 2.26). These two registers are the PC (Program Counter) and the SP (Stack Pointer). The higher and lower portions of these registers are labeled H and L to make it easier to refer to only eight bits within these registers. The lower and higher portions of the PC are called PCL and PCH, respectively. Similarly,

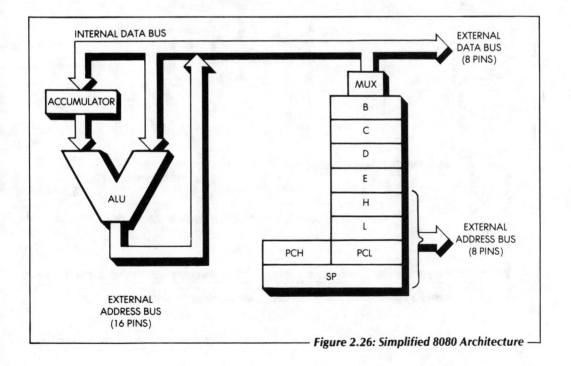

Figure 2.26: Simplified 8080 Architecture

the lower and higher eight bits of the SP are called SPL and SPH. The illustration in Figure 2.26 is simplified. Remember that the H and L registers are also connected to the *address bus*—and they can be manipulated as a single 16-bit register.

The abbreviation MUX in Figure 2.26 stands for *multiplexer*. Several registers are connected to a single path via the MUX. Only one register, or register-pair in the case of the address bus, is connected to a bus at any time. A detailed illustration of the architecture of the 8080 appears in Figure 2.27. Let us examine it.

The *internal data bus* appears at the top of the illustration. All functional modules are connected to it. It has eight bits. The *address bus* appears at the bottom of the illustration. It is equipped with an incrementer/decrementer, shown as ± 1, used to modify the contents of the address registers. The address bus is connected to PC, SP, and HL. The

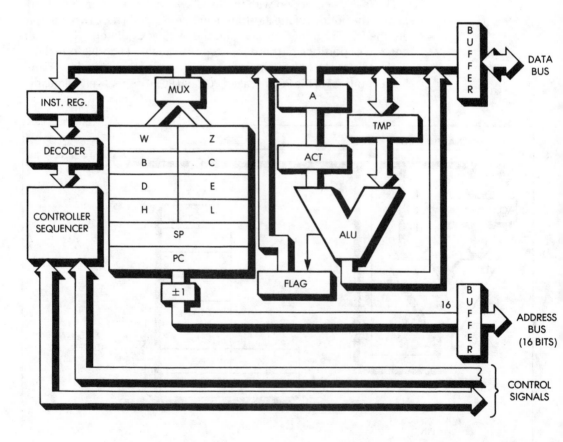

Figure 2.27: 8080 Internal Architecture

control bus appears at the bottom of the illustration. It is connected to the control unit. The *control unit* is on the left of Figure 2.27. The IR will hold one byte of the instruction fetched from the memory.

The *registers* are shown as a block and are in fact implemented as a RAM on the chip. Multiplexers are used to select a register in the RAM.

The *ALU* has an accumulator A, plus buffer (ACT for Temporary Accumulator), and a buffer register on the right input (TMP for Temporary). The ALU also has a flags register that stores exceptional conditions.

Figure 2.27 is a simplified illustration, but it is sufficient for our needs. It does not show all the actual connections, and some paths have been simplified.

We will next examine how the 8080 fetches and executes instructions, but, first, we will present some definitions.

8080 CYCLES AND STATES

Recall that the execution of an instruction in any processor starts with a *fetch* phase: the instruction must be brought from the memory into the IR, a special register of the control unit. In the case of the 8080, a fetch corresponds to a *machine-cycle* (with the exception of the DAD instruction).

The execution of each instruction requires from one to five machine-cycles, i.e., one to five memory accesses, depending on the length of the instruction. In the 8080, an instruction may be one, two, or three words in length and may, therefore, require one or two additional memory accesses after the first one.

Every machine cycle is implemented internally through a succession of microoperations. Each step in the sequence is called an *internal state*. Each machine cycle requires three to five such states, labeled T1 to T5 (see Figure 2.28). Each internal state is associated with the execution of a *microinstruction* of the sequencer's microprogram. The sequencing of microoperations is *clock-synchronous*, and *a state lasts for the duration of time between two successive pulses of the clock*. The 8080 indicates the start of each cycle with a pulse on the SYNC control signal (see Figure 2.28).

The 8080 uses a two-phase clock. The two phases are labeled $\phi1$ and $\phi2$, respectively. The duration of a phase is the period of Phase 1 of the clock. The standard 8080A uses a 2MHz clock. The duration of a state is, therefore, 500 ns (with the exception of the instructions WAIT, HLDA, and HLTA): $1/(2 \cdot 10^9) = 500 \cdot 10^{-6}$. The complete execution of an instruction requires from four to eighteen states. We can thus compute the duration of the execution of an 8080 instruction; it can vary from 4×500 ns $= 2000$ ns $= 2\,\mu s$ to 18×500 ns $= 9000$ ns $= 9\,\mu s$. This assumes a 2MHz clock.

Other versions of the 8080A are faster (for example, the 8080 A1 and the 8080 A2). The faster versions use a 3MHz clock and are 33% faster, requiring only 1.3 μs for a minimum cycle (4 states).

INSTRUCTION FORMATS

The 8080 instructions are listed in the tables of Figures 2.30 and 2.31 and are summarized in Appendix C. Like the instructions of many other microprocessors, the 8080 instructions may be formatted in one, two or three bytes.

The format of an instruction is shown in Figure 2.29. Every instruction includes an opcode followed by an optional *literal* or *address field* comprising one or two words.

The opcode field specifies the operation to be carried out. In strict computer terminology, the opcode represents only those bits that specify the operation to be performed, exclusive of the register pointers that might be necessary. In the microprocessor world, it is convenient to call the operation code, as well as any register pointers that it might incorporate, the opcode. For reasons of efficiency, this generalized opcode must reside in an 8-bit word. This constraint is a limiting factor on the number of instructions available in an 8-bit microprocessor.

Some instructions require that the opcode be followed by one word of data. In such a case, the instruction contains two words, the second word being the data. Let's look at some examples:

ADI data   (*add immediate data to A*)
MVI r,data   (*move immediate data to register r*)

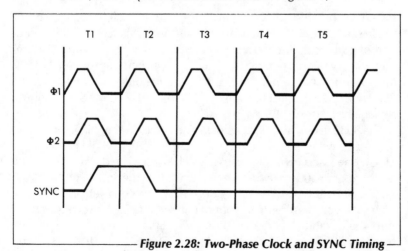

Figure 2.28: Two-Phase Clock and SYNC Timing

In other cases, the instruction might require that an address be specified. An address requires 16 bits or 2 bytes. In such cases, the instruction will be a 3-byte instruction.

A 3-word format is the longest format used in the 8080. Let's look at two more examples:

JMP addr   *(jump to specified address)*
CALL addr   *(call subroutine at specified address)*

For each byte of the instruction, the control unit must perform a memory fetch, which requires two µs. Thus, the shorter the instruction, the faster the execution.

Let us now examine the representation of some typical instructions in order to learn how to use the charts presented in Figures 2.30 and 2.31.

Representation of a One-Byte Instruction _____

In principle, 1-byte instructions are the fastest and are normally favored by the programmer. A typical 1-byte instruction for the 8080 is:

MOV r1,r2

This instruction means: "Transfer the contents of register r2 into r1." This is a typical "register-to-register" operation. Every microprocessor must be equipped with such instructions, which allow the programmer to transfer information from one register into another. Instructions referencing special registers of the machine, such as the accumulator or other special-purpose registers, often have a special opcode and a special name. The effect of this instruction is illustrated in Figure 2.33.

After the instruction is executed, the contents of r1 will be equal to the contents of r2. Note that the contents of r2 will not be modified by the read operation.

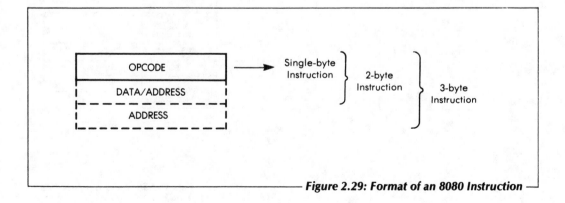

Figure 2.29: Format of an 8080 Instruction

MNEMONIC	OP CODE		M1[1]					M2		
	D7 D6 D5 D4	D3 D2 D1 D0	T1	T2[2]	T3	T4	T5	T1	T2[2]	T3
MOV r1, r2	0 1 D D	D S S S	PC OUT STATUS	PC = PC +1	INST→TMP/IR	(SSS)→TMP	(TMP)→DDD			
MOV r, M	0 1 D D	D 1 1 0				X[3]		HL OUT STATUS[6]	DATA→DDD	
MOV M, r	0 1 1 1	0 S S S				(SSS)→TMP		HL OUT STATUS[7]	(TMP)→DATA BUS	
SPHL	1 1 1 1	1 0 0 1				(HL) ____→SP				
MVI r, data	0 0 D D	D 1 1 0				X		PC OUT STATUS[6]	B2→DDDD	
MVI M, data	0 0 1 1	0 1 1 0				X			B2→TMP	
LXI rp, data	0 0 R P	0 0 0 1				X			PC = PC + 1	B2→r1
LDA addr	0 0 1 1	1 0 1 0				X			PC = PC + 1	B2→Z
STA addr	0 0 1 1	0 0 1 0				X			PC = PC + 1	B2→Z
LHLD addr	0 0 1 0	1 0 1 0				X			PC = PC + 1	B2→Z
SHLD addr	0 0 1 0	0 0 1 0				X		PC OUT STATUS[6]	PC = PC + 1	B2→Z
LDAX rp[4]	0 0 R P	1 0 1 0				X		rp OUT STATUS[6]	DATA→A	
STAX rp[4]	0 0 R P	0 0 1 0				X		rp OUT STATUS[7]	(A)→DATA BUS	
XCHG	1 1 1 0	1 0 1 1				(HL)↔(DE)				
ADD r	1 0 0 0	0 S S S				(SSS)→TMP (A)→ACT		[9]	(ACT)+(TMP)→A	
ADD M	1 0 0 0	0 1 1 0				(A)→ACT		HL OUT STATUS[6]	DATA→TMP	
ADI data	1 1 0 0	0 1 1 0				(A)→ACT		PC OUT STATUS[6]	PC = PC + 1	B2→TMP
ADC r	1 0 0 0	1 S S S				(SSS)→TMP (A)→ACT		[9]	(ACT)+(TMP)+CY→A	
ADC M	1 0 0 0	1 1 1 0				(A)→ACT		HL OUT STATUS[6]	DATA→TMP	
ACI data	1 1 0 0	1 1 1 0				(A)→ACT		PC OUT STATUS[6]	PC = PC + 1	B2→TMP
SUB r	1 0 0 1	0 S S S				(SSS)→TMP (A)→ACT		[9]	(ACT)-(TMP)→A	
SUB M	1 0 0 1	0 1 1 0				(A)→ACT		HL OUT STATUS[6]	DATA→TMP	
SUI data	1 1 0 1	0 1 1 0				(A)→ACT		PC OUT STATUS[6]	PC = PC + 1	B2→TMP
SBB r	1 0 0 1	1 S S S				(SSS)→TMP (A)→ACT		[9]	(ACT)-(TMP)-CY→A	
SBB M	1 0 0 1	1 1 1 0				(A)→ACT		HL OUT STATUS[6]	DATA→TMP	
SBI data	1 1 0 1	1 1 1 0				(A)→ACT		PC OUT STATUS[6]	PC = PC + 1	B2→TMP
INR r	0 0 D D	D 1 0 0				(DDD)→TMP (TMP) + 1→ALU	ALU→DDD			
INR M	0 0 1 1	0 1 0 0				X		HL OUT STATUS[6]	DATA→TMP (TMP)+1→ALU	
DCR r	0 0 D D	D 1 0 1				(DDD)→TMP (TMP)+1→ALU	ALU→DDD			
DCR M	0 0 1 1	0 1 0 1				X		HL OUT STATUS[6]	DATA→TMP (TMP)-1→ALU	
INX rp	0 0 R P	0 0 1 1				(RP) + 1 ____→RP				
DCX rp	0 0 R P	1 0 1 1				(RP) - 1 ____→RP				
DAD rp[8]	0 0 R P	1 0 0 1				X		(rl)→ACT	(L)→TMP, (ACT)+(TMP)→ALU	ALU→L, CY
DAA	0 0 1 0	0 1 1 1				DAA→A, FLAGS[10]				
ANA r	1 0 1 0	0 S S S				(SSS)→TMP (A)→ACT		[9]	(ACT)+(TMP)→A	
ANA M	1 0 1 0	0 1 1 0	PC OUT STATUS	PC = PC + 1	INST→TMP/IR	(A)→ACT		HL OUT STATUS[6]	DATA→TMP	

Figure 2.30: 8080 Instructions

	M3			M4			M5			
T1	T2[2]	T3	T1	T2[2]	T3	T1	T2[2]	T3	T4	T5
HL OUT STATUS[7]	(TMP) → DATA BUS									
PC OUT STATUS[6]	PC = PC + 1 B3 → rh									
	PC = PC + 1 B3 → W		WZ OUT STATUS[6]	DATA → A						
	PC = PC + 1 B3 → W		WZ OUT STATUS[7]	(A) → DATA BUS						
	PC = PC + 1 B3 → W		WZ OUT STATUS[6]	DATA → L WZ = WZ + 1		WZ OUT STATUS[6]	DATA → H			
PC OUT STATUS[6]	PC = PC + 1 B3 → W		WZ OUT STATUS[7]	(L) → DATA BUS WZ = WZ + 1		WZ OUT STATUS[7]	(H) → DATA BUS			
[9]	(ACT)+(TMP)→A									
[9]	(ACT)+(TMP)→A									
[9]	(ACT)+(TMP)+CY→A									
[9]	(ACT)+(TMP)+CY→A									
[9]	(ACT)-(TMP)→A									
[9]	(ACT)-(TMP)→A									
[9]	(ACT)-(TMP)-CY→A									
[9]	(ACT)-(TMP)-CY→A									
HL OUT STATUS[7]	ALU → DATA BUS									
HL OUT STATUS[7]	ALU → DATA BUS									
(rh)→ACT	(H)→TMP (ACT)+(TMP)+CY→ALU	ALU→H, CY								
[9]	(ACT)+(TMP)→A									

Figure 2.30: 8080 Instructions (cont.)

MNEMONIC	OP CODE		M1[1]					M2		
	D7 D6 D5 D4	D3 D2 D1 D0	T1	T2[2]	T3	T4	T5	T1	T2[2]	T3
ANI data	1 1 1 0	0 1 1 0	PC OUT STATUS	PC = PC + 1	INST→TMP/IR	(A)→ACT		PC OUT STATUS[6]	PC = PC + 1 B2 →TMP	
XRA r	1 0 1 0	1 S S S				(A)→ACT (SSS)→TMP		[9]	(ACT)+(TPM)→A	
XRA M	1 0 1 0	1 1 1 0				(A)→ACT		HL OUT STATUS[6]	DATA →TMP	
XRI data	1 1 1 0	1 1 1 0				(A)→ACT		PC OUT STATUS[6]	PC = PC + 1 B2 →TMP	
ORA r	1 0 1 1	0 S S S				(A)→ACT (SSS)→TMP		[9]	(ACT)+(TMP)→A	
ORA M	1 0 1 1	0 1 1 0				(A)→ACT		HL OUT STATUS[6]	DATA →TMP	
ORI data	1 1 1 1	0 1 1 0				(A)→ACT		PC OUT STATUS[6]	PC = PC + 1 B2 →TMP	
CMP r	1 0 1 1	1 S S S				(A)→ACT (SSS)→TMP		[9]	(ACT)-(TMP), FLAGS	
CMP M	1 0 1 1	1 1 1 0				(A)→ACT		HL OUT STATUS[6]	DATA →TMP	
CPI data	1 1 1 1	1 1 1 0				(A)→ACT		PC OUT STATUS[6]	PC = PC + 1 B2 →TMP	
RLC	0 0 0 0	0 1 1 1				(A)→ALU ROTATE		[9]	ALU→A, CY	
RRC	0 0 0 0	1 1 1 1				(A)→ALU ROTATE		[9]	ALU→A, CY	
RAL	0 0 0 1	0 1 1 1				(A), CY→ALU ROTATE		[9]	ALU→A, CY	
RAR	0 0 0 1	1 1 1 1				(A), CY→ALU ROTATE		[9]	ALU→A, CY	
CMA	0 0 1 0	1 1 1 1				(Ā)→A				
CMC	0 0 1 1	1 1 1 1				C̄Y→CY				
STC	0 0 1 1	0 1 1 1				1→CY				
JMP addr	1 1 0 0	0 0 1 1					X	PC OUT STATUS[6]	PC = PC + 1 B2 →Z	
J cond addr[17]	1 1 C C	C 0 1 0				JUDGE CONDITION		PC OUT STATUS[6]	PC = PC + 1 B2 →Z	
CALL addr	1 1 0 0	1 1 0 1				SP = SP - 1		PC OUT STATUS[6]	PC = PC + 1 B2 →Z	
C cond addr[17]	1 1 C C	C 1 0 0				JUDGE CONDITION IF TRUE, SP = SP - 1		PC OUT STATUS[6]	PC = PC + 1 B2 →Z	
RET	1 1 0 0	1 0 0 1				X		SP OUT STATUS[15]	SP = SP + 1 DATA →Z	
R cond addr[17]	1 1 C C	C 0 0 0			INST→TMP/IR	JUDGE CONDITION[14]		SP OUT STATUS[15]	SP = SP + 1 DATA →Z	
RST n	1 1 N N	N 1 1 1			φ→W INST→TMP/IR	SP = SP - 1		SP OUT STATUS[16]	SP = SP - 1 (PCH) →DATA BUS	
PCHL	1 1 1 0	1 0 0 1			INST→TMP/IR	(HL) → PC				
PUSH rp	1 1 R P	0 1 0 1				SP = SP - 1		SP OUT STATUS[16]	SP = SP - 1 (rh) →DATA BUS	
PUSH PSW	1 1 1 1	0 1 0 1				SP = SP - 1		SP OUT STATUS[16]	SP = SP - 1 (A) →DATA BUS	
POP rp	1 1 R P	0 0 0 1				X		SP OUT STATUS[15]	SP = SP + 1 DATA →rl	
POP PSW	1 1 1 1	0 0 0 1				X		SP OUT STATUS[15]	SP = SP + 1 DATA →FLAGS	
XTHL	1 1 1 0	0 0 1 1				X		SP OUT STATUS[15]	SP = SP + 1 DATA →Z	
IN port	1 1 0 1	1 0 1 1				X		PC OUT STATUS[6]	PC = PC + 1 B2 →Z, W	
OUT port	1 1 0 1	0 0 1 1				X		PC OUT STATUS[6]	PC = PC + 1 B2 →Z, W	
EI	1 1 1 1	1 0 1 1				SET INTE F/F				
DI	1 1 1 1	0 0 1 1				RESET INTE F/F				
HLT	0 1 1 1	0 1 1 0				X		PC OUT STATUS	HALT MODE[20]	
NOP	0 0 0 0	0 0 0 0	PC OUT STATUS	PC = PC + 1	INST→TMP/IR	X				

Figure 2.31: 8080 Instructions

M3			M4			M5				
T1	T2[2]	T3	T1	T2[2]	T3	T1	T2[2]	T3	T4	T5
[9]	(ACT)+(TMP)→A									
[9]	(ACT)+(TMP)→A									
[9]	(ACT)+(TMP)→A									
[9]	(ACT)+(TMP)→A									
[9]	(ACT)+(TMP)→A									
[9]	(ACT)–(TMP); FLAGS									
[9]	(ACT)–(TMP); FLAGS									
PC OUT STATUS[6]	PC = PC + 1 B3 →W							WZ OUT STATUS[11]	(WZ) + 1 → PC	
PC OUT STATUS[6]	PC = PC + 1 B3 →W							WZ OUT STATUS[11,12]	(WZ) + 1 → PC	
PC OUT STATUS[6]	PC = PC + 1 B3 →W		SP OUT STATUS[16]	(PCH) SP = SP – 1	→DATA BUS	SP OUT STATUS[16]	(PCL)→ DATA BUS	WZ OUT STATUS[11]	(WZ) + 1 → PC	
PC OUT STATUS[6]	PC = PC + 1 B3 →W[13]		SP OUT STATUS[16]	(PCH) SP = SP – 1	→DATA BUS	SP OUT STATUS[16]	(PCL)→ DATA BUS	WZ OUT STATUS[11,12]	(WZ) + 1 → PC	
SP OUT STATUS[15]	SP = SP + 1 DATA →W							WZ OUT STATUS[11]	(WZ) + 1 → PC	
SP OUT STATUS[15]	SP = SP + 1 DATA →W							WZ OUT STATUS[11,12]	(WZ) + 1 → PC	
SP OUT STATUS[16]	(TMP = 00NNN000) →Z (PCL) →DATA BUS							WZ OUT STATUS[11]	(WZ) + 1 → PC	
SP OUT STATUS[16]	(rl) →DATA BUS									
SP OUT STATUS[16]	FLAGS →DATA BUS									
SP OUT STATUS[15]	SP = SP + 1 DATA →rh									
SP OUT STATUS[15]	SP = SP + 1 DATA →A									
SP OUT STATUS[15]	DATA →W		SP OUT STATUS[16]	(H) →DATA BUS		SP OUT STATUS[16]	(L) → DATA BUS	(WZ) →HL		
WZ OUT STATUS[18]	DATA →A									
WZ OUT STATUS[16]	(A) →DATA BUS									

Figure 2.31: 8080 Instructions (cont.)

NOTES:

1.   The first memory cycle (M1) is always an instruction fetch; the first (or only) byte, containing the op code, is fetched during this cycle.

2.   If the READY input from memory is not high during T2 of each memory cycle, the processor will enter a wait state (TW) until READY is sampled as high.

3.   States T4 and T5 are present, as required, for operations which are completely internal to the CPU. The contents of the internal bus during T4 and T5 are available at the data bus; this is designed for testing purposes only. An "X" denotes that the state is present, but is only used for such internal operations as instruction decoding.

4.   Only register pairs rp = B (registers B and C) or rp = D (registers D and E) may be specified.

5.   These states are skipped.

6.   Memory read sub-cycles; an instruction or data word will be read.

7.   Memory write sub-cycle.

8.   The READY signal is not required during the second and third sub-cycles (M2 and M3). The HOLD signal is accepted during M2 and M3. The SYNC signal is not generated during M2 and M3. During the execution of DAD, M2 and M3 are required for an internal register-pair add; memory is not referenced.

9.   The results of these arithmetic, logical or rotate instructions are not moved into the accumulator (A) until state T2 of the next instruction cycle. That is, A is loaded while the next instruction is being fetched; this overlapping of operations allows for faster processing.

10.   If the value of the least significant 4 bits of the accumulator is greater than 9 or if the auxiliary carry bit is set, 6 is added to the accumulator. If the value of the most significant 4 bits of the accumulator is now greater than 9, or if the carry bit is set, 6 is added to the most significant 4 bits of the accumulator.

11.   This represents the first sub-cycle (the instruction fetch) of the next instruction cycle.

12.   If the condition was met, the contents of the register pair WZ are output on the address lines (A_{0-15}) instead of the contents of the program counter (PC).

13.   If the condition was not met, sub-cycles M4 and M5 are skipped; the processor instead proceeds immediately to the instruction fetch (M1) of the next instruction cycle.

14.   If the condition was not met, sub-cycles M2 and M3 are skipped; the processor instead proceeds immediately to the instruction fetch (M1) of the next instruction cycle.

15.   Stack read sub-cycle.

16.   Stack write sub-cycle.

17.   CONDITION   CCC

NZ	— not zero (Z = 0)	000
Z	— zero (Z = 1)	001
NC	— no carry (CY = 0)	010
C	— carry (CY = 1)	011
PO	— parity odd (P = 0)	100
PE	— parity even (P = 1)	101
P	— plus (S = 0)	110
M	— minus (S = 1)	111

18.   I/O sub-cycle: the I/O port's 8-bit select code is duplicated on address lines 0-7 (A_{0-7}) and 8-15 (A_{8-15}).

19.   Output sub-cycle.

20.   The processor will remain idle in the halt state until an interrupt, a reset or a hold is accepted. When a hold request is accepted, the CPU enters the hold mode; after the hold mode is terminated, the processor returns to the halt state. After a reset is accepted, the processor begins execution at memory location zero. After an interrupt is accepted, the processor executes the instruction forced onto the data bus (usually a restart instruction).

SSS or DDD	Value	rp	Value
A	111	B	00
B	000	D	01
C	001	H	10
D	010	SP	11
E	011		
H	100		
L	101		

Figure 2.32: Interpreting the 8080 Instructions

Internally, every instruction must be represented in a binary format. The representation "MOV r1,r2" is *symbolic* or *mnemonic*. It is called the *assembly-language* representation of an instruction. It is simply a convenient symbolic representation of the actual binary encoding for that instruction. The binary code that represents this instruction can be found in Figure 2.30, on the first line. It is:

```
7                    0
0  1  D  D  D  S  S  S
```

This representation is still partially symbolic. Each of the letters S and D stands for a binary bit. The three Ds represent the three bits pointing to the *destination* register. Three bits allow the selection of one register from eight possible registers. Similarly, SSS represents the three bits pointing to the *source* register. The convention here is that register 2 is the source, and register 1 is the destination. The codes for these registers appear in Figure 2.34. For example, the code for register B is 0 0 0, the code for register C is 0 0 1, and so on.

The abbreviations used in the 8080 instruction set are shown in Figure 2.35.

The placement of the opcode bits in the binary representation of an instruction is not meant for the convenience of the programmer; rather, it is for the control section of the microprocessor, which must decode and execute the instruction. The *assembly-language* representation, however, *is* meant for the convenience of the programmer. It can be argued that MOV r1,r2 should really mean: "Transfer the contents of r1 into r2." In this case, the convention, though arbitrary, has been chosen in order to maintain compatibility with the binary representation.

Another example of a one-byte instruction is:

ADD r

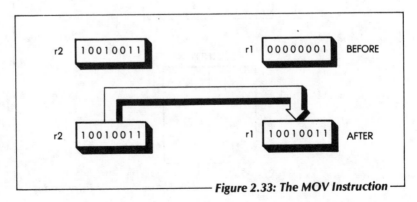

Figure 2.33: The MOV Instruction

This instruction adds the contents of a specified register (r) to the accumulator (A). Symbolically, this operation may be represented by: A = A + r. By inspecting Figure 2.30 it can be seen that the binary representation of this instruction is:

where SSS specifies the register to be added to the accumulator. For example, let us add register C to the accumulator. Using the codes given in Figure 2.32, the corresponding instruction is:

Representation of a Two-Byte Instruction

The simple two-word instruction:

ADI data

REGISTERS

000	B
001	C
010	D
011	E
100	H
101	L
110	—(Memory)
111	A

REGISTER PAIRS

00	BC
01	DE
10	HL
11	SP

Figure 2.34: Register Codes

adds the contents of the second word of the instruction to the accumulator. The effect of this instruction is shown in Figure 2.36. The second word of the instruction (byte 2) contains the data and is symbolically represented by B2 in the table in Figure 2.30. Abbreviations such as B2 are explained in Figure 2.35. The contents of the second word of the instruction are said to be the *literal* and are treated as eight bits of data without any particular significance. They could represent either a character or numerical data—a fact irrelevant to the operation. The code for this instruction:

1	1	0	0	0	1	1	0

is obtained by inspecting Figure 2.30.

The I in the mnemonic of the ADI instruction stands for an *immediate* operation. "Immediate" in most programming languages means that the next word (or words) within the instruction contains data that should be used as data and not be *interpreted* (in the same way that an opcode is interpreted). I generally means that the next one or two bytes are to be treated as *literals*. One byte is required for data; two bytes are required for an address.

The control unit is programmed to "know" the number of bytes in each instruction. It will, therefore, always fetch and execute the correct number of bytes for each instruction. However, the control unit's task of decoding the instructions becomes more complex as the maximum number of bytes increases.

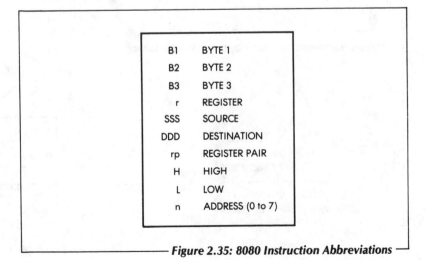

B1	BYTE 1
B2	BYTE 2
B3	BYTE 3
r	REGISTER
SSS	SOURCE
DDD	DESTINATION
rp	REGISTER PAIR
H	HIGH
L	LOW
n	ADDRESS (0 to 7)

Figure 2.35: 8080 Instruction Abbreviations

Representation of a Three-Byte Instruction _____

The instruction:

       LDA addr

requires three bytes. This instruction means: "Load the accumulator from the memory address specified in the next two bytes of the instruction." Since addresses are 16 bits long, they require two bytes. The binary representation of this instruction is obtained by inspecting Figure 2.30.

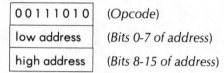

00111010	*(Opcode)*
low address	*(Bits 0-7 of address)*
high address	*(Bits 8-15 of address)*

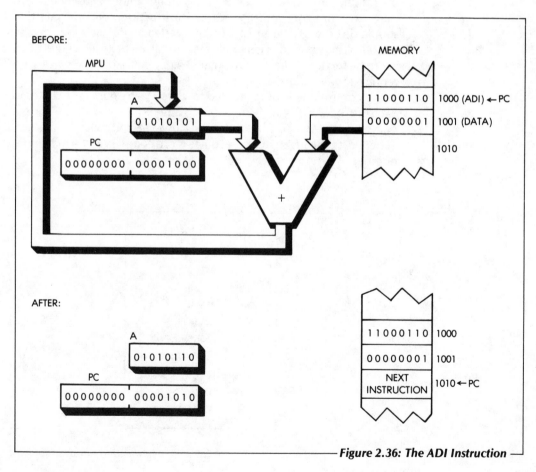

Figure 2.36: The ADI Instruction

By convention, the second and third bytes of a three-byte instruction are called B2 and B3, as shown in Figure 2.35. The tables presented in Figures 2.30 and 2.31 contain the complete specifications for the execution of any instruction within the 8080. The execution of instructions within other microprocessors is essentially similar.

We have seen how instructions are represented as one, two, or three bytes. We will now study the way they are executed inside the 8080.

EXECUTION OF INSTRUCTIONS WITHIN THE 8080

Let us first review the internal architecture of the 8080. The detailed internal architecture of the 8080 is shown again in Figure 2.37. The internal data bus appears at the top of the illustration. It propagates into the external world via a *buffer* that isolates it from the outside. External connection to this internal data bus is accomplished through pins D0

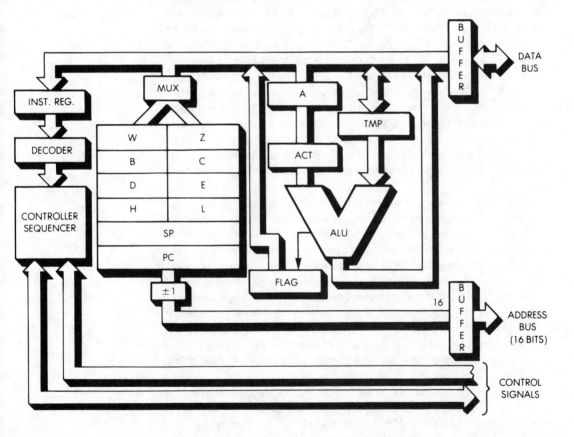

Figure 2.37: Internal Architecture of the 8080

through D7 of the package. The two other buses that are required for the operation of the system appear at the bottom of the illustration. The address bus originates from the double-length registers: PC, SP, HL, and WZ. (For simplicity, these connections are not detailed in the illustration.) On the left side of the illustration, the control bus is connected to the control unit.

Two buffer registers are used by the ALU. The accumulator (A) is followed by a buffer called ACT or "temporary accumulator." The right input of the ALU is buffered by the TMP or "temporary register."

Flags will not be considered here in detail. The programmer should be aware that operations carried out by the ALU will condition one or more flags within this register. However, this is not basic to the execution of instructions; thus we will not discuss them in detail here.

Grouped in a single block on the left side of the ALU are all of the general-purpose internal registers. They have been grouped because they are implemented as an internal RAM. These internal registers include the six general-purpose registers: B, C, D, E, H, and L, as well as the double registers: SP and PC. Further, B, C, D, E, H, and L have been grouped by pairs. This has been done because the 8080 is equipped with special instructions that allow the use of *register pairs* such as BC, DE, and HL. In addition, a special set of registers, W and Z, appear which are invisible to the user. Although invisible, they are necessary for the operation of the control unit. In fact, they are necessary for the internal execution of some instructions in nearly all microprocessors and must be provided, but they usually do not appear in the illustrations supplied by the manufacturer as they are not visible from the outside.

On top of the block of registers appears a multiplexer (MUX). This is the addressing mechanism that selects one of the registers within the block. It uses a field of 3 bits specified within the opcode to select a register. Below the block of registers appears a box containing ± 1. This symbolic representation indicates the availability of an *incrementer-decrementer* that can automatically increment or decrement the PC and the SP during some operations. The control unit appears on the far left of the illustration. The role of the control unit will be explained in detail shortly. The control unit is equipped with an *instruction register* (IR) that is connected to the data bus. The contents of this instruction register are decoded by a decoder, resulting in the execution of the specified instruction.

Let us once again study the table in Figure 2.30. Recall that this table presents the detailed internal sequencing of the 8080 instructions. On the left of the figure we find the *mnemonic* of each instruction (i.e., the way it is represented in assembly language). The next column contains the 8-bit binary code for its opcode, as previously explained. The next columns, labeled M1, M2, M3, M4, and M5, contain the detailed operations that are performed during successive *machine cycles*. Each instruction requires at least one machine cycle, and possibly more. Each machine cycle requires several *internal states* for its execution. During machine cycle M1, the instruction is fetched from the memory and brought into IR inside the microprocessor. Let us now examine the FETCH phase in detail.

THE FETCH PHASE

The FETCH phase of an instruction is implemented during the first three states of machine cycle M1. These three states are called T1, T2, and T3. They are shown in the table in Figure 2.30. The sequence corresponding to these three states is common to all instructions of the microprocessor because all instructions must be fetched prior to execution. The first FETCH phase of the instruction is accomplished during state T1 and represented by:

T1 : PC OUT

This line reads as: "PC is sent outside". The first step in the fetch process is to present the address of the next instruction to the memory. This address is contained in the program counter (PC). As with any instruction fetch, the contents of the PC are first placed on the address bus (see Figure 2.38). At this point, an address is presented to the memory, and the memory address decoders decode the address in order to select the appropriate location within the memory. Several hundred nanoseconds will elapse before the contents of the selected memory location become available on the output pins of the memory, which are connected to the data bus. It is standard computer design to use the memory access-time to perform an operation within the microprocessor. This operation is the incrementation of the program counter:

T2 : PC = PC + 1

While the memory is reading, the contents of the PC are incremented by 1 (see Figure 2.39). T2 requires 500 ns on the standard 8080. At the end of state T2, the contents of the memory are available and can then be transferred within the microprocessor. The corresponding operation is found by inspecting Figure 2.30:

T3 : INST into IR

During state T3, the instruction that was read out of the memory is deposited on the data bus and transferred into the instruction register of the 8080 where it will be decoded (see Figure 2.40). Note that state

T4 of M1 will be required. Once the instruction has been deposited into IR during T3, it is necessary to *decode* and *execute* it. This will require at least one state, T4.

A few instructions require an extra state of M1, i.e., state T5. However, for most instructions this state is not used and is skipped by the processor. Looking again at the table in Figure 2.30, the empty boxes in the column of T5 mean that the state is not used by the processor. Whenever the execution of an instruction requires more than machine cycle M1, i.e., M1, M2 or more cycles, the transition is made directly from state T4 of M1 into state T1 of M2. This sequencing is illustrated in Figure 2.41.

We will now study the detailed sequence of operations involved in executing typical instructions such as MOV D,C, ADD r, ADD M, and JMP addr. This will clarify and explain the role of all the registers, buses, and connections inside the microprocessor.

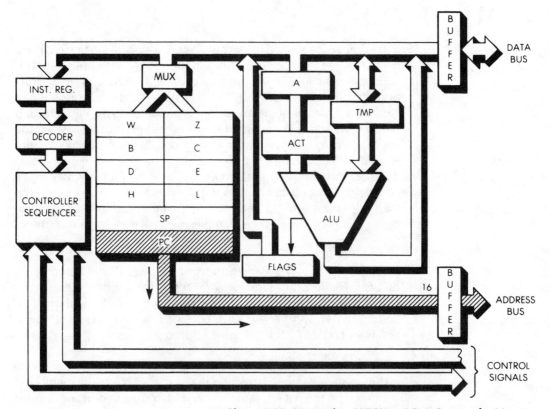

Figure 2.38: Instruction FETCH—(PC) Is Sent to the Memory

A Single-Byte Instruction: MOV D,C _____

The instruction MOV D,C transfers the contents of register C into
register D. Its code was described in the previous section. By coinci-
dence, the destination register in this example happens to be named D.
The transfer is illustrated in Figure 2.42. The corresponding 8080 internal
sequence is shown on line 1 in Figure 2.30 (MOV r1,r2). The corresponding entry is shown in Figure 2.43.

The first three states—T1, T2, T3—of cycle M1 are used to fetch the instruction from the memory, as previously described. At the end of T3,
the instruction is in IR, the Instruction Register, where it can be decoded.

During T4, the contents of C are deposited into TMP (see Figure
2.44):

T4 : (S S S)→TMP

In the instruction the parentheses mean "contents of," and in this case
SSS refers to register C.

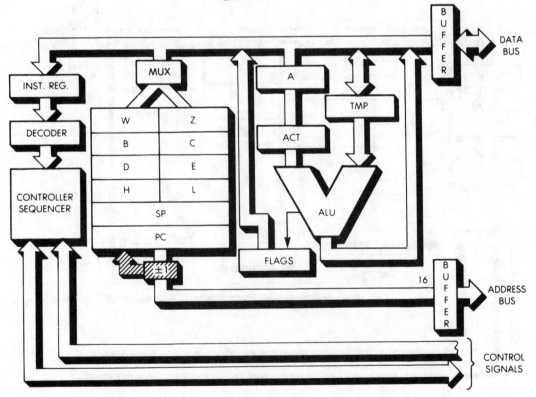

Figure 2.39: PC Is Incremented while the Memory Reads

During T5, the contents of TMP are deposited into D (see Figure 2.45):

T5 : (TMP)→D D D

Execution of the instruction is now complete. The contents of register C have been transferred into the specified destination, register D. This terminates execution of the instruction. The other machine cycles—M2, M3, M4, and M5—are not necessary and are not used. Execution stops at the end of M1.

The duration of this instruction can be easily computed. The duration of every state for the standard 8080A is the duration of Phase 1 of the clock: 500 ns. The duration of this instruction is the duration of the five states required to execute it, or $5 \times 500 = 2500$ ns $= 2.5\ \mu s$.

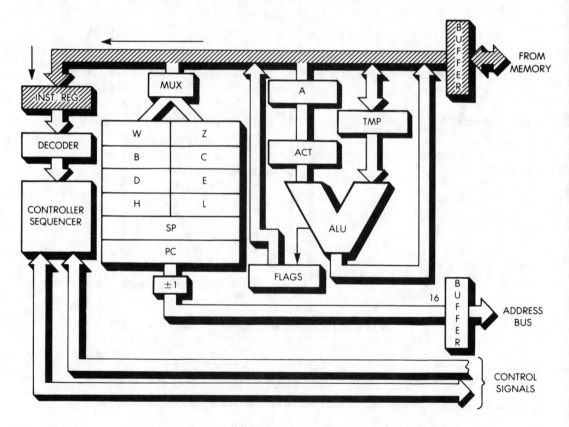

Figure 2.40: The Instruction Arrives from the Memory into IR

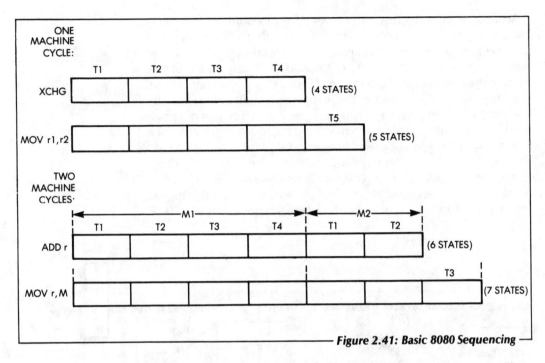

Figure 2.41: Basic 8080 Sequencing

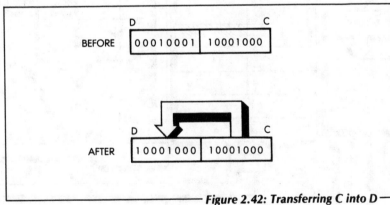

Figure 2.42: Transferring C into D

MNEMONIC	OPCODE	T1	T2	T3	T4	T5
MOV r1,r2	01DDDSSS	PC OUT STATUS	PC = PC + 1	INST → IR	(SSS) → TMP	(TMP) → DDD

Figure 2.43: MOV r1,r2

At this point one might ask why this instruction requires *two states* (T4 and T5) to transfer the contents of C into D. Two states are necessary because the instruction first transfers the contents of C into TMP and then the contents of TMP into D. It would obviously be simpler to transfer the contents of C directly into D within a single state. Unfortunately, this is not possible because of the implementation chosen for the internal registers. All the internal registers are, in fact, part of a single RAM, a read/write memory internal to the microprocessor chip, and only one word may be addressed or selected at a time through a RAM's single port. For this reason it is not possible to read from and write to two different locations simultaneously. Either two RAM cycles or a dual port RAM would be required. Thus, it becomes necessary first to read the data out of the register-RAM, storing it in a temporary register, TMP,

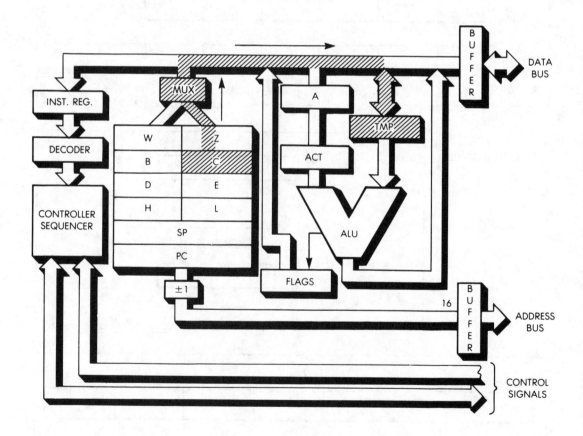

Figure 2.44: The Contents of C Are Deposited into TMP

and second, to write it back into the final destination register (in this case, D). This might rightly be viewed as a design inadequacy. However, this limitation is common to virtually all monolithic microprocessors. It is not intrinsic to processors and it is not normally found in bit-slice or large computers. This particular use of RAM in register design conserves precious area on the chip for other logic. As packing densities increase in the future, it may no longer be necessary.

At this point we recommend going back to Figure 2.42 and reviewing the sequencing of this simple instruction before proceeding on to more complex ones. A recommended exercise is to assemble a few small-sized "symbols" such as matches or paperclips, then refer to the table in Figure 2.30 and move the symbols in Figure 2.45 to simulate the flow of data from the registers into the buses. For example, deposit a symbol

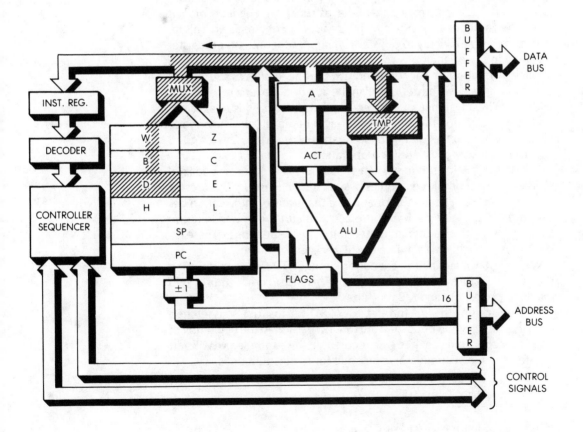

Figure 2.45: The Contents of TMP Are Deposited into D

into PC. Look at the entry for T1 in Figure 2.30. T1 will move the symbol contained in PC out on the address bus towards the memory. Continue simulating execution in this fashion until you feel comfortable with the transfers along the buses and between the registers. At this point, you should have acquired a reasonable understanding of the meaning of the microinstructions presented in the chart contained in the tables in Figures 2.30 and 2.31, and you should be ready to proceed.

We will now go on to study more complex instructions.

An Arithmetic Instruction: ADD r

Refer to the 15th line of the table in Figure 2.30. This instruction means: "Add the contents of register r (specified by a binary code S S S) to the accumulator (A), and deposit the results in the accumulator" (see Appendix C for the meanings of the instructions). This is an *implicit* instruction as it does not explicitly reference a second register. This instruction refers explicitly to register r. It *implies* that the other register involved in the operation is the accumulator. When used in such an implicit instruction, the accumulator is referenced *both as source and destination*. Data will be deposited in the accumulator as a result of this addition. The advantage of such an implicit instruction is to save opcode bits: the complete opcode is only eight bits in length. The opcode requires only a 3-bit register field for the specification of r. This is a good way to implement a fast addition operation.

Other implicit instructions exist that reference other specialized registers. More complex examples of such implicit instructions are, for example, the PUSH and POP operations that transfer information between the top of the stack and the accumulator while updating the Stack Pointer (SP) by either incrementing or decrementing it. These instructions implicitly manipulate the SP register.

We will now examine the execution of the ADD r instruction using the table in Figure 2.30 as a reference. This instruction requires two machine cycles, M1 and M2 this time.

As usual, during the first three states of M1 the instruction is fetched from the memory and deposited into the IR register. At the beginning of T4 it is decoded and can then be executed. In this example, we will add register B to the accumulator. The code for the instruction is:

(since the code for register B is 0 0 0).

During the fourth state of M1, the two operands are transferred to the

ALU input buffers:

T4 : (S S S)→TMP, (A)→ACT

Two transfers are executed simultaneously. The contents of the specified source register (here B) move into TMP, i.e., to the right input of the ALU (see Figure 2.46), and, at the same time, the contents of the accumulator move to the temporary accumulator (ACT). We see in Figure 2.46 that those transfers can occur in parallel because they use different paths within the system. The transfer from B to TMP uses the internal data bus while the transfer into ACT uses a short internal path (independent of this data bus). To save time, the transfers occur simultaneously. At this point, both the left and right inputs of the ALU are correctly conditioned. The right input of the ALU is now conditioned by the contents of register B. We are ready to perform the addition. Let us look again at the table in Figure 2.30. There is a surprise. If we look at

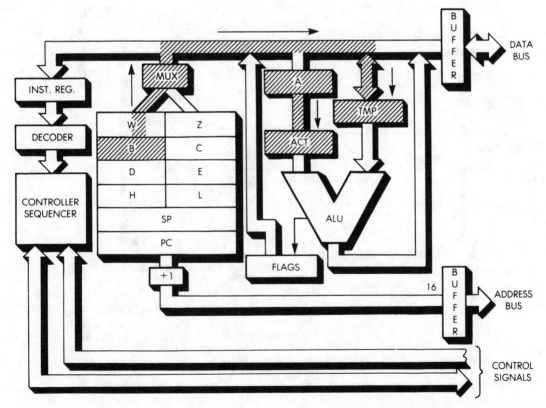

Figure 2.46: Two Transfers Occur Simultaneously

state T5 of M1, where we would normally expect to see the addition take place, we see that this state is simply not used. The addition is not performed.

Moving further to the right on the same line of the table, we enter machine cycle M2. During state T1, nothing happens; there is simply a reference (9) to the notes for the table (which will be explained later). It is only in state T2 of M2 that the addition takes place:

T2 of M2: (ACT) + (TMP)→A

The contents of ACT are added to the contents of TMP and the result is finally deposited in the accumulator. (See Figure 2.47.) The operation is now complete.

We might now be wondering why the addition took place during state T2 of machine cycle M2 rather than during state T5 of machine cycle M1. The answer to this question requires an understanding of CPU

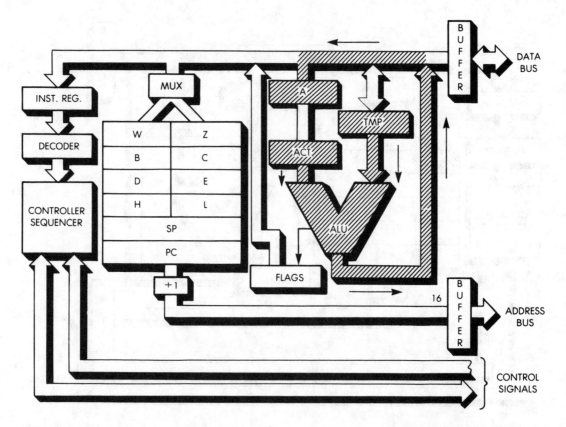

Figure 2.47: End of ADD r

design. The technique involved is fundamental to clock-synchronous CPU design; it is a standard "trick" called the *Fetch/Execute Overlap* and is used in the design of most CPUs. The basic idea is the following. Looking back at Figure 2.46, we see that the actual execution of the addition only requires the use of the ALU and the data bus. In particular, it does not access the register RAM (register block). We know that the next three states to be executed after completion of any instruction are T1, T2, and T3 of machine cycle M1 of the next instruction. Looking back at the execution of these three states, we recall that they only require access to the program counter (PC) and use of the address bus. Access to the program counter requires access to the register RAM. (This explains why the same trick could not be used in the instruction MOV r1,r2.) It is therefore possible to use the shaded area in Figure 2.47 and the shaded area in Figure 2.38 simultaneously. Unfortunately, there is one more fact that has not yet been explained that somewhat complicates the picture. Looking back at the tables, we notice that during state T1 of M1 two phenomena occurred: "PC out" and "status." This is due to the specific implementation of the 8080, which we will now explain.

The 8080 was the first powerful standard 8-bit microprocessor introduced on the market. The device requires three power supplies, +5V, −5V, and +12V, as was the requirement for dynamic memories at the time. Unfortunately, these power supplies used up four pins on the chip (three plus ground) rather than two as is the case in current systems. In addition, the external clock used in the 8080 system also required several pins. In view of the 40-pin limitation, it was no longer possible to supply all of the pins needed by the control bus. For this reason, control signals appear on the data bus, i.e., eight control signals are gated out on the data bus during state T1. This is indicated by the term "Status" in the chart in state T1 (Figure 2.34). Naturally, this creates an added complication. A special device is required for the 8080—the 8228 (system controller)—which demultiplexes the data bus. The 8228 creates a "clean" data bus carrying data and a separate control bus carrying control signals. In short, since the data bus is, in fact, used during state T1 of M1 to carry out *status* information, the same bus cannot be used for the *addition* that we would like to perform during T1 of M2. Thus, it becomes necessary to wait until state T2 before the addition can be carried out. This is what occurred in the chart (Figure 2.30). The addition was completed during state T2 of M2.

The Fetch/Execute Overlap mechanism has now been described. The advantage of this approach should be clear. Let us assume that we would have implemented a straightforward scheme, where the addition was performed during state T5 of machine cycle M1. The duration of the ADD instruction would have been 5 × 500 = 2500 ns. With the overlap approach that was described, once state T4 is executed the next instruction is immediately fetched. In other words, after four states have been used by the ADD instruction, the next instruction is initiated. In a manner that is invisible to this next instruction, the "clever" control unit uses state T2 of the next instruction to carry out the end of the addition.

On the chart, T2 is shown as a part of M2 for the first instruction. This is because, conceptually, M2 is the second machine cycle of the addition. In fact, M2 is overlapped. This overlapping occurs at the same time as machine cycle M1 of the next instruction. For the programmer, the delay introduced by ADD is only *four* states, i.e., 4 × 500 = 2000 ns rather than 2500 ns using the "straightforward" approach. The speed improvement is 500 ns or 20%.

This overlap technique, illustrated in Figure 2.48, is used whenever possible to speed up the (apparent) execution of the microprocessor. Naturally, it is not possible to overlap in all cases. Required buses or facilities must be available without conflict. The control unit "knows" whether or not an overlap is possible and this is indicated by Note 9 on the table in Figures 2.30 and 2.31.

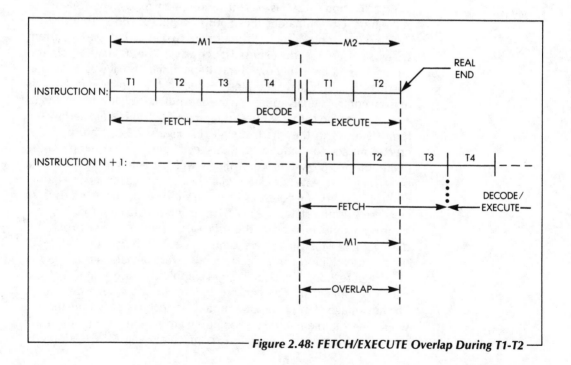

Figure 2.48: FETCH/EXECUTE Overlap During T1-T2

Let us take this scheme a step further and use state T3 of M2 to execute a longer instruction. We will now examine a more complex instruction.

Another Typical Instruction: ADD M

By inspecting Figure 2.30, we find that the opcode for this instruction is 10000110. This instruction means: "Add the contents of a memory location (M) to the accumulator." (See Appendix C.) By convention, the address of the memory location M is contained in registers H and L. This instruction assumes that these two special registers (H and L) have been loaded with appropriate contents by the programmer prior to the execution of the instruction. The 16-bit contents of these registers now specify the address in the memory where data resides. These data are added to the accumulator and the result is left in the accumulator. The process is illustrated by Figure 2.49.

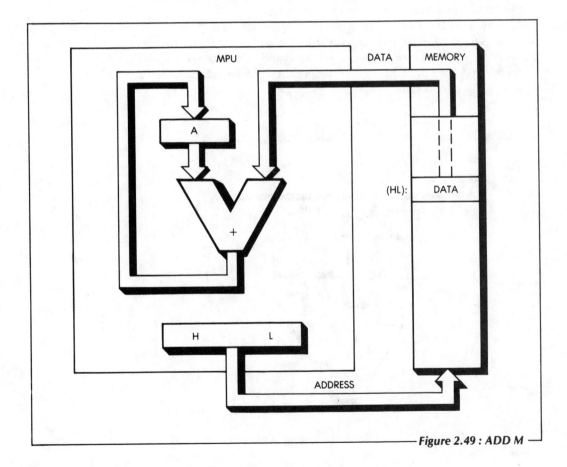

Figure 2.49 : ADD M

This instruction has a specific history. It was supplied in order to provide compatibility between the early 8008 and its successor, the 8080. Because the early 8008 was not equipped with a direct memory addressing capability, registers H and L were used to address memory. To access the contents of the memory, the two registers H and L are first loaded and then an instruction referencing H and L is executed. ADD M is an example of such an instruction. It must be stressed that the 8080 is not limited in its memory addressing capability in the same way as the 8008. The 8080 also has direct memory addressing. The facility allowing the use of the H and L registers becomes an added advantage and not a disadvantage as was the case with the 8008.

Using the table in Figure 2.30, let us now follow the execution of this instruction. States T1, T2, and T3 of M1 are used, as usual, to *fetch* the instruction. During state T4, the contents of the accumulator are transferred to its buffer register, ACT, and the left input of the ALU is conditioned. The situation is shown in Figure 2.50.

Memory must be accessed in order to provide the second byte of data that is to be added to the accumulator. The address of this byte of data is contained in H and L. The contents of H and L therefore need to be transferred onto the address bus, where they will be gated to the memory. This occurs during M2.

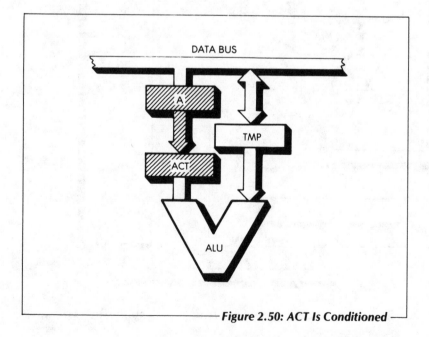

Figure 2.50: ACT Is Conditioned

Machine Cycle M2.   During the T1 phase of machine cycle M2, we read in Figure 2.30 that:

T1 : HL OUT

H and L are deposited on the address bus in the same way that PC was deposited on the bus during M1. This is shown in Figure 2.51. During state T1, *status* is also output on the data bus, but we will not make use of that information here. From a simplified point of view, M2 requires two states: one for the memory to respond to the address, and one for the data that has become available to be transferred onto the TMP, i.e., the right input of the ALU.

Both inputs of the ALU are now conditioned; the situation is analogous to the one in the previous instruction (ADD r). As before, we simply have to ADD. We use a *fetch/execute overlap* technique and,

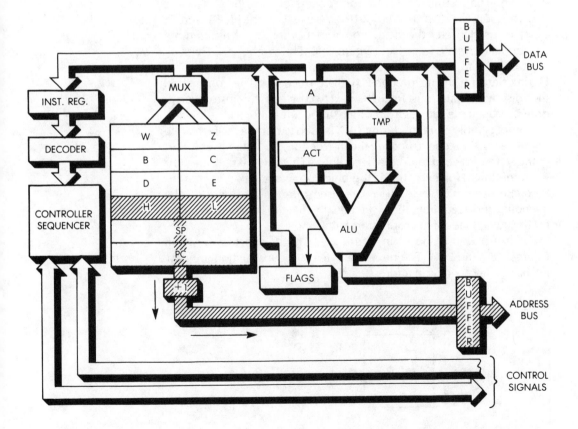

Figure 2.51: Transfer Contents of HL to Address Bus

rather than executing the addition within state T4 of M2, final execution is postponed until state T2 of M3. Looking at the table in Figure 2.30 it can be seen that, indeed, during T2 of M3 we do have:

T2 : (ACT) + (TMP)→A.

The addition is finally performed, the contents of ACT are added to TMP, and the result is deposited into the accumulator A.

Having described three typical instructions, we will now study a more complex direct memory addressing instruction that uses the invisible W and Z registers.

A Direct Memory Addressing Instruction: LDA addr

The effect of this instruction is to load the accumulator from the memory contents of the address specified in bytes 2 and 3 of the instruction. The instruction LDA addr appears on Line 8 of the table (Figure 2.30). The opcode is 00111010. As usual, states T1, T2, and T3 of M1 are used to fetch the instruction from the memory. A new symbol now appears in state T4 of M1 in Figure 2.30. This symbol is X. This X indicates that state T4 is used but that no visible result can be described. During state T4, the instruction is, in fact, decoded. The control unit then discovers that it must fetch the next two bytes of this instruction in order to obtain the address from which the accumulator will be loaded. As nothing visible happens during T4, X is used to denote the fact. Note that state T4 is needed to *decode* the instruction, but actually only part of the state is needed to do the decoding, so it could be considered a waste of time. However, this is the philosophy of *clock-synchronous logic*. Because *microinstructions* are used internally to perform the decoding and execution, this is the penalty that must be paid in return for the advantages of microprogramming.

The instruction is shown in Figure 2.52 and its effect is shown in Figures 2.53 and 2.54. The next two bytes of the instruction are now fetched. They specify an address.

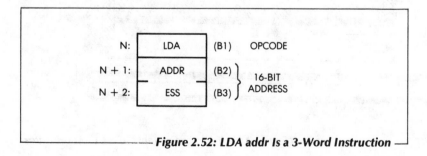

Figure 2.52: LDA addr Is a 3-Word Instruction

Machine Cycle M2. As usual, the first two states, T1 and T2, are used to fetch the contents of the memory location pointed to by PC. During T2, the program counter, PC, is incremented. Sometime by the end of T2, data becomes available from the memory and appears on the data bus. By the end of T3, the word that has been fetched from memory address PC (B2, second byte of the instruction) is available on the data bus. It must now be stored in a temporary register; it is deposited into Z: B2→Z. This is shown in Figure 2.55.

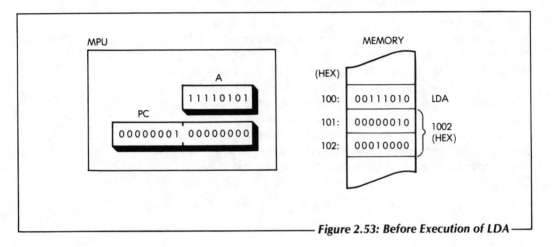

Figure 2.53: Before Execution of LDA

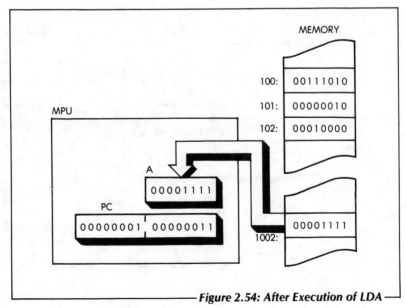

Figure 2.54: After Execution of LDA

Machine Cycle M3. Again, PC is deposited on the address bus, incremented, and finally the third byte, B3, is read from the memory and deposited into register W of the microprocessor. This is shown in Figure 2.56. At this point, by the end of state T3 of M3, registers W and Z inside the microprocessor contain B2 and B3, i.e., the complete 16-bit address that was originally contained in the two words following the instruction in the memory. W and Z contain an address; execution can now be completed. This address must be sent to the memory in order to extract the data. This is done in the next machine cycle.

Machine Cycle M4. This time, W and Z are output on the address bus. The 16-bit address is sent to the memory, and by the end of state T2, data corresponding to the contents of the specified memory location become available. The data are then finally deposited in A at the end of state T3, which terminates execution of this instruction.

This illustrates the use of an *immediate instruction*. This instruction required three bytes in order to store a 2-byte *explicit address*. It also required four memory cycles, as it needed to go to the memory three times in order to extract the three bytes of this 3-word instruction, plus one more memory access in order to fetch the data specified by the address. It is a long instruction; however, it is also a basic one for loading

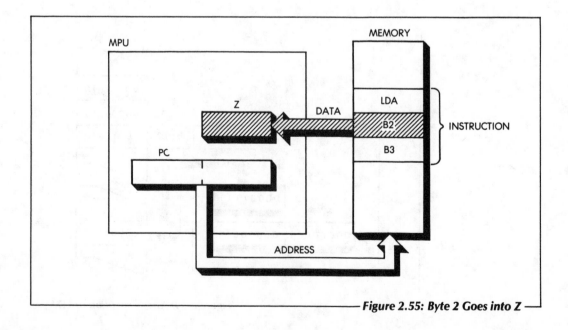

Figure 2.55: Byte 2 Goes into Z

the accumulator with specified contents residing at a known memory location. It can be noted that this instruction requires the use of W and Z registers.

Let us now consider the question: could this instruction have used registers other than W and Z within the system? The answer is no. If this instruction had used other registers, for example the H and L registers, it would have modified their contents. After execution of this instruction, the contents of H and L would have been lost. In a program, it is always assumed that an instruction will not modify any registers that it is not explicitly using. An instruction loading the accumulator should not destroy the contents of any other register. For this reason, it becomes necessary to supply the two additional registers, W and Z, for the internal use of the control unit.

Another question that comes to mind is: could PC have been used rather than W and Z? If you think about it, you will see that the answer to this question is definitely not; that would have been suicidal: the contents of PC would have been lost, and there would have been no way to find the next instruction to be executed.

One more type of instruction, a *branch* or *jump* instruction, will now be studied. This instruction modifies the sequence in which instructions are executed within the program. So far we have assumed that

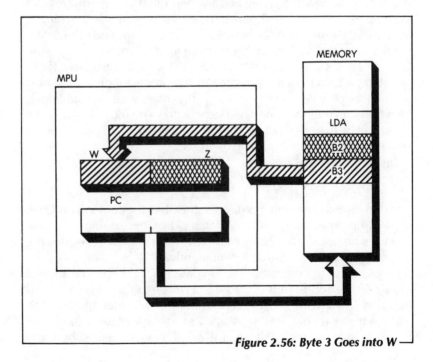

Figure 2.56: Byte 3 Goes into W

instructions were executed sequentially. However, there are instructions that allow the programmer to jump out of sequence to another instruction within the program or, in practical terms, to jump to another area of the memory.

The Jump Instruction: JMP addr

This instruction causes the instruction at address *addr* to be executed next. It appears on Line 18 of the table in Figure 2.31. Follow the horizontal line of the table where the instruction execution is described. This again is a 3-word instruction. The first word is the opcode and contains 11000011. The next two words contain the 16-bit address to which the jump will be made. Conceptually, the effect of this instruction is to replace the contents of the program counter with the 16 bits following the JMP opcode.   In practice, a different, more efficient approach will be implemented.

As before, the first three states of M1 correspond to the instruction-fetch. During state T4, the instruction is decoded and no other event is recorded (X).

The next two machine cycles are used to fetch bytes B2 and B3 of the instruction. During M2, B2 is fetched and deposited into the internal register Z. During M3, B3 is fetched and deposited into internal register W. If we refer to the table (Figure 2.31) we see something surprising. It looks as if the instruction has finished execution at the end of T3 of M3. But this is not the case. In the insert on the right side of the chart we see two more states which are overlapped with the next instruction. These two states are, in fact, implemented by the processor during the next instruction-fetch (as was previously the case with the addition). However, this time these next two steps, (shown on the right side of the table) will be executed *rather than the usual steps* for T1 and T2 of the next instruction. Let us examine them.

The next two steps are:

WZ OUT and (WZ) + 1→PC

In other words, the contents of WZ rather than the contents of PC are used during the next instruction-fetch. The control unit will have recorded that a jump was being executed, and it will have executed the beginning of the next instruction differently.

Let us look at the effect these two extra states will have. The address placed on the address bus of the system will be the address contained in W and Z. In other words, the next instruction will be fetched from the address that was contained in W and Z; this is effectively a *branch* or *jump*. In addition, the contents of WZ will be incremented by 1 and deposited in the program counter so that the next instruction will be correctly fetched in the normal way by using PC. The effect is therefore correct.

We might wonder why the contents of PC were not directly loaded and why the intermediate registers W and Z were used. This was done because it was not possible to use PC.

If we had loaded the lower part of PC (PCL) rather than Z with B2, we would have destroyed PC. It would then have become impossible to fetch B3. It would, however, have been possible to use only Z rather than W and Z, but this would have been slower. We could have loaded Z with B2, then fetched B3 and deposited it into the high order half of PC (PCH). However, then it would have become necessary to transfer Z into PCL before using the contents of PC. This would have slowed down the process, so W and Z are both used. Furthermore, to save time, W and Z are not transferred into PC but gated directly to the address bus for the next instruction fetch. Understanding this point is crucial to the understanding of efficient execution of instructions within the microprocessor—but it is not essential to the understanding of the rest of this book.

Other Instructions

It is a valuable exercise to follow the execution of other instructions on this chart while watching transfers of data on the 8080 diagram. Recommended instructions are: RAL (Rotate Accumulator Left), CMP r (compare contents of accumulator with the contents of register r), and PUSH or POP instructions, which appear in the table in Figure 2.30. The sequencing should now be easy to follow.

SUMMARY OF 8080 STUDY

We have described the detailed execution of the main types of instructions available in a "standard" microprocessor, the 8080. Using the tables in Figures 2.30 and 2.31, the interested reader should now be able to follow the execution of virtually any instruction within the microprocessor. The internal architecture and execution processes of most standard microprocessors are essentially similar. As an example, the architecture of the Motorola 6800 is shown in Figure 2.57. The 6800 has two accumulators (A and B) and an index register. It does not, however, have the general-purpose registers of the 8080 (B, C, D, E, H, L). Overall, the performance levels of these two microprocessors are essentially similar.

Similarly, the internal organization of the Z80 is shown in Figure 2.58. The Z80 has more registers but uses essentially the same architecture.

INTERNAL MICROPROCESSOR ARCHITECTURES

Having described the internal architecture of a standard microprocessor, let us review the limitations facing the designer. From a functional standpoint, there are three basic constraints imposed on the implementation of microprocessor architectures. They are:

1. 40-Pin Limitation.   It may be surprising to find that one of the main constraints imposed on the design of LSI components is the limitation to 40 or 42 pins. This limitation results from economic considerations. It is mostly due to the fact that industrial testers will not accept packages having more than 40 to 42 pins. Components having a higher number of pins (for example, 64) are available but are not easily tested by an industrial user. It is not expected that this constraint will be removed in the near future. Let us examine the impact of this limitation.

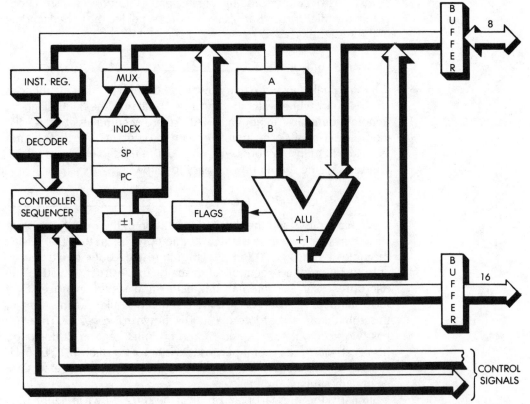

Figure 2.57: Architecture of the Motorola 6800

— The microprocessor must be equipped with a data bus. The data bus will require 8 (or 16) pins, depending on the microprocessor (see Figure 2.59).

— Sixteen additional pins are required for a 16-bit address bus (see Figure 2.60), making the total 24.

— The microprocessor will require at least two pins for power and ground (see Figure 2.61), making the total 26.

— It will also require at least two pins and usually four, for connection to an external crystal or clock (see Figure 2.62). Thus, with the total so far and these additional pins, we have 28 pins minimum (and usually 30).

At this point, only 10 to 12 pins are left to complete the design. These pins are needed for the control bus (see Figure 2.63). Typical signals used or needed by a control bus appear in Figure 2.25. It can be easily seen that the complexity of the control bus is seriously limited by the lack of available pins. Ten pins are an absolute minimum for synchronization with external events. In many conventional computer systems, it is not unusual to use 40 or 50 lines for control. In practice, this means that *16-bit microprocessors cannot be efficiently implemented in a 40-pin package.*

A 16-bit microprocessor implemented in a 40-pin package cannot communicate with the outside world via two 16-bit buses. Either the data bus or the address bus will have to be *multiplexed*. Let us now consider a multiplexed data bus: the lower part of the data will be input (or output) first, followed by the higher part. This means that instructions (16 bits in length) must be brought into the microprocessor in two successive operations. Such a 16-bit microprocessor is slowed down by bus multiplexing and may not be significantly faster than an 8-bit one. For this reason, this approach is often not pursued. The "clean" approach to designing a 16-bit microprocessor is to use more pins. Texas Instruments did just that with the TMS 9900. However, the 9900 requires *64 pins* and may not have gained wide acceptance because of this. Other manufacturers use 48 pins or they use a complex multiplexing scheme. It must be stressed here that we are referring to *microprocessors-on-a-chip*, not *microcomputers-on-a-chip*. The microcomputer-on-a-chip is not limited by the pins since the memory is inside the chip. No external address bus will be necessary, and 16 more pins are available for I/O. Thus, a 16-bit microcomputer-on-a-chip is able to communicate with the outside via a 16-bit (or wider) data bus and can be implemented with 40 pins or less.

2. Chip Area. The second essential constraint due to a technological limitation is the maximum amount of chip area that can be economically implemented at any time. In view of the limitations on the density of integration that can be achieved, the number of functions that must be implemented in the limited die area should be as high as possible.

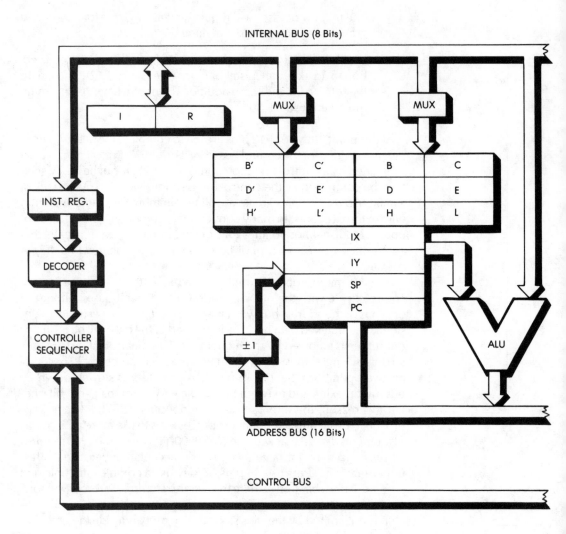

Figure 2.58: Architecture of the Z80

This is an essential constraint in the design. We have seen that this constraint has led to the implementation of single-bus, accumulator-based systems and to the use of microprogrammed control units as well as an internal RAM to contain the registers. The complexity of the operations carried out by the ALU is naturally also restricted by the size of the die.

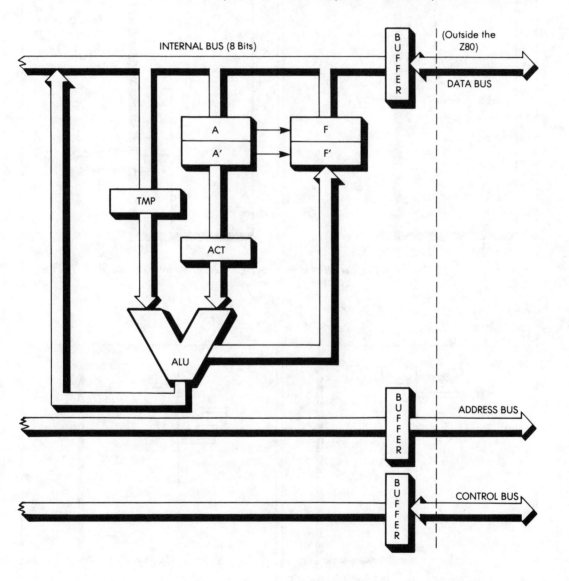

Figure 2.58: Architecture of the Z80 (cont.)

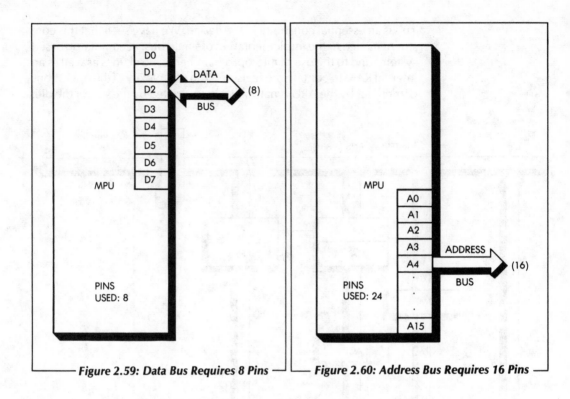

Figure 2.59: Data Bus Requires 8 Pins   *Figure 2.60: Address Bus Requires 16 Pins*

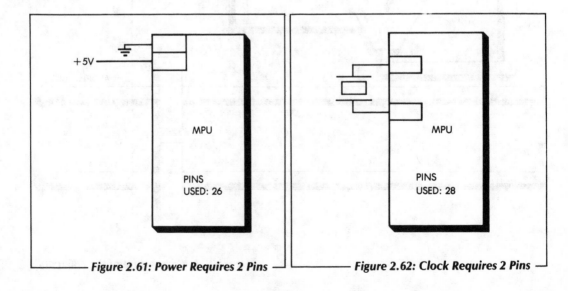

Figure 2.61: Power Requires 2 Pins   *Figure 2.62: Clock Requires 2 Pins*

In the case of 8-bit microprocessors, ALU complexity is also restricted by the 8-bit field used for opcodes. In view of the small number of bits available, most microprocessors cannot provide more than 60 to 80 different instructions. In the future, as chip areas expand, it will become feasible to consider other architectures, in particular more performing architectures that will result in higher speeds and more powerful functions.

3. Speed of Technology.   The third constraint is due to the limited speed of the technologies currently used to obtain the required density. These technologies are essentially NMOS (most widely used), PMOS (the oldest and therefore frequently used, but slower), and CMOS (used for space applications requiring very low power consumption).

Currently the maximum speed for the execution of a typical instruction is one microsecond. Major progress will have to be accomplished in the technology in order to obtain faster execution times. Some progress could be accomplished through architectural changes, such as equipping the ALU with a Q or extension register for the ALU, which is used for multiplication.

The faster technologies, mostly bipolar, result in a much lower density

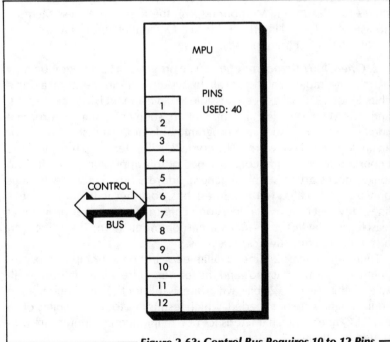

Figure 2.63: Control Bus Requires 10 to 12 Pins

and do not permit the implementation of the complete microprocessor on a single chip. They are reserved for bit slices.

THE FOUR MAIN ARCHITECTURES

As a result of the above limitations, three basic types of architecture for microprocessors have emerged. These types of architecture, as well as bit-slice architecture, are illustrated in Figure 2.64.

1. Standard Architecture.   The standard microprocessor architecture is characterized by an MPU that incorporates in one chip the functions of a traditional CPU. Memory and I/O are external to the chip. Until the end of 1976, MPUs had, in fact, not been able to supply all the functions of a CPU within a single chip. At the least they required the addition of an external clock and its crystal. Today, all new designs incorporate a clock within the MPU. However, because of its bulk the crystal cannot be incorporated on the chip.

The standard microprocessor architecture is characterized by the three buses that we previously described. Note that the illustrations in Figure 2.64 show only the data and address buses; they do not show the control bus. In the standard architecture, all other system components are connected to the buses. The illustration at the top of Figure 2.64 shows the Read Only Memory (ROM), the Random Access Memory (RAM), and a typical interface chip, a PIO (Parallel Input/Output), connected to the I/O (peripherals).

2. One-Chip Microcomputer.   The progress of LSI integration now permits the implementation of all the system's components on a single chip. Since 1976, it has been possible to have an MPU, a clock, a ROM, and a RAM on a single chip. In addition, such chips may incorporate additional facilities such as a programmable timer, a restart circuit, or an analog-digital converter. The crystal is still external to the chip. The important architectural consequence of this approach is that it is no longer necessary to supply a general address bus. Thus, the 16 lines previously allocated to the address bus, together with some control lines, now become available. A one-chip microcomputer provides at least three 8-bit I/O buses for external communication. These lines can be connected directly to I/O devices.

There are at least 24 lines available for I/O on a 1-chip microcomputer. The former data bus and the former address bus are now available, giving 8 + 16 = 24 bits, which are usable for I/O. In addition, some control signals are not needed, which results in a total availability of 26 or 27 I/O lines. The characteristics of 1-chip microcomputers are presented in Chapter 4.

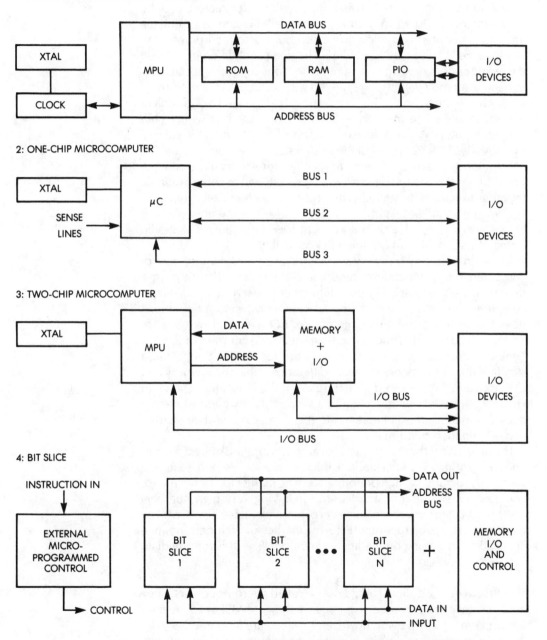

Figure 2.64: The Three Basic Architectures And Bit-Slice

3. Two-Chip Microcomputer. Conceptually, the 2-chip micro-computer lies somewhere between the standard architecture and the 1-chip microcomputer. In such a system the MPU chip is essentially analogous to a standard microprocessor, but it also incorporates the clock, as well as direct I/O capability. The significant difference lies on the memory-I/O side of the machine, where one or more special com-ponents are supplied that are equipped with ROM, RAM, and I/O on a single chip. With two chips it becomes possible to assemble a complete microcomputer. The memory is limited in size, as it is with 1-chip microcomputers. A typical size for a ROM is 2K × 8 and a typical size for a RAM is 512 × 8. In view of the limited size of the memory, the size of the address bus that is needed to specify addresses can be reduced, and the lines that are freed from the address bus will become available for other functions. In such a system, the MPU chip itself is typically equipped with at least eight lines of direct I/O. The memory plus I/O chip is also equipped with at least eight to sixteen lines. The 2-chip system then provides 24-bit direct I/O capability.

Although such a system may seem equivalent to the 1-chip micro-computer from a functional standpoint, it is quite different from a performance standpoint. The main difference is that on a 2-chip micro-computer, the microprocessor chip can reside on the complete chip; it does not need to share it with memory or I/O. Two-chip systems are characterized by a high microprocessor speed and complex functions. Typically, complexity and performance are essentially identical to a standard microprocessor. The main difference is that the memory and I/O (appearing at the top right-hand side of the illustration shown in Figure 2.64) have been merged into a single chip. By contrast, 1-chip microcomputers are still limited as to the complexity of their instruc-tion set and their performance.

The markets for these three types of architectures are quite different. The primary market for standard microprocessors is one requiring complex programs or high performance. The market for 1-chip micro-computers is simple industrial control involving very high numbers (over 100,000) in view of the necessity of masking the 1-chip ROM. The market for 2-chip microcomputers is the market for high-performance applications requiring only a limited memory size. It is intermediate between the previous two markets.

4. Bit-Slices. Bit-slices should not be called microprocessors. They are often called microprocessors because they use MSI or LSI devices and implement a processor; however, bit-slices are fundamentally dif-ferent from microprocessors. It is more correct to call them bit-slice devices, or bit-slice processors, as they are slices of a processor. The implementation of the processor with bit-slices is quite simple. Basically, slices are cascaded to assemble an ALU with its registers. A carry-look-ahead unit may be added to improve the arithmetic performance. Additional gates may still be added to further improve the speed of the multiplication and division operations. The real complexity in implementing a bit-slice computer does not lie in the assembly of the processor itself; it lies instead in the realization of the control unit and the associated circuitry, such as loop counter, decoder, condition logic, multiplexers, and bus management.

An ALU with registers can be assembled with four to six packages. The implementation of a complete control unit requires 20 to 50 packages. The market for the bit-slice devices is the market for fast CPUs. All bit-slices so far are bipolar. This is the fastest technology. A typical instruction can be executed in 100 to 200 ns for virtually any number of bits.

SUMMARY

The standard microprocessor has a single-bus, accumulator-based architecture. The internal structure of such a system includes the ALU, the flags, the registers, the buses, the stack, and the scratch-pad. These features were described in this chapter. The mechanism used for executing instructions, as well as the role of the buses and the registers, have been explained in detail. An actual step-by-step sequencing of each major type of instruction on the 8080 was also presented.

In Chapter 3 we will connect the external buses created by the microprocessor to LSI components and we will continue to assemble a system that will be completed in Chapter 5.

EXERCISES

2-1: Explain why chip designers like to implement RAMs on a chip.

2-2: What is the function of the pads around a chip?

2-3: Define the three standard external buses in a microprocessor system.

2-4: Examine Figure 2.2. Is the accumulator register on the left input of the ALU required? What is its role?

2-5: Explain the differences between single-bus architecture, double-bus architecture, and triple-bus architecture. What are the advantages and disadvantages of each approach?

2-6: What is the difference between a shift and a rotate operation?

2-7: What is the function of the flags within the flags or status register next to the ALU?

2-8: What is the function of the 16-bit address registers within the microprocessor? Describe several kinds of address registers.

2-9: Is the program counter a required register?

2-10: Is the stack pointer a required register? Are there other alternatives for implementing a stack?

2-11: What is an index register?

2-12: Explain the sequence of events required to read an instruction from the memory and execute it.

2-13: What is the function of the control unit? How does the control unit obtain the instruction that it must execute? How does it know the number of bytes in an instruction?

2-14: What is the IR?

2-15: Describe the role of each register and each bus within the 8080, as shown in Figure 2.27.

2-16: Explain the difference between a machine cycle and an internal state in the case of the 8080.

2-17: Assuming a standard 2MHz 8080, what is the duration of a state? What is the duration of a machine cycle?

2-18: Using the charts shown in Figures 2.30 and 2.31, what is the binary code corresponding to the following instructions:

a. Transfer the contents of register E into register C.

b. *Transfer the contents of H into L.*

c. *Load the accumulator with the contents of memory location 5.*

d. *Add the contents of register C to the accumulator.*

e. *Add the contents of memory location 9 to the accumulator.*

f. *Rotate the contents of the accumulator left by one position.*
Hint: A description of the 8080 instructions is shown in Appendix C, and the codes corresponding to the various registers are shown in Figure 2.32.

2-19: *What is the function of the two buffer registers labeled ACT and TMP on both inputs of the ALU of the 8080 as shown in Figure 2.27?*

2-20: *What is the function of the incrementer/decrementer shown below the register RAM of the 8080 in Figure 2.27?*

2-21: *Assuming a 2MHz 8080, what is the apparent execution time (for the programmer) of an ADD r instruction? Is it:*

a. 7.5μs   b. 5μs   c. 4.5μs   d. 4μs

2-22: *Does the internal organization shown in Figure 2.65 solve the critical race problem?*

2-23: *Using the internal organization shown in the illustration below, explain the detailed sequencing of operations required to execute the instruction R1 = R0 + R1. Does this result in a longer execution time than in the case of the standard organization shown in Figure 2.22?*

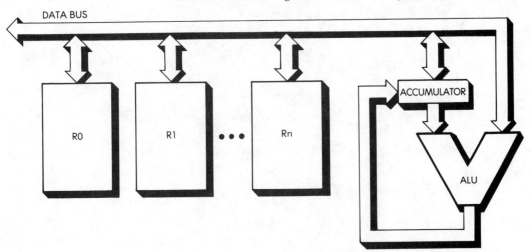

Figure 2.65: Alternative Internal Organization

2-24:   Using the chart in Figure 2.31, explain the sequence of operations involved in a PUSH rp.

2-25:   Using Figure 2.30, explain the sequence of operations involved in LHLD addr.

2-26:   Explain how the 40-pin limitation of a package restricts the speed of a microprocessor. Also explain why it does not affect the speed of a single-chip microcomputer.

2-27:   Why are at least 24 lines generally available for I/O on a one-chip microcomputer?

2-28:   What is the disadvantage of implementing a large number of registers on board the MPU chip?

2-29:   Why is the number of instructions generally small in the case of an 8-bit microprocessor?

2-30:   What is happening within the MPU while the memory reads the contents of a specified location?

2-31:   Assuming that a state lasts 250 ns, is it useful to have a memory that has an access time shorter than 250 ns?

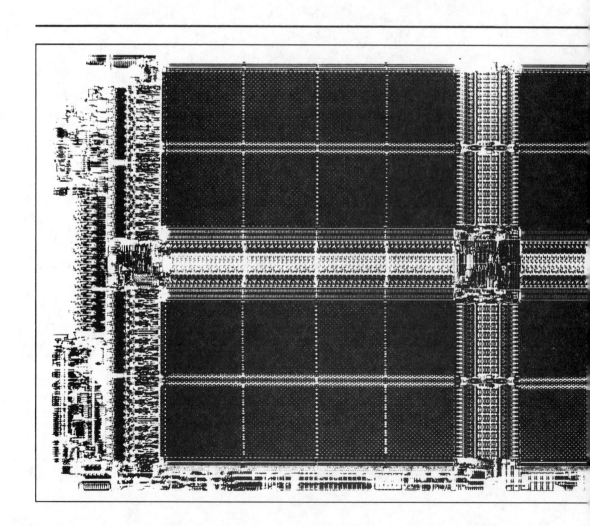

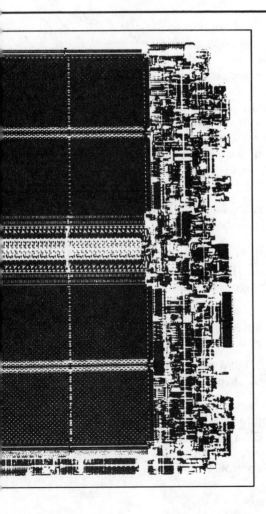

CHAPTER **3**

SYSTEM COMPONENTS

OBJECTIVE

In the previous chapter we examined the way a microprocessor operates. In this chapter we will introduce the additional chips, from memory to input/output, necessary to build a complete microcomputer system. We will learn about the various types of memories, from ROM to RAM, and static and dynamic. We will describe the three fundamental input/output techniques: polling, interrupts, and DMA, as well as the I/O chips that automate or facilitate these techniques.

In particular, we will examine the two basic I/O chips, the PIO for parallel transfers, and the UART for serial transfers. Then, we will study the priority interrupt controller (PIC), the Direct Memory Access Controller (DMAC) and the peripheral controller chips.

THE MICROPROCESSOR FAMILIES

Microprocessors today have families. A variety of LSI components have been introduced that are designed to be connected directly to the buses of specific microprocessors in order to assemble a complete computer system.

When the first microprocessors were introduced, memories (ROM, RAM) and UARTs were the only LSI circuits available. This made the design and assembly of a system difficult and it required many components. For example, early 8080-based systems had to have fairly complex circuitry to accomplish the required external demultiplexing of the 8080 data bus. Today this can be done with a single chip, the 8228.

The reason for the delay in introducing microprocessor support components is quite simple. When microprocessors first appeared, few manufacturers believed that there would be much of a market for them. Today, every manufacturer realizes that a microprocessor requires a large family of "support" components in order to be usable. All of the leading microprocessor manufacturers now supply a line of components for each type of microprocessor. Fortunately, many of these components are interchangeable. In this chapter we will study all the components required to assemble a complete system. We will begin by distinguishing three categories of components.

THE THREE BASIC SYSTEM COMPONENTS

We have shown in Chapter 1 that every computer system has five modules: control, ALU, memory, input and output. These functions are provided by specific LSI components that can be grouped by function. The three basic system components are:

1. *The microprocessor* (MPU), and any required additional support components, such as the clock and crystal.

2. *The memory,* which generally includes both ROM (for a fixed program) and RAM (for data or transient programs).

3. *The I/O interface chips:* the two main I/O chips are the UART (universal asynchronous receiver-transmitter), a serial-to-parallel converter; and the PIO (Parallel I/O), a parallel interface. Additional, more specialized *device controllers,* such as an FDC (floppy disk controller) or a CRTC (CRT controller) connect to these primary interface chips.

In addition, auxiliary circuits such as *latches* and *drivers* are usually necessary. *Latches* are used whenever it is necessary to preserve or freeze information. They are typically used to interface to I/O devices. Latches are generally internal to an input/output interface chip, such as the PIO. *Drivers* are generally necessary because of the bus driving limitation of MOS chips. Because a microprocessor is an MOS device, it can only accommodate one TTL load. Whenever more than about five chips must be connected to the system's buses, bus drivers must be used. Drivers are generally used on the data, address, and control buses, except in the case of the smallest systems.

A complete microprocessor system is shown in Figure 3.1. The microprocessor (MPU) appears on the left. It requires a crystal and often an external clock. The power supply (shown in the lower left corner of the figure) provides power to the entire system. Recently designed microprocessors usually require only one voltage level (say +5V), but

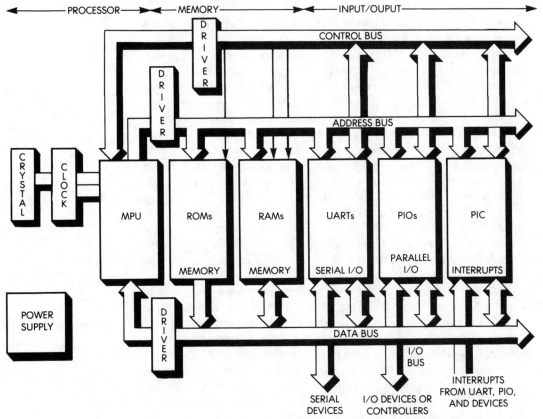

Figure 3.1: A Standard Microprocessor System

memories can require up to three levels (say +5V, −5V, and +12V). The I/O generally involves one or more UART and PIO connected to I/O devices or device controllers. In some systems, multiple interrupt priorities are used, and a priority interrupt controller (PIC) may be used. Other special purpose components, such as a direct memory access controller (DMAC), may also be required. As shown in Figure 3.1 all these devices connect to the three standard buses. We will now examine each component in turn.

THE MEMORY

We will first study the types of memories required in a system and then examine the technological characteristics and limitations of each type. Recall that the two main types of memories used in microprocessor systems are RAM and ROM.

The first type, RAM, is a read/write memory. Its contents can be written to or read from. Reading from a RAM is nondestructive, i.e., it will not destroy the information. The main disadvantage of an LSI RAM in the current state of the technology is that it is *volatile*: whenever power disappears, the contents of the RAM will be lost. For this reason a control program will seldom reside in RAM. In other words, if power goes off, then before the system can resume operation it is necessary to reload the control program from another permanent storage medium (such as a diskette or a cassette). A RAM is used to store *data* (for example, measurements or the results of intermediate computations, i.e., data not critical if lost during a power failure) or programs that can be conveniently reloaded. A RAM resident program can be any program whose temporary loss is not catastrophic.

The second type of memory is the ROM or read-only memory. Once the contents of this memory have been defined by a manufacturing process, they can no longer be altered. The contents can be read but no new contents may be written. A ROM, therefore, is used to store essential *programs*. It is non-volatile.

Thus, in an industrial control environment, programs are generally stored in ROM, as the programs are seldom changed and should not be reloaded every time power is turned off. The same applies to the programs of single-chip microcomputers, which are normally used as dedicated control devices and manufactured in quantity.

In a professional or business environment, many different programs are being executed all the time and any one program may fill all the available memory. Thus, programs are stored in RAM, which is easily changeable. A small ROM is also required for the *monitor program* which maintains communication with the system via a keyboard and loads other programs from disk or tape into RAM.

A typical memory configuration for an industrial control system is 4K ROM, and 1K RAM. A typical memory configuration for a business system is 2K ROM, and 62K RAM. Recall that 1K = 1024 and that a K in this context refers to the number of *bytes*.

Other types of memories also exist. We will now examine the different types of memory in detail.

RANDOM-ACCESS MEMORY (RAM)

RAM stands for random-access memory, and refers to the fact that any of its contents may be accessed at any time. This is in contrast to a serial memory, such as a magnetic tape, where access to the stored data is only in a fixed order, e.g., the serial order in which data passes under the tape head. Actually, both ROM and RAM are random-access memories, but the term random-access traditionally refers to *read/ write* memories and is, therefore, only used with RAM. Two technologies are used for RAM memories: static and dynamic.

STATIC VERSUS DYNAMIC

A *static* RAM stores a bit of information within a flip-flop. It is asynchronous and does not require a clock. The contents of a static RAM remain stable forever, as long as power is available.

A *dynamic* RAM stores a bit of information as a charge. A dynamic RAM uses the gate-substrate capacitance of an MOS transistor as an elementary memory cell. An illustration of a typical dynamic RAM appears in Figure 3.2. The obvious advantage of a dynamic RAM is that this elementary cell is smaller than a static RAM flip-flop, resulting in a much higher density. For example, a 64K-bit dynamic RAM resides on the same chip area as a 16K-bit static RAM. In addition, the simpler geometry of the elementary cell results in higher speed. The typical speed of a dynamic RAM memory today is 100 to 500 ns. Higher speeds can be achieved, but usually at the expense of chip density.

The photomicrographs of a 4K static RAM (the 2114) and of a 4K dynamic RAM are shown in Figures 3.3 and 3.4, respectively. They display the typical geometry of RAM chips.

The disadvantage of a dynamic RAM is the increased complexity of the memory board due to the necessity of additional logic. Like any charge, the charge stored in the capacitor leaks, and within a few milliseconds most of the charge is lost. To preserve the information contained in a dynamic RAM memory, the charge must be *refreshed* every 1 or 2 milliseconds. The refresh process consists of reading the information out of, and then writing it back into the memory, thus restoring a full charge. To save time, the refresh process reads out a complete row or column at a time. Note that the internal memory organization of a RAM does not correspond to its external appearance. In particular, a typical 4K dynamic RAM (illustrated in Figure 3.2) may have 64 columns × 64 rows. Thus, only 64 operations will be needed for the complete refresh of this memory.

The need to provide a refresh presents two disadvantages. First, refresh logic must be provided on the board. (In the future refresh may be implemented directly on the chip.) Second, the refresh slows the processor's execution time by delaying memory accesses while refresh is in progress. However, a good time refresh scheme will only degrade processor execution speed from one to five percent. The additional complexity of clever refresh circuitry, however, often reduces the reliability of the memory.

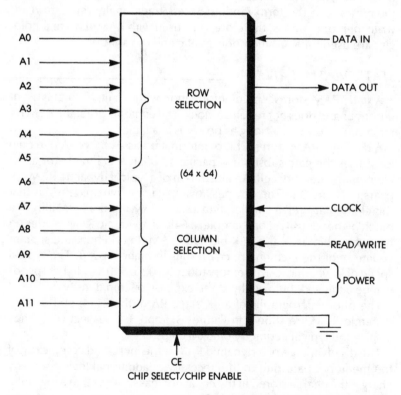

Figure 3.2: Typical 4K Dynamic RAM

Let us now consider an example of a standard RAM: the Intel 2107B. The 2107B has a 200 ns access time (time necessary for reading data out), a cycle time of 400 ns (time necessary to write data into the memory), and 22 pins. Each cell requires a single transistor. The 2107B is organized in a 4K × 1 bit format and requires three levels: + 5V, − 5V, + 12V.

Using the 2107B, it is necessary to connect eight of these chips in parallel in order to implement a 4K byte memory. Each data bit of each chip is connected to one of the eight lines of the data bus. Such standard RAMs (one bit wide) are the most economical, as they minimize the number of pins. For smaller memories, other chip architectures, such as 1K × 4 or 512 × 8 bits, may be used. Smaller memories require fewer components but cost more per chip.

INTEL   2114-D-19-0   02-03-77

Figure 3.3:
A Fabrication Mask for the 2114, a 4K Static RAM (The pattern is typical of a memory chip.)

Figure 3.4:
The 2107A Is a 4K × 1 Bit Dynamic RAM (The decoders are clearly visible outside the RAM areas.)

SUMMARY—STATIC VERSUS DYNAMIC

In summary, because of its higher density, a dynamic RAM circuit is less expensive than a static RAM circuit. However, a dynamic RAM requires an extra refresh circuit if one is not incorporated within the MPU.

Thus, for a *smaller* memory, a static RAM will usually be less expensive. This naturally assumes that there is no plan to expand to a larger memory at a later date. For a *medium* or *large* memory, a dynamic RAM is usually less expensive but may reduce reliability.

Let us now examine how memory chips operate and how they connect to the system.

READING FROM THE MEMORY

In order to read from or write onto a memory chip it is necessary to:

1. Signal to the device that it is being addressed. This is done by the chip-select (CS) or chip-enable (CE) signal, which selects one memory chip among the various chips connected to the address bus. In Chapter 5 we will examine ways to provide this signal.

2. Supply the address of the selected word within the memory.

For example, to select one bit from among the 4K bits that are available on the RAM illustrated in Figure 3.2, it is necessary to provide one chip-select in order to select a chip, plus 12 bits on A0-A15 in order to supply the address of the bit. In the case of a 4K × 1-bit chip, eight such chips are used in parallel to implement a 4K × 8 memory. All eight chips are connected to the same CS and the same address lines.

After a period of time called the *access-time*, data become available and appear on the data pins. The data are then transmitted along the data bus to the microprocessor.

In the case of a static memory, the contents of the data bus must be validated when data are presented (see Figure 3.5). The enable signal (the third signal from the top in Figure 3.5) accomplishes this task. The low-to-high transition of the signal indicates that the data presented in the data bus are presumed valid.

The address must be kept valid for the duration of the access time and usually longer in order to prevent race conditions. The *chip-select* or *chip-enable* signal is normally presented at the same time as the rest of the address bus, but this is not a necessity. The access time is measured from the moment that the chip-enable signal becomes good, i.e., from the time that the access actually starts. The *access time* is the time that elapses between the presentation of the CS signal and the availability of valid data on the output pin.

After each read cycle, the memory completes a write cycle in order to restore the data so that the data cannot be accessed again before the complete *cycle time* has elapsed. The cycle time is the time required by a read followed by a write operation.

WRITING IN THE MEMORY

The sequence of events involved in writing in the memory is analogous to the read operation just described. The memory chip(s) must be *selected* and the address within the memory must be specified via the address pins. In addition, the data to be written in memory must be presented on the data pins within a specified time, T1. After a time T2 called cycle time, the data will have been written at the specified memory address. Both the data and the address buses will be available again. The timing diagram for a static memory appears in Figure 3.6.

READ-MODIFY-WRITE CYCLE

This cycle allows the processor to read the contents of a word, then write back different contents at the same address, during a single cycle. This special cycle offers an important advantage during file handling when a user first reads a byte, then writes back into the same memory location.

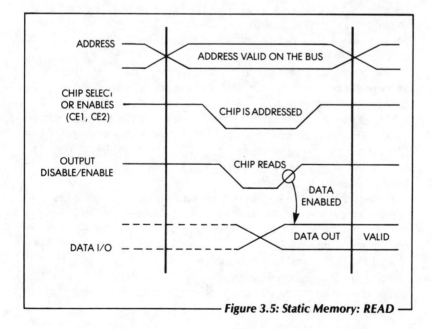

Figure 3.5: Static Memory: READ

THE MEMORY VOLATILITY PROBLEM

The main disadvantage of MOS RAM is *volatility*. Whenever power is removed, the contents of the RAM are lost. That is why read-only memories (ROMs) are preferred for storing programs that would otherwise need to be reloaded too frequently (for example, the BASIC interpreter, or operating system).

Conversely, under varying external conditions, such as the time of day, different programs may have to reside at the same address in memory, which is not possible with ROM. If ROM is used to provide non-volatile memory, then all the programs will have to reside at different addresses simultaneously (i.e, end to end) within the ROM, and this requires a very large ROM memory. For these reasons it is desirable in many cases to have a *non-volatile RAM*. Three solutions exist for this volatility problem:

1. Battery Back-up.   The simplest and most frequently used solution is to provide batteries for powering the RAM during temporary power failures. If a CMOS memory is used, power consumption can be very low. New batteries that can power a 4K memory card for weeks (derived from aerospace experience) are now available. Such batteries occupy little space.

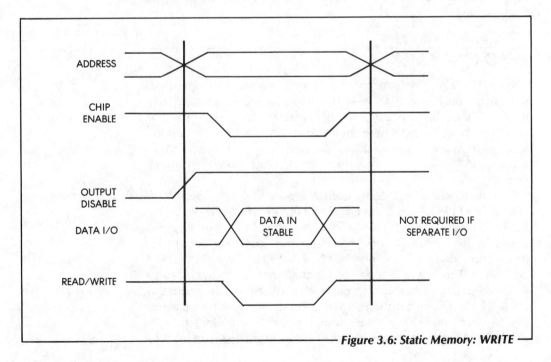

Figure 3.6: Static Memory: WRITE

Larger, more expensive batteries can power a memory board for months. When CMOS is used, not just the memory but also the decoders and refresh circuitry should be CMOS for minimum power consumption. Batteries are frequently used in portable or industrial systems where it is highly desirable to preserve data or programs during brief power failures that might range from milliseconds to minutes. The cost involved in restarting an industrial process is usually so high that it justifies the additional cost of providing this battery back-up. It is usually not necessary to provide a long memory survival period. In the case of a long power failure, the process being controlled will probably come to a stop anyway, so it is not essential to provide long-term survival.

2. EAROMs. EAROM (electrically alterable read only memory) is, in fact, a read/write memory, or more exactly, a "read-mostly" memory. This type of memory is described in the next section. Briefly, it is expensive, very slow during write operations, and has been used essentially for applications such as missile-guidance systems, where a small size is essential and cost is not a factor.

3. Bubble Memories. Bubble memories provide a large amount of memory at a reasonable cost. They retain information for long periods of time. However, they are slow and relatively expensive. They are generally used in portable computers to retain data over a period of hours or days.

READ-ONLY MEMORIES (ROM)

Recall that a read-only memory is a memory whose contents, once written, can only be read. Writing data in a ROM is generally called *programming* the ROM, since a program is what is usually written into it. However, programming here means that the specified bit patterns have been written into the memory. Because a read-only memory is intrinsically *non-volatile*, it is nearly always used to store *control programs*.

Four main types of ROMs are used: the pure ROM, the PROM, the EPROM (or RPROM), and the EAROM. Let us examine ROMs first. A ROM is a *mask-programmed* read-only memory that can only be produced by the manufacturer. The bit patterns corresponding to the desired contents of this memory must be supplied by the user in a standard format. The 0s and 1s are implemented on the memory by either establishing or not establishing connections between rows and columns. The last manufacturing step for a ROM chip is the metallization step by which these interconnections are established. Once the customer supplies the bit pattern, the manufacturer can realize a *mask* for the metallization step and perform this last manufacturing step. Thus, a ROM is said to be mask-programmed.

Because of the cost involved in the production of a mask and in the manufacturing process, the manufacturer normally requires that a minimum quantity of ROMs be produced before undertaking such a task. Typically, at least 1000 ROMs must be produced at one time. In addition, a delay of from three to six weeks is usually required for production. Although *masked ROMs* have many advantages, such as high bit density, non-volatility, and the lowest cost of any type of memory in large quantities, they *are only intended for large production volumes.* For example, Figure 3.7 shows the internal structure of a 16K static ROM, the 8316A. It is organized in 2048 words of 8 bits. Its access time is 850 ns maximum. Figure 3.8 shows a 64K dynamic ROM. Its access time is 150 ns.

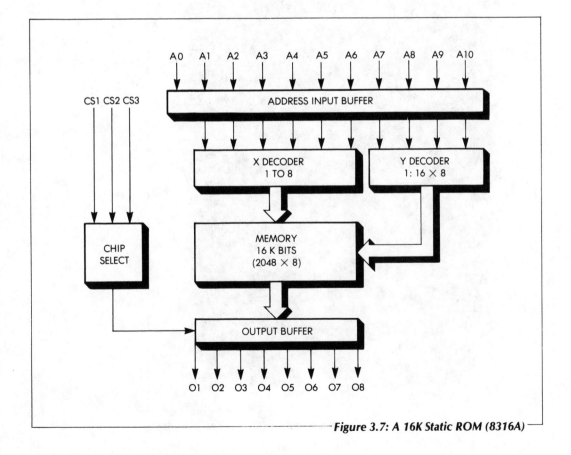

Figure 3.7: A 16K Static ROM (8316A)

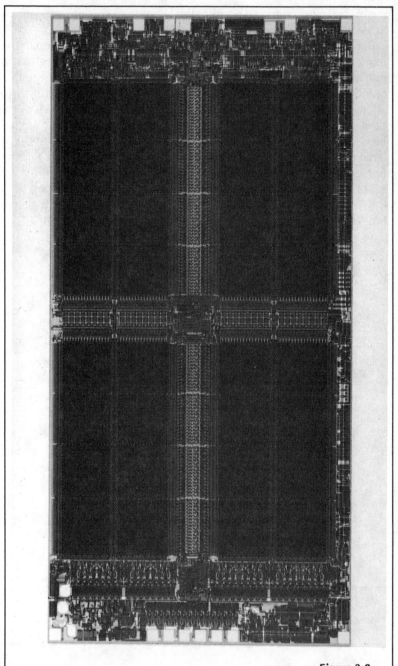

Figure 3.8:
Intel 2164 Dynamic ROM (It holds 64K bits, with a 150 ns access time.)

A typical timing diagram for reading a ROM appears in Figure 3.9. The address must be good for the cycle time of the memory, and the chip-select determines the time from which the memory will start to cycle. After the access time has elapsed, valid data is available on the output pins.

The three major disadvantages of a ROM are:

1. The delay involved in producing ROMs.

2. The large quantity that must be produced at one time.

3. The fact that once manufactured, a ROM cannot be modified. In other words, should an error be found in the program, it is impossible to effect a change within the ROM. The ROM must be replaced.

These constraints would retard the development phase of a system and inhibit the production of systems in small numbers. For these reasons several other types of read-only memories have been introduced, all of which can be directly programmed by the user. Three main types can be distinguished: PROM, EPROM/RPROM, and EAROM. They will be described in turn.

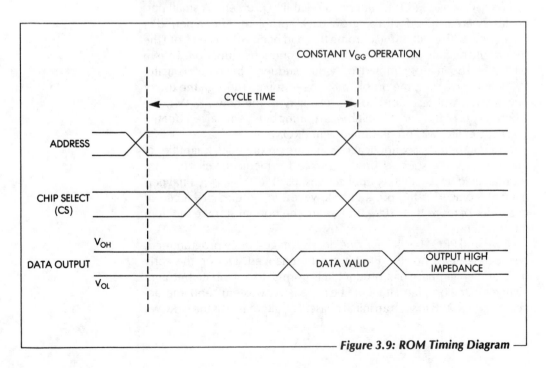

Figure 3.9: ROM Timing Diagram

1. PROM (User-Programmable Read-Only Memory). This is a read-only memory that can be programmed directly by the user using a special *PROM programmer*. It is also sometimes called a fusible-link PROM. In a PROM each memory cell is manufactured with a fuse. The fuse can be made of nichrome or polysilicon. Originally, all rows and columns are connected (logical 0s). During the programming process the PROM programmer generates trains of pulses. Fuses at appropriate locations within the memory are blown, causing the row-to-column junctions to be open at these locations, resulting in logical 1s. The colloquial expression is to "burn" a PROM. PROMs offer high density, high speed, and relatively low cost. Within a few minutes it is possible to burn a small PROM and to plug it into the application. In addition, most PROMs are pin-compatible with the ROM that may replace them at a future date, once the system is mass-produced. They present the same speed characteristics and the same pin-out. This is naturally a great advantage for developing prototype systems. Also, it is not necessary to burn all of the PROM locations in one operation. Typically, only one part of the PROM is programmed at a time. If program errors are detected it is then often possible to use the remainder of this PROM for changes and patches. Otherwise the PROM is thrown away and a new one is programmed.

A few years ago PROMs suffered a reliability problem. A small percentage were plagued with a "grow-back" problem. After a period of time, some of the nickel and chrome that had been volatilized from the fuse would migrate back and reestablish a conductive junction. Thus, a bit that had been programmed to 1 would suddenly become a 0 again. With time, however, the problem has been solved through the use of new alloys. As a testimony to the reliability of the new PROMs, the laboratory of Mars Lander, which was running biochemical tests for the presence of life, was programmed with PROMs.

Most microprocessor applications that are produced in quantities of fewer than 1000, such as products used for medical, scientific, industrial, avionic, or military applications, use PROMs as the final permanent storage for the program. However, in systems produced in quantities of more than 1000, ROMs are the normal storage medium for programs.

ROMs and PROMs still have one disadvantage—once programmed, neither the ROM nor the PROM can be changed. During the early developmental phase of a product, it is normal to anticipate frequent changes in the program. It would be expensive, wasteful, and impractical to use PROMs in such an initial phase. The alternative is the EPROM.

2. EPROM/RPROM (Erasable PROM or Reprogrammable PROM). The EPROM and RPROM are read-only user-programmable memories that can be *reprogrammed* a number of times. There are two main types: the UV-erasable PROM and the electrically-erasable PROM. Depending on the manufacturer, they are called either EPROM or RPROM. The principle of operation is the same for both.

A typical EPROM is erased by exposing it to hard (high-frequency) ultra-violet light for five to ten minutes, thus returning the contents of all the memory cells to zero by discharging them (see Figure 3.10). An EPROM package has a characteristic aspect: the seal on top of the chip is not opaque; it is a quartz window that allows ultra-violet light through. Once zeroed, the EPROM can be programmed with a special (E)PROM programmer. Selected locations within the EPROM can then be programmed and within a few minutes a bit pattern can be installed in the EPROM. The component can then be inserted in the application board. If errors are detected or changes are desired, the EPROM can be unplugged and reprogrammed within minutes. This process can be repeated many times.

EPROMs, however, are expensive. In addition, EPROMs are often not pin-for-pin compatible with the final ROM or PROM that will be installed on the board. The speed and density of the EPROM is also significantly different from that of a ROM or PROM. A board using an EPROM will therefore often require design changes in addressing and layout of final design that uses ROMs or PROMs.

Several technologies are used to implement EPROMs. The "floating-gate" technique is one of the best used. A charge is accumulated in a silicon gate "floating" above the silicon substrate but isolated from it by a silicon-dioxide layer (see Figure 3.11). The charge is induced in the silicon gate by trains of pulses. Once programmed, an EPROM is expected to retain its charge for ten years with only a 30% loss of charge. Erasure of the charge is accomplished with hard ultra-violet light. The photons hitting the floating silicon gate displace electrons from shallow energy levels and cause them to migrate to the silicon substrate where their charge is neutralized. This process is essentially analogous to the photoelectric effect. When a charge is neutralized, the corresponding bit reverts to 0.

Typical densities are 8K to 64K. An 8K-bit EPROM (the 8708) appears in Figure 3.12. Its access time is 450 ns.

A 64K EPROM is shown in Figure 3.13. RPROMs are also available that are erasable *electrically*. They often achieve performance levels on a par with UV-type EPROMs.

Figure 3.10: *Erasing an EPROM (The 2716 (Intel) is a 16K EPROM with a single + 5V power supply.*
(The light striking the 2716 is an art effect simulating the erasure of the chip by UV light.)

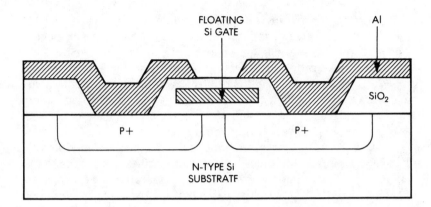

Figure 3.11: A Floating Gate Technology

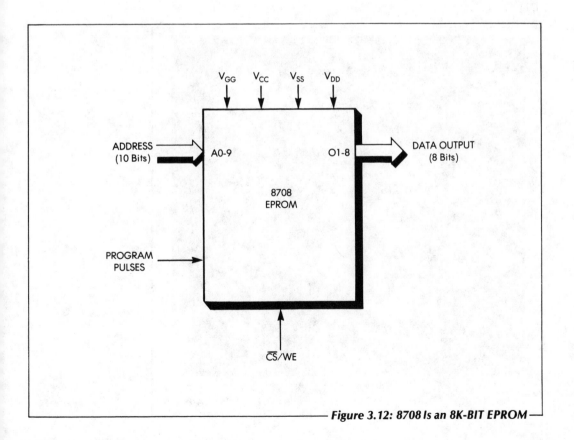

Figure 3.12: 8708 Is an 8K-BIT EPROM

3. EAROM (Electrically-Alterable ROM).   Another type of ROM, the EAROM, appeared on the market in 1976. The EAROM is an electrically alterable ROM and can be read from and written to. However, because the two processes (read and write) are significantly different, the EAROM can be called a "read-mostly" memory. In order to write into the EAROM, a *millisecond* is required, while the read operation can be performed in a *microsecond*. Thus, the EAROM cannot be used as a general-purpose read/write memory.

The EAROM uses complex technologies which require multiple voltage levels and provide only low storage densities. Its application is limited to critical industrial and military applications. Typically, an EAROM is used in cases in which it is necessary to store a small number of parameters infrequently. The advantage of the EAROM is that it is non-volatile and does not require an auxiliary power source (such as a battery). Because of these characteristics, an EAROM can be used, for example, for storing the guidance parameters of a missile-guidance

**Figure 3.13: TMS2564 Is a
64K-Bit EPROM Compatible with the Industry Standard 64K ROM**

system, where non-volatility is mandatory, the EAROM is read mostly, and updates are infrequent. This type of memory is intended to be used essentially as a ROM and infrequently as a non-volatile storage memory. The write-time for this memory is so slow that its widespread application in usual microprocessor systems cannot be considered at this time. The design of EAROMs is evolving toward higher densities, faster writing speeds, and lower costs.

We have described all the usual types of ROM. The main technologies will now be examined.

ROM TECHNOLOGIES

Three main technologies are used to implement the ROMs we have just described:

1. **Bipolar.** Bipolar technology is used for PROMs, i.e., user-programmable memories. Bipolar is the fastest of the three technologies. In fact, access time can be less than 100 ns. For smaller PROMs the access times get down to 40 ns or less. Thus, bipolar PROMs offer high speed and pin-for-pin compatibility with ROMs.

2. **MOS.** MOS technology is used for erasable PROMs, i.e., EPROMs and RPROMs. They are slower than bipolar devices; typical access times are 250 to 1000 ns. Typical densities are 8K to 32K bits. The cost of an EPROM programmer ranges from a few hundred dollars to more than a thousand dollars, depending on the options and the conveniences offered. A typical PROM programmer is shown in Figure 3.14.

3. **MNOS.** MNOS stands for *metal-nitride MOS*. (It must be carefully distinguished from *NMOS* (n-channel MOS).) MNOS is a leading technology for the implementation of EAROMs (electrically-alterable ROMs). Its essential characteristics have already been reviewed. It has an access time on the order of 1 microsecond and an erasure time of 1 to 100 milliseconds. Typical density now is 1K to 16K. The main manufacturers of MNOS are GI, Nitron (a division of McDonnell-Douglas), and NCR in the U.S. and Nippon Electric in Japan.

We have now described the most common types of memories. Three additional types are used in specific cases. These will be presented next.

OTHER TYPES OF MEMORIES

Three specific types of memories—bubble memory, CCD, and PLA—
have been developed in order to solve specific problems. Let's examine them.

BUBBLE MEMORY

Bubble memories are characterized by extremely high density and
non-volatility. A typical bubble memory chip can integrate from 64K to
1 million bits. However, bubble memories are slow and expensive. A
typical access time is 10 milliseconds.

Magnetic bubbles are used to store bits of information and are organized in loops. Data are thus organized in blocks of loops. A typical
data rate is 50K to 200K bits per second (see Figures 3.15 and 3.16).

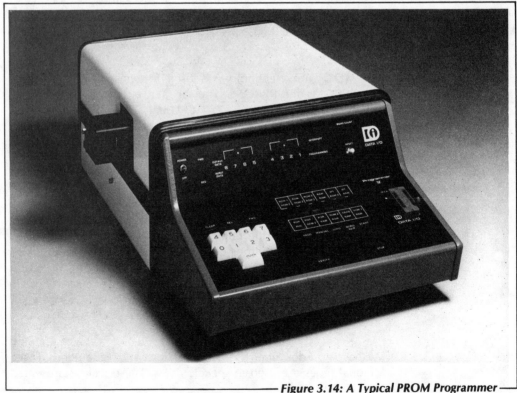

Figure 3.14: A Typical PROM Programmer

Figure 3.15: The Intel 7110
Bubble Memory (This is a non-volatile megabit (1,048,570-bit) device.)

Figure 3.16: 512 kbyte Bubble Memory
Board (uses the 7110 megabit memory and the 7220 bubble controller.)

CCD

CCD stands for *charge-coupled device*. These are MOS memories characterized by a very high density. The structure of a CCD memory appears in Figure 3.17. Small squares of aluminum are deposited on the silicon. Because of their very simple and highly repetitive geometry, very high densities can be achieved and 64K bits on one chip are common. The access time is slow (from 50 to 100 microseconds) and the cost relatively high. The market for CCD memories is analogous to the market for small or medium-size disks. Because of a drop in the price of disk drives, an increase in disk density, and the introduction of 1-chip disk controllers, CCD memories cannot yet compete with disks. They provide large amounts of fast storage in a smaller area than disks.

PLA

The PLA (or programmable-logic array) is not a simple memory. The structure of a PLA appears in Figure 3.18. A PLA is essentially a combination of two ROMs: the AND-ROM and the OR-ROM. It is used to encode or decode logic signals. The matrix equivalent is shown in Figure 3.19. PLAs are used specifically in the design of control units. They are sometimes used in monolithic microprocessor designs but are generally not used outside the MPU chip.

SUMMARY—MEMORY

All the memory types and technologies normally used in the design of a microprocessor system have now been described. The two main types of memory are ROM and RAM. ROM is permanent and required

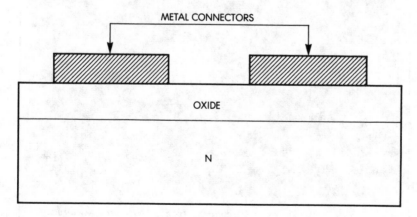

Figure 3.17: CCD Memory

for control programs. RAM is volatile and required for data and new programs. Specific types of ROMs such as PROMs and EPROMs have been designed to facilitate program development.

Having studied the memory let us now go on to examine the I/O devices required to complete the system.

INPUT/OUTPUT TECHNIQUES

A basic understanding of I/O techniques is necessary in order to understand the functions and merits of the various I/O devices needed to assemble a system. Therefore, in this section these concepts, including polling, interrupts, and direct memory access, will be presented first. Then the various types of I/O interface chips will be described and analyzed according to the functions they perform.

Connecting an input/output device to the system usually requires an *interface*. A *device interface* may range in complexity from a few registers or gates to one or more boards of logic. Two kinds of chips

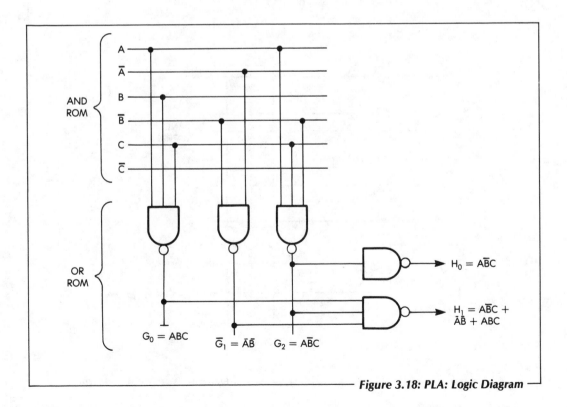

Figure 3.18: PLA: Logic Diagram

have been developed in order to simplify microprocessor interfacing: general-purpose interface chips and specific device controller chips. General-purpose interface chips are described in this section along with device controllers. Specific device controllers and interfacing techniques for the usual input/output devices are described in Chapter 7.

In order to be usable by a microprocessor system most I/O devices such as keyboards, disk drives, printers, CRTs and cassette drives require combinations of interface devices and programs. Most of these techniques and interfaces have been implemented as LSI chips that are used for direct device control. These device controllers connect to the standard I/O chips or even to the standard buses.

A device is generally microprocessor-dependent. It receives and executes program instructions and implements the specific control sequence required by the device. For example, a disk controller issues commands to advance a mechanical element (the read/write head) by a specified number of steps (using a *step-motor*). Complete device con-

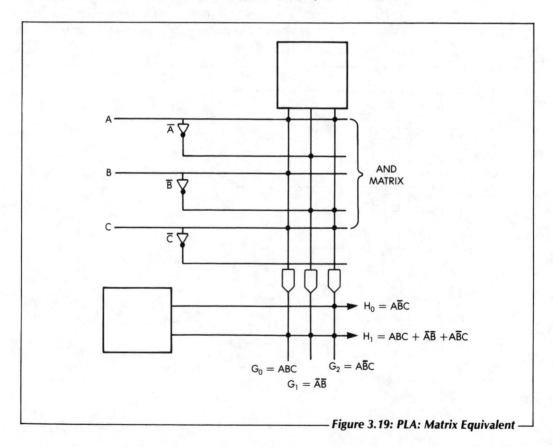

Figure 3.19: PLA: Matrix Equivalent

trollers may range from single chips to highly complex multi-board implementations.

Since all input/output devices are connected to the common system buses, a communication procedure must be established between the devices and the microprocessor. In order to transmit data along the data bus in an orderly manner, transfers must be scheduled. Three *scheduling techniques* have been devised for communicating with input/output devices: polling (or programmed I/O), interrupt, and DMA. Let us now study these three fundamental techniques.

POLLING

Polling, also called *programmed I/O*, is the simplest scheduling technique from a hardware standpoint. I/O devices are connected in the usual manner to the system's data and address buses via the required interface chips. (For clarity, only the data bus is shown in Figure 3.20.) Depending on the microprocessor system, they may also be connected to specific control bus lines. The goal of a scheduling technique is to implement an orderly procedure for determining the next input/ output device that requires, or will be given, service. The polling technique is called a *synchronous* technique, as it does not interrupt the program in execution.

Using polling, the microprocessor will periodically ask every device connected to its data bus: *"Do you require service?"* (as illustrated in Figure 3.20.) Each device will then answer with a "yes" or "no," usually on the data bus. If a "no" answer is received, the microprocessor will proceed to the next device and ask the same question. Thus, in the polling mode, the microprocessor calls each of the I/O devices successively and determines whether or not service is needed.

In practice, a flag is tested in a status register of the device or its interface (see Figure 3.21). If the test is successful, action will be initiated. A usual action is the transfer of a word or block of data to or from the device. The polling sequence is illustrated in Figure 3.22.

The program used to implement a polling algorithm is called a *polling loop*. The program executes the sequence shown in Figure 3.22, then some action, and eventually comes back to the beginning of the sequence. The process of asking a question of the device and receiving information in return is called *handshaking*. Every communication protocol between one device and the next one on an I/O chain will normally implement some form of handshaking. This chain may involve the MPU, a status register in the I/O interface chip, the I/O controller, and the device itself (see Figure 3.23). For example, before transmitting information to a device, the MPU checks a status bit in the I/O interface chip to determine whether or not the device is ready to accept data.

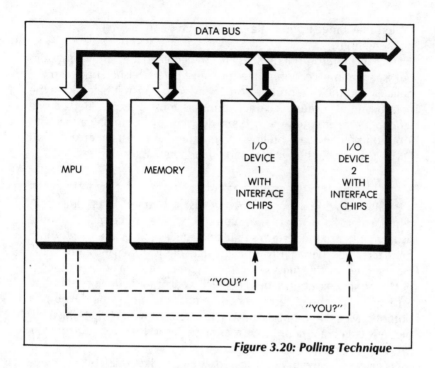

Figure 3.20: Polling Technique

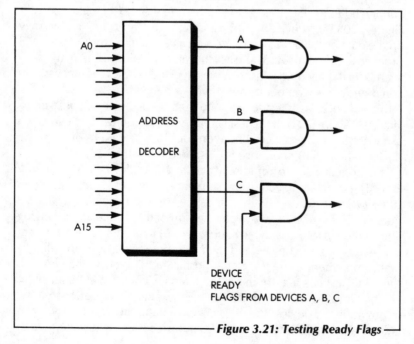

Figure 3.21: Testing Ready Flags

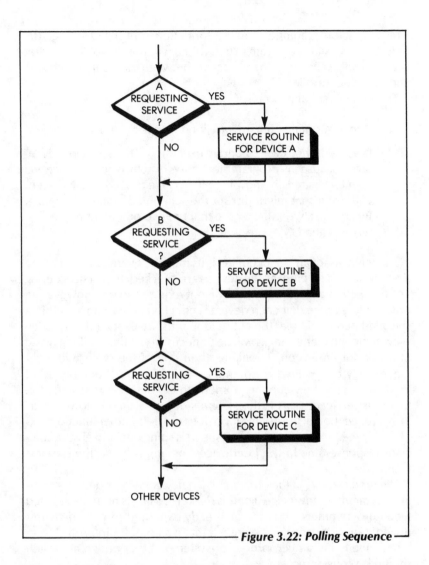

Figure 3.22: Polling Sequence

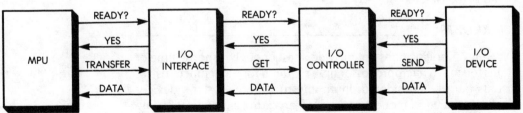

Figure 3.23: An I/O Handshaking Chain

Similarly, before reading a word of information from an I/O register, the MPU checks a status bit again to determine whether or not this register is indeed full. A similar exchange occurs between the I/O interface chip and the I/O controller.

The polling technique has several advantages:

1. It requires minimal hardware, and no special lines.

2. It is *synchronous* with program execution. This is a major advantage because the programmer knows exactly when a device will be interrogated and how long it will take to service it. No event will occur that might disrupt the scheduled polling sequence. By contrast, we will later see that the two other techniques, interrupts and DMA, are *asynchronous*.

The main disadvantage of polling is its intrinsic overhead. Every time a polling loop is entered, all the devices are checked. In practice, during any one poll, most of the devices will not require service. However, in order to guarantee that each device is checked at least once within a specified period of time, the entire loop must be executed frequently —even though many checks will be unnecessary. If the resulting waste of processor time is objectionable, then one of the other two techniques may be required. Also, in a polling scheme, a long period of time may elapse between the moment an I/O device is ready and the time it is serviced. (This is the system's *response time*.) However, as long as execution of the polling loop does not delay other functions excessively (i.e., the microprocessor speed is sufficient) and gives a sufficient response time to the I/O devices, polling is by far the simplest technique to use.

The predictability of the order in which devices will be polled is a major programming advantage. For this reason, polling is normally advised for all programmers who are not already experienced with interrupt-driven design. It can even be argued that if a complex interrupt structure is needed in a microprocessor system another design approach should be considered.

INTERRUPTS

Whenever polling does not provide a fast enough response time or wastes too much microprocessor time required for other functions, interrupts must be considered. In an interrupt-driven system, devices take the initiative for requesting service—an extra communication line is used (see the bottom of the illustration in Figure 3.24). This line, called the interrupt line, is connected to the MPU and part of the control bus.

Each I/O device is connected to this interrupt line. The situation is analogous to that of a passenger bus. When a passenger wishes to get off, a line can be pulled that will ring a bell and request service. Similarly, in our system every device that requires service may generate an interrupt pulse or level on the interrupt line. The microprocessor must *detect* the presence of interrupts on the line and *manage* them. The detailed management of interrupts is presented in the section on scheduling chips. Briefly, the microprocessor must accept the interrupt at the proper time, identify it, and then service it. As usual, interrupt management can be implemented in hardware, in software, or by a combination of both. Let us examine the operations involved.

Interrupts are automatically detected by the MPU through one or more interrupt inputs. However, interrupts must be prevented during some processes. To this end, an inhibit facility is provided (when required), either inside the MPU or outside it to prevent interrupts from being sensed.

The acceptance or refusal of an interrupt is implemented with an *internal mask* bit (called an interrupt mask), an *interrupt inhibit* signal, or an *interrupt-enable* signal. This mask bit, when internal to the MPU, is normally stored as a mask in the status register.

Once an interrupt is accepted, and assuming a single interrupt line, the microprocessor must determine which device originated the interrupt. Polling and other techniques may be used for this purpose. These techniques will be described in a later section.

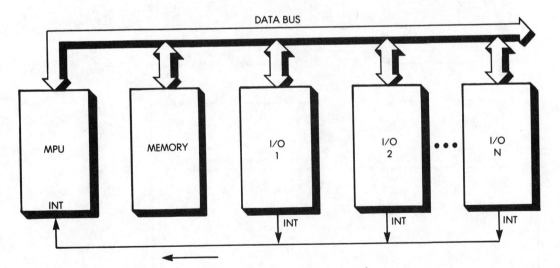

Figure 3.24: Interrupt Technique

However, several devices might generate interrupts *simultaneously* (see Figure 3.25). For this reason, whenever multiple devices are connected to the same interrupt line, *priorities* must be assigned. This task will be discussed in the next section.

Assuming that the interrupt has been accepted and the device has been identified, the service requested by the device must now be performed. The microprocessor must suspend the program it was executing and branch to an appropriate *interrupt handling routine* (or *interrupt handler*) for the interrupting device (see Figure 3.26). When the required branching address is available at the same time that the interrupt is presented to the microprocessor, it is a *vectored interrupt*.

The execution of the interrupt handler is *asynchronous* to program execution. Upon termination of the handler, the program that was suspended by the interrupt must be installed on the processor again. This requires several instructions and contributes to the *overhead*, i.e., the delay involved in managing the process, rather than servicing the device.

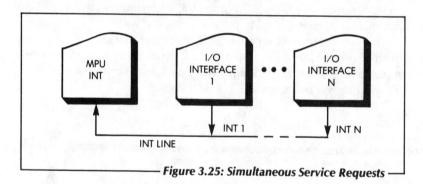

Figure 3.25: Simultaneous Service Requests

Figure 3.26: Program Is Suspended by Interrupt

The essential advantage of interrupts is that they provide a fast response. Assuming that no conflicting requests appear simultaneously, devices are serviced within a short period of time after service is requested. This response time is a measure of the microprocessor's efficiency in handling external interrupts. Interrupts are usually required in *real-time* systems, which must guarantee the best possible response time to external conditions.

The three disadvantages of interrupts are:

1. They usually require additional hardware, especially if priorities need to be resolved externally. (This point is explained in the next section.)

2. Overhead is incurred every time a program is interrupted by an external device.

3. Execution of the device handler is asynchronous with the execution of the main program. It would be desirable to compute the timing of interrupts and to anticipate all possible combinations in order to reserve appropriate areas in memory. In practice, this becomes quite complex in view of the asynchronous nature of interrupts.

Looking at Figure 3.24, we notice that only one interrupt line is used for all the input/output devices. Microprocessors seldom allow more than one or two interrupt lines. Why, then, don't microprocessors provide one interrupt line per device, as is done in larger computer systems? This would greatly simplify device identification.

The answer to this question should be obvious by now. There are *not enough pins* on the microprocessor to allocate any more lines to the control bus and, in particular, to interrupt lines. For this reason, the interrupt line(s) must be shared among the various devices. We will see how the resulting priority conflicts are solved either through the use of specialized programs or by specialized additional hardware (priority chips).

Interrupts may not be fast enough for some devices that require fast word or block transfers. Let us examine the overhead involved.

Whenever an interrupt is received, the microprocessor suspends the program in execution and switches to a new routine. This routine will then usually execute several instructions to transfer one word. Since many instructions must be executed before a word is actually transferred, many microseconds will usually elapse. This technique is too slow for devices such as floppy disks or CRT display terminals, that must be accessed quickly. The DMA technique is used to provide the additional speed required, at the expense of increased hardware complexity.

DIRECT MEMORY ACCESS (DMA) _____

Direct memory access is a "radical" technique whereby the microprocessor is suspended and disconnected from the buses. A special device, the DMA controller, then takes over and performs the required transfer at the full speed of the memory.

A direct memory access controller (DMA or DMAC) is a special *block-transfer processor*. It is a hardware device that automatically implements at hardware speed, a process that would normally be executed by a program within the microprocessor. The principle of DMAC operation is illustrated in Figure 3.27. When DMA is provided, specific I/O devices (or their interfaces) may send an interrupt directly to the DMAC rather than to the MPU. The DMAC then suspends the microprocessor by sending it a HOLD signal. Next, the DMAC takes over the buses of the system and automatically transfers one or more words between the memory and the I/O device. The detailed operation of the DMAC is explained in a later section. A DMAC is a complex device. Its complexity may be compared to the complexity of the microprocessor. Naturally, it is much more expensive than a microprocessor since it sells in smaller quantities.

In summary, a DMAC must be used in cases where the block-transfer

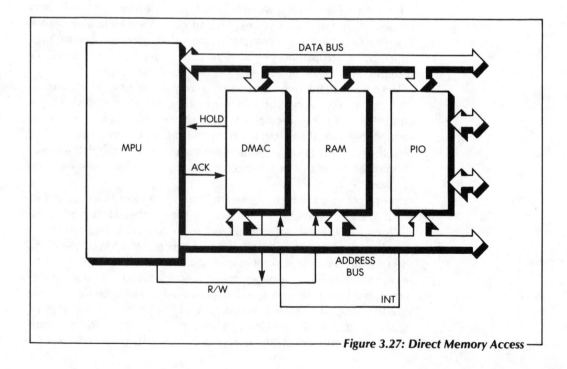

Figure 3.27: Direct Memory Access

speed of the MPU is not sufficient, even with interrupts. The DMAC provides high-speed word or block transfers between device and memory. A DMAC is typically used in the case of fast I/O devices, such as disks or CRTs. It contributes significantly to the system's cost and complexity and thus it is not normally used in small systems.

The previous discussion summarizes the essential principles of the three input/output scheduling techniques. We will now examine the various interface devices used to provide the required input/output facilities.

INPUT/OUTPUT INTERFACE CIRCUITS

Three types of I/O circuits have been developed to facilitate the connection and management of I/O devices to a microprocessor system:

1. interface chips
2. scheduling chips
3. device-controller chips.

The basic interface chips are essentially passive devices, i.e., devices that do not execute any complex operation. They are designed to facilitate the connection of I/O devices to microprocessor buses.

The scheduling chips are devices that facilitate or implement a scheduling algorithm. The device controller chips provide the required interfacing and sequencing for the specific device they control. Each type will be studied in turn.

BASIC I/O INTERFACE CHIPS

Two basic I/O interface chips are used: the universal serial interface (UART) and the parallel interface (PIO). In addition, a variety of analog-to-digital and digital-to-analog converter chips are also available for connecting analog devices. The two basic I/O interface chips will now be examined in detail. A good understanding of these chips is fundamental to the understanding of a microprocessor system.

THE UART

The UART is a universal serial interface. UART stands for *universal asynchronous receiver-transmitter*. It converts a serial input into a parallel output and can simultaneously convert a parallel input into a serial output. The asynchronous UART is most frequently used for low-to-medium-speed operation. A synchronous version, the USRT (universal synchronous receiver-transmitter) is used for high-speed transmission.

The basic function of a UART is serial/parallel conversion. The principle of serial-to-parallel conversion is illustrated in Figure 3.28. On the left of the UART a digital signal appears as a sequence of 0s and 1s. A 1 represents a high level; a 0 represents a low level. It can be seen that the input signal is (from right to left) 1000100010010. The 8-bit UART output appears on the right. It is 10001000. This output is supplied in parallel form on eight bits.

Let us examine what happens when the input signal is received by the UART. A problem arises that will require the clock signal shown in Figure 3.23. The problem in this example is that the first 1 will be correctly detected as a 1 but so will the 0. However, the next two 0s cannot be easily distinguished from the first one; so how is the UART to know that there are three 0s in succession rather than just one? This problem is solved by *timing*. The timing is supplied by an external *clock* synchronized with the external *signal*. This clock signal appears in the upper left corner of the illustration.

The external clock is always supplied from the *outside* and must be synchronized with the serial signal. One pulse of the clock (typically a half-period) will identify the presence (duration) of a bit. Three successive clock pulses will then delimit and identify in sequence the three 0s in the input signal.

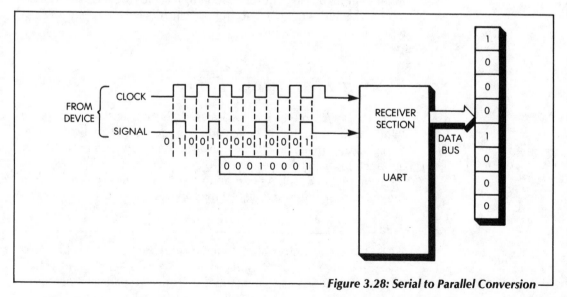

Figure 3.28: Serial to Parallel Conversion

The eight bits to be assembled as a parallel word are shown underneath the input signal on the left side of Figure 3.28. With the two input signals, clock and data, the receiver portion of the UART will automatically assemble an 8-bit word and output it to the data bus on an 8-bit connection.

Conversely, the UART will accept an 8-bit input signal (from the microprocessor data bus) and serialize it onto a serial output line under the control of an external clock supplied by the external device. The receiver and the transmitter portions of the UART are independent of each other.

UARTs were one of the first LSI chips to be standardized. As a result, most UARTs available today are essentially similar. Some microprocessor manufacturers have added a few features or merged several devices into one in order to make them different or better adapted to their own microprocessors. However, their characteristics are essentially analogous, with the exception of speed, and most UARTs can be used with any microprocessor.

A standard UART has three sections: a receiver, a transmitter, and a control section. These three modules are shown in Figure 3.29. The

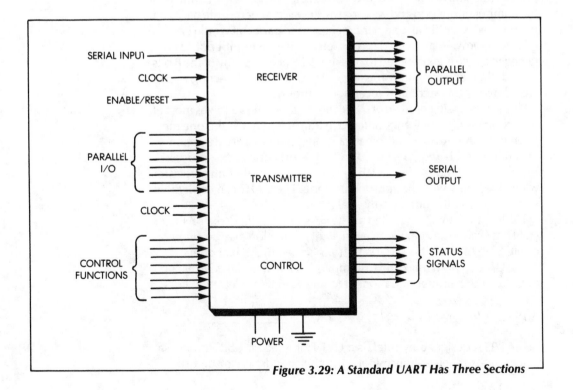

Figure 3.29: A Standard UART Has Three Sections

receiver module receives a serial input (plus clock) and supplies a parallel 8-bit output. The transmitter module receives an 8-bit parallel input (plus clock) and supplies a serial output. The control module receives control information from the microprocessor and implements the required operations. It also supplies status and control information as an output.

In addition to the serial/parallel conversion process, a UART provides a number of additional functions. It automatically manages the *start* and *stop bits* and automatically verifies, using *parity* if requested, the correct transmission of data.

In standard 8-bit transmissions, each 8-bit character is framed by one *start* and one or two *stop* bits. The input section of the UART automatically strips each character from its start and stop bits and retains only the 8-bit value. Similarly, during transmission the UART adds the required start and stop bits to the outgoing signals.

The *parity* bit is an extra bit that is often used to verify the correct transmission of data. With the parity technique, an extra bit called the parity bit is added to a 7-bit code, resulting in an 8-bit format. It is then possible to detect that a single bit has accidentally been changed. The principle of parity is the following. The 1s in a 7-bit code are counted. If the number of 1s is odd and we use an *even parity* scheme, the parity bit to be added is a 1. (In an *odd parity* scheme the parity bit would be a 0.) In other words, in an even parity scheme the total number of 1s contained in a byte is guaranteed to be *even*. If by accident any of the 8 bits should change during transmission, a special parity detecting circuit would detect this fact upon reception of the byte.

Parity detects single-bit errors. Because this technique solves most of the problems normally encountered in transmission, it is the one most often used. A UART will automatically implement parity detection or generation if it is required to do so by the processor. The processor issues a command to the UART by loading a special control register within the UART with the appropriate code. The UART can implement even or odd parity, or no parity at all.

The length of a word handled by the UART may be five, six, seven, or eight bits. Parity may be odd or even. Parity detection may be either on or off. Stop bits may be 1, 2, or 1½ (this is used in a 5-bit code).

The UART is primarily used to communicate with serial devices such as a teletype, a printer or a modem (connected to a telephone line).

An Example: The Intel 8251 USART (PCI)

The 8251, designed by Intel, is a UART; it is also a USRT (universal *synchronous* receiver-transmitter). In other words, it can be used as either an asynchronous or a synchronous device, and is called USART (universal synchronous-asynchronous receiver-transmitter) by Intel. This feature, however, is of questionable value to the user. In most designs the system is configured for either asynchronous communications *or* synchronous communications. A switch during the design is not likely. However, inasmuch as the price of the 8251 is essentially comparable to that of other UARTs on the market, the availability of a synchronous mode may be considered an advantage. The logical organization of the device appears in Figure 3.30.

The three functional blocks of any UART can be clearly identified: the transmitter section, the receiver section, and the control section. For clarity, a separate block has been allocated to the data bus buffer, which communicates with the other zones. The connections of the device to the microprocessor are all on the left side of the illustration. The connections of the device to the peripherals are all on its right side.

Let us examine the I/O device side first. As usual, there are two signals per I/O function: a data line and a clock signal. In addition, there is a synchronization line for use in synchronous mode, SYNDET. The serial input is RxD; the serial output is TxD.

The 8251 is selected by a CS (chip-select) signal gated at the bottom of Figure 3.30. Whenever CS is 1 the device is selected. The microprocessor may send the device four basic orders, which are shown in Figure 3.31. These orders will read from or write to the 8251 data bus buffer, i.e., read its status, or write a control word into its control section.

A typical application of the 8251 in asynchronous mode is shown in Figure 3.32. In this example, the UART is used to read serial information from a keyboard and to display information onto a CRT. The *baud rate generator*, which appears in the illustration, is a standard module designed to supply the appropriate clock pulses for the transmission. The slowest mode of operation is normally 110 baud. (In the binary world, a baud is a bit-per-second, or bps. A speed of 110 baud corresponds to 10 characters per second, the standard teletype speed.) Most CRT controllers are equipped with a baud-rate generator whose baud rate can be selected from 110 baud to 9600 or 19,200 baud.

When used in synchronous mode, the USART will typically be connected to a modem for communication on a high-speed data line with another computer, such as a minicomputer. In synchronous mode the 8251 will operate at up to 56 Kbaud, compared to a maximum of 9.6 Kbaud in asynchronous mode.

In summary, the UART is a basic interface chip used to communicate with a serial device. It can be "programmed" by the MPU to use virtually any serial data transmission technique.

The second basic interface chip is the PIO. It will be described now.

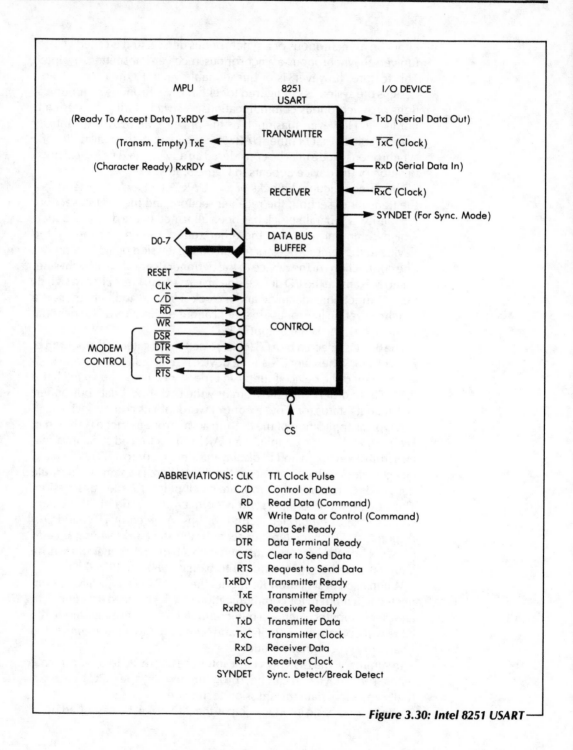

Figure 3.30: Intel 8251 USART

C̄/D	R̄D̄	W̄R̄	C̄S̄	OPERATION
0	0	1	0	8251 to Data Bus (Read)
0	1	0	0	Data Bus to 8251 (Write)
1	0	1	0	Status to Data Bus
1	1	0	0	Data Bus to Control
—	—	—	1	Data Bus to 3-State

Figure 3.31: USART Commands

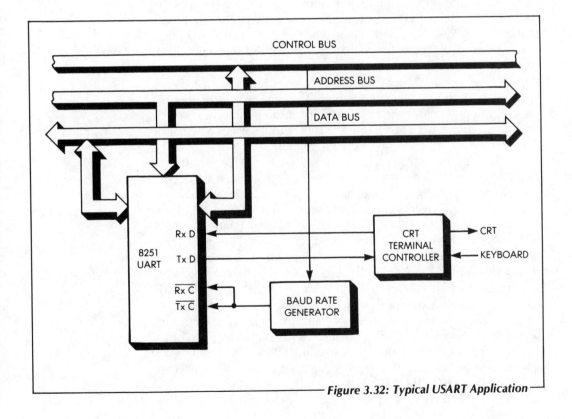

Figure 3.32: Typical USART Application

THE PIO

PIO stands for "parallel input/output" interface chip or "programmable input/output" chip. The PIO is a *programmable* device that provides a basic input and output interface for eight bits or more of parallel data. (The acronym PIO is not used industry-wide. There has never been an industry standard established for these devices as is the case for UARTs. Thus, depending on the manufacturer, this device is known by a variety of names, such as PIA (Motorola), PPI (Intel), PDC (Rockwell), and PIO (Zilog). In this book we use the term PIO to designate this type of device.)

In order to connect an input or output device to a microprocessor data bus, at a minimum latches for input and output must be provided. The *input latch* keeps data valid long enough for the microprocessor to read the data. It also isolates the data signals from the bus. Similarly, an output latch is used to "freeze" the output data for a long enough period of time for the output device to make use of it. For example, data presented on an 8080 bus will typically be valid for less than 500 nanoseconds, which is not long enough for most input/output devices to use it. In addition to the input and output latches, the *status* of the latches or registers must be available to implement a *handshaking* communication procedure. Before reading the contents of an input buffer, the microprocessor must know that the contents of this register are valid. Either a status bit must be supplied or an interrupt must be sent to the microprocessor. Conversely, a status bit is required to indicate whether the output buffer is full or empty. The microprocessor uses this status bit to determine whether or not it can output the next word. Other status bits may also be required to tell output devices whether or not they can use the contents of the PIO buffer.

Thus, any general-purpose parallel input/output interface must supply at least one input register, one output register, several status bits, and interrupt logic. Eight I/O lines are not sufficient for most input/output applications. Typical applications require 16 or 24 lines of I/O at a minimum. It would be complex and uneconomical to connect a single 8-bit interface for each 8-bit connection. The general-purpose interface chip must therefore provide several *channels*. A *channel*, or *port*, is an 8-bit connection that may be used either as input or output. The PIO must now *multiplex* a single connection to the microprocessor data bus into two or three external ports. Each port will be equipped with its buffer register(s) and with its status information. It would be desirable to provide as many input/output ports as possible, but, once again, the practical limitation is the pin count (40 pins maximum). For this reason no more than three ports can be provided. Most devices provide either two or three 8-bit parallel I/O ports.

We have now defined the main elements of a standard PIO device. The fundamental difference between a PIO and the usual standard multi-component interfaces, which were previously designed on a board, is that the PIO is *programmable*. A PIO is programmable in at least two ways:

1. The functions of the control logic are programmable for each port. For example, the microprocessor can specify the I/O line to be used for the handshaking process, the direction in which it is to be used, and often its function. The programmer can also specify whether or not a device signal will trigger interrupts, and whether or not a device signal will generate sense *levels* or *pulses*, or use positive or negative logic. These specifications are obtained by loading appropriate control registers within the PIO.

2. A PIO has "programmable" data lines. Each data line (or group of data lines) on a port *is programmable in direction*; in other words, each line may be individually defined as an input or output line. Using a PIO, it is possible to program all of the lines as outputs in the morning and then use all of the lines as inputs in the afternoon. This feature, though it is heresy to a traditional hardware designer, makes the PIO a truly general-purpose interface device that can be used in every standard situation. It is possible to connect any combination of input and output lines to the same PIO or group of PIOs. A standard microcomputer board equipped with standard PIOs can essentially be interfaced to any standard I/O device without modifying the board. The required modifications are accomplished by the program.

The internal structure of a PIO appears in Figure 3.33. This PIO has two ports (eight bits each) plus control lines. Various combinations of I/O lines and control signals are possible, depending on the manufacturer.

In Figure 3.33 each port is equipped with three registers:

1. *The data-buffer register*. This register accumulates the data for input or output on each of the eight I/O lines.

2. *The direction register*. A 0 or a 1 written into a bit position of this register will identify the corresponding line as input or output. A 0 usually denotes input and a 1 usually denotes output. This convention may seem odd. Input starts with 1 and output with 0, yet 0 and 1 are used, respectively. The reason for this convention is due to a safety consideration during start-up. When the system is initialized, the contents of all the registers are normally

reset to 0. During system start-up, spurious signals might be generated on output lines that could cause false settings in the outside world. It is therefore crucial that, if any potentially dangerous signal could be generated on the I/O lines, these lines be configured as *input* during start-up rather than as output.

3. *The control register*. This register stores the control bits issued by the microprocessor for the port. For each port, the microprocessor can specify whether or not interrupts are to be generated and which control signals are to be logically associated with the port. This means, in particular, that an appropriate status bit will be set within the control register when the data buffer is full or empty. Typically, this control register provides storage for both

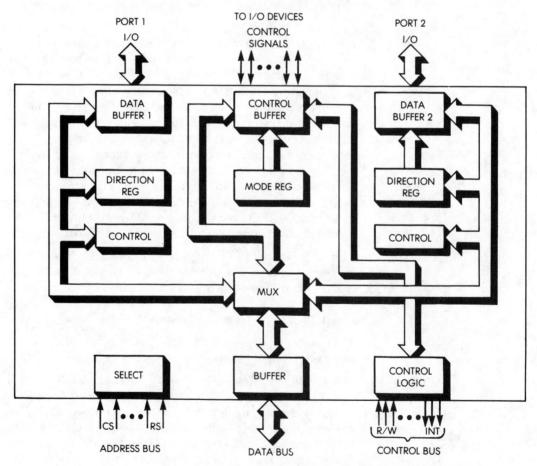

Figure 3.33: The Internal Structure of the PIO

the command word issued by the microprocessor and the status information generated by the device; status information may require only one or two bits.

The above statement may seem surprising: the "same register" is used for two different functions. Let us examine what this means, as this is a common occurrence.

The register in question consists, in fact, of two distinct registers (or latches): one for input and one for output. Both halves are referred to as the same register because they have the same address. One is selected by a read operation, the other one by a write operation.

Since each internal address inside the device adds to the complexity and may create a need for additional pins, the number of addresses is always minimized. Monodirectional registers (input or output) may, and do, share common addresses.

Let us illustrate this point with a simple example. Using a straightforward design, a PIO with four internal addresses (registers) requires two RS (register-select) pins for register selection (2 bits can specify $2^2 = 4$ codes). A PIO with six or eight registers requires three RS pins.

Let us now examine the way a PIO is used. Before using the PIO, the microprocessor must configure it by executing two basic operations:

1. *Specifying the mode.* The microprocessor must load the control registers and specify the mode in which the control signals will be generated or will operate.

2. *Designating the line direction.* Next, the microprocessor must load the direction registers of the two ports in order to designate the lines of the ports as inputs or outputs.

These two operations must be done for every port. Once the contents of the control register and the direction register of a port are valid, the port may be used.

A data transfer operation can then be performed by a standard transfer instruction such as the MOV instruction that was described for the 8080. Specialized input and output instructions are also sometimes available. Using such an instruction, a byte of data can be transferred between the MPU and the PIO, provided that the PIO register is ready (this is ascertained by examining the appropriate PIO status bit).

Let us now examine how the internal PIO registers are selected and loaded with contents.

All data transmitted by the microprocessor normally appear on the data bus. The data to be loaded in a PIO register will therefore be placed by the MPU on the data bus and, simultaneously, a register-select (RS) will be performed. Register selection is accomplished by providing an address on the address bus. At least one bit must be supplied to select the chip (CS) and, assuming that our PIO has eight, or fewer, internal registers, three lines of the address bus must be used to select one of the registers (RS lines). Three lines generate eight binary patterns, thus allowing the selection among eight possible registers.

Thus, the microprocessor selects one of the internal PIO registers by putting the appropriate pattern on the address bus and it then supplies eight data bits to be transferred into one of these registers on the data bus. An internal multiplexer (MUX) within the PIO then gates the 8-bit data to the appropriate register. Once the appropriate internal registers have been loaded, the PIO is ready to be used and data may be freely exchanged between its data buffers and the microprocessor. To read information from a data buffer, the microprocessor, i.e., the programmer, provides the appropriate RS signals for selecting the data buffer register and simultaneously generates a read order on the control bus. In the case of a write operation it supplies a W signal rather than an R signal on the control bus. To read status from the PIO, the contents of the appropriate control register are read. Normally, once the PIO has been *configured*—that is, once its control and direction registers have been loaded—no further change is necessary and the microprocessor can communicate directly with the data buffers by using a single instruction.

Complex as it may seem, the PIO is conceptually a very simple device. One of the essential advantages of the PIO is that it is programmable. The programmability of this device is, in fact, rudimentary; selections may be performed, but there are no complex automated sequences. In the future, the power of PIOs will probably be increased by supplying them with more programmed functions. We will show later that the concept of LSI evolution is towards *vertical integration*, i.e., supplying more functions per chip. Future PIOs will be equipped with elementary processors that will provide them with local processing capabilities.

PIO Example 1: The Motorola 6820 PIA

PIA stands for "peripheral-interface adapter" and is Motorola's name for a PIO device. The internal structure of the Motorola 6820 appears in Figure 3.34. It is essentially identical to the structure of our "standard" PIO shown in Figure 3.33. The PIA is equipped with two 8-bit input/output ports. Each line may be individually programmed as an input or an output. A 0 in the data direction register specifies an input; a 1 specifies an output. The 6820 is equipped with two control lines per input/output port: CA1 and CA2 for Port A, CB1 and CB2 for Port B.

The second control line on each port may be programmed separately as either an input or an output. For example, one of the lines may be used as a *ready* signal and the second one as an *acknowledge* signal. In addition, this ready signal may be programmed to generate an interrupt automatically. The PIA is also equipped with two interrupt request lines, IRQA and IRQB—one per port.

Unlike the Motorola 6800 or the Intel 8080, which have a single interrupt input, the Motorola 6820 has two separate interrupt lines. This

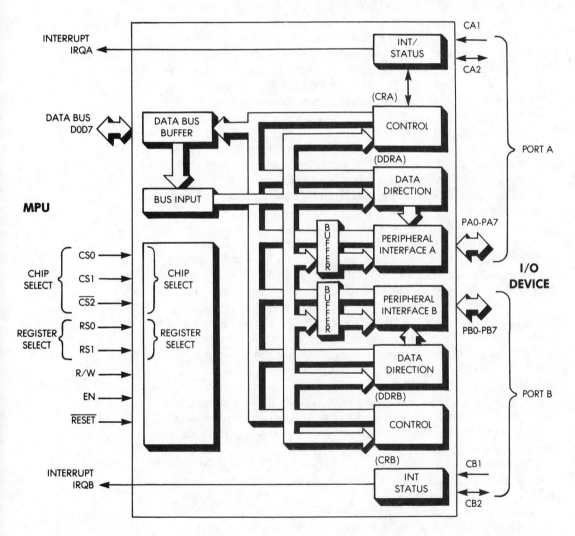

Figure 3.34: The Motorola 6820 PIA

may seem surprising since, in a simple system, both interrupt lines A and B will normally be tied to the single microprocessor interrupt line. In a more complex system, however, a more elaborate priority structure will be used for interrupts. Such priority structures are described later in this chapter. In such a case, each of the PIA interrupt-request lines is connected to a separate interrupt input on a special priority chip (a PIC).

The role of the pins on the 6820 should be clear. Two sets of signals on the left—CS0, CS1, CS2, and RS0, RS1—are used to implement chip select and register select, respectively. This approach corresponded to Motorola's philosophy. Most of the components of the 6800 family have three or more chip-select pins. In small systems, this will eliminate the need to use address decoders, since up to eight chips may be connected to the address bus; however, the components require more pins. Since a higher number of pins results in a larger size and an increased cost at the board level, Motorola made every attempt to minimize the number of pins.

In particular, one of the features of the 6820 register-selection scheme is probably due to the lack of a sufficient number of pins on the device. We see only *two* register-select signals, RS0 and RS1. However, the 6820 is equipped with *six* internal registers. How can *two* RS signals select one of the *six* registers? Clearly, two signals may only select one of *four* register addresses. This is exactly the case here. The two remaining registers—the peripheral interface register and the data direction register—*share a common address* on a port. The selection between either register is accomplished by a bit within the control register. A 0 in bit position 2 of the control register selects the DDR and a 1 selects the peripheral interface register. The manufacturer presents this situation as an advantage. Whenever the system is initialized, that is, when a reset is applied, the contents of the control register will be 0, automatically selecting the data direction register. Thus, no spurious signal would be generated on the peripheral interface register, which is not selected. This is correct. However, it can also be argued that this selection system leads to awkward programming. If the DDR and the peripheral interface registers must be accessed in succession, the contents of the control register must be changed between the two accesses, a definite nuisance.

All the same, the 6820 is a powerful and flexible I/O interface device and the possible shortcoming of its register-access scheme should not be a significant consideration.

As a simple example, we will examine the signals required to implement a handshaking process between the 6820 and a device such as a paper tape reader (PTR). We assume that the paper tape reader is equipped with an 8-bit buffer. The microprocessor wants to read one byte of data from the PTR. It must first verify whether or not the contents of the PTR buffer are valid. CA1 can be used to connect the "buffer-full" or "ready" signal from the PTR to the PIA (see Figure 3.35). Whenever the "ready" signal comes in, it will be known that the contents of the PTR buffer are good and can be read. The data present on Port A can then be read. Subsequently, an "acknowledge" signal will be transmitted back to the device. This acknowledge tells the device: *"Your buffer has been emptied, you may reload it."* In addition, most devices are equipped with a "data overrun" signal or flag, which indicates that data have been written in a buffer when the previous contents had not yet been emptied. This is an error that is normally detected in hardware.

Automatically, whenever the contents of the data register on Port A or B are read onto the microprocessor data bus, an acknowledge signal may be transmitted on CA2 to CB2 towards the peripheral, indicating that the read operation is being performed.

Similarly, when communicating with an output device such as a buffer-equipped teletype, the PIA must interrogate the device prior to sending it information. The PIA must check to see if the buffer of the

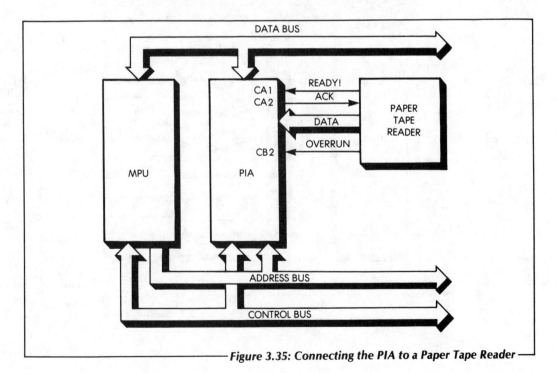

Figure 3.35: Connecting the PIA to a Paper Tape Reader

device is empty before loading additional data into it. This time a
"ready" signal from the device means: *My input buffer is empty, you
may supply me with the next character. Go ahead.* The microprocessor can then send the next byte to the peripheral.

Once the PIA has been properly connected, its use by the programmer is straightforward:

1. The control register for Port A is loaded with the appropriate
    contents (see Figure 3.36).

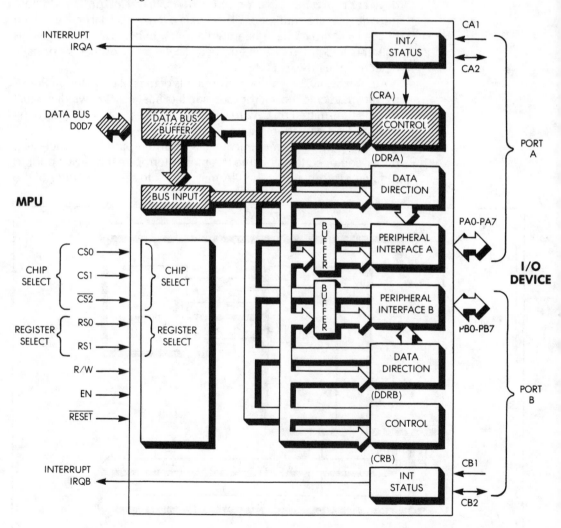

Figure 3.36: PIA: Loading the Control Register

2. The data direction register is loaded (see Figure 3.37). For example, 00000000 will configure Port A as eight input lines, 11111111 will configure it as eight output lines.

3. Port A is now configured and ready to be used. The (output portion of the) control register is tested for device status (see Figure 3.38).

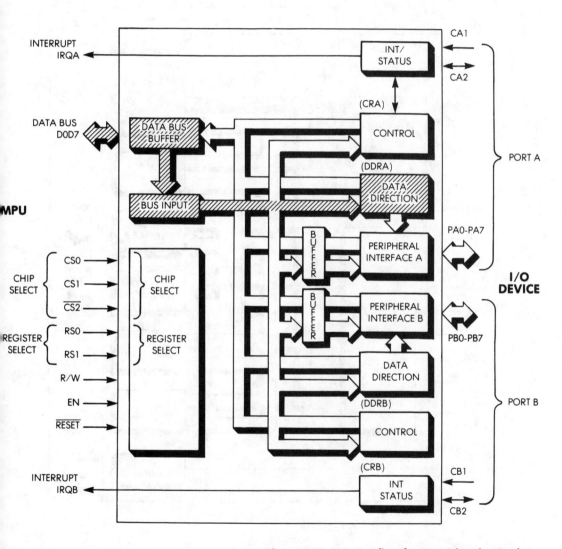

Figure 3.37: PIA: Loading the Data Direction Register

4.   Data is read by the MPU from the device (see Figure 3.39).

Steps 3 and 4 can now be repeated indefinitely. In summary, the PIA is a typical PIO device (and may be used in an 8080 system). Let us examine a second PIO example.

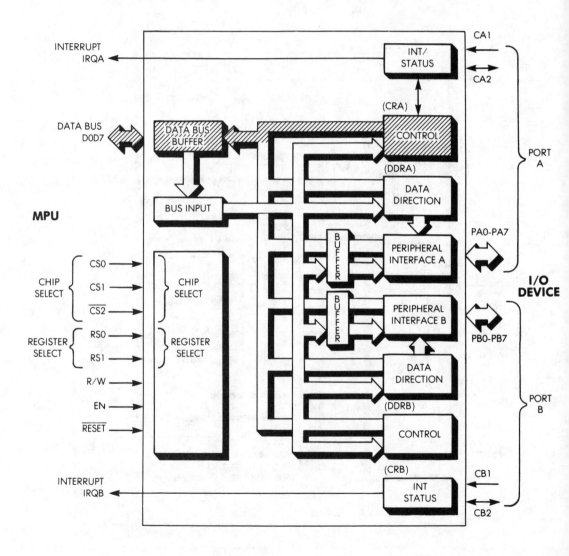

Figure 3.38: PIA: Reading the Status

PIO EXAMPLE 2: THE INTEL 8255 PPI

PPI stands for "programmable peripheral interface." It is Intel's version of a PIO (Figure 3.40). This device is equipped with 24 input/output lines. These lines are normally grouped into three ports. At first it might appear that this device is more powerful than the PIA because of the

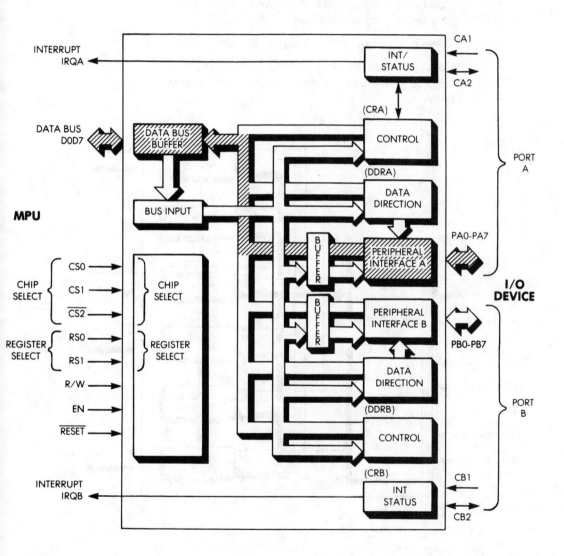

Figure 3.39: PIA: Read Input

larger number of lines, but this is not the case. Although this component is equipped with three ports, at least four lines on one of the ports must be used for control functions. In this respect it is essentially analogous to the previous device.

The PPI, however, is not programmable by line but by groups of four lines. This reduces the PPI's flexibility. This is not a significant drawback as, in most practical cases, lines are used in groups of four or more.

The PPI may be programmed in three modes:

1. Mode 0 allows each group of four lines to be input or output.

2. Mode 1 programs eight lines as input or output within a group of twelve lines. The four remaining lines are then reserved for control functions.

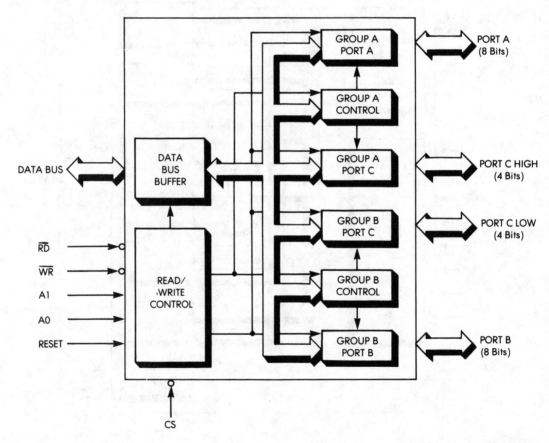

Figure 3.40: Intel 8255 PPI

3. Mode 2 is called "bidirectional-buffer" mode; eight lines are available for data and five lines for handshaking.

Internal 8225 addressing is performed in the usual manner. The signal combinations are shown in Figure 3.41. CS is the chip-select signal, which tells the device that it is being selected. A0 and A1 are used in combination with the read and write lines to transfer information to or from the PPI registers.

Two typical applications of the 8255 are shown in Figures 3.42 and 3.43. In the upper part of Figure 3.42, the 8255 is programmed in mode 1 and is used as input. The lower part of the 8255 is programmed in mode 0 and Port B is used as output; the upper half of the device is used to communicate with an 8-bit paper tape reader and the lower half is used to control the operation of the machine tool. The paper tape contains a stored program that has been punched on tape. This program specifies the sequence of steps to be accomplished by the machine tool. Data or instructions on the tape are usually encoded in an 8-bit format (with parity). The byte coming out of the paper tape reader is shown as R0-R7 on Figure 3.42 and is read through Port A of the PIO.

The paper tape reader accepts only two commands: STOP/GO, transmitted via line PC6 of the PIO. A strobe signal STB is available from the paper tape reader to indicate that a byte is available. Once the byte has been read, a confirmation ACK is sent back by the microprocessor via line PC5 of the PIO so that the paper tape reader can read the next byte.

This signal is required in order to avoid an *overrun*, a situation in which a byte is read by the paper tape reader while the previous one

$\overline{CS}$	A1	A0	$\overline{RD}$	$\overline{WR}$	OPERATION	
0	0	0	0	1	PORT A TO DATA BUS	MPU
0	0	1	0	1	PORT B TO DATA BUS	READ
0	1	0	0	1	PORT C TO DATA BUS	(A, B, C)
0	0	0	1	0	DATA BUS TO PORT A	
0	0	1	1	0	DATA BUS TO PORT B	MPU
0	1	0	1	0	DATA BUS TO PORT C	WRITE
0	1	1	1	0	DATA BUS TO CONTROL	
0	1	1	0	1	ILLEGAL	
1	—	—	—	—	DATA BUS TO 3-STATE	DISABLE

Figure 3.41: Addressing the 8255

has not yet been picked up by the microprocessor, thus destroying the previous one. This simple communication protocol is another example of a handshaking procedure:

STB (to PIO): *(I have a byte ready (PTR).)*
READ (to PIO): *(MPU reads byte.)*
ACK (to PTR): *(Thank you. I am done (MPU). Get the next one.)*

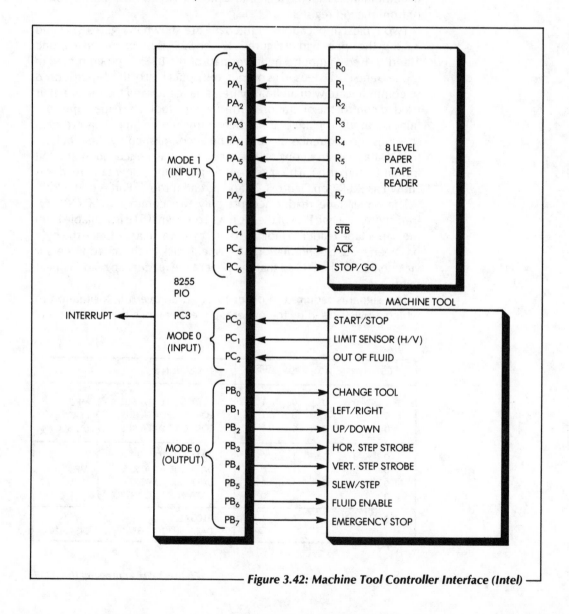

Figure 3.42: Machine Tool Controller Interface (Intel)

The machine tool shown at the bottom of Figure 3.42 is equipped with three sensors and it accepts eight commands. The three sensors are:

— start/stop
— limit sensor (horizontal/vertical)
— out of fluid.

They are connected to lines PC0, PC1 and PC2 of Port C.

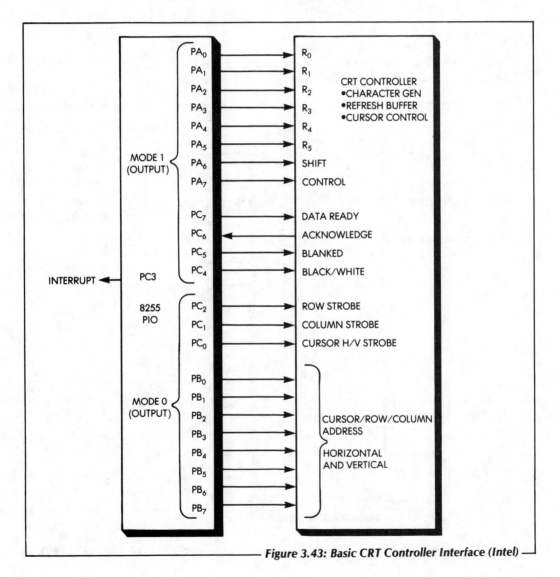

Figure 3.43: Basic CRT Controller Interface (Intel)

The eight commands are issued on lines PB0 to PB7 of Port B. These commands position the cutting tool up/down, right/left; they also lubricate it, stop it, or cause an alternative tool to be used. This example illustrates the use of the many I/O lines of such a PIO.

One point still needs to be clarified. The function of the data lines seems identical to the function of the control lines. Their function is similar but not identical. In particular, a control line used as an input may be programmed to generate an automatic acknowledge or interrupt. This is shown on line PC3 of Figure 3.42.

SUMMARY—PIO

All major microprocessor manufacturers have a PIO or its equivalent. As an example, Rockwell's GPI/O is shown in Figure 3.44. Rockwell also

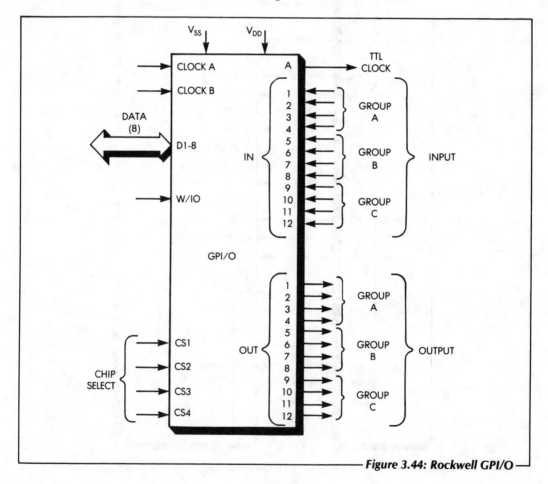

Figure 3.44: Rockwell GPI/O

uses a multiple address selection scheme in order to save external address decoders. Four pins are used for SC1 to SC4 on Figure 3.44.

All PIOs accomplish the same basic purpose. They are parallel interface devices with at least two ports and four control lines for handshaking (two per 8-bit port). The lines are programmable in direction, and the operation of the control signals may also be programmed. At least one PIO is used in almost any microprocessor system.

Scheduling chips have been designed to facilitate the scheduling of I/O devices, using one or more of the three basic techniques we have described: polling, interrupts, and DMA.

Since a polling technique is generally used to minimize the number of chips and since it can be completely done in software, no polling chips have been created. However, polling *could* be done in hardware. Sophisticated priority chips also provide automatic polling facilities. This is done in a system of higher complexity that already requires a priority management chip.

Interrupt handling is greatly facilitated by interrupt management chips, but DMA requires a hardware controller. We will now examine the chips that implement these two scheduling techniques, i.e., interrupts and DMA.

INTERRUPT MANAGEMENT CHIP

Interrupts are used to obtain fast response time from a microprocessor in order to service I/O devices. Two problems arise:

1. Simultaneous interrupts may occur. A decision must be made as to which device to service first. This problem is solved by a *priority* scheme.

2. The availability of a single interrupt line imposes the need to identify the device that triggered the interrupt. This is the *interrupt-identification problem*.

We will now study these two problems and the techniques and components available to solve them. First we will examine interrupt identification techniques, then priority techniques.

Interrupt Identification Techniques

Because of the pin number limitation on the package, we have seen that most microprocessors have only one or two interrupt lines. This is not sufficient to dedicate one interrupt line to one device when more than two I/O devices are used. Consequently, several devices will be connected to the same interrupt line. Whenever an interrupt signal is sent, the microprocessor must determine which device caused the interrupt in order to execute the correct interrupt-handling routine. As usual, two methods may be used: a software method and a hardware method.

1. The Software Method.   In the software method, a polling program checks each of the devices connected to the interrupt line one by one to determine which is the interrupting device. In the simplest form of this method, the polling routine reads an interrupt status bit on each device to determine whether or not that device caused the interrupt. When the interrupting device is found, the routine then branches to the appropriate interrupt handler.

Identifying the device that caused the interrupt may be assisted by external hardware. The *daisy-chain* method uses an extra line from the microprocessor to the I/O device, then from I/O-device-1 to I/O-device-2, and then from I/O-device-2 to I/O-device-3, and so on, back to the microprocessor. A signal is generated onto this line. Device-1 receives the signal. If it did not generate an interrupt it lets the signal flow to the next I/O device, and so on. Whenever the signal reaches the device that triggered the interrupt, the device will place an identification number (vector) on the data bus, where it can be read by the microprocessor. Still other methods can be used to improve the efficiency of this scheme.

2. The Hardware Method.   This method is more efficient than the software method. The software scheme is simple in terms of the connections required, but it requires appreciable time from the processor, thus increasing the overhead for responding to an interrupt. The hardware scheme makes it the responsibility of a hardware device to automatically supply the address of the appropriate interrupt-handling routine. This is called an automated *interrupt-vectoring* technique. A vectored interrupt is an interrupt that supplies the branching address to the interrupt-handling routine at the time it occurs. To provide this facility, the component that manages the interrupt(s) has to be equipped with one 16-bit address register per device. This address register will contain the required branching address. The detailed operation of such a component, called a PIC, is presented in a later section.

Priority Techniques _____

The remaining problem is to determine which I/O device should be granted service in the event that simultaneous interrupts occur. The solution is to implement a priority scheme. In its simplest but most often used form, the priority scheme assigns a fixed priority number to each device. For example, the floppy disk will have priority level 1; a power-failure detect will have priority level 0. By convention, priority 0 is normally the highest in the system.

A more complex priority scheme is to give an initial priority to each device, then modify these priorities by program, according to some algorithm. However, managing priorities that vary dynamically is such a complex software proposition that it is seldom used. It is generally impossible to predict all possible combinations of interrupts, so that the system's behavior could become erratic.

One simple improvement to the fixed-priority scheme is the *masking* facility. It has become a standard facility when managing interrupts. With this technique, a mask bit that can either enable or disable the interrupt is associated with each interrupt.

This facility is best described using an actual circuit. A basic interrupt-management circuit, exclusive of the priority-encoding and of the vectoring facility, appears in Figure 3.45. This circuit will manage eight interrupts labeled INT0 to INT7, which appear on the right side of the illustration. The mask register appears at the bottom of the illustration. Whenever a bit of the mask contains a 0, the 0 blocks the propagation of the corresponding interrupt signal toward the left of the illustration. The corresponding interrupt level (0 to 7) is then said to be masked. The presence of a 1 bit in the mask register allows the corresponding interrupt to propagate left. If all interrupt lines are to be used or allowed, the mask register will contain all 1s. If interrupt line 2 is to be ignored, bit 2 of the mask register will be set to 0. Interrupt levels that have not been masked out can set a bit in an interrupt register on the left of the illustration. The contents of this register may be read out of the circuit onto the data bus (top of illustration) in order to be examined by the MPU. We will see below how this register allows the easy implementation of software priority decoding. Finally, an inclusive OR of the lines of this register provides the final INT interrupt signal appearing on the left side of the illustration. This interrupt request is connected to the single microprocessor interrupt line and alerts it to the occurrence of one or more interrupts. The MPU then reads the contents of the interrupt register to identify the device that caused the interrupt.

In normal operation the mask register is loaded by the programmer with an appropriate bit pattern that will enable the selected interrupt levels. Assuming that all interrupt lines are used, the mask will be all 1s. If one or more interrupts are triggered, they will propagate to the left of the illustration and an interrupt request will result. The microprocessor will then read the contents of the interrupt register and find a 1 in every bit position where a device has requested service. Assuming that several devices have requested service simultaneously, it is then easy

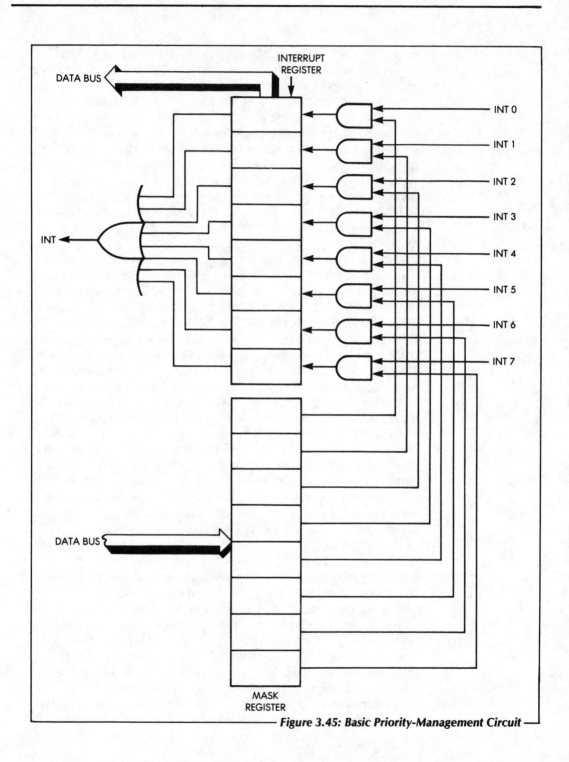

Figure 3.45: Basic Priority-Management Circuit

to implement a priority scheme. We will assume here that interrupt 0 is the highest priority, interrupt 1 the next highest, and so on. The microprocessor will then simply test bit 0 of the interrupt register, then bit 1, and then bit 2 until it finds a 1. When it finds a 1, the corresponding interrupt level will be serviced. This guarantees that the highest level of interrupt is serviced first. If INT is still true after this interrupt has been serviced, the microprocessor will have to read anew the contents of the interrupt register in order to service the other waiting interrupts. This is a simple software implementation of a priority-interrupt scheme.

We have described the techniques used to implement interrupts and solve the two essential problems associated with interrupts: identifying the interrupt and handling simultaneous interrupts. We have also described the basic interrupt management circuit required to implement priorities and mask interrupt levels selectively.

In order to facilitate interrupt management further, a specialized chip has been created, the programmable interrupt controller, or PIC. It will be described now. Then, specific examples will be given, using actual chips.

PROGRAMMABLE INTERRUPT CONTROLLER (PIC)

The PIC facilitates and automates the management of multiple interrupts in a microprocessor system (Figure 3.46). It manages eight interrupt levels, provides masking, multiple priorities, and automatic interrupt vectoring. In interrupt vectoring, when an interrupt level has been detected and accepted by the MPU, the program branches automatically to the required address in memory where the interrupt service routine resides. In addition, this component may automate additional scheduling techniques such as polling and round-robin. The *round-robin* is a simple technique whereby each device is merely serviced in turn. The operation of a PIC in the case of an actual device, the Intel 8259, will now be described.

PIC Example: Intel 8259

The 8259 PIC provides complete interrupt management including managing priorities, interrupt mask, and automatic interrupt vectoring. It is implemented on a static NMOS 28-pin device. In addition, the device is cascadable: it can be associated with up to 8 other PICs to manage 64 separate interrupt levels. This PIC is specifically adapted to the 8080. Let us therefore examine the 8080 interrupt management in more detail.

By itself, the 8080 provides minimum internal interrupt management facilities. In response to an interrupt signal, provided that interrupts are enabled, the 8080 will accept the interrupt and return an "interrupt-acknowledge" signal on INTA. (Interrupts are enabled via the INTE line.) The microprocessor takes no other action and stops in a special state where it waits for an *instruction* to be forced onto the *data* bus. Whenever the instruction appears on the data bus it will be transmitted directly into the instruction register of the control unit, where it will be decoded. This is minimal interrupt management indeed.

Whenever an interrupt occurs, the program in execution on the MPU is suspended so that the proper interrupt handling routine can be executed. In order to restart the interrupted program upon completion of the interrupt handler, all the MPU registers that will be used (and therefore changed) by the interrupt handler must be preserved prior to execution of the interrupt handler. At a minimum, the program counter, the status flags, and the accumulator must be saved in the stack.

The 8080 does not even preserve the program counter or the status automatically. It is the responsibility of the interrupt handler to save the program counter. This is why, in the case of the 8080, the instruction

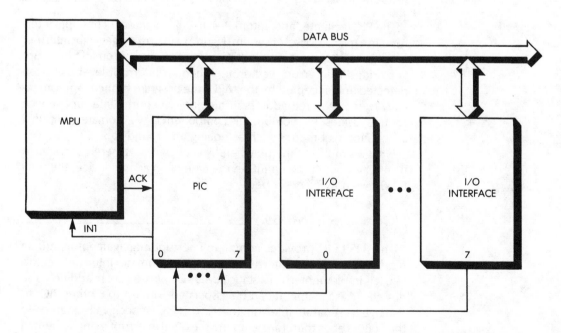

Figure 3.46: PIC Intercepts and Manages Interrupts

placed on the data bus by the PIC must be an instruction that automatically saves PC on the stack. Before the introduction of PICs, the usual instruction forced on the data bus was the restart (RST). The RST instruction is a special 1-byte call. A *call* is a jump that saves the PC in the stack first. The 1-byte format presents a speed advantage since a usual program call would require three bytes. The RST instruction includes a 3-bit field which allows a direct call to one of eight memory locations: 0, 8, 16, 24, 32, 40, 48, 56. The interrupt-handling routine must start at one of these addresses. The RST instruction automatically preserves the program counter on the stack. However, it is the responsibility of the interrupt handler to preserve any or all of the other internal 8080 registers. When the 8080 was introduced, this was considered a deficiency. Interrupt response was slow since most of the processing was done by software, thus generating a large overhead.

The 8259 PIC has changed this situation. The 8259 provides highly automated interrupt management, including automatic vectoring. It does not, however, implement automatic preservation of the registers in the stack. It is the programmer's responsibility to preserve the registers when executing the interrupt handler.

In response to an INTA from the 8080, the 8259 places a 3-byte instruction—a CALL (11001101) followed by a 2-byte address—on the data bus automatically. The two bytes are the *vectoring address* and they contain the address of the interrupt handler. The 8259 can handle eight interrupt levels, and is therefore equipped with eight internal 16-bit registers containing the interrupt vectors. The 8259's internal organization is shown in Figure 3.47. These registers must be loaded by the programmer prior to their use. Two 8-bit transfers are needed to load each 16-bit register before the corresponding interrupt level may be used. Generally, however, this task is accomplished during the initialization phase of the system. The contents of these registers normally are not changed during system operation, so that the 8259 continues to place the same 16-bit vectoring address on the data bus for each interrupt level. This is clearly an efficient way to provide interrupt vectoring. For example, should an interrupt occur on level 4, assuming that its priority level is enabled, the contents of the fifth 16-bit address register will be used to provide the automatic vectoring.

As shown in Figure 3.47, the 8259 includes the usual interrupt mask (called IMR), and any one of the eight interrupt levels may be inhibited by placing a 0 in the appropriate bit position of the mask register.

The 8259 also includes a priority facility that automatically allows the inhibiting of any interrupt that has a priority lower than a specified level. The described priority level is loaded into the "in-service register" (ISR). A simple comparison is performed between the priority level of the actual interrupt and the value of the level stored in the ISR register before allowing the interrupt to trigger the external INT signal. This effectively filters out interrupts with levels that are higher than the specified threshold. (The priority of an interrupt increases when its level decreases.)

Finally, several modes of operation of the device are provided that automate various priority scheduling schemes, and multiple PICs can be cascaded to manage additional interrupt levels, as shown in Figure 3.48. One to eight "slaves" may be cascaded.

INTEL VERSUS MOTOROLA INTERRUPTS

It is interesting to compare the interrupt management approach taken in the 8080 to the one implemented in the 6800 since these two microprocessors were early competitors. The 8080 interrupt response has been described. The 6800 implements a completely different interrupt philosophy.

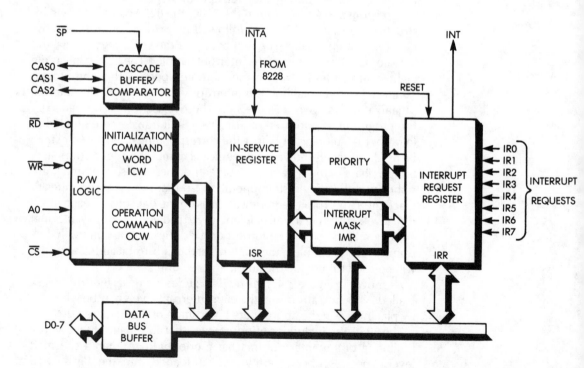

Figure 3.47: 8259 PIC Internal Organization

One difference is that interrupts are enabled or disabled by a bit of the internal mask register, which may be set by the programmer. Recall that interrupts are enabled or disabled by an external INTE signal in the case of the 8080. The 6800 approach has the advantage of saving the microprocessor pin used by the INTE in the 8080.

The main difference, however, is in the automatic response to interrupts. In response to an interrupt, provided that the interrupt is enabled, the 6800 saves *all the internal registers* in the stack automatically and reads the contents of a reserved memory location (FFF8, FFF9 in hexadecimal notation; hexadecimal is explained in Chapter 8). Addresses FFF8-FFF9 contain the interrupt vector. The 6800 reads the contents of this memory location, then branches automatically to the 16-bit address that was contained in FFF8, FFF9.

Thus, by preserving all the MPU registers and branching to a programmed address in the memory automatically, the 6800 by itself provides a faster interrupt response than the 8080 by itself, at least in the case of a single interrupt. The required logic inside the microprocessor is naturally more complex, but this is not the main problem.

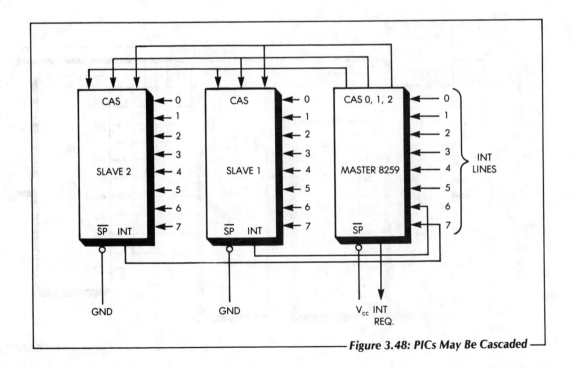

Figure 3.48: PICs May Be Cascaded

This approach has disadvantages. The scheme used by Motorola does not easily lend itself to automatic vectoring in the case of multiple interrupts. When an interrupt occurs, a branch will take place automatically to the address stored at FFF8, FFF9, regardless of the interrupt level. A software routine must then determine the final vectoring address, i.e., which interrupt handler to activate.

A special PIC has been introduced by Motorola to solve this problem. As usual, the PIC manages eight interrupt levels. Its internal architecture is shown in Figure 3.49. To provide automatic vectoring, the PIC monitors the address bus continuously. Whenever the device sees FFF8-FFF9 on the address bus, it takes control of the data bus. The *PIC* then supplies the branching address, rather than allowing the *memory* to supply one from the contents of FFF8-FFF9. The PIC is equipped with eight 16-bit registers, and, depending on the interrupt level that has been activated, it will provide the correct branching address for the level by reading out the contents of the appropriate 16-bit register. In other words, this PIC will substitute the correct 16-bit vectoring address for one of eight interrupt levels to the 16-bit address that was contained in the memory at address FFF8-FFF9. The problem has been solved. This approach is clearly efficient for the 6800 (see Figure 3.49).

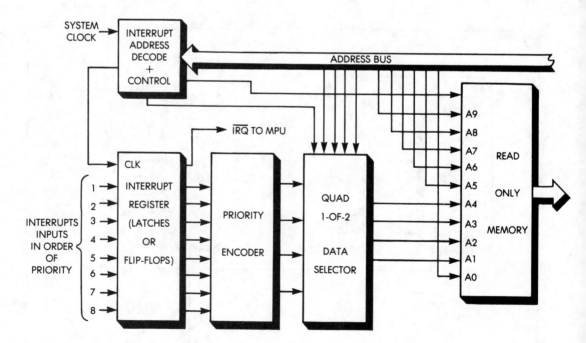

Figure 3.49: 6800 PIC

We can see that Motorola's PIC is incompatible with Intel's PIC. The results are essentially similar with the exception that the 6800 will automatically preserve all of the machine registers. The 8080 must accomplish this through the use of a short software routine. In some situations it is not necessary to store all the machine registers, and in these situations the 8080 has a faster response. When all the registers must be saved, the 6800 is faster. Since the 8080 has more internal registers than the 6800, saving all the internal registers of the 8080 might be undesirable as well as inefficient.

The role and operation of a PIC has been described. The PIC automates the management of multiple interrupts and improves the response time. In cases where a minimal overhead is required, a DMAC must be used.

DIRECT MEMORY ACCESS CONTROLLER (DMAC)

The DMA concept was introduced at the beginning of the chapter. The parallel transfer speed of a microprocessor is limited by the software overhead involved in transferring successive words. Several instructions must be executed in order to transfer a word or a chain of words. This constraint may become critical. The block transfer speed may not be sufficient for a floppy disk or a CRT. A DMAC is then required. A DMAC implements the transfer algorithm in hardware and automates word or block transfers between the memory and an I/O device. Two main DMA techniques are used to allow a peripheral to communicate directly with the memory:

1. The processor is halted or suspended by the DMAC. The DMAC gains control of the buses and lets the I/O device communicate directly with the memory.

2. The DMAC steals a memory cycle from the microprocessor, giving it to the data transfer between the memory and the I/O device.

A combination of these methods can also be used.

Conceptually, the DMAC is a specialized block transfer processor that disconnects or isolates the MPU from the buses and manages the required transfers between the memory and an I/O device. The sequence of operations involved in using a DMAC will now be described in the case of a real DMAC.

Rockwell DMAC

A system using the Rockwell DMAC appears in Figure 3.50. The sequence of operations is:

1. The PDC (Rockwell's PIO, connected to the peripheral) requests service from the DMAC on line DMA0 (the highest priority line; see Figure 3.51).

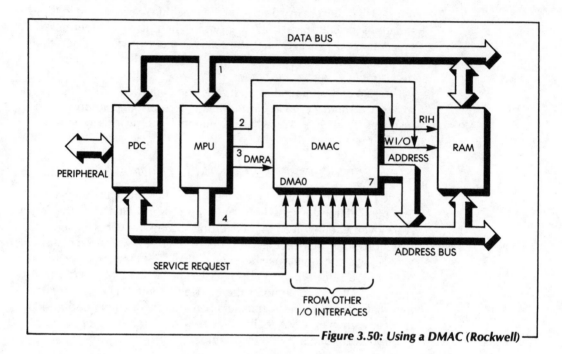

Figure 3.50: Using a DMAC (Rockwell)

Figure 3.51: DMA Sequence, Step 1

2. The DMAC forwards the request to the microprocessor (MPU) on the DMRA line in order to "disconnect" the MPU (see Figure 3.52).

3. The MPU finishes the instruction it was executing (with the exception of an I/O operation) and returns an acknowledge signal on the bidirectional line DMRA back to the DMAC (see Figure 3.53). The MPU has now entered a WAIT state. It releases the data bus and the address bus in the high-impedance or "floating" state (hence the requirement for tri-state buses on microprocessors).

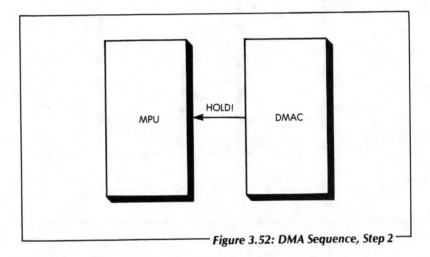

Figure 3.52: DMA Sequence, Step 2

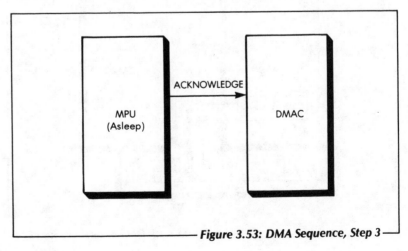

Figure 3.53: DMA Sequence, Step 3

4. The DMAC forwards an "acknowledge" signal to the PDC, telling it that the processor has been suspended and that the transfer may occur (see Figure 3.54).

5. The DMAC loads the appropriate transfer address on the address bus (see Figure 3.55). The DMAC is equipped with eight internal 16-bit registers that provide the beginning address of the

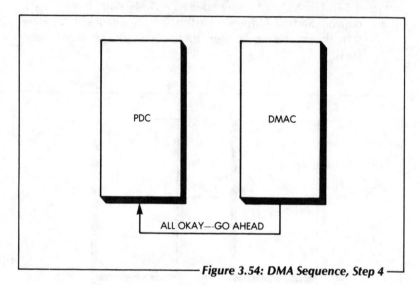

Figure 3.54: DMA Sequence, Step 4

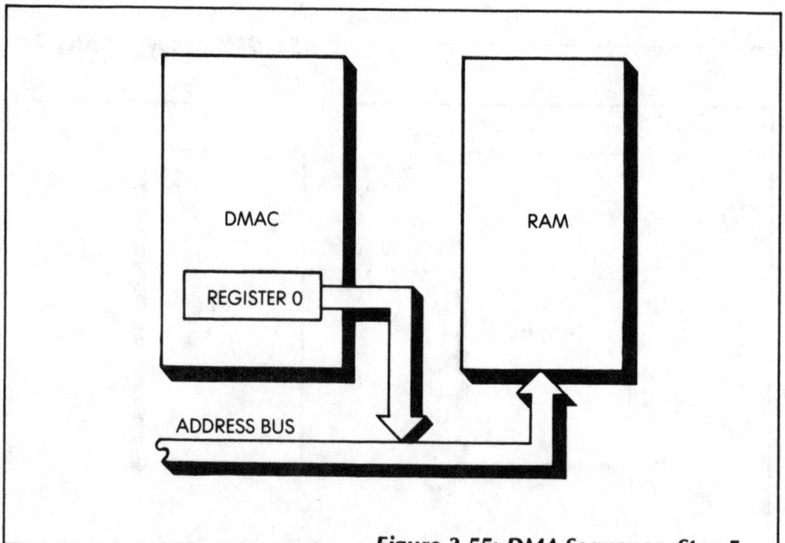

Figure 3.55: DMA Sequence, Step 5

word or block transfer to be performed. The DMAC also contains additional registers, such as a counter register (one for each DMA level), specifying the number of words to be transferred. The contents of these registers must naturally be preloaded by the program prior to their use. Once activated, the DMAC substitutes its own logic to the microprocessor and supplies successive addresses to the address bus for the required memory transfer.

6. The DMAC then supplies a read or write signal on RIH or WIO. At this point, the memory has received its address and its read or write order. The memory starts cycling. If a write order was specified, the PDC supplies the data word to the memory. Otherwise, the PDC reads the data coming out of the memory. A write is shown in Figure 3.56. The PDC, i.e., the I/O device, can now input or output its data word.

7. After each word transfer, the DMAC increments its internal address register automatically and updates its word counter. This is shown in Figure 3.57.

The block transfer operation continues until one of the following occurs:

*   The I/O device drops its DMA request.

*   The word counter goes through the value 0. The end of the specified block of words has then been reached and transfer is stopped.

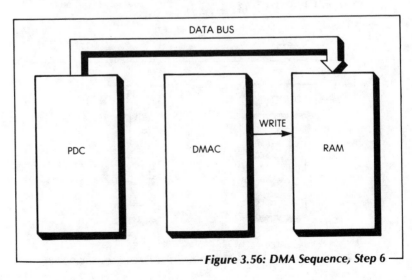

Figure 3.56: DMA Sequence, Step 6

- The lower half of the internal DMAC address register goes from value 11111111 to value 00000000. This is a special feature of the device due to the paged organization of its memory. Whenever a page boundary (i.e., a multiple of 256) is crossed, a page register must be incremented. The DMA transfer must be interrupted. This is specific to Rockwell's device.

- An interrupt at level 0 is received by the MPU. On most systems, interrupt level 0 corresponds to a power failure. In such a case a few milliseconds of processing time are still available to preserve as much of the system state as possible. Normally this time is used to preserve the contents of the internal microprocessor registers and to shut down the I/O in an orderly fashion. DMA transfer as well as any other I/O operation is then immediately stopped, and a branch occurs to a special power failure routine for the orderly shutdown. Preserving the contents of the internal microprocessor registers is possible only if the memory is battery-assisted so that the RAM contents are not lost for the duration of the power failure.

- The DMAC receives a request at a higher priority level. The highest priority level is DMA0; the lowest priority level is DMA7. If, for example, we were honoring a request at DMA3, any request on DMA0, DMA1 or DMA2 would result in a suspension of DMA3. The higher priority level (e.g., DMA0) would then be honored. Whenever the block at the high priority level is completely transferred, the transfer for the lower level would resume automatically.

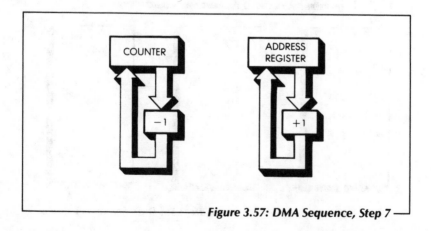

Figure 3.57: DMA Sequence, Step 7

Other DMACs

Other manufacturers have introduced DMACs for their systems. Intel's 8257 appears in Figure 3.58. This DMAC can control four devices. The internal organization of a DMAC is shown in Figure 3.59.

The 8257 requires an external latch (8212) to preserve eight address bits. An application of the 8257 is shown in Figure 3.60. Four DMA levels are available, and the 8257 is shown controlling four different disk units, each of them connected to its own DMA level.

Another application is shown in Figure 3.61, where the DMAC is used to implement a high-speed communication link by automating block transfers.

In summary, the DMAC is a specialized block transfer sequencer that takes over the buses and automates transfers between an I/O device and the memory. The overhead introduced by a DMAC is minimal. It is only the time required to suspend the MPU and generate the required memory address. Afterwards, the transfer proceeds at the speed of the memory.

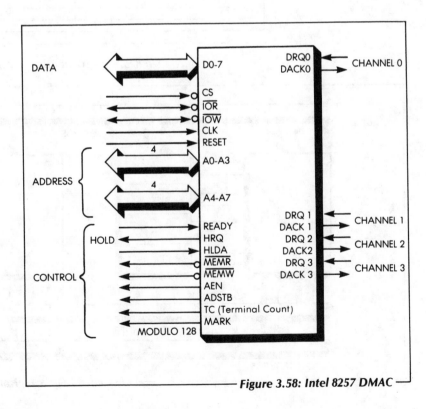

Figure 3.58: Intel 8257 DMAC

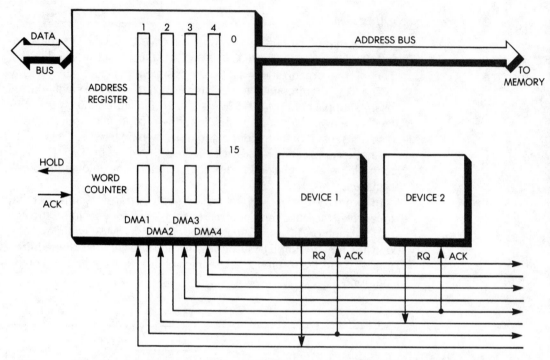

Figure 3.59: 8257 Has 16-Bit Address Registers and 8-Bit Counters

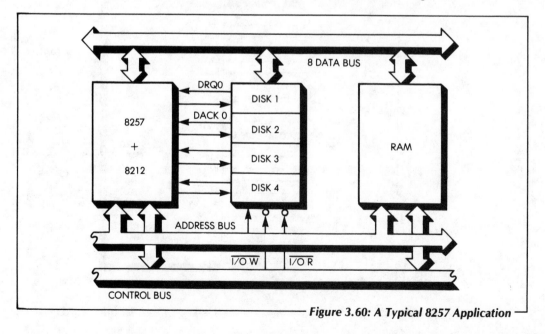

Figure 3.60: A Typical 8257 Application

The PIC and the DMAC are two important scheduling chips that automate interrupt handling and DMA control. Various simpler chips have been introduced to facilitate I/O management and can be used by themselves or in conjunction with a PIC or a DMAC. The most important one is the programmable interval timer, or PIT, which will be described now.

PROGRAMMABLE INTERVAL TIMER (PIT)

Most microprocessor programs must generate or measure delays. A *delay* corresponds, for example, to the length of time between two successive pulses on input or output. A delay can be measured by incrementing a counter variable in the program. This software method is simple and does not require external hardware. However, it wastes the processor's time. If wasting processor time is objectionable, a hardware

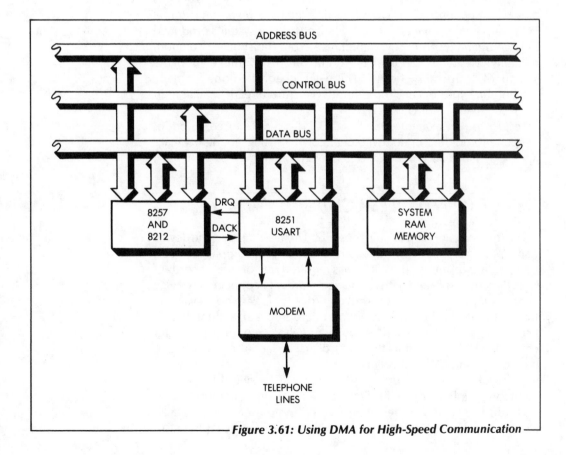

Figure 3.61: Using DMA for High-Speed Communication

method can be used by replacing the program with a timing circuit. This is achieved by the *programmable interval timer* or PIT.

The PIT is not just a simple timer. The PIT is equipped with seven independent counters. It may operate in either input mode or output mode or both. In input mode the PIT measures the duration of one or more external pulses. In output mode a counter register is preloaded with a value expressed in microseconds or milliseconds. Whenever the counter goes to 0, a status bit is set or an interrupt is generated. In other words, a signal is generated after the specified period of time has elapsed.

The PIT improves the processing capability of a microprocessor by eliminating the need for counting programs. Using the PIT frees the MPU for other tasks and also guarantees exact delays.

A PIT is usually required in the case of a *real-time* application. In a system using interrupts, software counters cannot be used with any degree of accuracy to provide timing. A counter might be interrupted at any time by an external event, which would result in an erroneous time measurement. A PIT avoids this problem. However, an external PIT means adding an extra chip, a disadvantage for systems produced in large quantities in order to minimize cost. The simplest solution, naturally, would be to implement a PIT on one of the other chips of the system: MPU, memory, or PIO. This will probably be done for many system chips introduced in the future. PITs are already available in chips such as PIOs or UARTs.

To provide an example, Intel's 8253 PIT supplies three 16-bit independent counters, operates at speeds of 0 to 2 MHz, counts in binary and BCD, and has six modes of operation, programmable by the user.

DEVICE CONTROLLER CHIPS

The third category of I/O chips described in this chapter is the *device* or *peripheral controller*. Traditionally, the control of complex devices, such as disks, printers, and CRTs, has required one or more boards of logic directly associated with the device in order to connect the device to any computer system. Powerful controller chips are now available for most usual devices connected to a microprocessor system. In particular, there are now display controllers, keyboard controllers, printer controllers, telecommunication controllers, disk controllers, cassette controllers, and CRT controllers.

In the future, 1-chip interfaces will eventually be available for every common peripheral that is likely to be interfaced in a microprocessor. This is the logical step in integrating each sub-system into LSI. Typically, a controller chip will be interfaced directly to one or more PIOs, or to a

UART. Peripheral controllers will be described in Chapter 7. Here is a list of some typical controllers:

— Programmable floppy disk controller (FDC)

— Programmable CRT controller (CRTC)

— Programmable keyboard controller

— Printer controller

— HDLC/SDLC protocol controller

— GPIB controller

For completeness, we will review the main peripherals connected to a typical microprocessor system.

TYPICAL PERIPHERALS

The three main types of peripherals connected to a microprocessor system are input devices, output devices, and mass-memory or ''bulk-memory'' devices.

In the microprocessor world, the keyboard is the input device most frequently used. The simplest keyboard is the hexadecimal keyboard, a 16-key keyboard similar to the one used in pocket calculators. Hexadecimal keyboards are very inexpensive when purchased in quantity and are found on most microprocessor-equipped appliances. Today, many appliances such as television sets or washing machines incorporate microprocessors in their control system, using a keyboard as an input device. Soon every appliance user will be ''interfacing'' to his or her appliances through a keyboard.

The most frequently used low-cost output devices are light-emitting diodes (LEDs) and liquid-crystal displays (LCDs). These devices can be described as 7-segment displays that can generally represent the digits 0 through 9 and the letters A through F. (They can thus display each of the 16 hexadecimal digits.) These devices are the least expensive display devices available and are used extensively on digital watches, pocket calculators, and other mass-produced, low-cost devices. Since each LED or LCD can display a hexadecimal digit, a minimum microprocessor development system requires six LEDs—four to display the address (four hexadecimal digits will represent sixteen bits) and two to display data (eight bits).

The two most common complete output devices are the printer and the CRT display. When a microprocessor system is used for industrial control, it can be connected to any external control mechanism, such as a relay or a step-motor.

Tapes and disks are the two *mass memories* that are most frequently used with microprocessors. The *cassette tape* is the least expensive mass memory available. By using a standard audio-type tape recorder, a large number of programs can be easily stored on a standard cassette. The disadvantages of the cassette tape are: (1) the tape recorder and the record switch must usually be turned on and off manually; (2) the tape recorder is slow and sometimes unreliable. Loading a long program may require 30 seconds of winding time. Overall, the cassette recorder is economical and reliability is sufficient for usual needs in a nonindustrial situation. The connection of a cassette recorder to a system equipped with the proper interface is completely straightforward. Direct connections are made to the microphone input and from the audio (external jack) output.

The mass-memory device most often used in "professional" systems is the floppy disk. A floppy disk is a soft magnetic disk. Bits are recorded on the surface of the disk using a movable head. The disk surface is logically divided into *tracks* and *sectors*. Tracks are concentric rings. A typical size of a *data block* on a track within a sector is 128 words. A floppy disk supplies at least 110K bytes at 125K bits per second. When it is operating, a floppy disk consumes only 7 to 15 watts. Most systems have two floppy disks, for both conceptual and financial reasons. The conceptual reason is that two floppy disks are required to copy files containing programs or data. The financial reason is that a dual-disk drive is only slightly more expensive than a single disk drive and can use the same controller.

COMBINATION CHIPS

The components we have described improve system performance and free the microprocessor for other tasks. A disadvantage of these components is that they introduce extra chips into the system. To eliminate this disadvantage, new chips are being introduced that offer a combination of the above facilities. As the integration of components onto a single chip improves, the space required to implement the various functions decreases and it becomes possible to build *combination chips*. In particular, memory-and-I/O combination chips now exist. The Intel 8085 can, for example, implement a complete system with only three chips, using memory-and-I/O combination chips.

Similarly, other combination chips exist for input/output functions: serial-to-parallel conversion with parallel interface, analog-to-digital with serial-to-parallel conversion, and microprocessor with analog-to-serial conversion.

As an example, the Texas Instruments TMS5501 supplies one-half of a PIO with an 8-bit input port, an 8-bit output port, a single asynchronous serial line, two interrupts, and five programmable interval timers. The 5501 interfaces directly with the 8080; it does not require the 8228. This component is, essentially, a combination of a partial PIO, a partial UART, and a PIT (programmable-interval timer).

Similarly, the Intel 8741 is a combination of a processor, ROM, RAM, PIO, timer, and clock.

SUMMARY

In the future, any reasonable combination might be implemented on a single chip. Already, microprocessors with built-in analog-to-digital conversion are available for industrial control. These microprocessors are still digital, but they can manage external analog signals. However, the reader who understands the basic chips that have been presented in this chapter should easily understand these new combination chips.

We have now studied all the techniques and components required to assemble a complete system. We are almost ready to interconnect these components. However, design differences may arise, depending on the microprocessor chosen. In Chapter 4 we will survey the characteristics of all the major microprocessors available today.

EXERCISES

3-1: Describe the function of each chip in the standard microprocessor system shown in Figure 3.1.

3-2: Why does a system need both ROM and RAM?

3-3: Describe the differences between dynamic RAM and static RAM. Which one is more dense?

3-4: What is the function of the CS pin on a memory chip? Why do some manufacturers use three CS pins?

3-5: Describe those methods that solve the RAM volatility problem.

3-6: What does "programming a ROM" mean?

3-7: Are ROMs used in low volume applications?

3-8: What is the difference between a ROM and a PROM?

3-9: What does "burning a PROM" mean?

3-10: What is an EPROM? When is it used?

3-11: How is an EPROM erased? How is it programmed?

3-12: What is an EAROM?

3-13: What are bubble memories? What are their main characteristics?

3-14: What is a CCD memory?

3-15: What are the three basic scheduling techniques used for I/O control?

3-16: Describe the polling technique for handling external signals.

3-17: Describe the interrupt approach to the handling of external signals.

3-18: Explain why most microprocessors have either one or two interrupt pins even though more interrupts may be required in a system.

3-19: What does an interrupt handler do?

3-20: What is a vectored interrupt?

3-21: What is direct memory access?

3-22: What is a UART? Is it mandatory to connect the clock to the input of the UART's receiver?

3-23: Is a clock output required on the output of the UART?

3-24: What is a baud rate generator?

3-25: Explain the role of the PIO.

3-26: Explain the role of each register in Figure 3.33 showing the internal organization of a PIO.

3-27: Referring to the Motorola 6820 PIO, which contents must be loaded in DDRA and DDRB in order to configure Port A as input and Port B as output?

3-28: What contents must be loaded in DDRA in order to configure the port as follows (from lines 0 to 7)?:
output output input output input output output input

3-29: Explain the function of the handshaking signals on a PIO.

3-30: When is an interrupt management chip (PIC) required?

3-31: Explain interrupt priorities. Are they handled by software or by hardware?

3-32: Describe the role of the PIC.

3-33: Describe the vectoring of interrupts in the 8080 microprocessor, with and without a PIC.

3-34: Describe the sequence of operations involved in a DMAC.

3-35: Describe the ways in which the number of chips in a system can be minimized.

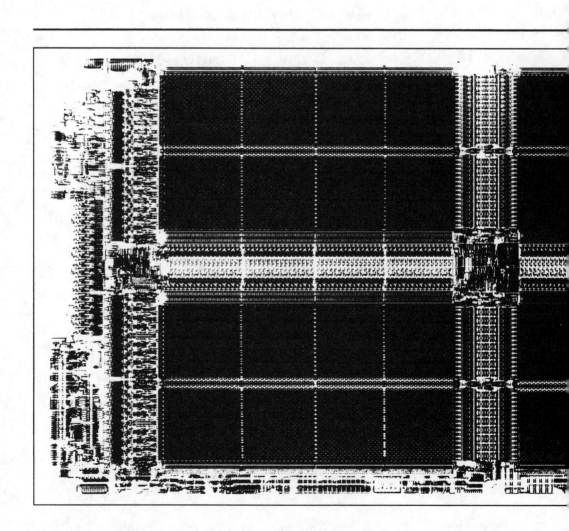

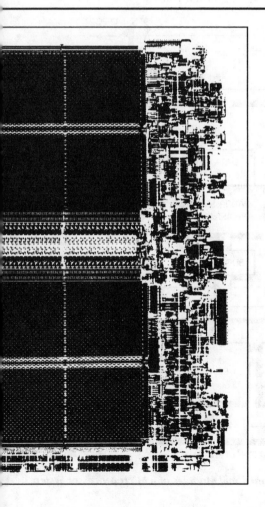

CHAPTER **4**

COMPARATIVE
MICROPROCESSOR
EVALUATION

OBJECTIVE

This chapter provides a comparative overview of the microprocessors available on the market today. The advantages and disadvantages of each microprocessor are analyzed and the specific characteristics that qualify each product for specific applications are discussed. Finally, the essential criteria for selecting a microprocessor are presented.

FUNCTIONAL ELEMENTS OF AN MPU

A number of criteria, both technical and non-technical, may be used to evaluate the suitability of the many microprocessors available today for a given application. From a technical standpoint, one of the essential characteristics of a microprocessor is the nature of the functions implemented on board the chip. In this chapter we use this criterion to characterize the various microprocessors. Therefore, we will examine this concept first.

In the first three chapters we studied the set of functions required for the operation of a complete system. The actual modules that perform these functions appear in the illustration in Figure 4.1, and their roles

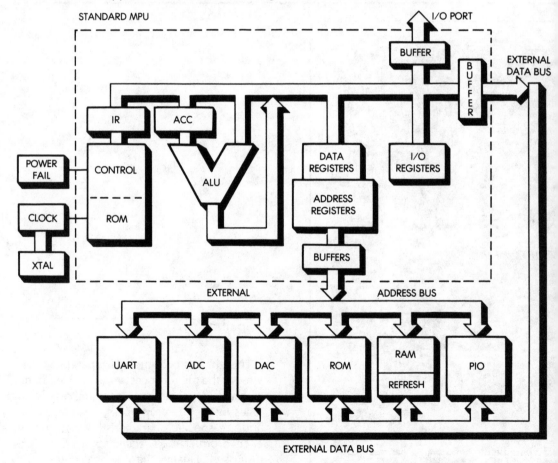

Figure 4.1: The Functional Modules of a Microprocessor System

will be reviewed in this chapter. The upper half of the illustration in Figure 4.1 represents those functions that are incorporated on a standard microprocessor chip. The lower half of the illustration represents the various functions that are usually required to complete the system. In a "standard system" they are provided by separate chips, as shown in Figure 4.1.

In order to understand the technical comments that will be presented about the various microprocessors, these modules must be well understood. Let us briefly examine them again.

First, let us study the upper half of the illustration. Every microprocessor must at least have a control unit, an ALU, and registers. The control unit of most microprocessors is implemented with a microprogram. This explains the presence of the ROM in the control-unit module in Figure 4.1. The ROM stores the microprogram and generates the sequence of microoperations required to fetch and execute external instructions. Using a ROM for sequencing the control unit offers two advantages for the manufacturer:

1. The ROM improves the utilization of the limited chip area by providing more logic per square millimeter than would be achieved by using a conventional random logic design.

2. A microprogrammed CU can be easily modified by changing the microprogram. This is a major advantage for correcting early design mistakes and for adding functions or making improvements later. (In manufacturing jargon, "corrections" are always made at the design stage, while "improvements" are made later. For example, the 8080A is the "improved" version of the 8080.)

The ALU in the illustration is equipped with an accumulator; this is the standard architecture for microprocessors today. Moving now to the right in the illustration we see the data and address registers. The data registers are 8 bits wide and the address registers are 16 bits wide. The address registers include such registers as PC, SP, and any additional address pointers that might be provided (IX, for example). On the right of the illustration we find a set of I/O registers. These registers are only available on a few microprocessors. They are included on a chip in order to provide on-board input/output facilities. They are always provided when the memory is incorporated on the chip, since this releases a number of pins for input and output (the pins freed by the former address bus).

Appearing at the bottom of the illustration are the chips necessary to complete the design of the system. These chips include:

— ROM and RAM (whenever they are not included on the chip itself)

— UART for serial communications

— PIO for parallel communication

— ADC and DAC for analog-to-digital and digital-to-analog conversion.

A complex system might also require a PIC (programmable interrupt controller), a PIT (programmable interval timer), or a DMA (direct memory access) for efficient I/O management.

Finally, on the left of the illustration we find two modules that are now generally integrated on the chip itself: the oscillator circuit (clock) and the power-fail restart circuit (PFR).

When evaluating a given microprocessor, an easy way to examine the functions implemented on the microprocessor chip is to circle those modules in Figure 4.1 that are provided within the chip. Note that when assembling a system, any required modules not provided within the microprocessor chip itself must be provided by external chips. As an example, an 8080 or a 6800 will provide all the functions displayed at the top of the illustration, with the exception of the clock, power-fail, and I/O registers. To assemble an 8080- or 6800-based system, it is necessary to add ROM, RAM, UART, PIO, and any other specialized chips that might be needed.

A 1-chip microcomputer, such as an 8048 or a 3870, provides all the facilities displayed in the upper half of the illustration plus several of the modules that appear at the bottom (i.e., ROM, RAM, and PIT) on a single chip; and it can function as a complete, although limited system.

In time, single-chip microcomputers will incorporate most or all of these functions on a single chip so that no external chips will be needed in order to implement a complete system. More complex devices will also appear either through the creation of chips that provide more powerful functions, or through the implementation of various combinations of these functions. However, all the concepts presented so far should still apply.

CLASSIFYING MICROPROCESSORS

Several functional classifications can be used to classify microprocessors. We have already presented the four architectural classes:

the standard microprocessor, the 1-chip microcomputer, the 2-chip system, and bit-slices. A chart showing the historical evolution of microprocessors is given in Figure 4.2.

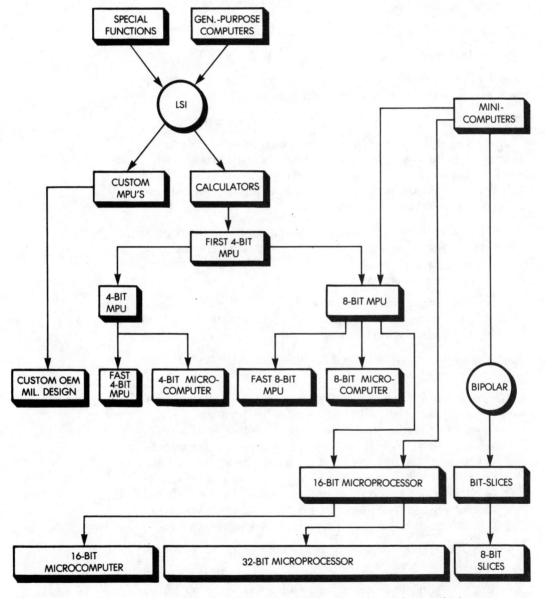

Figure 4.2: The Evolution of Microprocessors

In this chapter we will use a different classification, one that is more convenient for table comparisons and relates to the computational power. It is based on the bit width, i.e., the number of bits that the ALU can process in parallel. Thus, we will distinguish three classes:

1.   4-bit microprocessors

2.   8- or 12-bit microprocessors

3.   16-bit microprocessors

In addition, for completeness, we will describe a fourth class of processing components that are not microprocessors:

4.   Bit-slices.

For each type, we will present a comprehensive table listing the technical characteristics of each microprocessor in a comparative format. For example, a chart for 4-bit microprocessors appears in Figure 4.4. All the terms used in the chart refer to the microprocessor and have the following meanings:

—   *Standard:* the usual architecture. A "standard" microprocessor architecture implements a CPU-on-a-chip and creates three buses: data, address, and control. The memory and I/O are external to a standard MPU.

—   *µC:* a microcomputer residing on one or two chips. It is a microprocessor incorporating the CPU and memory (ROM and RAM), plus some I/O facilities.

—   *Cycle time:* the typical execution time of an instruction (not the clock cycle time).

—   *Number of instructions:* an often misleading and thus not significant characteristic. The number of instructions can vary depending on the conventions chosen to distinguish them. (For example, it is possible to increase the number of instructions by a power of two by simply listing separately the instructions that manipulate different registers.) The number of instructions for 8-bit microprocessors is essentially limited by the required availability of 1-byte instructions, leaving approximately 6 bits for the opcode. These 6 bits represent 64 different opcodes.

—   *PMOS or NMOS:* the technology used (P-channel or N-channel Metal Oxide Semiconductor).

—   *Stack:* "hard" indicates a hardware implementation of the stack, i.e., a set of internal hardware registers supplied within the MPU for stack operation. "Soft" indicates a software implementation of the stack, that is, the availability of a stack pointer pointing to the top of the stack area within the memory.

— *Interrupts:* the availability of interrupts and the number of levels available. A 0 or NO indicates that none are available.

We will now examine in turn the characteristics of each category we have defined.

4-BIT MICROPROCESSORS

Historically, the 4-bit microprocessor was the first general-purpose microprocessor introduced on the market. The basic design of the early microprocessors was derived from that of the desk calculator.

The design of a 4-bit microprocessor is less complex than that of an 8-bit microprocessor, and a 4-bit microprocessor can generally be produced with a better yield, resulting in a lower cost for these components. In particular, in the field of 1-chip microcomputers (used for volume applications), cost is an important and often dominant criterion. 4-bit microcomputers have therefore remained competitive despite the availability of 8-bit designs. In the distant future we can expect the dominance of 8-bit or even 16-bit designs, and no doubt even "wider" designs will become available.

Let us now examine the main manufacturers of 4-bit microprocessors. A genealogy is shown in Figure 4.3, and a comparative chart is shown in Figure 4.4.

INTEL (4-BIT MICROPROCESSORS)

The Intel 4004 is the grandfather of microprocessors. Introduced in late 1971, the 4004 was originally designed for a Japanese manufacturer as the processing element of a desk calculator; it was not designed

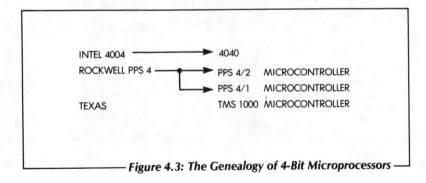

Figure 4.3: The Genealogy of 4-Bit Microprocessors

as a general-purpose computer. The shortcomings of the 4004 were recognized as soon as it was introduced. But it was the first general-purpose computing device on a chip to be placed on the market. Many of the chips introduced at about the same time by other companies (and called "microprocessors") were, in fact, mere calculator chips. Some of them were even serial-by-bit devices.

Within a short period of time, the 4004 became obsolete and was replaced by the 4040. Then, the powerful 8-bit microprocessors were introduced at a price that was only slightly higher than the price of the 4040. Even so, a significant number of devices are still being sold that use the 4040. The reasons for this are simple. First, it originally took a long time to educate the engineering community and management on the advantages of using a microprocessor, and for many companies it was simply not profitable to go through another educational process for another microprocessor.

Second, once a product has been designed, it is often not worthwhile to change a part that is performing sufficiently well. Also, the additional power of an 8-bit microprocessor is often not needed.

As we just explained, the 4004 was soon replaced by an improved version, the 4040. To preserve the software investment of 4004 users,

	INTEL 4004	INTEL 4040	ROCKWELL PPS4	ROCKWELL PPS4/1	ROCKWELL PPS4/2	TMS 1000
TYPE	STANDARD	STANDARD	STANDARD	μC	2-CHIP μC	μC
TECHNOLOGY	PMOS	PMOS	PMOS	PMOS	PMOS	PMOS
NBR OF INSTRUCTIONS	46	60	50	50	50	SMALL
CYCLE TIME (μS)	10.8	10.8	5	12.5	5	15
DIRECT ADDRESSING (BITS)	12	12	12	11	11	10 or 11
REGISTERS	16	24	4	3 + RAM	2 + RAM	4
STACK (LEVELS)	HARD (3)	HARD (7)	HARD (1)	HARD (2)	—	HARD (1)
INTERRUPTS	—	1	1	2	—	—
ON-CHIP CLOCK	—	—	—	—	YES	YES
ROM (BYTES)	—	—	—	1K	—	2K
RAM (WORDS)	—	—	—	96	—	128
TIMER	—	—	—	—	—	—
PFR	—	—	—	—	—	—
OTHER	—	—	—	—	—	—
I/O LINES	—	—	12	26	12	19 to 24
PACKAGE (PINS)	16	16, 24	42	42	42	40 or 28
POWER SUPPLY (V)	15	15	17	15	15	15
REMARKS		I-SET COMPATIBLE WITH 4004	BCD ADD IN 30 μS		PPS 4 INSTRN SET	

Figure 4.4: Comparative Chart—4 Bits

the 4040 instruction set is compatible with that of the 4004. However, the 4040 offers significant improvements. In particular, it is equipped with an interrupt capability, a large number of internal registers, and three register banks (3 × 8 registers). These three register banks can be used to provide very fast interrupt response. Whenever an interrupt occurs, rather than saving the registers in the stack, a switch is made from one bank of registers to the next, provided there are no more than two interrupt levels. Unfortunately, the program counter and the status word are not replicated within the three register banks. Thus, for complete switching, several program instructions must still be executed.

The performance of the 4040 is limited, but sufficient for many simple applications. As a result, the 4040 has been incorporated in a large number of industrial applications. Because it is now possible to purchase an 8-bit processor at about the same price as a 4040, the 4040 will gradually lose a part of its share of the market. However, even with its limitations, the 4040 will still be used for a long time to come in a replacement market. Once a microprocessor has been proved effective for a design, there is no direct benefit in replacing this microprocessor with another one.

Additional functions can be obtained in the 4040 through programming. This is a typical characteristic of microprocessor systems whereby a standardized hardware design can be modified through software changes. This can be very advantageous, since the cost of redesigning a board or a complete industrial product including packaging, documentation, training, programming, etc., is simply overwhelming. However, most *new* designs are likely to use 8-bit microprocessors.

ROCKWELL (4-BIT MICROPROCESSORS)

In 1971, at the time the 4004 was introduced, Rockwell manufactured a variety of calculator chips. Following an evolution similar to that of the Intel products, the PPS-4 was introduced as the evolution of a calculator design. However, it was introduced late and by the time it appeared, 8-bit microprocessor designs were already preempting the field. The successor to the PPS-4 was the PPS-4/2, a complete computer on two chips. The instruction set of the PPS-4/2 is compatible with the PPS-4. The PPS-4/2 is a competitor of the Intel 4040 for large volume applications, offering a simple and low-cost design, as long as the memory and I/O limitations are acceptable.

Rockwell's most competitive product, the PPS-4/1 introduced in 1976, was one of the first complete microcomputers-on-a-chip, since it incorporates ROM, RAM, and clock circuitry directly on the chip. The PPS-4/1 is a powerful design with a large number of input and output lines. The internal organization of the PPS-4/1 is shown in Figure 4.5. The PPS-4/1, like all single-chip microcomputers, exists in several versions, depending on the amount of memory incorporated on the chip and the number of pins. If bought in large quantities, the price of the PPS-4/1 is very low. Typical applications for the PPS-4/1 are consumer appliances, which justify the cost of producing several thousand units incorporating a masked ROM. The PPS-4/1 now faces strong competition from several other microcomputers-on-a-chip (described in the next section), such as the TMS-1000 from Texas Instruments.

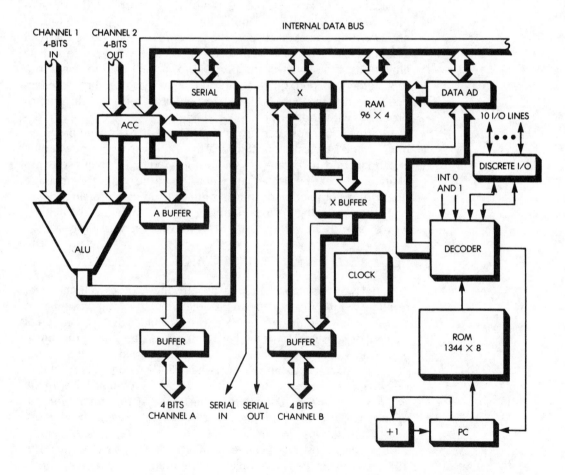

Figure 4.5: Rockwell PPS-4/1 1-Chip Microcomputer

TEXAS INSTRUMENTS (4-BIT MICROPROCESSORS)

Texas Instruments was late in entering the field of microprocessor design when it introduced the TMS-1000 family, a complete 4-bit microcomputer-on-a-chip. The TMS-1000 family incorporates ROM, RAM, and clock circuitry on a single chip. It is intended for use with consumer applications and large volume industrial products. The internal architecture of the TMS-1000 is shown in Figure 4.6. It is significantly different from the standard computer design that has been described so far. It provides a number of control signals internally decoded by a programmable logic array (PLA). Using an internal PLA offers the following advantages:

1. The user's application is encrypted in a way that is difficult to decipher and therefore difficult to copy.

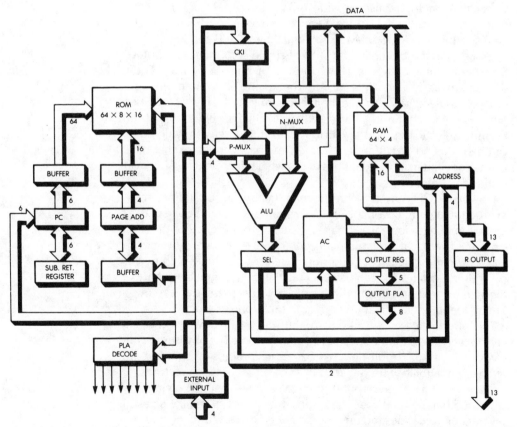

Figure 4.6: Texas TMS-1000 1-Chip Microcomputer

2. The PLA replaces a much larger amount of ROM for providing output signals in response to combinations of input signals.

The TMS-1000 does not, however, have the many direct 4-bit I/O ports of the PPS-4/1. While it is particularly well suited to complex control in response to 4-bit instructions, it is not well suited to the direct processing of a 4-bit stream. Like the PPS-4/1, the price of the TMS-1000 is very low when purchased in quantity.

4-BIT 1-CHIP MICROCOMPUTERS

The Rockwell PPS-4/1 and the Texas Instruments TMS-1000 families were the first 4-bit, 1-chip microcomputers on the market. Now both of these microcomputers have various family members that vary the amount of memory on board the chip as well as the number of pins. Other manufacturers also provide 4-bit microprocessors, but most tend to be specialized: National Semiconductor (COPs), Hitachi, OKI Semiconductor (CMOS MSM 5840), and AMI (S2200 and 2300).

Let us examine the characteristics of single-chip microcomputers. Single-chip microcomputers use mask-programmed ROMs. These devices are therefore not intended for the small user. A minimum order of 10,000 is necessary to make them economical. Their low cost when purchased in quantity is their essential advantage. Beyond cost, an essential selection criterion is support, i.e., the ease with which they can be used and programmed. Prime candidates are chips that have been produced in large quantities and have been proved reliable over a period of time.

However, it is now possible to manufacture an 8-bit single-chip microcomputer and even a 16-bit microcomputer. If the price of 8-bit microcomputers decreases to a level similar to the price of the 4-bit ones, it is likely that 8-bit microcomputers will dominate. Since cost is usually the most significant criterion in selecting a single-chip microcomputer, 4-bit designs can be expected to retain a significant share of the market for a time. Eventually this share will decrease in an evolution similar to the standardization of the 8-bit microprocessor.

The introduction of new designs in the 4-bit field is now unlikely, except for very high volume specialized applications. The obvious advantages of 8-bit and 16-bit designs are higher processing speeds and, often, compatibility with previous instruction sets or architectures.

Since a 1-chip microcomputer is aimed at applications involving very large numbers, a chip manufacturer who wishes to realize sales of several hundred thousand units could lower prices of 8-bit microcomputers to a level beneath those of the best-selling 4-bit design. The incentive is to develop the most complex design that the chip manufacturer will be able to sell in large quantities.

8-BIT MICROPROCESSORS

We have seen that an important limitation of microprocessors today is the pin limitation of 40 to a package. Because of this limitation, 16-bit microprocessors on 40-pin packages cannot communicate with the outside world without multiplexing information; and using a larger package raises the cost. As a result, 8-bit microprocessors have become the standard design today. With the exception of the single-chip microcomputers, the standard 1-chip microprocessor is the most frequently used type of microprocessor in any design. 8-bit microprocessors provide a more powerful processing capability than a 4-bit design at a similar cost and have displaced the early 4-bit designs. Further, most information processing is performed on bytes, thus requiring an 8-bit microprocessor (4-bit devices are used for control applications).

The genealogy of existing 8-bit microprocessors appears in Figure 4.7. We will trace the evolution of these products and compare their characteristics, manufacturer by manufacturer. We will distinguish standard 8-bit microprocessors and 8-bit single-chip microcomputers. Let us examine standard 8-bit microprocessors first. Comparative charts are shown in Figures 4.8 to 4.11.

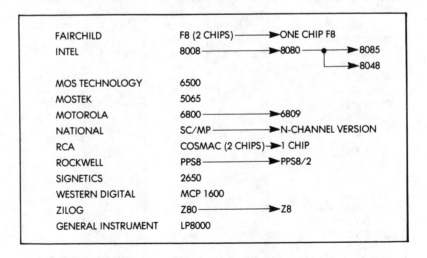

FAIRCHILD	F8 (2 CHIPS) ──────▶ ONE CHIP F8
INTEL	8008 ──────────────▶ 8080 ──●──▶ 8085
	└──▶ 8048
MOS TECHNOLOGY	6500
MOSTEK	5065
MOTOROLA	6800 ──────────────▶ 6809
NATIONAL	SC/MP ──────────────▶ N-CHANNEL VERSION
RCA	COSMAC (2 CHIPS) ──▶ 1 CHIP
ROCKWELL	PPS8 ───────────────▶ PPS8/2
SIGNETICS	2650
WESTERN DIGITAL	MCP 1600
ZILOG	Z80 ────────────────▶ Z8
GENERAL INSTRUMENT	LP8000

Figure 4.7: The Genealogy of 8-Bit Microprocessors

	INTEL 8008	INTEL 8080	INTEL 8085	INTEL 8048
TYPE	STANDARD	STANDARD	STANDARD	μC
TECHNOLOGY	PMOS	NMOS	NMOS	NMOS
NBR OF INSTRUCTIONS	48	69	71	50
CYCLE TIME (μS)	12.5, 20.0	1.3, 1.5, 2.0	1.3	2.5
DIRECT ADDRESSING (BITS)	14	16	8 + 8	—
REGISTERS	7	7	7	1
STACK (LEVELS)	HARD (7)	SOFT	SOFT	HARD (8)
INTERRUPTS	1	1	4	1
ON-CHIP CLOCK	—	—	YES	YES
ROM (BYTES)	—	—	—	1K
RAM (WORDS)	—	—	—	64
TIMER	—	—	—	YES
PFR	—	—	—	—
OTHER	—	—	8228	—
I/O LINES	—	—	2	27
PACKAGE (PINS)	18	40	40	40
POWER SUPPLY (V)	−9, +5	+5, −5, +12	5	5
SECOND SOURCE	—	AMD, TI, NEC, NS, SIEMENS	—	—
REMARKS				

Figure 4.8: Comparative Chart—8 Bits

	FAIRCHILD F8	F8 (1-CHIP 3859)	MOS TECH 6502	GI LP8000
TYPE	μC	μC	STANDARD	μC (2-CHIP)
TECHNOLOGY	NMOS	NMOS	NMOS	NMOS
NBR OF INSTRUCTIONS	70	70	LIKE 6800	—
CYCLE TIME (μS)	2 to 13	1.5	—	—
DIRECT ADDRESSING (BITS)	16	—	12 to 16	11
REGISTERS	1 + RAM	1 + RAM	3	RAM + AC
STACK (LEVELS)	EXTERNAL SP	SOFT	SOFT (8 BITS)	HARD (4)
INTERRUPTS	1	1	1	—
ON-CHIP CLOCK	—	YES	YES	—
ROM (BYTES)	—	1K	—	—
RAM (WORDS)	64	64	—	48
TIMER	—	YES	—	—
PFR	—	—	—	—
OTHER	—	—	—	—
I/O LINES	16	32	—	8
PACKAGE (PINS)	40	40	28/40	—
POWER SUPPLY (V)	+5, +12	—	—	—
SECOND SOURCE	MOSTEK	MOSTEK	SYNERTEK	—
REMARKS	—	—	—	—

Figure 4.9: Comparative Chart—8 Bits

INTEL (8-BIT MICROPROCESSORS)

The ancestor of 8-bit microprocessors is the Intel 8008 introduced in 1972-1973. The 8008 was not intended to be a general-purpose microprocessor. It was to be a CRT display controller for Datapoint. (The conditions surrounding its introduction are described in Chapter 1.) Taking into account all of its design inadequacies and its limited performance, the 8008 was an overwhelming success.

This success motivated Intel as well as a number of leading semiconductor manufacturers to produce competing designs. The 8080 was designed as a successor to the 8008 and had to maintain compatibility. To do this, the 8080 included all of the 8008 registers (plus more), as well as all of the 8008 instructions (plus more).

The 8080 was the first powerful microprocessor introduced on the market, and it continues to sell well in its class. Several other microprocessors of similar performance were introduced on the market within a year after the 8080 appeared, and several additional powerful designs were introduced later. Technically, the 8080 was not the most powerful product on the market for a long time. However, Intel was the first

	MOSTEK 5065	MOTOROLA 6800	NS SC/MP	RCA COSMAC	SIGNETICS 2650
TYPE	STANDARD	STANDARD	STANDARD	STANDARD	STANDARD
TECHNOLOGY	PMOS	NMOS	PMOS	CMOS	NMOS
NBR OF INSTRUCTIONS	51	71	50	59	75
CYCLE TIME (μS)	10	2	5 to 25	3	4.8 to 9.6
DIRECT ADDRESSING (BITS)	15	16	12	16	15
REGISTERS	3	4	6	16(RAM)	7
STACK (LEVELS)	—	SOFT	SOFT	—	HARD (8)
INTERRUPTS	2	1	1	1	1
ON-CHIP CLOCK	—	—	YES	YES	—
ROM (BYTES)	—	—	—	—	—
RAM (WORDS)	—	—	—	YES	—
TIMER	—	—	—	—	—
PFR	—	—	—	—	—
OTHER	—	—	—	—	—
I/O LINES	—	—	2	—	—
PACKAGE (PINS)	40	40	40	40	40
POWER SUPPLY (V)	−12, −5, +5	5	+5, −7	3 to 10	5
SECOND SOURCE	—	AMI, SESCOSEM	—	—	—
REMARKS	—	—	—	—	STATIC ADDRESS ADDER

Figures 4.10: Comparative Chart—8 Bits

company to invest in the development of support chips and software for its products. This insured the continued success of the 8080 because its performance was then sufficient for many applications. The early 8080 competitors were introduced with at least a nine-month delay and failed to dislodge it. Today, the 8080 is out-performed by (but not out-priced by) the Z80. It is, however, often out-priced by the 6502. The 8080 also has a successor product: the 8085. We will describe this microprocessor later on in this chapter, once we have established a basis for comparison. Let us temporarily leave Intel.

MOTOROLA (8-BIT MICROPROCESSORS)

The 6800 was introduced by Motorola as a direct competitor to the 8080. The design of the 6800 was obviously inspired by the 8008 and the then prevalent minicomputer philosophy. The 6800 has essentially

	ROCKWELL PPS 8	ROCKWELL PPS 8/2	WEST DIG MCP 1600	ZILOG Z80	INTERSIL IN 6100
TYPE	STANDARD	μC	MICRO-PROGRAMMED	STANDARD	ST, 12 BIT
TECHNOLOGY	PMOS	PMOS	NMOS	NMOS	CMOS
NBR OF INSTRUCTIONS	90	109	—	8080 + MANY	PDP8
CYCLE TIME (μS)	4	5	—	1.6	2.5 to 11.0
DIRECT ADDRESSING (BITS)	15	14	16	(16)	12
REGISTERS	3	3	—	17	3
STACK (LEVELS)	SOFT (5-BIT SP)	SOFT (5-BIT)	—	SOFT	—
INTERRUPTS	3	3	—	3	1
ON-CHIP CLOCK	—	YES	—	YES	YES
ROM (BYTES)	—	—	—	—	—
RAM (WORDS)	—	—	—	—	—
TIMER	—	—	—	—	—
PFR	YES	YES	—	—	—
OTHER	—	—	—	INTERNAL 8228 + MEM REFRESH	—
I/O LINES	—	—	—		—
PACKAGE (PINS)	42	42	—	40	40, 28
POWER SUPPLY (V)	17	17	—	5	5
SECOND SOURCE	—	—	—	MOSTEK	HARRIS
REMARKS	BCD ADD = 12 μS		PDP 11	8080 INSTN SET	PDP8 INSTN SET STATIC 10 mW

Figures 4.11: Comparative Chart—8 Bits

the same internal architecture as the 8080, though there are some differences at the register level. The internal architecture of the 6800 is shown in Figure 4.12. The 6800 is equipped with two accumulators (the 8080 has only one), but the 6800 has a smaller number of general-purpose registers. The 6800 has a special index register (IX) that facilitates access to tables stored in the memory. The 8080 does not have an index register but is equipped with register pairs that can be used to provide a similar facility. The 6800 instructions reflect the fact that it was introduced after the 8080. They tend to be somewhat more complex but generally similar to those of the 8080. Depending on the function used in the comparison, either of the two microprocessors can be said to be marginally faster.

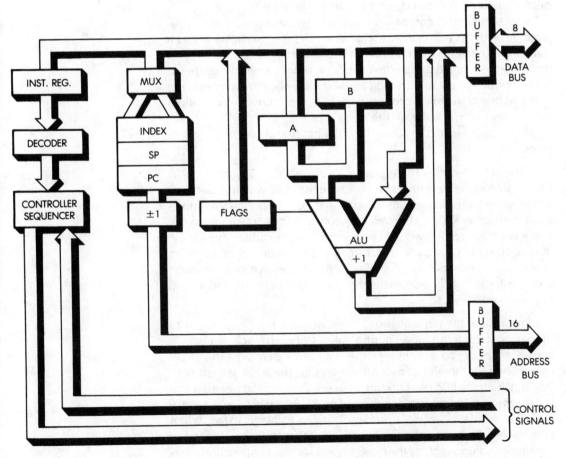

Figure 4.12: The Internal Architecture of the 6800

The most significant difference in performance is achieved not by comparing a standard 8080 to a standard 6800—their performance is essentially similar—but by considering a faster version of either the 8080 or the 6800. The 8080 is available in three versions: the standard 8080A with a 2MHz clock, the 8080A-2 and the 8080A-1 with a 3MHz clock. The 6800 is also available in two versions. The standard 6800 uses a 1MHz clock. However, the clock rates do not mean that the standard 6800 is half as fast as the standard 8080A. The clock simply supplies the pulses needed by the internal microprogram of the control unit. On the average, the 8080 uses simpler microinstructions and requires twice as many microinstructions as the 6800. It therefore uses a faster clock. The overall performances of the 8080 and the 6800 are similar. A typical instruction is executed in two microseconds on either microcomputer. A detailed comparison is inconclusive.

The best method of comparison would be to execute a standard program on both microprocessors. However, there is no such thing as a standard program. When comparing the 8080 and the 6800, it is found that, due to so-called design "features" (in other words, design peculiarities or design errors), an 8-bit by 8-bit multiplication may execute faster on one of the microprocessors, while an 8-bit by 16-bit multiplication may execute faster on the other one.

When compared to the 6800, the 8080 has two apparent disadvantages:

1. The 8080 requires three power levels: +5V, −5V, and +12V. These three levels were necessary because the 8080 was introduced at a time when Intel was using its dynamic memory technology to implement the register RAM on the MPU. By contrast, the 6800 requires only one level, thus freeing two pins on the package, an advantage for the manufacturer in gating additional signals. The argument of a simpler power supply may not be valid. If the system uses dynamic memory, then it will still usually require the three levels, +5V, −5V, and +12V, on the board.

2. Because of the pin limitation, the 8080 must use the data bus to propagate status information during state T1 of each machine cycle. It is then necessary to demultiplex the data bus externally. This is accomplished by the addition of an extra chip, the 8228 system controller. When the 8080 was first introduced, this chip did not exist and the scheme was definitely a drawback. The 8228, however, was quickly introduced and successfully overcame this disadvantage. In fact, when considering the complete system, the 8080 system has the same number of components as the 6800 system for most applications. It is true that the 8080 requires the 8228; however, the 8228 provides not

only the data bus demultiplexing but also a bidirectional driver for the data bus. A system built around the 6800 or the 8080 is usually not a system of minimal complexity, i.e., a system requiring a minimal number of chips. Most systems using the 8080 or the 6800 need to have their buses drive more than one TTL load. They must use drivers for both the address and data buses. The 8080 does not require an extra driver for its data bus, but the 6800 does. Chip for chip, the component count is the same. Note that both of these early microprocessors require an external oscillator circuit (a clock chip and crystal).

THE SECOND SOURCES

Within the industry there are two types of second sources for a microprocessor: *authorized* and *unauthorized*. An authorized second source has entered into licensing agreements with the original manufacturer. An unauthorized one has "copied" the design but laid down a different chip. The result is the same: another manufacturer produces a component that is supposedly identical to the original model (and sometimes better). The new component could cut into the sales of the first component; however, it usually provides the market stability required by most industrial and military purchasers and actually contributes to the overall acceptance of the component.

For example, the 8080 has several authorized second sources. These authorized second sources have the masks and process necessary to manufacture the chip. However, the majority of the 8080 second sources are unauthorized. They are, for example, the AMD 9080 from AMD, a fully compatible version of the 8080 that is claimed to be faster and more reliable; and the 8080 versions from Texas Instruments, NEC (in Japan), and National Semiconductor. Most of these components are claimed to be totally compatible with the 8080, i.e., both pin-for-pin and software compatible. However, some of the earlier versions of these products were not completely compatible and resulted in some surprises for the users.

Most best-selling microprocessors have been copied by a variety of manufacturers, both for profit and for purposes of acquiring experience in technology and processor design. Unauthorized copies are also known as "scanning-electron microscope" versions (the original chip is studied in detail and in secret by competitors in a laboratory using such a microscope).

The impact of second sources on the market can be very significant. AMD, for example, can be credited with starting the major price wars on the early microprocessors. The resulting price drop on the 8080 and similar products was one of the most spectacular events of 1975. At a time when Intel was selling the 8080 for $70 (in quantities of at least 100), AMD announced the sale of the 9080 for $35. Within days, Intel followed, lowering the price of the 8080 to $35. A year later, the price of the 9080 from AMD was around $12 or less, but Intel did not follow suit immediately. Naturally this also forced other manufacturers that were competing with the same chip to realign their prices, and since then additional manufacturers (in particular Texas Instruments) have entered the price war. As a result, it is obvious that the manufacturers of microprocessors that do not sell their products in significant quantities are in fact losing money with every chip. The price is just too low now for any manufacturer to realize a profit if small quantities are involved.

All widely used microprocessors have second sources. The 6800, for example, is also produced by American Microsystems (AMI) in the U.S. and by the Sescosem Division of Thomson CSF in Europe, as well as other manufacturers.

At the end of 1976 the Intel 8080 and the Motorola 6800 were the two best-selling standard microprocessors. These two microprocessors, along with the TI 9900 (16 bits) and the AMD 2901 were the first microprocessors to qualify under the military 38510 reliability program (JAN).

In 1976 the 6800 was the second-best-selling standard microprocessor. However, Motorola was not the only manufacturer to introduce competitive designs. Some manufacturers, such as MOS Technology brought out direct competitors to the 6800 (the 6502), while others brought out direct competitors to the 8080 (the Z80). Let us examine the other designs.

ROCKWELL

The Rockwell PPS-8 was introduced to compete with the 8080 and 6800. Even though implemented in PMOS technology, it is a powerful microprocessor. Rockwell used their processor design expertise derived from the manufacture of similar chips for military and aerospace applications to design the PPS-8. Despite the many interesting features of the PPS-8, it arrived late on the market and has not achieved the sales volumes of the 8080 or the 6800. The set of microprocessor support chips introduced at the time by Rockwell—including the first one-chip disk controller, display controller, keyboard controller, and DMAC—was probably the best on the market. Obviously convinced that the advantages of these impressive support chips would generate large sales, Rockwell decided to make these peripheral chips incompatible with the 8080 and 6800. As a result, neither those chips nor the PPS-80 have achieved large sales. A 2-chip microcomputer version, the

PPS-8/2, implements a microcomputer on two chips and is compatible with the PPS-8 instruction set. Rockwell also manufactures the 6502 as a second source.

SIGNETICS

The Signetics 2650 was also a long time in coming. Originally Signetics was troubled by financial difficulties. During the recession of the mid-1970s when the dollar was hitting an all-time low, investing in U.S. companies was a particularly attractive option and Signetics was purchased by Phillips, the large Dutch electronics manufacturer.

With the financial resources and purchasing power of Phillips, the 2650 has achieved limited success. The 2650 is an interesting processor. Although it is slower than the 8080 and the 6800 from an arithmetic standpoint, it has a powerful instruction set and an original architecture. The concept behind the product is that "communications are more expensive than processing." As a result of this philosophy, the address bus is equipped with a limited processing unit. This makes it possible to compute complex addresses using sophisticated addressing techniques. The 2650 is equipped with a complex instruction set for addressing memory. It implements all the addressing techniques expected on a traditional computer, such as indirect addressing, indexed addressing, and indexed indirect addressing. In view of the facilities provided for addressing memory in a complex way, the 2650 is ideally suited for complex memory word retrievals. For example, it is well suited for word processing and accessing chains of characters. Because of Phillips' investment in the 2650, this microprocessor will be produced and supported even though it cannot compete directly with the 8080 or the 6800 for arithmetic-oriented applications.

NATIONAL SEMICONDUCTOR

The first 8-bit design by National Semiconductor was the SC/MP. SC/MP stands for "simple cost effective microprocessor." The SC/MP was intended as a simple, inexpensive microprocessor requiring few extra chips. It is indeed a simplified microprocessor and it is indeed inexpensive; however, the low cost of the MPU is not sufficient by itself to generate large sales. The original P-channel version of the SC/MP was too slow. An N-channel version was later introduced to improve speed. This microprocessor is well suited for simple applications in which component economy is desired. It does not, however, have the processing power of the 8080, the 6800 or the 2650.

In 1976, National also introduced another 8-bit microprocessor: its own 8080 implementation that is compatible with Intel's.

MOS TECHNOLOGY

MOS Technology was formed, in part, by former Motorola employees who were a part of the 6800 design team. As a result, the 6502 has strong analogies with the 6800 and competes directly with it. The 6502's bus organization, internal registers, and instruction set are all very close to that of the 6800. In fact, the 6502 support devices can be used with either the 6502 or the 6800. The 6502 is faster than the 6800 and the special components introduced by MOS Technology, such as combination chips including memory and I/O, result in systems with fewer chips. They are also low in price, which results in inexpensive small- to medium-sized systems with a processing power greater than or equal to the 6800. In 1978, MOS Technology was acquired by Commodore International.

GENERAL INSTRUMENT

General Instrument (GI) is a manufacturer specializing in custom-design chips. As a result, General Instrument discovers from time to time that one of their custom designs, whose development has already been paid for, can be sold as a general-purpose microprocessor. However, these microprocessors were usually not designed from the start to be general-purpose processors, so that no component support exists. One such 8-bit processor is the LP-8000. However, due to the lack of support chips, systems and software, it cannot be considered a competitor to the other 8-bit microprocessors. General Instrument certainly has the capability to produce advanced designs, but they have not yet decided to use this capability to produce general-purpose chips, at least in the case of microprocessors.

WESTERN DIGITAL

The MCP 1600 set introduced by Western Digital is unusual in that it is a microprogrammed design in two chips. The MPU requires an external controller ROM containing the microprogram. The set of components is used to implement the Digital Equipment LSI-11. In view of early production difficulties, Digital Equipment is now manufacturing its own components on the East Coast. The LSI-11 is software-compatible with the PDP-11 line from Digital. It is equivalent to the PDP-11/03. Western Digital has introduced other chip-sets derived from this early experience that are used in specific microcomputers (for example, the Pascal Microengine).

INTERSIL

One of Intersil's strengths is in the area of CMOS technology. The Intersil 6100 is a 12-bit CMOS microprocessor. It was designed specifically to emulate (i.e., to execute the same instruction set as) the PDP-8, a 12-bit processor from Digital Equipment, which has proved to be the most successful minicomputer in the world. Intersil's motivation was to introduce a 1-chip portable implementation of the PDP-8 CPU that could replace it economically. The Intersil 6100 that resulted from this development is the only 12-bit microprocessor on the market (excluding the Toshiba TLCS-12 developed by the Japanese for Ford Motor Co.). The 6100 is software-compatible with the PDP-8 and allows the user to program directly in PDP-8 instructions. The PDP-8 compatibility proved to be no advantage. However, the use of CMOS technology did. A complete Intersil system can be powered with ordinary batteries. However, it is not possible to use ROM memory with this microprocessor in the same way that it could be used with a standard microprocessor. A peculiarity of the PDP-8 is that the return address of subroutines is stored within the subroutine itself, at the beginning, thus requiring that the subroutine be stored in RAM. Thus, if Intersil 6100 programs are to be stored in ROM rather than RAM, an "adaptation" of the PDP-8 program is needed in order to store the return addresses in a separate RAM.

ZILOG

Three of the 8080 designers left Intel and created their own company, Zilog, in Los Altos (overlooking Silicon Valley). Zilog is an affiliate of Exxon, the oil corporation. The story of Zilog is similar to the story of most Silicon Valley companies. Started by a small group of engineers, Zilog has grown in size and has become an important semiconductor manufacturing company. Its first product was the Z80 microprocessor, designed to compete with the 8080. The Z80 incorporates the 8080, the 8224 clock, the 8228 system controller, and some additional facilities on a single chip. The Z80 instruction set is upwards compatible with the 8080 instruction set. An 8080 ROM can run "as is" on a Z80 system, and the Z80 has additional instructions. The standard Z80 is as fast as the fast version of the 8080. A faster version, the Z80A, operates with a 4MHz clock (the fastest 8080, 8080-A2 operates on 3MHz).

The internal organization of the Z80 is shown in Figure 4.13. The architecture of the Z80 closely follows the architecture of the 8080. It provides, however, one main improvement. It is equipped with two banks of registers. These registers can be used to provide either a large number of internal registers or a very fast response to a single level of interrupt. These register banks are implemented correctly for interrupt handling. The accumulator and the status register are also duplicated. Thus, in response to a single interrupt, no register needs to be copied to

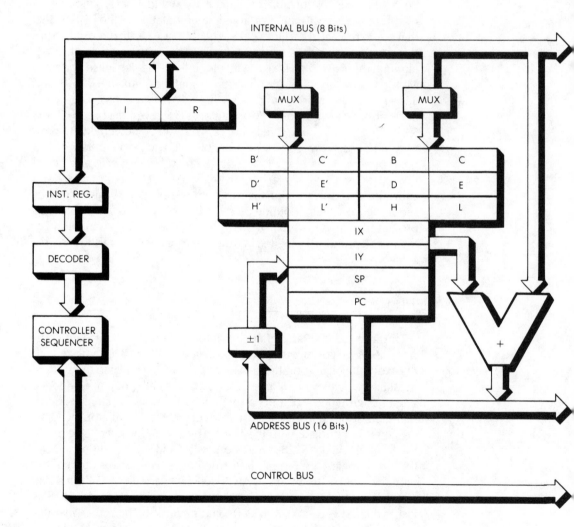

Figure 4.13: The Internal Organization of the Z80

the stack, except naturally the PC. Instead, a bank switch is performed. Each register bank includes all the 8080 registers, plus a set of index registers, thus enhancing the addressing ability of the Z80.

The Z80 is also equipped with a dynamic memory refresh facility that allows certain dynamic RAMs to be connected directly to the system

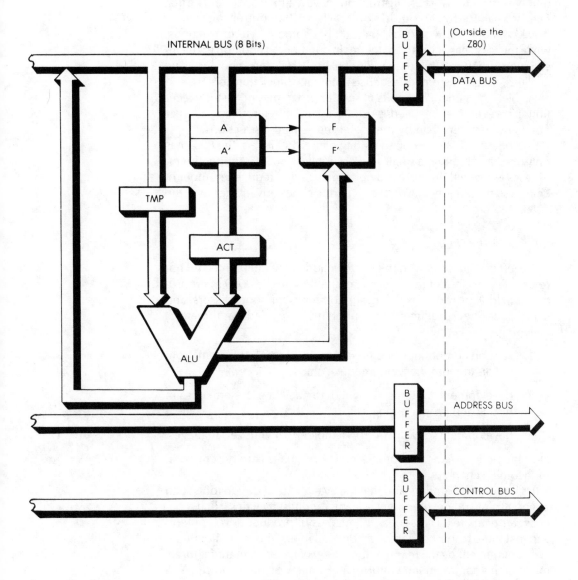

Figure 4.13: The Internal Organization of the Z80 (cont.)

without the need for an external refresh circuit. However, more powerful dynamic RAM refresh chips are now also available, so that the Z80 refresh output is often used as a random number generator.

The Z80 also has other less important advantages over the 8080. First, two of the unused instruction codes of the 8080 are used to provide additional instructions. These instructions have a 2-byte opcode. The first byte is the unused 8080 code. It simply tells the Z80 control unit that the "real" opcode follows. Thus, the Z80 has some 4-byte instructions, while the 8080 has at most 3 bytes per instruction. In addition to the instructions required by the additional Z80 registers and indexing facilities, special instructions such as automatic block transfers are also available. This generally results in shorter programs and faster execution. However, higher speed is usually attained by providing a larger number of registers than by the use of specialized instructions.

Second, the Z80 is equipped with two interrupt levels (the 8080 has only one), and requires a single power supply (the 8080 requires three). In cases where either improved performance or a reduced number of chips is significant, the Z80 presents performance advantages over the 8080.

INTEL (REVISITED)

We left off with Intel with the introduction of the 8080. Intel did not remain idle in front of the intense competition in the 8080 microprocessor field. It provided excellent support for its microprocessors, and it introduced new products. The support Intel provided was threefold, including:

1. support components required to build a complete system, from clocks to memories and interface chips

2. development systems designed to facilitate system design, testing and programming

3. development software from assemblers to high-level languages.

Development systems and programming languages are described in forthcoming chapters.

It is important to understand that the availability of design tools such as good software, development systems, and test facilities (such as an *in-circuit emulator*) is essential for successful product development, and that these resources can be made available without a major financial commitment by the manufacturer. Few of the early manufacturers made such a commitment. Unfortunately, many of them introduced a microprocessor chip, which may have been an excellent product, but they then left it unsupported, so that few users could integrate it into a system at a reasonable cost.

Intel must be credited with having immediately recognized the need for complete user support. We will see later that the "best microprocessor" is the one that solves a problem, within given cost and performance specifications. It is not necessarily the fastest one or the latest model. Such manufacturer support was an essential reason for the immense success of the 8080.

Let us now go back to the successor products to the 8080. With the progress of technology, the additional chips required by the 8080 could be integrated on a single chip. Thus Intel designed the 8085, which incorporates the 8224 clock, the 8228 system controller and the 8080 microprocessor within a single chip. The normal 8085 operates at a speed equivalent to the fastest 8080 (3MHz).

Like the Z80, the 8085 is software-compatible with the 8080 and provides additional instructions, but the resemblance stops there. The 8085 was designed for small- or medium-sized systems in which the number of chips must be minimized. Special memory-plus-I/O combination chips that can be connected directly to the 8085 buses were introduced at the same time as the 8085. A minimal 8085 system can be assembled with just three chips, including microprocessor, memory (2K of ROM and 256 words of RAM), and I/O facilities.

In view of the large amount of software developed for the 8080, software compatibility with the 8080 is a major advantage, since 8080 programs can be easily adapted to 8085 programs. A comparison between the 8080 and the 8085 is presented in Figure 4.14.

	8080	8085
CPU	3 CHIPS:8080+8228+CLOCK	1 CHIP
SPEED	2μS TO 1.3μS (8080 A-1)	1.3μS
REQUIRED MEMORY ACCESS	300 NS	450 NS
POWER SUPPLIES	3	1 (+5V)
INSTRUCTION SET	SEE 8080	SAME 2 INSTRUCTIONS
READ TIME	--------IDENTICAL--------	
INTERRUPTS	1	5 (3 Maskable)
SERIAL I/O	0	ONE IN, ONE OUT

Figure 4.14: 8080 Versus 8085

In the case of large systems where a difference of one or two chips in the total chip count is not essential, the 8085 is at a disadvantage. The 8085 provides four hardware interrupt levels (plus a software level). To achieve this within the traditional 40-pin limitation of the package, more pins were required than were available. As a result, multiplexing was required. The reader will recall that the 8080 multiplexes control information over the data bus. This time, the 8085 provides clean control signals over dedicated lines. However, it multiplexes the data bus. Thus, the data bus is used to transmit both data and eight bits of address. When a 16-bit address is transmitted, the lower eight bits appear on the data bus. The upper eight bits appear on the 8-bit address bus.

In view of this multiplexing of the data bus, external latching and multiplexing of the bus are required. These functions are internal to the special memory-plus-I/O combinations that were introduced together with the 8085. However, they must be performed externally in the case of conventional memory and I/O chips. A sample 8085 system is presented in the next chapter, with a complete interconnect.

In summary, the 8085, when compared to the 8080, presents several advantages in the case of small systems: a higher speed, a lower component count, a single power supply, five interrupt levels, and two I/O lines. When compared to the Z80, the 8085 is at a disadvantage in the case of large systems, since it has fewer registers, fewer instructions, and a slower speed. The fact that the Z80 has a dynamic refresh register for dynamic RAMs is not an important consideration in the case of large systems. However, remember that technical performance is often not the main criterion for selecting the proper microprocessor. Other criteria will be presented at the end of this chapter.

MOTOROLA (8-BIT MICROPROCESSORS—REVISITED) _____

Motorola introduced several chips derived from the 6800 and one significantly different one, the 6809. The 6809 is an 8-bit microprocessor designed for high performance. The internal architecture of the 6809 is shown in Figure 4.15. The 6809 provides enhanced addressing capabilities with two stack pointers (U and S) and two index registers (X and Y). As in the 6800, only two data registers are provided, the two accumulators A and B. The 6809 instruction set is upward compatible with the 6800, i.e., 6800 programs can be easily adapted to the 6809. In addition, the 6809 provides many 16-bit instructions, such as 16-bit add, subtract, load, store, and compare. The 6809 is also bus-compatible with the 6800 and can use common support devices. The 6809 qualifies as a high-performance replacement product for the 6800.

Various other 8-bit microprocessors are manufactured for exotic purposes, such as aerospace, military applications, or in-house custom applications. However, they are not generally available or supported as general-purpose microprocessors. This includes companies like Hewlett Packard, IBM, Texas Instruments, General Instrument, Mostek, Rockwell, AMI, and National Semiconductor.

RCA deserves a special mention with the COSMAC, a CMOS 8-bit microprocessor designed for aerospace applications, but otherwise non-competitive with the usual microprocessors.

8-BIT SINGLE-CHIP MICROCOMPUTERS

With the increasing component densities of LSI technologies, all the functional elements of a computer can be integrated on a single chip. However, this limited chip area does, in fact, limit the complexity of each function.

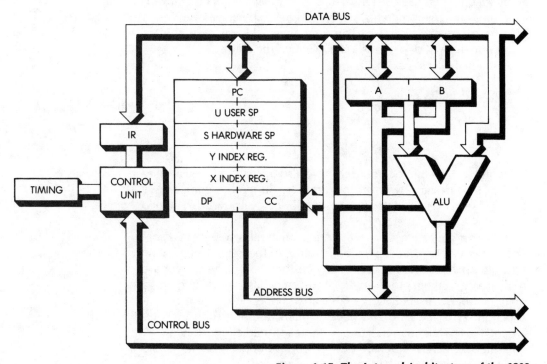

Figure 4.15: The Internal Architecture of the 6809

Typical features of an 8-bit, single-chip microcomputer are a 1K or 2K × 8 ROM containing the internal program and a 256- or 512-word RAM containing the internal registers, the stack, and the scratch-pad memory. The 16 lines necessary in a standard architecture for implementing the address bus are no longer necessary, since the memory is on board the chip. These 16 lines are therefore released to I/O functions. A single-chip, 8-bit microcomputer generally has three 8-bit I/O ports plus additional lines. These three ports correspond to the 8-bit data bus and the 16-bit address bus of a standard microprocessor. In addition, the chip normally includes a clock circuit as well as a programmable timer/event counter (important for I/O).

Since a single-chip microcomputer is equipped with a ROM memory, it must be manufactured in large quantities (i.e., thousands), in order to be economical. Typical markets for such microcomputers are toys, appliances, and device controllers. They usually involve quantities of over 10,000. In large quantities the cost of a single-chip microcomputer can drop below $2.

One obvious disadvantage of a single-chip microcomputer is that the ROM is on the chip. Therefore, if a single error is found in the program, all microcomputers must be replaced, since a ROM cannot be changed. This rules out large programs, which can never be error-free. This is why there is no real incentive to produce single-chip microcomputers with more than 2K or perhaps 4K of ROM on the chip.

The main devices are:

Fairchild/Mostek	3870 (F8)
Intel	8048
Zilog	Z8

Additional 8-bit microcomputers have also been introduced as spin-offs of 16-bit designs by Texas Instruments and Intel. A comparative table is shown in Figure 4.16. The various devices will now be examined in turn.

One other general fact is worth noting. High sales volume of a chip does not mean wide acceptance of a chip. In the case of single-chip microcomputers, as in the case of any custom design, these chips are sold in large quantities to a very small customer base. As a result, only a small number of users become familiar with the architecture and instruction set of the chip and develop hardware and software tools around them. Thus, manufacturer support and marketing are essential. This intrinsic market limitation does not bring about the same "habit-forming" results as standard microprocessors do.

FAIRCHILD/MOSTEK F8/3870

The 2-chip version of the F8 by Fairchild was the first true microcomputer-on-two-chips to be introduced on the market. The rather unconventional architecture and unusual instruction set of the F8 stems from its historical evolution. A custom chip built by General Instrument (per the specifications of a German company) led to the 2-chip F8, which was introduced by Fairchild in a design essentially similar to the GI product. Since then, all of the F8's functions have been implemented on a single chip, the 3870 by Mostek and later by Fairchild. This was one of the first widely-used general-purpose single-chip microcomputers.

The early F8 design required two chips, the 3850 MPU and the 3851 PSU. It is shown in Figure 4.17. The internal organization of the 3850 is shown in Figure 4.18, and the 3851 is shown in Figure 4.19.

Because the F8 was not originally designed to be a single-chip microcomputer, its organization is complex, and its instruction set is more difficult to use and to understand than most other instruction sets. For the first-time user, the F8, as well as its successor product, the 3870, is difficult to program. The cost of programming, however, is not a significant selection criterion when considering a microcomputer like the F8. This cost, when divided by the number of units sold, becomes minimal. For the typical applications of a single-chip microcomputer, the two essential criteria are sufficient performance and a low quantity-purchase price.

MICRO-COMPUTER	FAIRCHILD MOSTEK 3870	INTEL 8048H	INTEL 8022	ROCKWELL 6500/1-41P	ZILOG Z8	GI PIC 1670	MOTOROLA 6801	TEXAS INSTRUMENTS 9940
TECHNOLOGY	NMOS	NMOS	NMOS	NMOS	NMOS	NMOS	NMOS	NMOS
CLOCK (MHz)	4	8	3	2	8	4	4	3
ROM (bytes)	2K	1K	2K	1.5K	2K	1K × 13 BITS	2K	2K
RAM (bytes)	64	64	64	64	128	64	128	128
SERIAL I/O	YES	YES		YES	YES	NO	YES	YES
FEATURES	F8 COMPATIBLE	MANY VERSIONS	A/D CONVERTER	MANY VERSIONS	MANY VERSIONS			SIMILAR TO 9900

Figure 4.16: 8-Bit Single-Chip Microcomputers

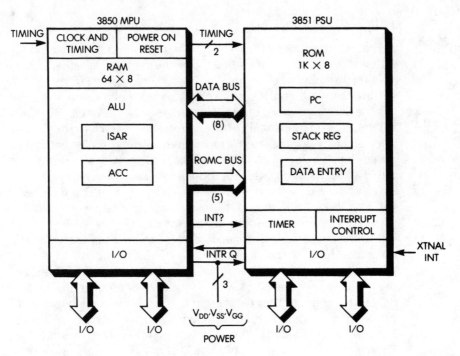

Figure 4.17: 2-Chip F8

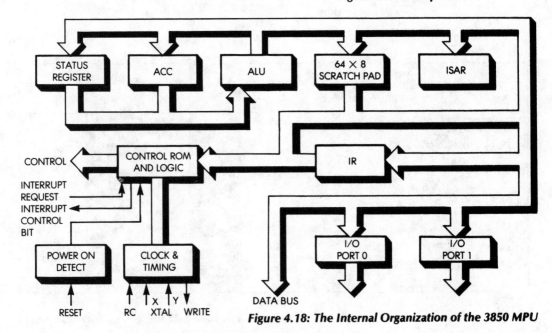

Figure 4.18: The Internal Organization of the 3850 MPU

INTEL 8048

The architecture of the 8048 was inspired by the architecture of the 8080, but the two microprocessors are not compatible. The internal architecture of the 8048 is shown in Figure 4.20. The 8048 has a 1K × 8 ROM on the chip, plus a 64-byte RAM. The RAM contains eight working registers, an 8-byte stack, a second register bank, and additional scratch-pad storage. As usual, the 8048 uses an accumulator-based, single-bus architecture. It provides three 8-bit I/O ports that replace the usual data bus (8 bits) and address bus (16 bits).

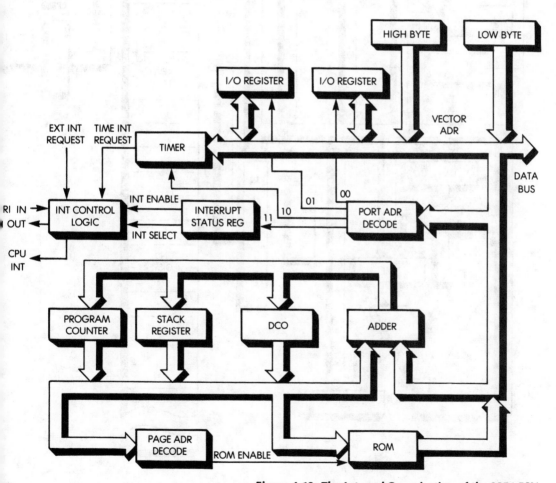

Figure 4.19: The Internal Organization of the 3851 PSU

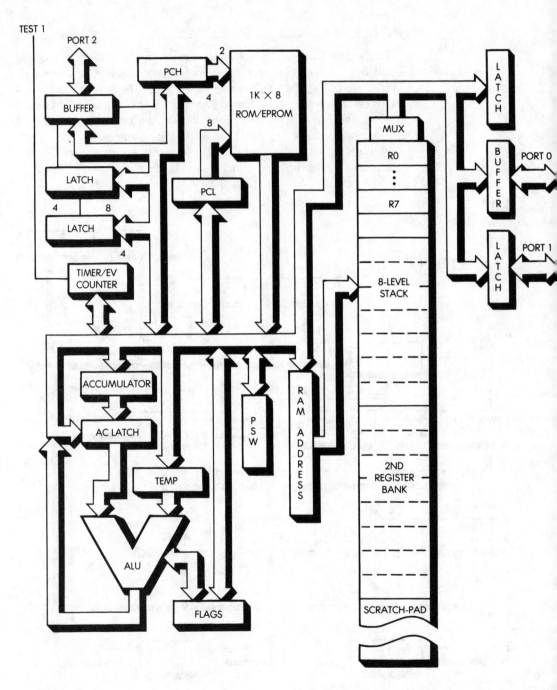

Figure 4.20: The Internal Architecture of the 80

The 8048 has a clean instruction set distinct from the 8080 instruction set. In particular, the 8048 provides the capability for testing any bit within the accumulator (and, depending on the bit used, jumping directly to an address). The 8048 was introduced later than the 3870, the 1-chip version of the F8, but it implements a cleaner design and is easier to use. Therefore, the impact of being first on the market might not be as significant in this case as it was with standard microprocessors. The performance level of the 8048 is somewhat higher than that of the 3870. However, when used by a skilled programmer, the performance level of the 3870 is almost on a par in many areas with the performance of the 8048. When comparing these two chips, cost and convenience are the most important selection criteria.

A convenient feature of the 8048 is the availability of an EPROM version (the 8748) for development work, when the program must be tested and modified. The 8748 is an 8048 equipped with a UV-erasable EPROM (rather than the standard ROM). Thus, it can be erased with ultraviolet light and then reprogrammed. This feature is advantageous during the developmental phase. Other single-chip microcomputers are almost always available in a development version, where an EPROM chip can be "piggy-backed" on the microcomputer (see Figure 4.21).

Figure 4.21: EPROM Piggy-Backed on a Single-Chip Microcomputer

ZILOG Z8

The Z8 single-chip microcomputer incorporates a 2K ROM and a 144-byte RAM. Using an 8MHz clock rate, it executes instructions in 1.5 to 2.5 μs. It provides two timer-counters, a UART, and six vectored interrupts on board the chips. As usual, it offers three I/O ports.

The 144-byte RAM of the Z8 includes a 124-byte scratch-pad (general-purpose registers), 16 control registers, and 4 I/O port registers. The general-purpose registers are indexable. The on-chip RAM's organization is shown in Figure 4.22. In addition, two of the ports may be used to transmit (multiplexed) address and data externally, thereby extending the addressing capability of the Z8 (see Figure 4.23).

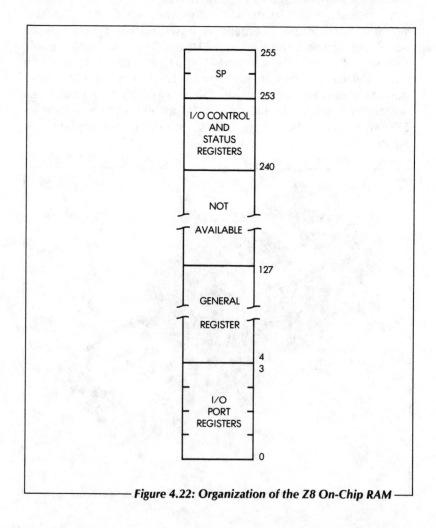

Figure 4.22: Organization of the Z8 On-Chip RAM

16-BIT MICROPROCESSORS

A limitation of the 16-bit microprocessors was pointed out previously. It was shown that with only 40 pins available it is not possible to implement a 16-bit address bus, and a 16-bit data bus, as well as a sufficient control bus. If only 40 pins are used, then one of the buses must be multiplexed. This results in the need for external address latches, demultiplexing circuits, and a possible system slowdown. Once 16-bit data or instructions are in the microprocessor, the processing speed of a 16-bit microprocessor is significantly higher than in the case of an 8-bit microprocessor. However, 16-bit transfers to and from the MPU must occur 8 bits at a time, slowing the processor down.

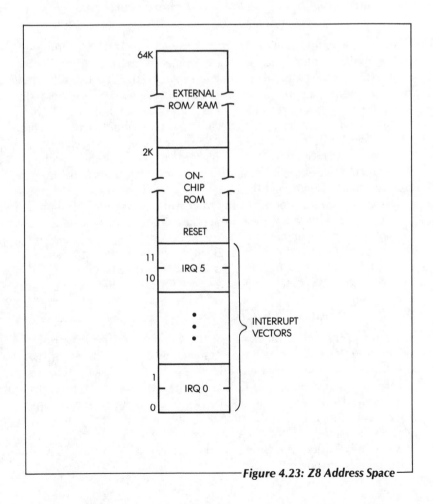

Figure 4.23: Z8 Address Space

As a result of this constraint, two types of packaging for the 16-bit microprocessors have been used. They include:

1. "full-power" designs that use a 64-pin package. The buses no longer need to be multiplexed, and 16-bit transfers may be performed at the processor's speed. However, the use of a 64-pin package results in a high unit cost and restricts the possibility of incoming testing by the user, since most industrial chip testers do not accommodate more than 40 or 42 pins.

2. "general purpose" designs that use 40- to 48-pin packages. One bus (16 bits) or half of one bus (8 bits) must be multiplexed. 8-bit transfers occur at full speed, but 16-bit transfers are generally slower than in the case of a 64-pin package. However, the standard packaging results in lower cost, both for the component and in terms of board space.

Most of the early 16-bit microprocessors were designed to compete in the minicomputer, CPU replacement market because of the high cost of CPUs at the time. All failed, since replacing the CPU by itself was not worthwhile, except for those microprocessors that were created and used for in-house replacement of 16-bit CPUs. For example, the Texas Instruments 9900 did well because it was designed as the CPU of Texas Instruments' "minicomputer," and therefore it was used mostly in-house. But competitive CPU replacements, such as the Fairchild 9440, did not fare as well. These early products are shown in the comparative chart in Figure 4.24.

The next generation of 16-bit microprocessors was designed specifically as general-purpose processors. They did not attempt to emulate or to maintain compatibility with existing products. Therefore they resulted in powerful designs. Examples of these microprocessors are the Intel 8086, the Zilog Z8000, and the Motorola M68000. We will now examine them in turn: the older ones first, then the newer ones.

NATIONAL SEMICONDUCTOR PACE

National Semiconductor was the first company to introduce a 16-bit design, the PACE. The PACE was designed as a replacement for the IMP-16, a 16-bit minicomputer CPU. The IMP-16 was a system based on National Semiconductor's GP/CP bit-slice set, which was too slow and required too many components. The PACE instruction set is compatible with the IMP-16 instruction set. Unfortunately, the first PACE was implemented in PMOS technology and was slow. The IMP-16 never achieved success as a minicomputer. The PACE has not achieved widespread diffusion either.

GENERAL INSTRUMENT CP1600

General Instrument introduced the CP1600, a fast NMOS 16-bit processor. Next, ITT announced that they would sell and second source the product, indicating that the 16-bit microprocessor would be used for internal ITT designs. However, no real effort was made to market the device as a general-purpose fully supported product.

DATA GENERAL MN601 (MICRONOVA)

Data General introduced the Mn601 to compete in the low end minicomputer market. The Mn601 implements, on one chip, most of the NOVA/3 CPU (the slowest NOVA minicomputer manufactured by Data General). Minicomputer manufacturers have been facing competition from companies who are implementing slow ("low end") minicomputers using microprocessors and other LSI devices. The use of large-scale integration results in a lower component count and thus in a

	DATA GENERAL MN 601	GEN. INST. CP 1600	NS PACE	TEXAS TMS 9900	FAIRCHILD 9440
TYPE	STANDARD	STANDARD	STANDARD	STANDARD	STANDARD
TECHNOLOGY	NMOS	NMOS	PMOS	NMOS	I^2L
NBR OF INSTRUCTIONS	NOVA 3 INSTR.	87	50	69	NOVA 1200 SET
CYCLE TIME (μS)	2.4 to 10	2.4	8 to 10	15	1 to 2.5
DIRECT ADDRESSING (BITS)	16	16	16	16	16
REGISTERS	4	7	4	RAM (16)	4
STACK (LEVELS)	HARD	SOFT	HARD (10)	—	HARD
INTERRUPTS	1	2	6	16	1
ON-CHIP CLOCK	YES	—	—	—	—
ROM (BYTES)	—	—	—	—	—
RAM (WORDS)	—	—	—	—	—
TIMER	YES	—	—	—	—
PFR	YES	—	—	—	—
OTHER	—	—	—	—	—
I/O LINES	—	—	—	—	—
PACKAGE (PINS)	40	40	40	64	40
POWER SUPPLY (V)	−4.25, +5 +10, +14	+12, +5, −3	+5, −12	−5, +5, +12	+5, +1
SECOND SOURCE	—	ITT	—	—	—
REMARKS	NOVA 3 EMULATOR	—	IMP 16 COMPATIBLE	MULT/DIV INS TRNS	NOVA 1200 EMULATOR

Figure 4.24: Comparative Chart—Early 16 Bits

lower cost. To compete in this area, minicomputer manufacturers must now produce their own LSI designs. Data General sells the Mn601 as a NOVA board and shows no interest in supporting the Mn601 as a general-purpose microprocessor device. The Mn601 is designed for internal use by Data General. For the Mn601 board user, the essential advantage is that all the software developed for it is compatible with the NOVA and can be developed directly on a NOVA minicomputer.

FAIRCHILD 9440 (FLAME)

Fairchild introduced the 9440 16-bit microprocessor, which implements most of the functions of a NOVA 1200 CPU on one chip and competes head-on with Data General's CPU. In view of the complexity of the design, however, Fairchild faced production problems very early on. Before the device could gain wide customer acceptance, Fairchild became entangled in litigation with Data General, thus effectively grounding the product.

TEXAS INSTRUMENTS 9900

Texas Instruments introduced the TMS 9900, a fast microprocessor equipped with hardware multiply and divide operations. Because it uses a 64-pin package, the TMS 9900 is a powerful processor that is no longer constrained by the usual 40-pin limitation and communicates with the outside world via a 16-pin address bus as well as a 16-pin data bus. The 9900 is a powerful 1-chip minicomputer CPU equivalent. It is well supported by Texas Instruments, which has introduced several support devices that are compatible with the 9900 as well as with their second source 8080. The 9900 is used internally by Texas Instruments for their 990 minicomputer/microcomputer.

Because Texas Instruments has used this chip as the CPU of their 990 system, any 9900 user will in fact be implementing a minicomputer-like processor with the same instruction set as the 990, which could be a possible disadvantage in smaller dedicated microprocessor applications. As long as it was the only 16-bit microprocessor on the market, the 9900 could interest users seeking powerful processing ability in a single chip. However, since this is no longer the case, the 9900 is mostly used within Texas Instruments systems and by traditional Texas Instruments customers, including military designers. Like the most recent 16-bit microprocessors, the 9900 has a family of other devices code-compatible with the 9900. In particular the 9940, the new 1-chip microcomputer from Texas Instruments, has an instruction set that is compatible with the 9900. The advantage of this is that, if the 9940 establishes a market, it will in turn support the instruction set and therefore the sales of the 9900 itself. Other 9900-like devices are also available in 8-bit format.

INTEL 8086-8088

The Intel 8086, introduced on the market just after the TMS 9900, was the first truly general-purpose microprocessor. It inherited many of the architectural features of the 8080, but, fortunately, there was not an attempt to maintain direct compatibility. Thus, many of the exotic or ir-ritating "features" of the 8080 do not exist with the 8086. An illustration showing the internal architecture of the 8086 appears in Figure 4.25. The actual chip is shown in Figure 4.26.

The 8088 is actually an 8086 that has been restricted to 8-bit external transfers. Both the 8086 and the 8088 use a standard 40-pin package.

In Figure 4.23 we saw that the microprocessor is partitioned into two logical units: the *execution unit* (EU) and the *bus interface unit* (BIU). The execution unit of the 8086 implements the standard single-bus, accumulator-based architecture, although the accumulator is shown as part of the register block.

The registers shown in Figure 4.27 include all of the 8080 registers plus many additional ones. The general registers group is characterized by the fact that all its registers are byte addressable, i.e., they may be used as 16-bit registers or as 8-bit registers. Because some 8086 instructions use specific registers, they have names such as *base* and *count*. The four 16-bit registers are used primarily for addressing purposes and are not byte addressable.

The *bus interface unit* (BIU) manages all bus communications with the outside world. Because of its 40-pin limitation, the 8086 multi-plexes the data and the address over the same 16 pins. The BIU manages this process. In addition, the BIU implements *instruction-pipelining* in order to speed up execution in the 8086. This is accomplished by pre-fetching up to six instructions and storing them in an internal instruction queue RAM, (which is shown on the far left of the illustration in Figure 4.25). This prefetching, or *look ahead*, is accomplished during periods of time when the EU is busy executing instructions; thus, fetching is overlapped with execution.

As long as the program does not contain a successful branch, i.e., as long as program execution is sequential, the next instruction to be ex-ecuted is generally available in the instruction queue at the time that it is needed. This results in an improved speed.

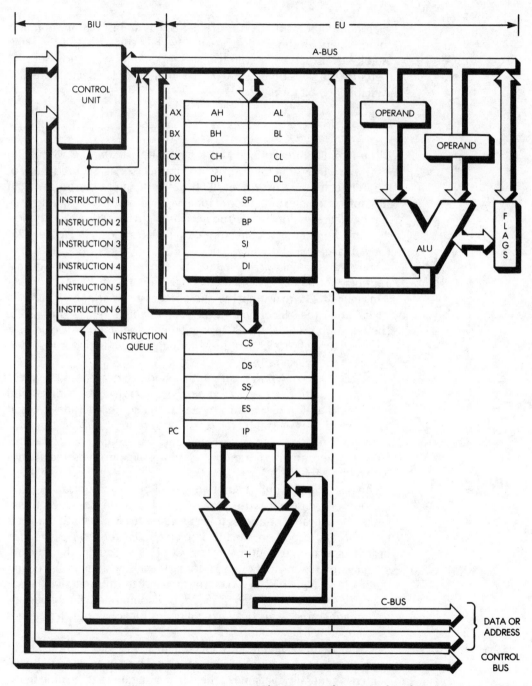

Figure 4.25: The Internal Architecture of the 8086

The BIU is also equipped with four segment registers which are shown at the bottom of Figure 4.27. These registers are designed to facilitate the addressing of a large memory (up to one megabyte) using *segmentation*. Segmentation allows the programmer to address 64K segments anywhere in a large memory without having to worry about their exact location. Thus, within a segment pointer any word is addressed

Figure 4.26: Photomicrograph of the Intel 8086

as a 16-bit address. Four kinds of segments are provided by the system. This requires the availability of four segment pointers. These are the four registers shown as CS, DS, SS, and ES in Figures 4.25 and 4.27. The actual, physical address of a word within the 1-megabyte address space is obtained by adding the 16-bit word address to the segment address, as shown in Figure 4.28.

All of the early microprocessors were limited to a 64K memory. Having anticipated the use of these devices for executing large programs or operating on large amounts of data, or executing in a multi-user or multi-program environment, the more recent designers have provided

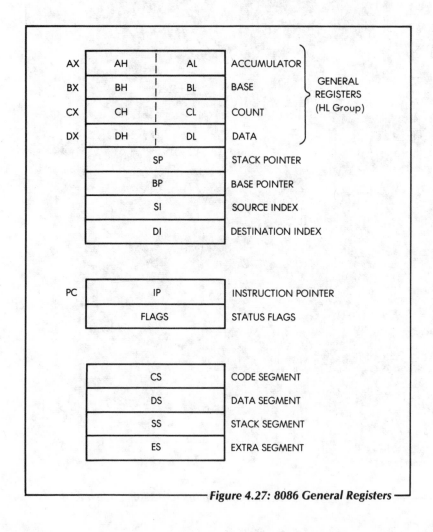

Figure 4.27: 8086 General Registers

the capabilities to address much larger memories directly. Each micro-processor provides a different solution to this problem.

Note that the capability of addressing up to one megabyte refers to the *logical* addressing capability, and not to the *physical* amount of memory actually used, which may, in fact, be much less. This facility simplifies program design and does not require an actual 1-megabyte (LSI) main memory. Programs may address up to one megabyte as if the segments were in main memory. However, the segments may actually reside on disk, for example, and may be brought to the main memory as needed, so that a small main memory may be used.

The 8086 is offered in a standard 5MHz version and an even faster 8MHz version. The corresponding required memory access times are 440 ns to 490 ns at 5MHz and 215 ns to 265 ns at 8MHz.

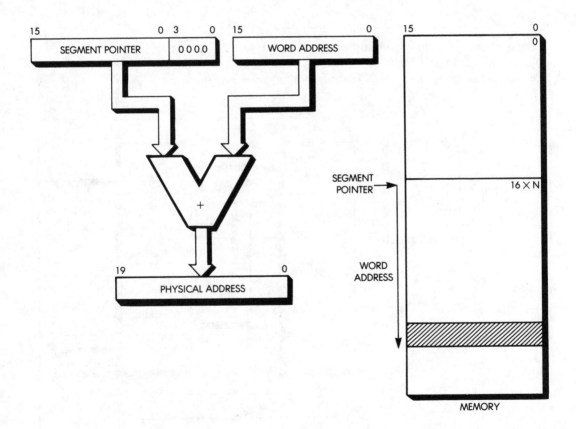

Figure 4.28: Computing the Physical Address

Finally, the 8086, like other more recent microprocessors, was designed for multiprocessing environments in which several processors share common buses or a common memory. It is for this reason that the LOCK signal was provided on one of the pins. Specific instructions have also been provided to facilitate multiprocessor communications using *semaphores*, for example. (A semaphore is a flag that indicates whether or not a shared resource is available.)

Sixteen pins on the 8086 are shared by the data bus and the address bus. Thus, these two buses must be demultiplexed externally, using the ALE (address latch enable) signal functions. A minimal system is shown in Figure 4.29.

In summary, the 8086 was the first general-purpose 16-bit microprocessor to be used on a wide scale. Although it is not the fastest 16-bit microprocessor available, it is well supported and thus easy to use.

INTEL 8089

The 8089 is an important support component that was designed to enhance the efficiency of an 8086 system. It is also compatible with the 8080 and 8085. The 8089 is an I/O processor that can simultaneously

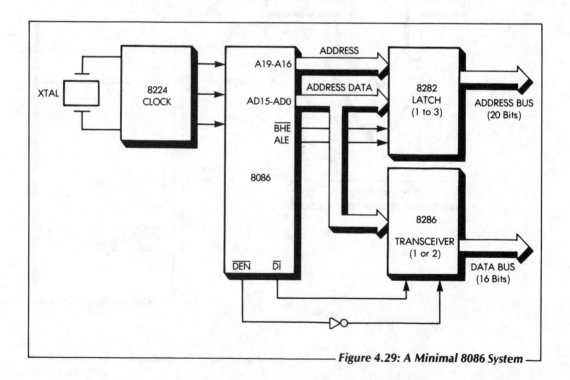

Figure 4.29: A Minimal 8086 System

manage two DMA channels. Because it is programmable, it can act as a processor and process information to or from the I/O devices in parallel with the main processor. A combination of the 8086 and 8089 results in high speed processing and very fast I/O handling and processing.

ZILOG Z8000

The Z8000 was the second general-purpose 16-bit microprocessor introduced on the market. The Z8000 is available in two versions, either with a special memory management chip or without one. Using the special memory management chip, the address space is expanded to eight megabytes. The two chips are shown in Figure 4.30.

Figure 4.30: Zilog's Z8001A (48-Pin) and Z8002A (40-Pin) 16-Bit Microprocessors

The Z8000 registers are shown in Figure 4.31. Sixteen general-purpose registers are provided. Fifteen are indexable. One or two registers are normally used as stack pointers. The Z8000 provides for two modes of operation: system and normal, with two separate stacks. This facility, as well as the segmentation facility, shows the influence of operating system designers on the chip's architecture.

The first microprocessors were designed simply to execute binary instructions, and little consideration was given to the ease with which these early microprocessors could be used to execute a high-level language such as BASIC or Pascal. However, it became obvious that ease in implementing complex software, such as language compilers and operating systems, would become a major selling point. Thus, the more recent models have been designed to facilitate the implementation of high-level languages, such as BASIC, Pascal or ADA, and to facilitate or automate basic operating system chores such as memory management and multiple modes of operation.

In a multi-user or multi-programming environment, the operating system is often designed to run in two modes:

1. in *executive* or *supervisory* mode, where all system resources are available to the program

2. in *user* or *slave* mode, where only some resources can be accessed by the program being executed.

The two sets of stack pointers provided by the Z8000 are intended to facilitate such a two-mode design.

Finally, like the Z80, the Z8000 contains a dynamic refresh register for dynamic memories. The non-segmented version of the Z8000 uses 40 pins and addresses 64K bytes. The segmented version uses 48 pins and addresses 8 MB (8,388,608 bytes). Twenty-three bits are used to provide the 8 MB address space: 7 bits for the segment number and 16 bits for the address within the segment, or offset. Thus, there are 128 segments of 0 to 64K bytes.

The memory management unit automates two functions:

1. It maps a 23-bit logical address into a 24-bit physical address, using an internal RAM, thus expanding the physical address space to 16 MB.

2. It provides memory protection by checking attributes associated with each segment, such as read-only, read/write, user mode, or executive mode.

This is illustrated in Figure 4.32.

The Z8000, like the 8086, multiplexes a 16-bit address and data bus.

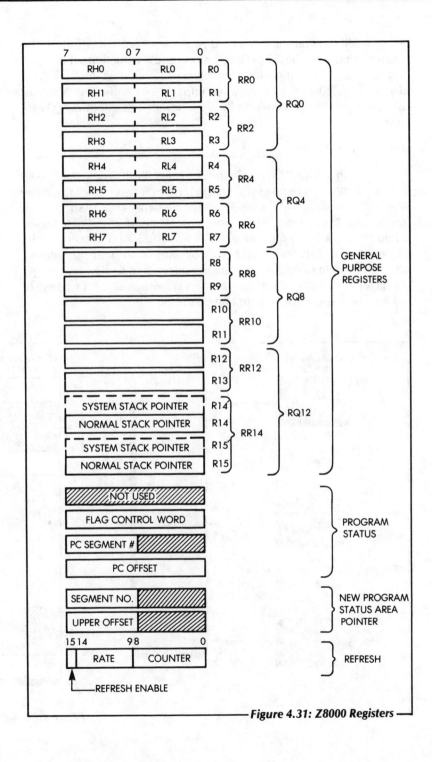

Figure 4.31: Z8000 Registers

Seven additional pins are required in the segmented version for the segment number. The Z8000 offers a powerful instruction set of 32-bit moves and 32-bit arithmetic instructions, including multiply and divide. The Z8000 is not software-compatible with the Z80, but most Z80 programs can be converted with reasonable ease into Z8000 programs.

MOTOROLA 68000 _____

The Motorola MC68000 was introduced after the 8086 and the Z8000. It implements a more powerful design but has suffered from the delay and lack of availability. The MC68000 implements a "pure speed" approach and uses 64 pins to provide separate address and data buses. Although it is a 16-bit microprocessor, the MC68000 has many of the same internal features as a 32-bit processor. Note that the internal registers, shown in Figure 4.33, are organized into two banks of eight 32-bit registers. Naturally, these registers are also available on a byte or on a 16-bit basis. Eight interrupt levels are provided.

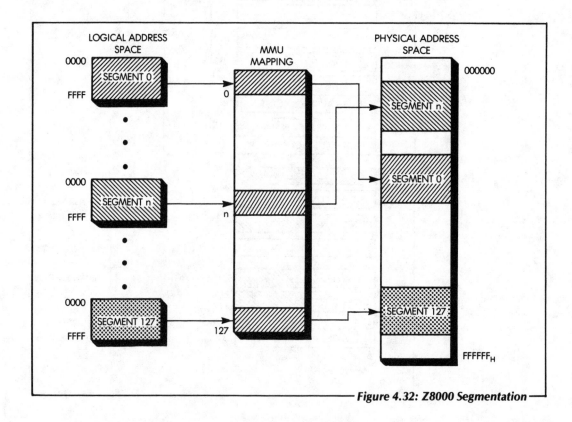

Figure 4.32: Z8000 Segmentation

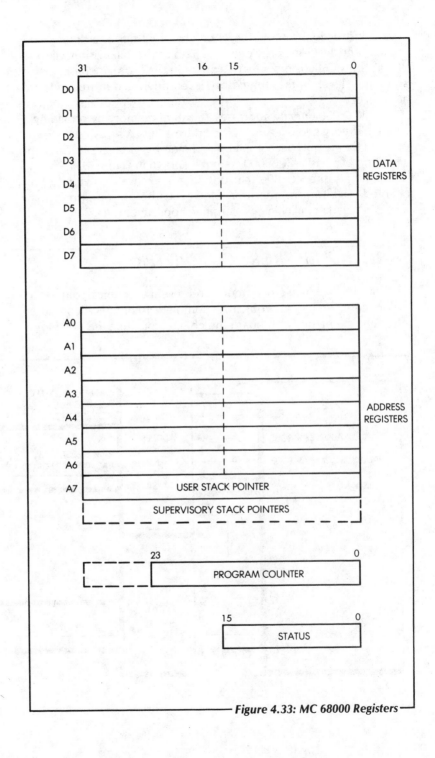

Figure 4.33: MC 68000 Registers

Most instructions operate on either 16 or 32 bits at a time. 16-bit multiply and divide are provided, plus 32-bit by 16-bit division. Like the Z8000, the MC68000 provides two operating levels: a supervisory level and a user level. In the supervisory level, privileged instructions are authorized.

The MC68000 directly addresses 16 MB of memory by providing a 24-bit address gated over the 16-bit address bus. A separate device is planned for memory segmentation and memory protection. The configuration of a basic MC68000 system is shown in Figure 4.34.

In summary, the MC68000 can be characterized as a powerful 32-bit oriented, 16-bit microprocessor. However, the use of 64 pins may restrict its marketability in cost-sensitive applications.

16-BIT 1-CHIP MICROCOMPUTERS

16-bit, single-chip microcomputers represent a technical solution to the pin-count limitation problem. A complete 1-chip microcomputer integrates the memory on board the chip, eliminating the need for a

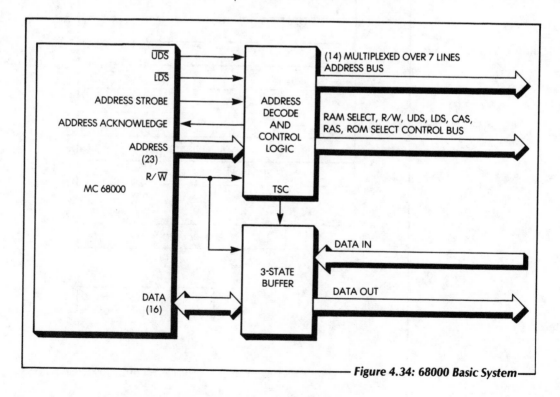

Figure 4.34: 68000 Basic System

16-bit address bus plus a 16-bit data bus. Thus the available pins can be used for input/output functions. This is indeed the solution of the future. In addition, if such a microcomputer is instruction set compatible with an existing microprocessor or minicomputer, there will be a less significant software development problem.

A 16-bit chip results in improved execution speed for arithmetic and logical operations. In addition, a 16-bit chip permits the use of 16-bit opcodes (similar to those of a minicomputer), which results, in turn, in more powerful and varied instructions. 16-bit microcomputers have the potential for taking in a significant share of the market that was previously held by smaller computers.

However, the incentive to produce single-chip microcomputers is low because the design cost is high and the market is limited. Single-chip microcomputers are used for simple I/O control in appliances, games, cars, and industrial machines, where the programs are generally simple and do not require high performance, and cost must be minimized. As a result, there is a large market for 4-bit, single-chip microcomputers and 8-bit microcomputers, but a much smaller one for 16-bit microcomputers. 16-bit designs are therefore a spin-off of a general 16-bit microprocessor.

The first 16-bit, single-chip microcomputer was the 9940 from Texas Instruments. The 9940 is a microcomputer version of the 16-bit 9900 microprocessor, which has already been described.

BIT-SLICE PROCESSORS

A *bit-slice* device should not be called a *microprocessor*; however, the term "microprocessor" is often used to describe bit-slice devices because they are integrated circuits used to implement the functions of a CPU. However, bit-slices are not complete CPUs, and for this reason, we will not label them *microprocessors*.

A *bit-slice* is a slice of a complete arithmetic logical unit with multiplexers and data paths. A bit-slice includes a complete data path within the CPU of a traditional processor (including registers), the corresponding n-bit ALU slice, flags, multiplexers, and buses. The bit-slice specifically excludes the control functions. The control section of a bit-slice system must be implemented by external devices and is generally microprogrammed. The central section generally requires many additional devices that make the bit-slice design complex.

Currently, the optimum size for bit-slices is four bits. Thus, four slices are used to make a 16-bit processor. Bit-slices have provided a basic tool for building powerful processors today and have reduced the number of parts necessary in a CPU. In addition, they have opened the way to novel multi-bit-slice designs with decentralized processing units on various units and buses.

The introduction of bit-slices stemmed from a search for increased speed. In order to implement the fastest possible switching speed, component designers turned to the fastest available technologies, such as bipolar and, in particular, low-power Schottky (LPS) TTL. Unfortunately, bipolar is characterized by a large power consumption and power dissipation, which in turn require a large area of silicon on a chip. The resulting component integration is low, and it is not possible to integrate a complete 16-bit bipolar microprocessor on a single chip. Thus, designers were forced to limit the number and the complexity of the functions they were implementing on a chip. It can be easily shown that vertical function integration rather than horizontal design is the logical solution in the field of bipolar MSI/LSI components. Large component densities cannot be achieved with a horizontal design. As a result, a highly vertically-integrated slice across a complete CPU was created; and it became the standard 4-bit slice device. A number of companies had previously introduced *ALU slices*, but these were not true *bit-slice devices*.

4-bit ALU slices are used to implement 8-bit, 16-bit, and 32-bit ALUs. However, they are just that, *ALU slices*. A bit-slice incorporates all of the multiplexers, buses, registers and flags. In short, putting four 4-bit bit-slices in parallel results in a complete 16-bit ALU with registers, at least three buses, and the usual flags. Control is external (see Figure 4.35). Let us now review the brief history of bit-slice devices. A comparative chart of bit-slice devices is presented in Figure 4.36.

NATIONAL SEMICONDUCTOR GP/CP

The first company to introduce a bit-slice device was National Semiconductor, which introduced the GP/CP set in PMOS technology. The GP/CP was used to implement the IMP series of minicomputer systems. The result was a 16-bit IMP-16 minicomputer implemented with four slices (RALUs) plus control elements (the CROMs). The influence of the Data General Nova minicomputer can be seen in this system. This design implemented a complete minicomputer with a small number of chips. Unfortunately, it was very slow. Some companies, such as Teledyne, have used these slices in hybrid form for military applications (e.g., TDY 52B). Although obsolete today, the GP/CP can be considered the grandfather of bit-slices.

INTEL 3000 _____

Intel was the first company to introduce a fast bipolar bit-slice device, the 3000. The 3000 is a true bit-slice and operates at high speed (100 ns). The 3000 offers the advantage of speed but it also has several disadvantages. One disadvantage is that it operates on only *two* bits and therefore requires more components than are required by a 4-bit slice. Another disadvantage is its limited instruction set. However, these points may not be significant drawbacks in view of the great versatility of the chip, which provides a large number of buses and thus can provide high speed.

Another feature of the 3000, which is both an advantage and a disadvantage, is that it is *horizontally microprogrammable*, i.e., a microinstruction has several fields and can specify several events

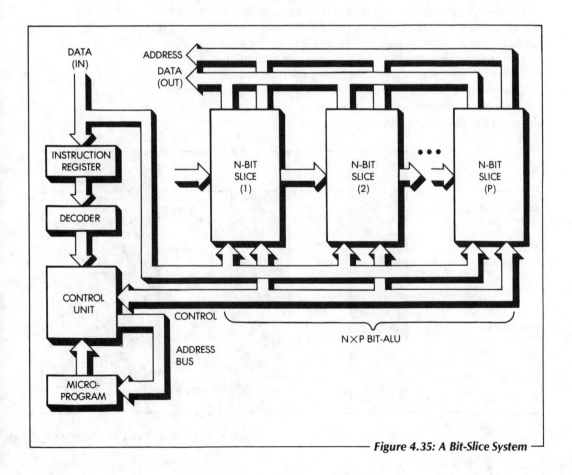

Figure 4.35: A Bit-Slice System

simultaneously. As a result, it is possible to execute many operations simultaneously and achieve great speed, provided that the microprogrammer knows how to take advantage of this feature. Unfortunately, many microprogrammers are easily discouraged by the apparent complexity of the device and consider the feature a disadvantage.

The 3000 is particularly well suited to the real-time control of sophisticated processes. The 3000 has been used for disk controllers as well as for numerous avionic applications (e.g., signal processing). It has also been used by military computer manufacturers (such as Hughes, which used the 3000 in the design of the AN/UYK 30).

One of the programming disadvantages of the 3000 is inherent to the horizontal microprogramming philosophy. Each microinstruction contains the address of the next one. Because of limitations on the number of pins, the address field is limited to seven bits. This limitation results in complex jump conventions, i.e., it is not possible to jump out of sequence to any address. In practice, this means that the microinstructions must be deposited in memory by a special program that places the microinstructions in such a way that it is legal (i.e., possible) to jump from one instruction to the next. One additional problem arises in the debugging phase. Once an error is found, the complete program must be remapped into the memory. This is acceptable practice in complex applications; however, it is normally judged an obstacle in simple applications.

	NS IMP	INTEL 3000	MMI 5701	AMD 2901	MOTOROLA XC 10800	TEXAS SBP0400
NUMBER OF BITS	4	2	4	4	4	4
TECHNOLOGY	PMOS	SCHOTTKY	SCHOTTKY	SCHOTTKY	MECL	I^2L
INSTRUCTIONS	4 + SHIFT	MINIMAL	36	36	COMPLEX	16
CYCLE TIME (NS)	9200	100	200	95, 125	55	1000
ON-CHIP REGISTERS	7	12	16	16	—	7
MEMORY REGISTERS	—	YES	—	—	—	—
EXT ACC.	—	—	YES	YES	—	—
STACK	YES (16)	—	—	—	—	—
STATUS	YES	YES	YES	YES	YES	YES
PACKAGING	24, 40	28	40	40	48	40
SECOND SOURCE	—	SIGNETICS	—	RAYTHEON, MOTOROLA THOMSON	—	—
REMARKS	—	—	—	SAME ARCHITECTURE AS 5701	—	128mW

Figure 4.36: Comparative Chart—Bit-Slices

MONOLITHIC MEMORIES 5701/6701

The 5701/6701 was introduced by Monolithic Memories (MMI) as the precursor of the standard 4-bit design used today. The MMI design was quickly followed by the AMD 2901 (described in the next section). The MMI 5701 emulated the Data General Nova 800 or 1200 architecture. Using the 6701, MMI created boards implementing a Data General Nova CPU with fewer components than Data General and 10% faster speed. However, the introduction of the 2901 by AMD superseded the 5701/6701 by offering identical functions and higher speed.

ADVANCED MICRO DEVICES AMD 2901

The AMD 2901 has become the standard 4-bit bit-slice. The 2901 architecture is essentially identical to that of the 5701; however, several improvements were made. Its performance is significantly improved (125 ns in the standard version rather than 200 ns, and an even faster speed for the 2901A, the faster version). Improvements made on the 2901 with respect to the 5701 are, for example, the addition of an extra bit in the microinstruction field, which results in twice as many micro-instructions and an external connection on the internal bus. The 2901 chip is shown in Figure 4.37.

A 16-bit ALU may be easily assembled using this device by cascading four slices (or putting them in parallel). For reasons of efficiency in performing arithmetic operations, a carry-look-ahead unit is usually added as well as several discrete components. The real complexity of bit-slice design lies in the *control section*, which includes the control logic, the loop counter, and bus multiplexers. (An example of the architecture of a bit-slice device was shown in Figure 4.35.)

The complexity of designing the external control functions required to build a system has been simplified by the introduction of new control components. The successful use of bit-slice devices for building larger CPUs has stimulated the design of sequencing chips. These chips significantly reduce the parts count necessary for the control logic. Bit-slices have become a standard design tool for CPUs today. As an example, a CPU implemented with the standard 2901 bit-slice device achieves a speed of 220 to 300 ns for 16, 32 or more bits. The AMD 2901 is second-sourced by a number of manufacturers, including Motorola, Signetics, and Thomson-CSF in Europe. It is used in many minicomputer designs as well as military processors, such as the ATAC 16 and the LSI-11M.

Other bit-slice devices have been introduced on the market but have been less successful. They will now be examined, along with the characteristics that make them valuable for specific applications.

MOTOROLA 10800

Motorola introduced an ECL component known as the 10800, which achieves very high speed with a cycle time of 55 ns. Unfortunately, this component requires an external register chip, which increases the component count and reduces the speed of the system. If this technology could achieve a higher integration factor, it could provide an efficient implementation of bit-slice devices for very fast applications.

TEXAS INSTRUMENTS 0400

The Texas Instruments 0400 and the later 0401 were the first bit-slice devices implemented in I²L technology. I²L (integrated injection logic)

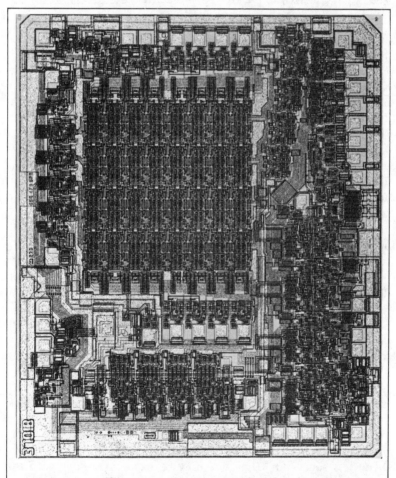

Figure 4.37: AMD 2901 Bit-Slice Shows Register RAM

is a bipolar technology that is characterized (in principle) by bipolar speed and a very low power consumption. This low power consumption makes it possible to implement a completely portable I^2L system. The I^2L technology evolved as a direct result of the portability requirements of pocket calculators and digital watches. I^2L was developed to solve the problem of limited power availability that characterizes these devices. Unfortunately, I^2L devices have not achieved the speed characteristic of bipolar technology. As an example, the 0400 achieved only 1 μs cycle time (versus approximately 100 ns for the AMD 2901). Laboratory experiments have indicated that much higher speeds can be achieved. If I^2L achieves these higher speeds, its capability for high component integration, high speed, and low power consumption could make it a good candidate for the implementation of battery-powered large scale computers. This result, however, is not immediately in sight.

FAIRCHILD MACROLOGIC

Fairchild has introduced a number of devices in the 9440 Macrologic family that are more than simple ALU slices but do not represent complete bit-slice devices. These devices are intermediate between usual MSI devices and true bit-slices and are used in standard computer designs.

In summary, the 2901 design has become the standard design for 4-bit slices. As new technologies are developed and improved, this design could be displaced by another one.

SELECTING A MICROPROCESSOR

We have presented a comparative evaluation of the various microprocessors and their manufacturers. Although this discussion may have answered questions on the many products available, it probably has not answered one of the most basic questions: "Which microprocessor is best for you?" In this section, we will consider the criteria that should be considered when selecting a microprocessor.

CRITERION 1: PERFORMANCE

The essential consideration when selecting a microprocessor is whether or not the microprocessor will do the job. The microprocessor must provide a sufficient performance for the application it is used for.

In order to evaluate the required performance, the first question to be asked is the following: "Does the application require 'super-speed,' such as the execution of complex instructions within less than a micro-second?" If it does, then a monolithic microprocessor is not fast enough. It will be necessary to consider a bit-slice design, a fast (bipolar) mini-computer, or some other fast processor.

If, however, the required instructions are like those currently available on microprocessors and no "super-speed" is required, then all types of microprocessors can be considered. But, if high speed is still a requirement, then 8-bit or 16-bit microprocessors can be considered. However, if speed is not a requirement, 4-bit microprocessors may be used, and other criteria such as price will then be used in making the selection.

Evaluating the required speed is often difficult. If the task to be per-formed is specific enough, *benchmark programs* should be established. *Benchmark programs* are "typical" programs written by the user to test the operating speed of the processor being considered in actual cases. For example, block-transfer programs or serialization programs are often used as benchmarks. Unfortunately, in most cases the applica-tion programs contain a mixture of functions, and it is therefore not easy to select "typical" benchmarks. In that case, an approximate evaluation is made, and if sufficient time and resources are available, simulation is used. In most control applications, the jobs performed by microprocessors can be performed by *virtually any standard 4- or 8-bit microprocessor*. These two categories have captured the largest part of the market. Fewer applications require the power (and fewer users can afford the cost) of 16-bit microprocessors.

CRITERION 2: NUMBER OF UNITS TO BE PRODUCED _____

The anticipated volume of units is an essential cost criterion. Low volumes rule out one-chip microcomputers. High volumes stress low cost and require a minimum number of components. A possible deci-sion chart for selecting the appropriate microprocessor appears in Figure 4.38.

Let us consider the case of a large production run. The chart in Figure 4.38 shows: "Consider a custom chip." A large production run implies minimum hardware cost, i.e., minimum chip count. Very large runs thus provide incentive for using a custom chip. In addition, a custom chip offers the advantage of a proprietary design, i.e., it is difficult to copy. If the performance of a single chip is not sufficient, the solution is to use a 2- or 3-chip microcomputer, depending on the memory size and I/O needed.

Let us again examine the chart in Figure 4.38. We see that in volumes of less than 100, two criteria should be considered:

1. If high performance is a requirement, then a 16- or 32-bit microprocessor should be used.

2. If minimizing cost is an important goal, then a 4-bit microprocessor should be considered. In the majority of cases, however, the domain of small to medium volumes is dominated by the standard 8-bit microprocessor that provides sufficient power at low cost.

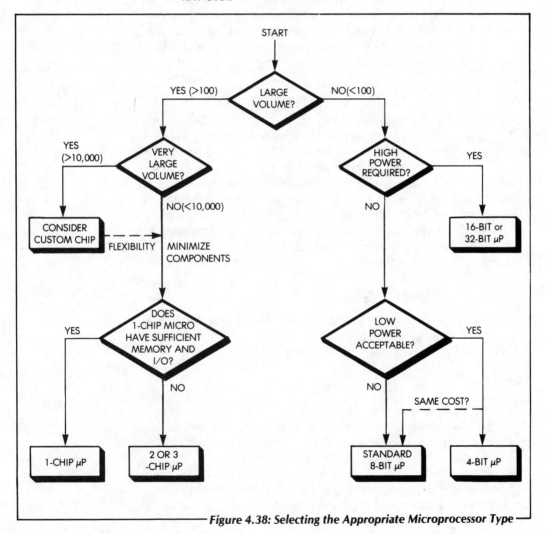

Figure 4.38: Selecting the Appropriate Microprocessor Type

CRITERION 3: AVAILABILITY

An essential criterion to consider when evaluating a *system* is whether or not it is available. A system requires not only a microprocessor, but also support chips, e.g., memory chips, I/O chips, interface chips, and sometimes device controllers. It is not reasonable to consider the implementation of a complete system on a single board and then to have to implement the required input/output interfaces on additional boards of logic. The complete system should be LSI and include as few extra components as possible. However, not all systems meet this qualification. Some manufacturers could not justify the cost of such a design effort and thus, did not introduce the support chips. Once the complete functions of the system are well defined, the selection process requires an evaluation of the microprocessors available as well as the required LSI components.

CRITERION 4: SOFTWARE

The difficulties of programming may represent a major obstacle in a first development effort on a new microprocessor. Assembling a microprocessor system is a relatively simple task. The real problems in the first implementation often lie in the programming phase. There are a variety of resources available to facilitate programming. These resources are described in Chapter 9. If a user needs a high-level language for a particular microprocessor in order to make programming easier, this requirement should be a significant selection criterion. On the other hand, if the user is capable of programming in assembly language, a good assembler and an editor are required.

CRITERION 5: DEVELOPMENT TOOLS

For most systems, a good *development system* is available that allows easy software development and easy testing of prototype boards. Development systems are described in Chapter 9.

CRITERION 6: SPECIAL CRITERIA

Special criteria may restrict the selection because of non-standard customer requirements. Thus, if low power consumption is essential, then a CMOS design is imperative. Other technologies, such as SOS and I²L, might qualify for consideration in the future.

For military designs, special environmental characteristics are often required. Most microprocessors today are available in an "M" version that will meet the extended temperature range, as well as some of the other military specifications. Many microprocessors are also MIL-qualified to the specifications of 38510 (JAN reliability program).

CRITERION 7: COST

Cost is often the most elusive—and deceptive—criterion because of errors of judgment by the user. The total cost of a product is the sum of many costs. The main expenses are:

— hardware cost

— software cost

— debugging/integration cost

— documentation cost

— maintenance cost

In the case of systems sold in very large quantities, the hardware cost is usually dominant and one of the main selection criteria (provided performance is sufficient). In most other cases, the cost of software is as important as, or more important than, the cost of hardware. Thus, the development of efficient support tools, including high-level languages and development systems, becomes a prime factor in minimizing cost.

Experience is required to evaluate the cost of software. For programming in assembler, the regularity of the internal architecture, the number of registers, and the convenience of the instructions are prime considerations. For programming in a high-level language, the efficiency and convenience of the compiler is the major consideration.

SUMMARY OF SELECTION CRITERIA

Selecting the proper microprocessor is generally an easy task once the requirements of a given application have been clearly identified. Large volumes often favor a single-chip microcomputer. Most other applications are served by 8-bit microprocessors. Low-cost applications may use a 4-bit microprocessor. Highly complex applications may require a 16-bit microprocessor.

SUMMARY

The various types of microprocessors have been presented, compared and evaluated in this chapter. The process of selecting the "right" microprocessor today is a much simpler task than it might at first seem. Whenever one criterion, such as the search for high speed, low cost, or low power consumption, is significantly more important than other factors, the choice is restricted and therefore simple. But when there is no dominant criterion the choice is, as usual, a compromise. The criteria presented in this chapter should help the buyer narrow down the list of microprocessors to be considered.

To understand and benefit completely from the guidelines given in this chapter, it is important that the reader understand both the hardware and software aspects of microprocessors. To achieve such an understanding, familiarity with the concepts of system interconnect, interfacing, software, and system development is necessary. (All of these topics are covered in later chapters.) It is, therefore, suggested that this chapter be read through a second time after the reader has studied the entire book. At that point, this chapter should contribute significantly to the clarification of important similarities and differences between the products available on the market today, which should make the task of choosing the "right" microprocessor easier.

EXERCISES

4-1: Draw a diagram showing all the possible functional elements of a microprocessor-based system. Then draw a line around those functional elements that are included in the following microprocessors:

a. 8080

b. Z80

c. 6800

d. 8086

e. Z8000

f. 8048

4-2: What are the advantages of 4-bit microprocessors?

4-3: What is a second source?

4-4: What is a bit-slice processor?

4-5: Is it valuable to have more registers inside a microprocessor chip? Are there any disadvantages to having many registers on board the chip?

4-6: What are the specific disadvantages of implementing the internal registers as an on-chip RAM memory?

4-7: Is it possible to implement a 16-bit microprocessor on a package with only 40 pins?

4-8: What are the important selection criteria when selecting a microprocessor?

4-9: Describe several cases where performance would be the main selection criterion.

4-10: Describe several cases where price would be the main selection criterion.

4-11: Assuming that a microprocessor-based system will be produced in quantities of more than 100,000, what are the essential selection criteria?

4-12: When is a microprocessor not a suitable choice for a control device?

4-13: What are the advantages of an 8-bit microprocessor compared to a 4-bit microprocessor? What are the disadvantages?

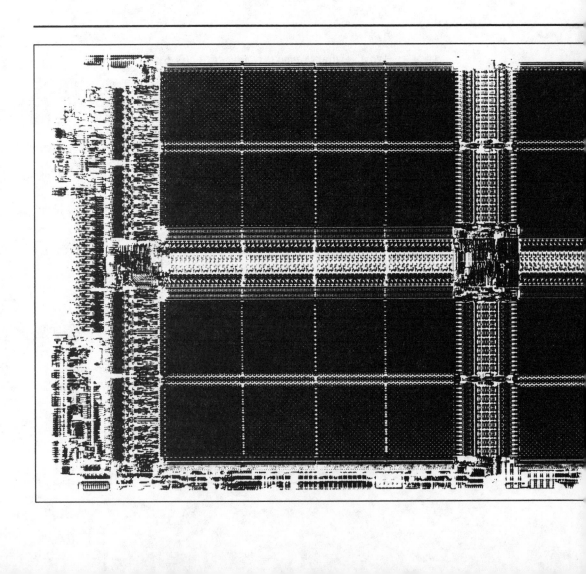

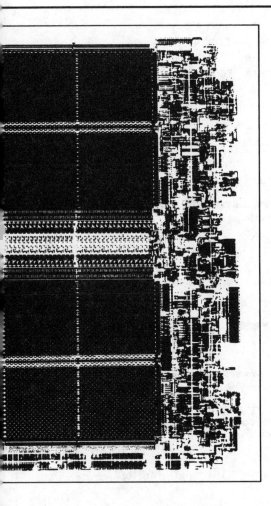

CHAPTER **5**

SYSTEM INTERCONNECT

OBJECTIVE

In the previous chapters we studied all the components necessary to assemble a microprocessor system. In this chapter we are going to interconnect them and build a complete system. We will first assemble a complete central processing unit, then connect memory to it, and finally, interface the input/output devices. At that point we will have assembled a "standard microcomputer system." We will then examine the actual interconnect of a number of real systems, based on various microprocessors.

Throughout this chapter, we will present design principles followed by actual application examples. We will see that a detailed knowledge of hardware is not needed to assemble a microcomputer. By the end of this chapter the complete interconnect of a system should be clear and unintimidating.

STANDARD SYSTEM ARCHITECTURE

The architecture of our "standard" microprocessor system is shown in Figure 5.1. We will see later on that "non-standard" systems normally vary only slightly from the system shown in this diagram; therefore, this diagram has wide applicability.

The system shown in Figure 5.1 is characterized by the three standard buses: the 8-bit bidirectional data bus, the 16-bit monodirectional address bus, and the control bus. All standard system components are connected to these three buses. Let us review these standard components.

Shown on the left side of the illustration is the CPU. It includes the microprocessor (MPU), plus the required clock and crystal. The CPU may also require bus drivers for the three buses, but these are not shown in this illustration. The other standard system components that will be connected to the buses are the memory (ROM and RAM) and the standard input/output interfaces: UART (for serial-parallel conversion)

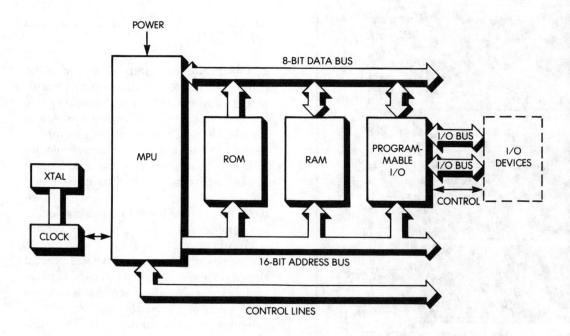

Figure 5.1: A Standard Microprocessor System

and PIO (for parallel interfaces). Other specialized components, such as peripheral controllers, may also be required for specific I/O devices, as well as scheduling chips, such as a PIC (to manage priorities), a DMA (for automatic block transfers) or a PIT (for precise interval timing). Naturally, a power supply is necessary to provide the required power levels to the system. All LSI components will be connected either directly to the buses or to the basic set of LSI components we have described.

We will now examine a standard system in detail and evaluate the various options available. In particular, we will study the common interconnection problems that are frequently encountered. We will first assemble a CPU, and then connect the address bus, the data bus, and the required control signals. When we have done this, we will have assembled a complete system. We will then study examples using actual microprocessors.

ASSEMBLING A CPU

A *central processing unit* includes an ALU (plus registers) and a control unit (CU). The earlier CPUs required, at the least, a microprocessor unit (an MPU), an external clock, a crystal, and other applicable "support circuits" (such as bus drivers and controllers). For processors developed after 1976, the clock circuit has been integrated within the MPU. However, the resulting architecture and three standard buses have remained unchanged.

As an example of a basic CPU, the actual interconnect of an 8080 CPU appears in Figure 5.2. The 8080 requires at least three LSI chips to implement a CPU: the 8080 microprocessor, the 8224 clock (plus the crystal), and the 8228 system controller. Recall that the 8080 was one of the first powerful 8-bit microprocessors to be introduced and that it requires three power supplies ($+5V$, $-5V$, $+12V$). In addition, its clock uses five pins. As a result, there is not a sufficient number of pins left to gate all the lines required by the control bus. Because the number of pins is limited to 40, control signals must be gated on pins already used for another purpose.

The 8080 multiplexes eight lines of the data bus for control purposes. During state T1 of every machine cycle, the data bus transmits status information on its pins. This creates the need for externally demultiplexing the data bus and for latching the control signals. These eight signals are shown in the table in Figure 5.3. Since eight pins were available on the data bus, the 8080 designers decided to transmit eight control signals. However, in practice, only five of these signals are used.

To facilitate this demultiplexing, a special component, the 8228, was introduced by Intel. The 8228 separates data from control information and also acts as a bus driver. The connection of the 8228 is shown in Figure 5.2. The 8228 provides five "clean" control signals for the external control bus: MEMR, MEMW (read and write for memory or I/O),

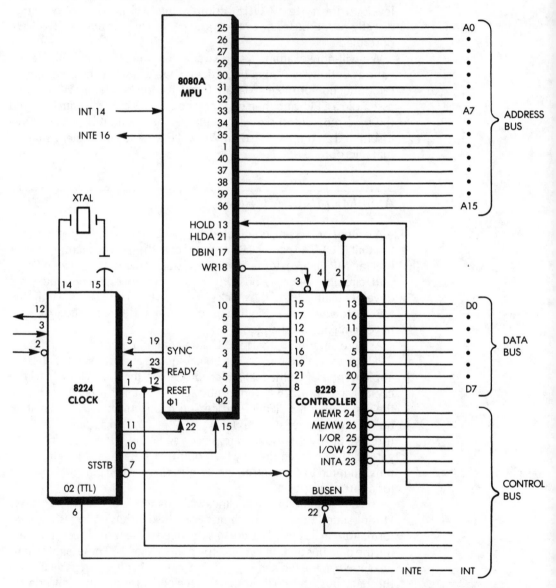

Figure 5.2: 8080 CPU Requires Three Chips

I/OR and I/OW (read and write for I/O devices), and INTA (interrupt acknowledge). An important feature of the 8228 is that it incorporates a data bus driver. The 8080 CPU has a "free" driver on its data bus because of the 8228 (other microprocessors such as the 6800 or the Z80 usually require a bus driver there). As a result, the chip count for an 8080 CPU is identical to that of other microprocessors.

Any time that a microprocessor multiplexes a bus, an external latch is required to demultiplex, i.e., separate, the signals. This latch is generally a separate component. Such a latch is shown in Figure 5.4. Pins AD0 to

DATA LINE	SIGNAL	MEANING
0	INTA	INTERRUPT ACKNOWLEDGE
1	$\overline{\text{WO}}$	WRITE OR OUTPUT/READ OR INPUT
2	STACK	SP IS ON ADDRESS BUS
3	HALT	HALT ACKNOWLEDGE
4	OUT	OUTPUT DEVICE ADDRESS ON AD-BUS
5	M1	MPU IN FETCH MODE
6	INP	INPUT DEVICE AD ON AD-BUS
7	MEMR	DATA BUS WILL HAVE MEMORY DATA

Figure 5.3: Eight Status Signals Appearing on the 8080 Data Bus

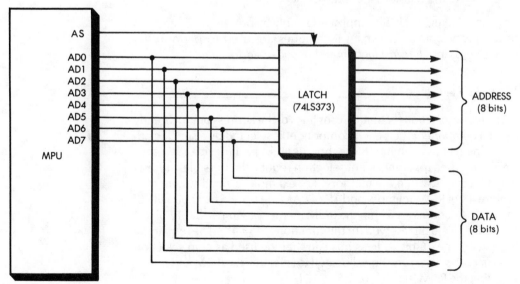

Figure 5.4: A Latch Demultiplexes a Shared Bus

AD7 on the MPU are multiplexed between two functions, such as address and data in the example.

An *address strobe* (AS) or *address enable* is used to tell the latch that the eight bits coming out of the MPU are an address to be latched. This approach can be used with any pin-multiplexed microprocessors. Often, special latches are provided by the manufacturer, as in the case of the 8080. Sometimes the latch is integrated with the memory or I/O chips. This latter approach is used by the 8085.

The role of the quartz *crystal* is to provide a precise time reference. In cases where accuracy is not essential, a simple oscillating circuit (resistor-capacitor, or RC) may be used.

We have now assembled the CPU, creating three buses. Let us connect each of the buses in turn. Connecting the data bus is straightforward. It is connected to the relevant pins of each device. Connecting the address bus is more complex. Let us study it.

CONNECTING THE ADDRESS BUS

The address bus is used to *select a register or a location* within a component. To accomplish this function, the address bus must:

1. select the device

2. select the register within the device.

Selecting the register is accomplished simply by presenting an address to the proper pins. Two main techniques are used to perform the device selection: *linear selection* and *decoded addressing*.

LINEAR SELECTION _____

The *linear selection* technique uses lines of the address bus to directly *select a component*, i.e., each component is selected by a specific address line. Let us examine this technique. It is used for small systems, since lines used for component selection reduce the possible addressing of locations within the memory. For example, a small system may require 4K of ROM memory and 1K of RAM memory. The capability of selecting 4K addresses within the ROM memory requires that 12 bits of the address field be reserved for this function ($2^{12} = 4K$). The remaining four bits of the 16-bit address bus can then be used as chip selection lines or *chip-selects*: one line allocated to selecting the ROM and one to selecting the RAM (see Figure 5.5).

Since the RAM dimensions in our example are smaller than the ROM dimensions, the 12 bits allocated to word selection also provide the necessary addressing within the RAM (when it is selected). Let us illustrate the connections so far by looking at examples.

Placing

0001000000000000

on the address bus has the following effects:

— the ROM is selected by the 1 in bit position 12

— address 0 within the ROM is selected.

Similarly, placing

0010000000000010

on the address bus has this effect:

— the RAM is selected by the 1 in bit position 13

— address 2 within the RAM is selected.

Thus, the 12-bit address field may be used for selecting an address within either ROM or RAM.

One potential problem is readily apparent. Placing

0011------------

on the address bus is illegal (a hyphen (-) can be either 0 or 1), since this would simultaneously select ROM and RAM.

Let us now go back to our 16-line bus, as shown in Figure 5.5. Only two bits, bits 14 and 15, are left for addressing I/O chips, such as I/O. The registers within the chips are selected by lines 0 to 11 (the address field). This example illustrates *pure linear addressing*, where a line selects a device. However, the addressing capability of the 16 lines can be enhanced at the cost of some hardware components by adding decoders.

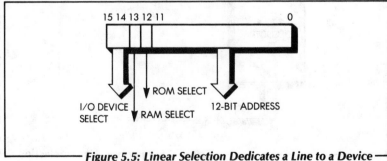

Figure 5.5: Linear Selection Dedicates a Line to a Device

For example, let us consider the selection strategy of Figure 5.6. This time, bits 13-14-15 are decoded as a group of three bits by an external 3-to-8 decoder chip and can be used to select up to eight devices. However, the bit combination 000 on lines 13-14-15 is used to specify memory addressing. A 1 in bit position 12 selects the RAM, while a 0 in bit position 12 selects the ROM.

One problem has been eliminated. The ROM and the RAM can no longer be addressed simultaneously. In addition, up to seven I/O devices can be selected rather than just two. The cost of this addition was an extra decoder chip. In the next section, we will push this approach even further and examine the decoded addressing technique, where decoders are used systematically.

Despite its limitation on the number of addressable devices, linear selection is the technique used most frequently for small systems because of its simplicity and economy. In systems that require only a modest amount of memory and a small number of I/O chips, address decoders are not needed. Bits 15, 14, 13 and others of the address field can be directly connected to the chip-select pin of a specific component. This minimizes the chip count and hence the cost.

However, should the system be expanded later, then rewiring and reprogramming would be needed in addition to the required address decoders. For this reason, medium-sized systems generally include a modest amount of decoding directly on the board from the beginning

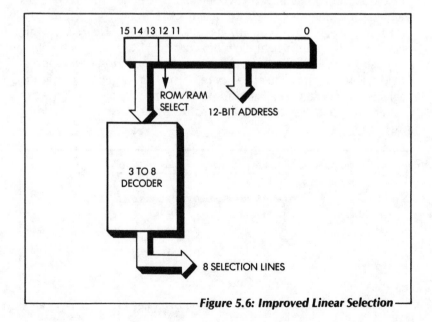

Figure 5.6: Improved Linear Selection

so that additional memory or other devices can be conveniently added at a later time. Conversely, the disadvantage of doing this is that initially the design uses a larger number of components than is necessary.

Another disadvantage of the linear selection technique is the fragmenting of the address space. The address space resulting from the addressing scheme of Figure 5.5 is shown in Figure 5.7. In theory, 16 bits may specify up to 64K locations.

In practice, using the linear addressing scheme of Figure 5.5, the ROM is addressed by placing a 0 in bit position 12. Thus, ROM addresses start at:

> 0000000000000000

and go to:

> 0000111111111111

i.e., in decimal, address 4K (exclusive). Similarly, RAM addresses start at address 4K. In our example, the RAM has only 1K bytes but could have up to 4K bytes on the chip.

Finally, the two I/O devices selected by lines 14 and 15 are selected at addresses 16K and 32K. The shaded areas in Figure 5.7 indicate unused areas of the address space.

Every time a dedicated address line is used for chip selection, the actual addressing space is divided by two. This results in discrete address

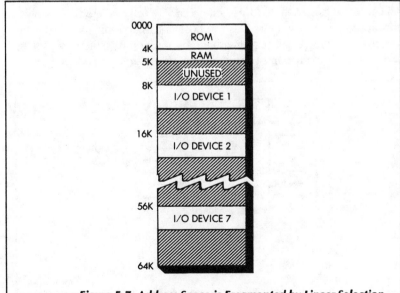

Figure 5.7: Address Space is Fragmented by Linear Selection

blocks within the addressing space. The waste of potential memory addressing space may be acceptable since we assumed that the system would require fewer than 2^{16} memory locations. However, there is an obstacle. These blocks are discrete, making programming more difficult because of the caution involved in addressing the various blocks. In our example, addresses 0 to 4K − 1 may not be used for addressing the ROM, and addresses 12K to 16K − 1 may not be used for addressing RAM. A 1 in bit positions 12 and 13 would select ROM at the same time as the RAM.

In summary, linear addressing is simple and economical but limited to small systems. This technique restricts possibilities for expansion at a later date without having to rewrite the programs. Let us now consider the alternative technique, that of decoded addressing.

DECODED ADDRESSING

With the *decoded addressing* technique, several lines are connected to a decoder, which then linearly selects one of many components. A group of n lines can be used to generate up to 2^n combinations of signals. Thus, n lines can be decoded into 2^n lines. Popular single-chip decoders are 3-to-8 decoders and 4-to-16 decoders. For example, the 8205, shown in Figure 5.8, is a 3-to-8 decoder. It accepts three inputs and selects one of eight (2^3) possible outputs.

More complex decoders or combinations of decoders may be used to decode any number of bits. In theory, if enough decoders are used, all 64K locations of the address space can be fully utilized. However, this approach clearly increases the cost of this system. Therefore the approach is traditionally used with large- or medium-sized computers. In the case of microcomputers, the cost of multiple decoders may be

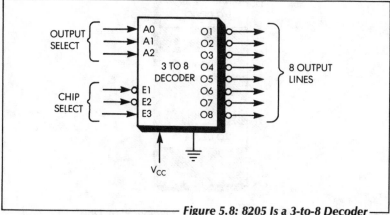

Figure 5.8: 8205 Is a 3-to-8 Decoder

objectionable, so that partial decoding is often used, thus reducing the number of components but leaving some gaps in the address space, i.e., "wasting" some addresses. An example of partial decoding is shown in Figure 5.9. We will study partial decoding in detail later.

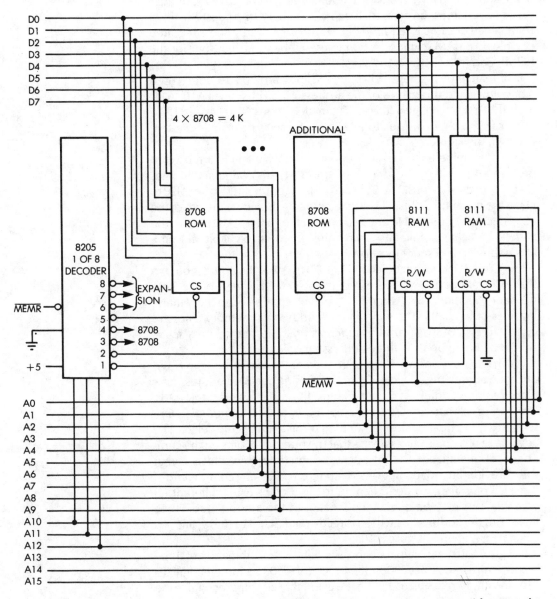

Figure 5.9: Interfacing Memory to an 8080 with a Decoder

In the example in Figure 5.9, an 8708 ROM and multiple 8111 RAMs are used. The 8708 ROM is a 1K × 8 ROM and the 8111 is a 128 × 4 RAM. Two 8111s are used in parallel to form a 128 × 8 RAM. Thus, the ROM requires ten address lines and the RAM requires seven. Lines A0 to A9 of the address bus will be used to address a ROM or RAM location.

This system must be expandable to 4K × 8 of ROM and 512 bytes of RAM. Since one line is required per 1K × 8 ROM and 1 line is required per 128 × 8 RAM, eight selection lines will be required: four for the ROMs, and four for the RAM pairs.

In order to provide these eight selection lines, an 8205 decoder is used that connects to three lines of the address bus. Thus, lines A10, A11, and A12 are used by the 8205 (see Figure 5.9). Lines A13, A14, and A15 remain free and can be used to select I/O devices. The resulting system is shown in Figure 5.9.

Let us examine each memory connection. Two 8111s are used to provide a 128 × 8 memory. The rightmost 8111 is connected to lines D4 to D7 of the data bus. The 8111 on the left is connected to lines D0 to D3 of the data bus. Both 8111s are selected by the same line out of the 8205 decoder. Both 8111s are also connected to lines A0 to A6 of the address bus, thus simultaneously reading or writing eight bits at a time at the specified memory location.

The 8708 ROM is connected to lines A0 to A9 of the address bus, so that 1K locations may be addressed. It is selected by line 5 of the 8205 decoder. Additional 8708s and 8111s can be connected to the remaining lines of the 8205. The way in which additional memory chips are connected is not irrelevant—as much as possible, the address space should be contiguous, with no addressing holes.

We have now shown how to implement linear addressing and decoded addressing. The disadvantage of using decoded addressing is that it requires additional decoder chips. In simple systems, this problem can be eliminated by using chips equipped with *multiple chip-selects* (CS, or chip-enables) rather than using a single chip-select. The advantage of a *single* chip-select is that the number of pins on the component is minimized. The advantage of *multiple* chip-selects is that they provide automatic address decoding *within the component*. If three CS pins are provided, then up to eight chips using different CS combinations may be directly connected to the address bus. Three lines from the address bus will be directly connected to these pins. An example is shown in Figure 5.10.

In Figure 5.10 each chip recognizes a different combination of three inputs. Chip 0 recognizes 000, chip 1 recognizes 001, chip 2 recognizes 010, and chip 7 recognizes 111. In the event that all chips recognize the same combination, inverters can be used on appropriate pins of the chips to recognize the eight combinations.

If several chips recognize a combination such as 010, three chips may still be selected without inverters by just exchanging address lines. For example, chip 6 will be enabled with the combination 110. This approach is equivalent to decoding the 110 combination inside the chip. Provided that all chips to be connected to the system decode a different combination, then the need for external decoders disappears. The disadvantage of this approach is that it requires a larger number of pins on the chips to be selected. This increases the cost per component. As an example, this approach has been used extensively in the 6800 system. Each device has three chip-selects or more, so that a medium-sized system can be built without decoders.

The multiple chip-select approach is particularly advantageous for small- and medium-sized systems. Many peripheral interface chips as well as memories are available with multiple chip-selects.

Let us now consider an important application example of the techniques we have described—that of connecting the memory.

CONNECTING THE MEMORY

We have assumed so far that memory chips are organized by four or eight bits. This is generally the case in small systems. However, in the case of large memories, many chips are required and economy is essential. The required economy is achieved by manufacturing a component that has as few pins as possible. Pins are required on a memory chip for three purposes: addressing, control, and data.

In the case of addressing, economy is achieved by using single chip-select pins. In the case of large memory chips, the number of address

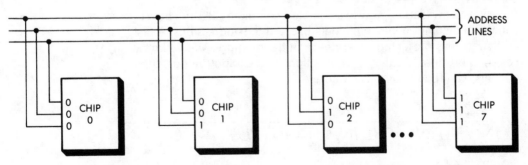

Figure 5.10: Using Multiple Chip Selects

pins may also be minimized by multiplexing the address pins. On large chips, the complete address may be sent in two successive strobes: RAS (row address-select) and CAS (column address-select).

Control pins are usually few in number and cannot be reduced further. Data pins, however, can be reduced in number, and usually are. The pin count can be reduced to a single pin. Thus, the lowest-cost general purpose RAM provides only one bit of data in and one bit of data out. This clearly minimizes the number of pins. To assemble an 8-bit system, eight memory chips must be connected *in parallel*. Naturally, they will all be selected by the same address. Each of their data input/outputs will be connected to one of the lines of the data bus.

Similarly, if a 4-bit memory such as an 8111 is used, then two chips must be connected in parallel, as in Figure 5.9. If an 8-bit memory is used, each data bit is connected to a data line. Clearly, the number of pins on the package is greater, resulting in a higher cost per bit, so that this approach is used only to minimize the number of chips in a small system.

We might ask why all standard (1-bit wide) memories provide a *separate data input* pin and a *separate output* pin since all microprocessors have a bidirectional data bus. The answer to this question is simply that such memories are *standard* components that are not designed solely for microprocessor applications. They are intended for general computer applications. Larger computers are not restricted to a bidirectional data bus and are normally equipped with separate data-in and data-out buses. General-purpose memories must therefore provide separate input and output connections. In the case of microprocessors the two pins are simply connected together (by using two quad transceivers, for example).

Other pins on the memory chip include the read and write signals and the power supply. Sometimes a synchronization signal is also required. Typical densities for standard memory chips are 4K bits to 64K bits for dynamic RAMs or ROMs.

We have now learned how to assemble a complete CPU and how to connect the components to the data bus and the address bus. A first case-study was presented on connecting the memory. We will now consider in more detail the connection of the input/output components required to complete a system.

CONNECTING THE INPUT/OUTPUT

The selection of input/output interface chips for addressing purposes is accomplished in the same way as for the memory. The selection of specific registers within the I/O chips is accomplished by using the address bus in the same way as it was used for addressing a memory location. For example, if a chip is equipped with eight internal registers, normally three pins are provided for internal register selection. These three signals will be internally decoded to select one of the eight registers.

Let us now examine typical connections. To provide an input or output facility, at the very least a latch is required. The simplest possible connection of a latch is illustrated in Figure 5.11.

The 8212 is selected by pins $\overline{DS1}$ and DS2. A strobe is sent via the address bus to these pins and selects the device. The contents of the data bus can then be output by the latch.

In the case of microprocessor systems, the PIO (rather than multiple latches) is the standard device for providing bidirectional facilities. The

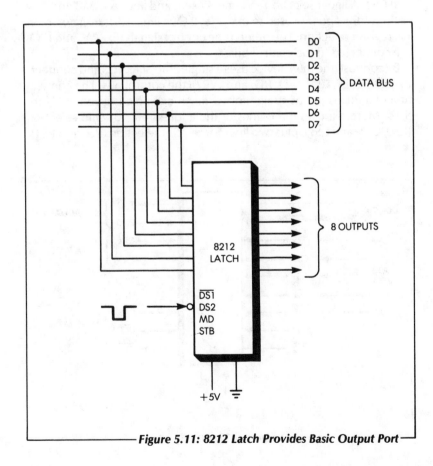

Figure 5.11: 8212 Latch Provides Basic Output Port

UART is used when serial communications are required. The connection of the PIO and the UART is straightforward. Both connect to the
data bus. The address bus provides chip-select and register-select as
previously explained. Finally, the connection to the control bus is
specific to the microprocessor used. However, the following rules
generally apply. The devices are connected to the read and write lines
in order to specify read or write operations within the registers. They
are also connected to RESET in order to zero the registers to the clock,
and to the interrupt lines if interrupts are used. Other connections may
be required by specific MPUs for synchronization purposes.

To illustrate the connections of two UARTs, the connections of an
ACIA (Motorola's UART) and an 8251 (Intel's UART) are shown in
Figures 5.12 and 5.13, respectively. Both connect to the data bus, the
address bus (for chip-select and register-select), and the control bus.

The Motorola device uses three chip-select pins, shown as CS0, CS1
and $\overline{CS2}$. A linear selection scheme is used, and lines A3, A13 and A14
of the address bus are used to that effect. One line, A0, is used for internal register selection. The other three control signals (E, R/W, and $\overline{IRQ}$)
are connected to the control bus.

By contrast, the Intel device uses a single chip-select CS and connects
to lines RESET, CLK, C/$\overline{D}$, $\overline{RD}$, and $\overline{WR}$ of the control bus. The connection of a PIO is just as straightforward. An example is given in Figure
5.14. Motorola uses three lines of the address bus for chip selection
(CS0, CS1, and $\overline{CS2}$), plus two lines for register selection (RS0 and RS1).

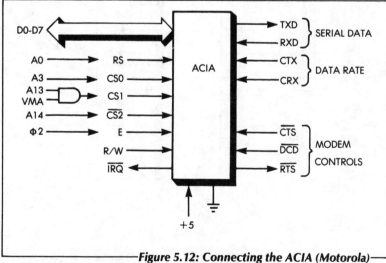

Figure 5.12: Connecting the ACIA (Motorola)

Five lines are connected to the control bus: E, R/W, $\overline{RESET}$, $\overline{IRQA}$, and $\overline{IRQB}$.

We have now connected all the basic components of a system separately. Let us examine the result.

STANDARD SYSTEM INTERCONNECT

The actual interconnect of our standard 8-bit microprocessor system appears in Figure 5.15. We will now discuss it.

The three standard buses are the data bus, the address bus, and the control bus. The data bus and the address bus are the same for nearly all standard 8-bit microprocessors. However, the signals of the control bus are specific to each microprocessor.

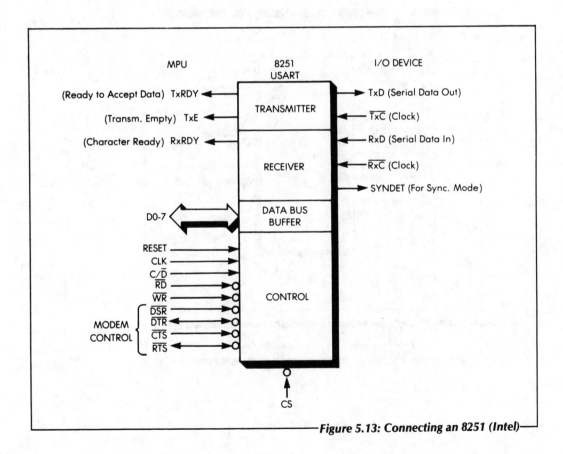

Figure 5.13: Connecting an 8251 (Intel)

Two types of devices are connected to the buses: the memory (here a ROM) and input/output (here a PIO). Other devices such as a RAM or a UART are connected in essentially the same way.

Let us now examine the detailed connections. Because this is a small system, linear selection is used. The chip-select (CS) pin appears at the top of the ROM and PIO chips. The ROM is selected by line A15 of the address bus and the PIO is selected by line A14 of the address bus. Let us assume that this is a 1K × 8 ROM.

The resulting connection is shown in Figure 5.15. Appearing on the left side of the ROM is the connection to the 8-bit data bus and on the right side is the connection to the address bus. 1K addresses require 10

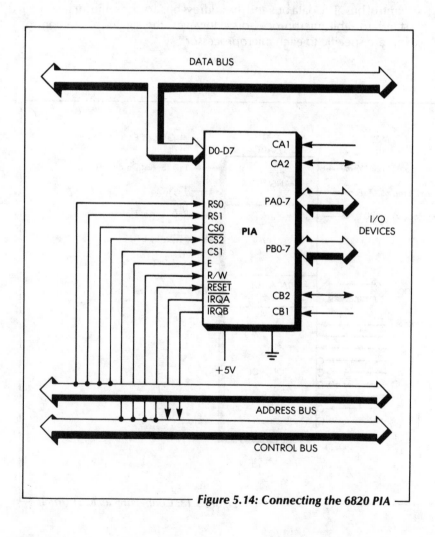

Figure 5.14: Connecting the 6820 PIA

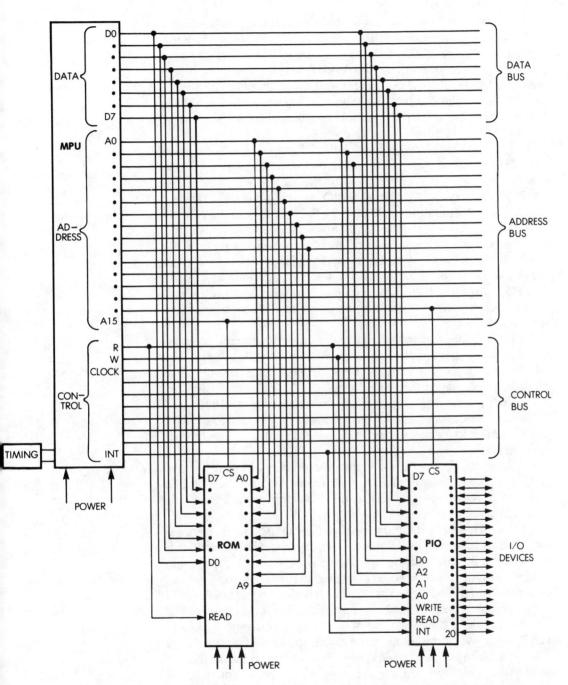

Figure 5.15: Standard System Interconnect

bits, and connections are established to lines A0 through A9 of the address bus. In addition, the ROM requires a synchronization signal, which could be the READ (R) line on the control bus. (The ROM does not require a connection to the WRITE line as this is read-only memory.) The power connections of the ROM are shown at the bottom of the ROM. If the ROM had been only four bits wide, we would have simply connected two of these components in parallel, using the same line A15 to select both chips.

The PIO is selected by A14, gated to the CS input. Let us assume that the PIO is equipped with no more than eight internal registers. These registers are selected by A0, A1, and A2 of the address bus, and the connections appear on the left side of the PIO. An apparent conflict arises if A0, A1, and A2 are connected to both the PIO and the ROM. Will both chips then be enabled at the same time? The answer should be obvious. The three bits A0, A1 and A2 may be enabled for both the PIO and the ROM; however, the ROM will be selected only when A15 equals 1, and the PIO will be selected only when A14 equals 1. As long as A15 and A14 are not on simultaneously, no conflict will occur. (It is the programmer's responsibility to make sure that A14 and A15 are not enabled simultaneously.)

The PIO is connected to the eight lines of the data bus and provides twenty input/output lines that appear on its right side. (In addition, the PIO is connected to the READ and WRITE lines of the control bus so that its registers may be read or written.) The PIO is also normally connected to the interrupt line and sometimes to special control lines used by specific microprocessors. A RAM requires a connection to a WRITE line in addition to the connection to the READ line. The rest of the connections are essentially the same.

The basic interconnect of this system should now be clear. The diagram in Figure 5.15 demonstrates how simple the interconnect of a standard microprocessor system can be. The diagram applies to nearly all standard microprocessors.

There are a few basic differences between systems, however. For example, in the case of a 16-bit microprocessor, the data bus is 16 bits wide. The address bus may be 15 or 20 bits wide. However, this would not change any of the techniques that have been presented so far. Also, decoders may be used rather than the linear addressing technique used in this diagram. Finally, every microprocessor has a different control bus. For example, the 8080 control bus has two separate READ and WRITE lines, while the 6800 uses a single READ/WRITE line plus a memory address validation line (VMA). Both microprocessors require two control lines. However, the use of these lines is different for each.

In summary, despite minor differences at the level of the control signals, this diagram applies to nearly all standard microprocessors and illustrates the interconnection techniques that have been presented in this chapter.

Although this diagram applies only to a standard system, we will see now that the understanding gained so far can be applied to any type of microprocessor system. We will therefore examine the other possible types of systems: a multiplexed system and a 2-chip system.

A MULTIPLEXED BUS SYSTEM

We will study a multiplexed bus system by examining a real microprocessor, the 8085. The interconnect of an 8085 is presented in Figure 5.16. The 8085 incorporates on a single chip the 8080, the 8224 clock, and the 8228 system controller.

The 8085 is compatible with the 8080 instruction set. The 8085 provides many control signals but runs short of pins. Unlike the 8080, the control bus is no longer multiplexed. This time, half of the address bus is multiplexed on the data bus. The address bus of the 8085 has only eight lines, which are used to gate out A8 through A15. The eight bits of the lower part of the address are gated out D0 through D7. A special line ALE (address latch enable) indicates that an *address* rather than *data* is being transmitted on the multiplexed data bus. The data bus must be externally demultiplexed and a latch must be provided. The same approach is used by 16-bit microprocessors that use only 40 pins.

The real value of the 8085 lies in the availability of two special components: the 8155 (RAM plus I/O) and the 8355 (ROM plus I/O). Because these components simultaneously provide memory, I/O, and demultiplexing of the data bus, a complete system can be assembled with only three chips. This makes the 8085 an ideal substitute for the 8080 in small systems. It does not, however, replace the 8080 in larger systems.

The 8155 incorporates a 256 × 8 RAM on a single chip and also supplies a PIO (equivalent to three external ports), two 8-bit ports (Ports A and B) for which every line can be programmed independently, and a 6-bit port (Port C) normally utilized for handshaking. In addition, it includes an interval timer. (The signals "timer in" and "timer out" are shown in Figure 5.16.)

The 8355 provides 2K × 8 ROM plus I/O. Alternatively, the 8755 provides EPROM plus I/O. Both also provide two 8-bit input/output ports.

Let us now go back to the illustration and examine the actual interconnect of the system. The 8085 is equipped with five interrupt lines,

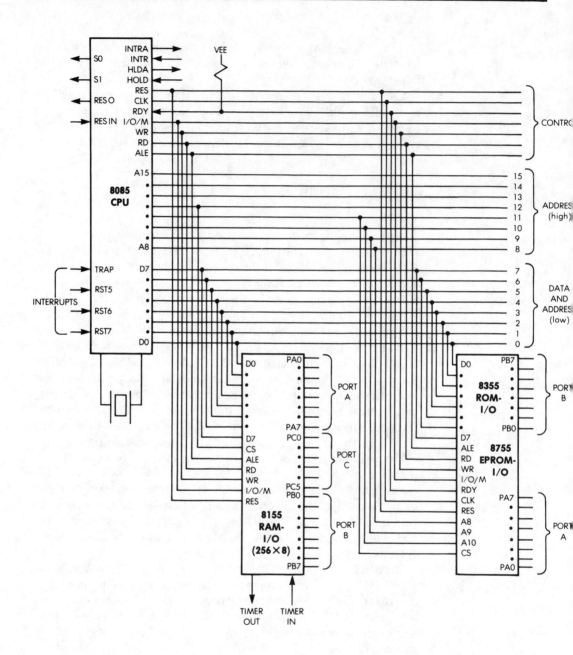

Figure 5.16: 8085 Interconnect

four of which appear on the left side of the illustration (TRAP, RST5, RST6, RST7), and one on the right (INTR). Two pins are used by the external crystal and two pins are allocated to the power supply. Appearing on the right side of the illustration are the essential lines of the control bus, as well as the address and data buses.

Let us examine in detail the connection of the 8155 chip (RAM plus I/O) to the buses. Moving from top to bottom, we see that the eight lines of the data bus are connected to pins D0 to D7 and that a linear selection is used for the chip select. A12 of the address bus selects the 8155. Continuing from top to bottom, the signal ALE (address latch enable), as well as the signals RD (READ), WR (WRITE), I/O/M (used to select between the I/O and memory section of the component), and, finally, the reset signal RES (used to set the contents of the internal registers to 0), are derived from the control bus. On the right side of the component we find the three buses that connect to external I/O devices. On the bottom we find the two lines of the internal timer. These lines are used to measure time elapsed in and out.

Looking carefully at the illustration we see that there does not seem to be a connection to the address bus. Is there an error in the diagram? Although it is not immediately obvious when looking at the illustration, this device is connected to the address bus. It is connected to D0 through D7, which are also bits A0 through A7 of the address bus. The next question then is: how does the device know when the bits presented on D0 through D7 represent an address? It knows through ALE. Whenever ALE is true, the eight bits on the data bus are interpreted as an address and are latched internally. Whenever ALE is not true, these bits are interpreted as data. Since this component includes only 256 words of RAM, eight bits are sufficient to select any RAM location within the device.

It is also possible to select I/O registers instead of memory within the device by using the I/O/M signal. I/O specifies an access to an I/O port, and M specifies an access to the memory portion of the device. READ or WRITE specify the required operation in the register or in the memory.

The connection to the 8355 (ROM plus I/O) is essentially similar. The 8355 includes 2K bytes (plus I/O ports), requiring 11 address bits. Accordingly, it is also connected to A8, A9, and A10 of the address bus. (The lower eight bits are supplied by the data bus.) The chip-select (CS) for the component is supplied by line A11 of the address bus. Line A11 is specifically used in order to have a *continuous* address space. Finally, the other control signals ALE, RD, WR, I/O/M, RDY (ready, a synchronization signal), CLK (clock), and RES, are connected to the component.

Note that lines A13, A14, and A15 of the address bus have not been used on this system and could be used to connect additional chips.

The internal organization of the 8155 is shown in Figure 5.17 and the organization of an 8755 is shown in Figure 5.18.

Now that we are familiar with the interconnect of a system using a multiplexed bus, let us consider the last possibility: a 2-chip system.

CONNECTING MINIMAL SYSTEMS

The task of connecting a 2-chip microcomputer is a simpler task than connecting the 3-chip system (presented for the 8085). As an example, the connection of a Rockwell PPS-4/2 system appears in Figure 5.19. Buses for the two chips are connected directly.

A final alternative exists when expanding the capabilities of the 1-chip microcomputer—that of adding external memory and I/O. This involves little more than connecting additional chips to the buses. As an example, Figure 5.20 shows the connection of an additional memory-plus-I/O chip to an 8048.

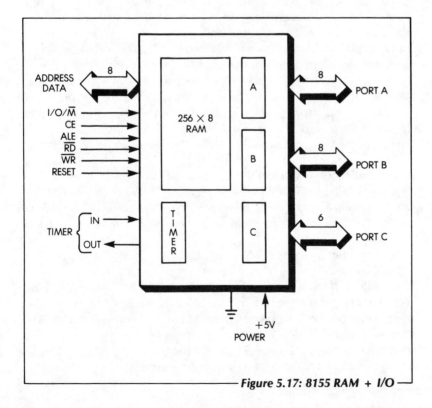

Figure 5.17: 8155 RAM + I/O

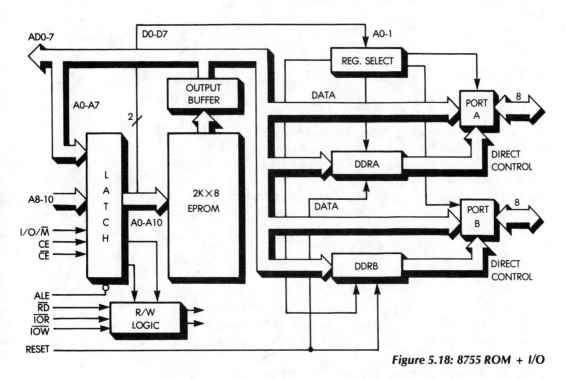

Figure 5.18: 8755 ROM + I/O

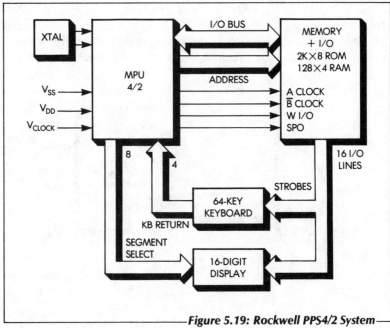

Figure 5.19: Rockwell PPS4/2 System

We have just learned how to connect a basic system. We will now connect peripherals to it.

CONNECTING OTHER DEVICES

Depending on the input/output scheduling philosophy implemented in the system (polling, interrupts, or DMA), it may be necessary to connect additional scheduling chips. The connection of a PIC is described in Chapter 3, as well as the connection of the DMAC. As another example, the complete connection of a set of AMD 9517 DMACs to an 8080 system appears in Figure 5.21.

In order to connect peripherals, we will add additional components such as peripheral controllers to the standard ones previously described. This subject will be discussed in Chapter 7.

SUMMARY

Interconnecting the various elements of a microprocessor system can be a simple task. Now, with the availability of LSI components that connect directly to the three system buses, all connections are simple and standardized. Assembling a complete system should not pose significant problems. However, because all chips are now in LSI, it is not possible to change the architecture of a system based on a microprocessor. Given a microprocessor and its support chips, there are virtually no variations in the logical system architecture short of multi-microprocessor systems. Common techniques apply to all systems.

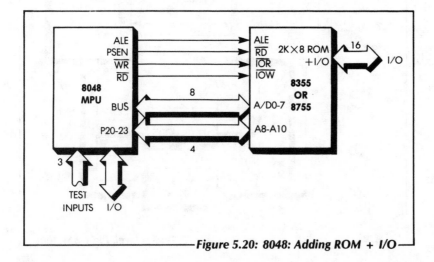

Figure 5.20: 8048: Adding ROM + I/O

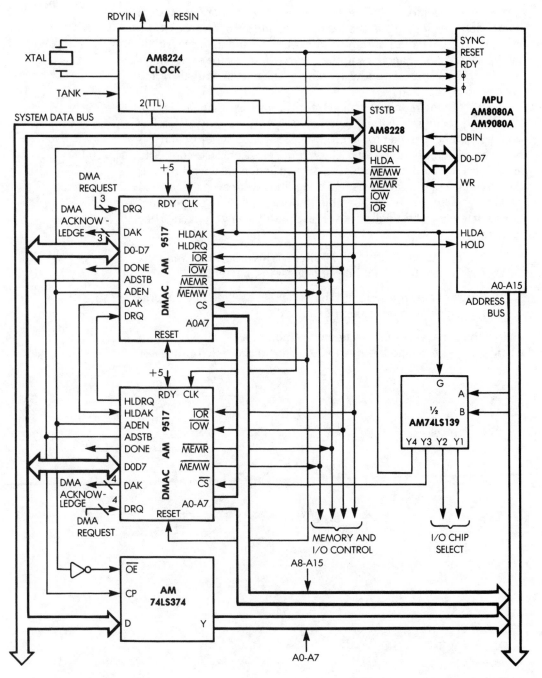

Figure 5.21: Connecting a DMAC

We have presented all the techniques required to connect system components to the data bus, the address bus, and the control bus. Connections to the data bus and the address bus are independent of the microprocessor. Connections to the control bus vary for each microprocessor, and an exact understanding of the specific signals of the control bus is required.

Overall, the interconnect of a system is a process that can be implemented rapidly. Previous experience is not necessary. This has opened up a new market for microprocessor-based systems, and it is now possible for nonspecialists without prior electronic experience to assemble a standard microprocessor system and make it work. This is the way many of the early personal computers were born.

Once a system has been assembled, there are only two significant tasks that remain. These will be covered in the following chapters. They include:

1. The actual interfacing of I/O devices. (This procedure is addressed for standard input/output devices in Chapter 7.)

2. Programming the system. (The principles and methods of programming are presented in Chapter 8.)

Now that a basic system has been assembled, we shall proceed to Chapter 6 and examine the possible applications of microprocessor systems.

EXERCISES

5-1: What is the function of the 8228 system controller in an 8080 system?

5-2: Why is the data bus multiplexed by the 8080?

5-3: Why does the 8228 receive eight control signals via the 8080 data bus, as well as five additional ones, and then only gate out five control signals?

5-4: What is the function of the crystal in a system? Is it indispensable? Is there an alternative?

5-5: Describe linear selection.

5-6: Describe decoded addressing.

5-7: Is linear selection also used with decoded addressing?

5-8: In what kinds of systems is linear addressing used? What are its advantages and disadvantages?

5-9: Using the example in Figure 5.6, draw an interconnection diagram of a system that has 16K of ROM memory and 128 bits of RAM.

5-10: Why do standard computer memories provide a separate data input pin as well as a separate output pin, even though all microprocessors have a bidirectional data bus?

5-11: Why do some I/O and memory chips have several chip-select inputs?

5-12: How are the internal registers inside an I/O chip addressed by the program?

5-13: Explain the purpose of each connection in Figure 5.15 (showing a standard system interconnect). Expand the diagram by connecting a 4K by 8 RAM and a UART of your choice.

5-14: Explain the function of each line connected to the 8155 and to the 8355 in Figure 5.16 (showing the interconnect of an 8085 system).

5-15: Why does the 8085 multiplex the address on its data bus?

5-16: If an 8085 must be connected to standard memory chips, what kind of interface is required?

5-17: Why is the WR (write) signal connected to an 8355 ROM, even though the 8355 is a read-only memory?

5-18: Draw the address space diagram for the systems shown in Figures 5.15 and 5.16.

5-19: List the names and functions of common signals that are used in the control bus of most microprocessors.

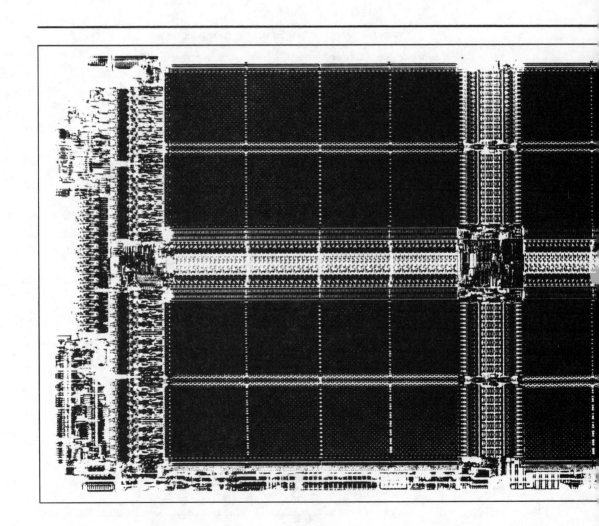

MICROPROCESSOR APPLICATIONS

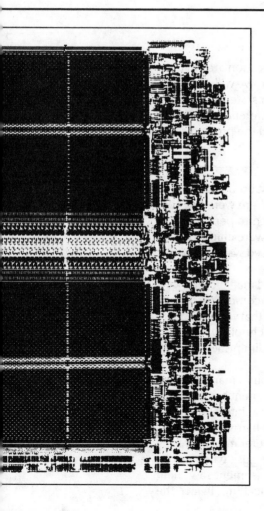

OBJECTIVE

This chapter presents typical application examples for microprocessor systems. The functions performed in each application are different; yet, as we will see, the overall architecture of the microprocessor system is the same. The requirements specific to each application are met by adding hardware and software components. The additional chips are simply connected to the buses. The programs specific to each application are developed to reside in ROM or RAM.

In this chapter we will build progressively more complex applications by connecting additional components to a standard microprocessor system. We will show that designing a microprocessor application is generally a simple task, unless the application imposes unusual demands. A complete system can be assembled easily with a small number of standard LSI components.

Once a microprocessor system has been assembled, two significant tasks remain: interfacing and programming. These techniques are addressed in the next two chapters.

APPLICATION AREAS

Because the elements of a microprocessor system can be assembled easily, the development of a new application is only limited by the skill and imagination of the designer. Cost or complexity are no longer relevant factors. Thus, no list of applications will ever be exhaustive.

In this chapter we will distinguish four essential application areas that correspond to specific microprocessor architectures. These include:

1.   computer systems

2.   industrial systems

3.   consumer devices

4.   specialized applications.

We will examine the main features of each application area in turn. Each area introduces specific constraints. However, we will see that in the end, the overall organization of microprocessor systems, as well as the techniques used, remain the same. The main differences are the interfaces required, the number of components, and the programs.

COMPUTER SYSTEMS

When microprocessors appeared, they were first used in computer systems for a negative reason. In the early 1970s there were few support chips, and microprocessors were programmed to perform functions that are now done by a wide variety of hardware chips. For this reason, assembling a complete microprocessor-based system required both hardware and software expertise.

Only five years later, in 1976, companies realized that microprocessors could be used to build inexpensive personal computers. It then took several more years to manufacture computers that were adequate for business and professional purposes. Yet, the technology had been there all along. (Naturally, with time, costs have diminished, and integrated circuits have been improved.)

Many of the early microprocessor applications found markets by accident rather than by design. New product development has generally been a direct result of the dissemination of technical information.

In the early 1970s, the necessary combination of hardware and software expertise was rarely found outside the computer manufacturing industry. This was not perceived as a problem, because when microprocessors were introduced, the computer establishment saw them only as low-cost processors for simple control applications. In fact, the first 8-bit microprocessor, the Intel 8008, was designed for direct control of a CRT display (recall the contracts between Datapoint, Texas Instruments and Intel).

Microprocessors are now used for controlling virtually every computer peripheral that does not require bipolar speeds. Initially, such applications were limited by the relatively low speed of early microprocessors. But now, with the faster microprocessors coupled with specialized peripheral controller chips, such as CRT and floppy disk controllers (CRTC and FDC), it is possible to control fast devices such as CRTs and disks. This can be done because the fast transfer rate required by high speed peripherals can be achieved by special device controllers and DMACs. Of course, there are still cases where microprocessors are not fast enough. For example, controlling fast disks, such as hard disks, still requires bipolar speeds. However, these are notable exceptions. Microprocessors are generally used to control slower devices such as paper-tape readers, paper-tape punches, printers, keyboards, relays, and analog-to-digital converters.

Also, the implementation philosophy of computer systems has changed. In all of the medium- to low-cost systems (systems equivalent to the former minicomputers), the processing unit (the microprocessor) is now available at a cost of only a few dollars. It has become one of the least expensive components of the system. For this reason, the old philosophy of computer design—to *share* the most expensive resource in the system, i.e., the CPU—would no longer be valid in small- to medium-sized systems. It would be a basic design error in these systems to share (i.e., to multiplex) the processor's time. (This practice, however, is still relevant in very large systems where the CPU represents a major cost.) Thus, the complex "executive" and other time-sharing operating systems for small computers have almost disappeared. (An essential goal of the "executives" was to provide timesharing: the processor time was shared among a number of tasks that were being executed in parallel.)

As a general rule, timesharing does not make sense anymore. (One notable exception is when a large data base must be shared.) The least expensive, least complex, and most efficient solution now is to dedicate a processor to each process. Provided that the processor does not require unusual resources or a large amount of memory, it may even be possible to implement the entire system on a single-chip microcomputer at a cost of only a few dollars.

With microprocessors, we have now entered the era of *distributed systems*. In distributed systems, intercommunication between a number of processors is reduced to a minimum because they do not interact in real time but exchange data words or blocks. Each processor is then a direct process controller that completely controls a process. Such a network may involve multiple microprocessors. Traditionally, a multiprocessor system is one in which several processors interact with each other in real time for control purposes. Most systems involving networks of microprocessors do not interact so closely and therefore do not qualify as "multimicroprocessor systems."

With the continuing progress of LSI technology, most microprocessor systems actually use multiple processors distributed over several chips. Processors can often be found in the peripheral chips of the system, i.e., the PIO, the UART, or other system chips. This makes the programming task more difficult than with traditional systems; however, it does result in standardized systems. All of the traditional chips that were merely interface devices in the past are now fully programmable. Programmed instructions are sent to these devices by the microprocessor. These processors, residing in peripheral devices, should be considered as *slaves*. Let us consider such a network of processors.

Multimicroprocessors

Practically and conceptually it is an easy task to interconnect a number of microprocessors into one network or *multimicroprocessor* system. In cases where there is one main processor and a number of slave microprocessors, the system is actually a "distributed system" rather than a multimicroprocessor system. A true multimicroprocessor system is a system in which any number of processors may assume the role of *master*. Thus, a complex interconnect and a specialized operating system are required to synchronize the operation of the entire system. In any cost-conscious implementation this approach is generally unreasonable, as the cost of developing a complex operating system that is capable of synchronizing a number of processors operating simultaneously is overwhelming. In addition, it implies a high level of unreliability for the system as it can never be proven that the system will operate correctly under all circumstances. Thus, the cost and risk involved in developing such complex software is generally unreasonable when compared to the cost of the hardware involved. The correct implementation philosophy, then, is to use *dedicated processors* on site whenever necessary and to synchronize their operation as loosely as possible to simplify overall system operation. This results in simplicity, higher reliability, and lower cost.

There are exceptions to this claim. For the reasons just indicated, it is indeed usually unreasonable to consider using multimicroprocessor systems involving monolithic microprocessors. However, it is perfectly reasonable and highly desirable to consider using multiprocessor implementations with bit-slice devices. Bit-slice devices were created specifically for easy operation when used in parallel. It is possible to design a number of novel computer architectures that use slices operating simultaneously on various instruction streams. In fact, this is the correct design philosophy to use when it is necessary to improve speed in any stream-processing device. (This topic is beyond the scope of this book and it will not be addressed further here.)

There is one more exception to the above claim. It involves any system that is replicated enough times to distribute the cost of software over a large number of units. In view of the complexity of a multimicroprocessor system, such a large-scale distribution is not frequent.

Multimicroprocessor systems are used in special cases, such as military and avionic applications, where cost is no obstacle and microminiaturization is essential. Typical communication mechanisms for multimicroprocessors are presented at the end of this chapter.

Personal Computers

Recall that microprocessors were first used in computer-related applications. They were used to implement controller boards for printers, tape drives, plotters, and keyboards. This was due to the availability of hardware and software talent that was required in the early days.

Since then, a major new application of microprocessors has emerged in the computer field: personal computers. Personal computers were first introduced in the late 1970s as kits. However, they quickly became full-blown computer systems. Most popular designs now use the Z80 or the 6502 microprocessors. Typically, a personal computer is a small general-purpose computer, equipped with a minimal amount of ROM (say 1K) and 4K to 63K of RAM memory, and one or two serial ports, for communication with a printer or a CRT terminal.

Low cost personal computers incorporate a BASIC interpreter in ROM, while some business computers incorporate a CP/M operating system in ROM. Most personal and business computers are single-board microcomputers with a motherboard that can receive additional memory, I/O or interface boards. In the case of the 8080, 8085 and Z80-based systems, the motherboard connectors often conform to the S-100 bus standard.

These systems illustrate again how a standard hardware design may be used for a variety of applications by merely using different software or adding a few standardized hardware modules.

INDUSTRIAL SYSTEMS

Industrial microprocessor applications generally replace minicomputers or complex hardwired logic with low-cost microprocessors. The main impact of microprocessors in the industrial world has been to provide a number of new functions that make process control simpler, more powerful and more "intelligent" without increasing costs. At times, microprocessors have even reduced costs.

Microprocessors have also introduced software, with its many advantages, into the hardware world, thus making it possible to use standardized products over a much longer period of time. This, in turn, has resulted in significantly lower costs when enough systems are produced. Specific case studies are presented later in this chapter.

Industrial microprocessor applications are characterized by two essential technical features. First, most industrial applications require processors with analog inputs and outputs. The resulting processor system is the equivalent of a traditional analog controller with a number of *control loops*. (A control loop is simply the implementation of an algorithm (a technique) that will regulate an output as a function of one or more inputs. The term "control loop" stems from the graphic representation of the control technique that shows a loop, as illustrated in Figure 6.1.)

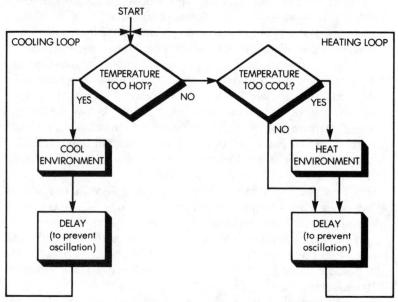

Figure 6.1: A Temperature Control Loop

Second, most industrial applications are characterized by costly sensors and control mechanisms. The cost of the sensors required for input and the cost of the control devices required for output are typically much higher than the cost of a standard microprocessor system.

In view of the overall cost of the process control facility, the low cost of the microprocessor system itself is therefore generally not a significant advantage by itself. The essential advantage of a microprocessor system is the use of software in cases where complex and expensive hardware was previously required. The resulting advantages of software are those of *programmed logic*.

Programming permits the implementation of functions of unlimited complexity that could not be implemented previously with hard-wired logic. Changes are easy to make and algorithms can be improved or even replaced with few or no hardware changes. These advantages are documented in Chapter 8. Microprocessors are now used to control processes and flows, whether discrete or continuous, (from traffic control to the distribution of water through pipelines to telecommunications), and to regulate virtually any control process.

A typical process control application might be the regulation of a fermentation reactor. The microprocessor system is equipped with sensors for temperature, pressure, and other process parameters, such as pH, speed of the fluid, and measurements of input fluids or gases. Using the information supplied by the sensors, the system monitors the reactor and regulates the control parameters, which will optimize the reaction. The system will control, for example, temperature, pressure, and the flows of liquids and gases, resulting in optimum performance. In addition, the program will improve reliability by detecting or correcting malfunctions. The system's data collection capability may result in a later improvement of the control strategy.

Whenever a microprocessor is used for process control, a resulting advantage is the availability of the processor for functions not previously provided. For example, it becomes a simple matter to add a bulk memory device such as a cassette recorder or a floppy disk to the system, thus enabling it to log data continuously. During idle times or at regular intervals, the microprocessor can then not only monitor the state of the system but also record for future reference all of the parameters in its bulk memory. It can also use this historical information to improve upon the performance of the process. This process is called *dynamic optimization*, whereby the system looks up previous values of the control parameters that were found to be successful in improving the operation of the system and attempts to improve the operation even further by trying out new alternatives.

Industrial applications are characterized by specific software techniques that are now being used universally. We will explain here the techniques of status feedback (including soft fail), reasonableness testing, confidence weighing and programmed filtering. Later we will discuss analog to digital conversion.

Status Feedback

For reliable operation every industrial control system must be equipped with a *status feedback*. A microprocessor must have the means to verify the correct operation of any output device that it controls. This concept is illustrated in Figure 6.2. For example, whenever an order is given to the output device, such as *"close relay A,"* the microprocessor should verify that relay A has indeed been closed. Every control device should be monitored in this manner and must provide status information. The status will be gated back to the microprocessor, which will verify it. This is known as the *status-feedback loop*.

As an example, let us follow the sequence of events that might result from the order, *"close relay A."* A specified number of milliseconds after giving this order, the microprocessor reads the status of relay A. If the status bit is 1 the microprocessor determines that the relay has been closed correctly. If the status is not 1, this indicates a malfunction. When this is the case, the microprocessor repeats the order a second or

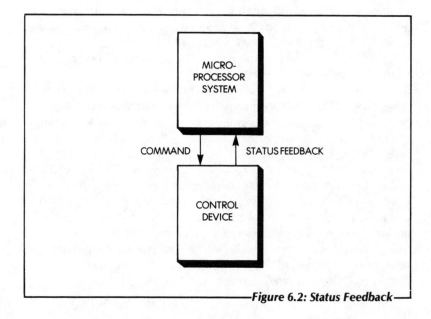

Figure 6.2: Status Feedback

third time. If the relay then closes, status information tells the micro-processor that the order has been executed. Typically, the "malfunc-tion" is then ignored as "noise," and execution proceeds normally. If this "noise" ever occurs repeatedly, the microprocessor sounds an alarm, requesting preventive maintenance. If the relay should refuse to close at all, after several attempts, a number of alternatives might be considered.

These alternatives are called *soft-fail techniques*. Soft-fail techniques involve a progressive degradation of the system rather than a complete shut-down whenever one of the system components fails. Unfortu-nately it is usually difficult to remedy the failure of *output* control devices as they are expensive and usually not easily duplicated. Ideally the microprocessor should activate an alternate control device. At worst it would execute a backup algorithm, ignore the control device and sound an external alarm.

A similar monitoring must also be performed on input devices (the sensors). This technique, however, is different. It uses *reasonableness* testing.

Reasonableness Testing

Whenever the microprocessor reads values of input sensors, it should determine whether or not they are reasonable. This is accom-plished by *reasonableness testing*. Normally a *bracket* of reasonable values can be defined for every input parameter at any given time (see Figure 6.3). For example, a system controlling traffic at an intersection will sense incoming cars through the use of *loop detectors*. It will use the information provided by two consecutive detectors to compute the speed of a vehicle. A speed of 200 miles per hour in an urban environ-ment is deemed "unreasonable" and would indicate a failure of the detector (the input mechanism). Similarly, in a process controller measuring an external temperature, unreasonable temperature levels can be detected by comparing the actual measurement to a predefined temperature bracket: [Temp min, Temp max].

The usual procedure is the following. A value is first read, then it is compared to an acceptable minimum and an acceptable maximum (the reasonableness bracket). Whenever there is a single occurrence of an "unreasonable" input value, this value is simply considered as "noise" and ignored. This simple technique performs, in fact, a *filtering* of spurious input values.

Whenever there is a repeated failure, this indicates a malfunction of the input device. A diagnosis will be generated and the device may have to be "disconnected" from the system. (The device itself does not need to be physically disconnected from the system; rather, its measurements are merely ignored.) It is interesting to note that the device can be automatically "reconnected" to the system once its input becomes reasonable again. There might be a *temporary* malfunction, so the microprocessor will continue to monitor the input device. When the input device is once again giving reasonable indications for a suitable period of time, it will be deemed "reasonable" again, and it will automatically reconnect to the system. Recall that with a microprocessor system it is not necessary to connect and disconnect this input device physically to or from the hardware of the system. This is normally accomplished internally by *software*. In order to improve the accuracy of measurements and to improve reliability, multiple sensors are often used. For example, five temperature sensors may be used at various points inside an oven. In this case, a weighing technique is used.

Confidence Weighing

With the *confidence-weighing* technique, every sensor is assigned a confidence ratio or weight. A measurement is obtained from several in-

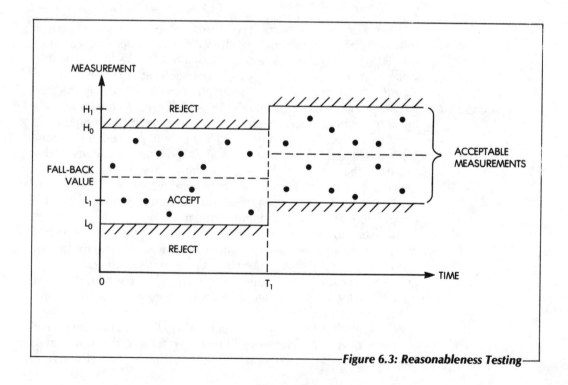

Figure 6.3: Reasonableness Testing

put sensors by multiplying the input value of each by the weight, and computing the final averaged input value. The formula is:

$$M = \frac{M_1W_1 + M_2W_2 + \ldots + M_iW_i}{W_1 + W_2 + \ldots + W_i}$$

where M_i is the ith measurement, and W_i is the corresponding weight.

For example, two temperature sensors might be available. One is assigned a 40% weight and a second is assigned a 60% weight. The resulting temperature measurement is the value of the first measurement multiplied by .4 plus the value of the second measurement multiplied by .6. Should the first sensor fail, its weight will be set to 0 by the program and its value will thus be automatically ignored. The input temperature will be derived directly from the second sensor. The first sensor will have been effectively "disconnected" by reducing its weight to zero. If the first sensor should again give reasonable values, it will be "reconnected" by simply reinstating a non-0 weight.

In the case of the traffic controller, another example of unreasonable input would be a continuous speed indication of 0 mph by one of the loop detectors. This might occur because of an actual malfunction or perhaps because a car is parked directly on top of the loop detector. We will now see the advantage of this automatic connection-disconnection mechanism. The processor will determine that the loop is giving unreasonable values since the other loops are indicating a speed of 25 mph. The faulty loop will automatically be disconnected and a diagnostic will be generated. Fifteen minutes later, the microprocessor, which keeps monitoring this "defective" loop (even though it does not use its results), will notice that the speed indicated by the loop is once again 25 mph, a "reasonable" speed. If the loop behaves reasonably for a period of several minutes, the processor will reconnect it to the system. This incident might occur because a car is stalled on top of the loop detector and is later towed away. The loop is automatically reconnected to the system in this instance, whereas in a less "intelligent" system the detector would be "lost" or would cause erratic system behavior.

These testing techniques are not new. They have been used for a long time now by those that have been able to afford minicomputers in industrial process control. The essential point to remember is that these techniques can now be used with microprocessor systems. Reasonableness testing, for example, provides a higher level of system performance and reliability. In essence, these techniques filter out transient malfunctions and allow for the best possible system operation with available resources. Their cost is generally very small, as they are accomplished by software.

Let us present one more important programmed technique.

Programmed Filtering

Whenever a microprocessor system samples a number of inputs during a specific period of time, the input measurements must be *filtered* in order to eliminate spurious indications and to obtain the most precise results possible. This filtering can be easily accomplished by software. For example, in a digital multimeter (DMM), the voltage being measured will usually be sampled several thousand times per second. The simplest possible filtering technique, and one of the most effective, is averaging. If the voltage is sampled 50,000 times a second, the 50,000 measurements are added together and then divided by 50,000. The resulting value is the filtered, averaged input voltage. Naturally, it is assumed that:

1. the input value remains stable during a second sampling

2. any unreasonable values would have been filtered out.

The resulting voltage measurement then has a high precision.

In summary, software techniques are now universally used to improve the system's intelligence, reliability, and convenience. These techniques include status monitoring, programmed soft-fail, reasonableness testing, and programmed filtering. In addition, software techniques can be used to eliminate hardware devices, thus reducing the cost of a system.

In the case of industrial systems, microprocessors offer two essential advantages: lower cost and improved performance.

CONSUMER DEVICES

Consumer devices are characterized by a large volume and the lowest possible cost. This is the main application area of 1-chip and 2-chip microcomputers. Other microprocessor architectures are simply not well suited to consumer-type applications, as they require more components. For example, a 1-chip microcomputer is sufficient for simple control functions, such as those required by a washing machine or a microwave oven controller. The technical advantages are obvious. The microprocessor eliminates electro-mechanical or hard-wired logic and provides more functions. It may also implement reasonableness testing. For example, should the user of the washing machine request a hot cycle for delicate fabrics, the microprocessor may flash a warning signal or even refuse to execute an "erroneous" command. Microprocessors provide added "intelligence" to such consumer devices. As an example, the early F8 had been used successfully in Germany in advanced color televisions to provide tuning and automated long-term "programming" of the set (user-programmed selection of channels over time). Naturally, once a microprocessor is installed in a television set, it is tempting to provide a "free" digital clock as well as other program functions.

Because there are hundreds of thousands of units involved, there is a strong incentive for manufacturers in this market to develop suitable LSI chips. However, because this market is so tempting, the competition is tough. The buyers of 1-chip microcomputers are generally large, well-financed companies who can get the components at the lowest price possible. As a result, manufacturers may have to set unrealistically low prices and then develop the required functions. Thus, they may not make a profit immediately. In the long run, however, the leading suppliers can make a significant profit with such a large market.

One technical problem that occurs when manufacturers try to incorporate microprocessors into consumer goods is that of providing a non-volatile memory. Since they are changed frequently, many of the parameters supplied by the user of a device must be stored in a read/write memory. In the washing machine example, the microprocessor system has to "remember" the type of clothes that are being washed and the specific instructions indicated by the user. (In a traditional machine, a rotating knob mechanically keeps track of the part of the cycle being executed.) There is, however, the possibility that the user might accidentally disconnect the machine, or that there may be a power failure. In this case, it is important that the machine recover as smoothly as possible. A customer would not be very happy if after a power disconnection the machine did not remember where it was interrupted. Thus, some amount of non-volatile memory must be provided.

Providing non-volatile memory is often an expensive proposition when compared to the cost of the microprocessor itself, unless the required memory is small. Several solutions are available. An EAROM or a small battery-assisted CMOS memory could be used, or even bubble memory when a large amount of storage is required. Vital parameters may also be specified via mechanical switches that can be read at any time. This technical problem has generally been solved by using CMOS technology, as in the case of digital watches and pocket calculators.

Examples of microprocessor-equipped consumer goods include washing machines, sewing machines (the Singer Athena 2000 is equipped with a custom microprocessor built by AMI), microwave ovens, color televisions, coffee machines, and electronic games. Also, many of the expensive office machines (for example, word processing typewriters, copying machines, telephone switchboards, etc.) are becoming microprocessor-equipped.

These various consumer devices, which did not exist before the advent of pocket calculators, are now opening up a large new market to semiconductor manufacturers.

In the case of consumer devices, because of the large quantities involved, custom designed chips may be considered. They offer two advantages:

1. They are more immune to direct copying by competition.

2. They are better adapted to a given application, and may reduce the number of components (and are therefore less expensive).

Custom designs also have two essential disadvantages:

1. Since they are tailored to the application, they are usually more difficult to reprogram when improvements are found.

2. They might require a long time for debugging before they become truly reliable.

For the reasons given above, custom designs are in the minority. Whenever a market is firmly established, custom designs are then created to cater to it. Generally standard microprocessors are used to establish new market areas. Then custom designs are created once the market is well established. One such market is that of electronic games.

The first games implemented on television sets were created with standard logic. At that time, low-cost microprocessors made it particularly tempting for many manufacturers to use a microprocessor system in order to provide several games on the screen; and a new market was established. Suddenly, electronic games were selling by the tens of thousands. This resulted in manufacturers turning to specialized companies, such as General Instrument, for the direct implementation of electronic games within a single chip ("game chips"). These new custom chips were then introduced, eliminating previous microprocessor-based implementations from the market. The chips could accomplish the same function at a much lower cost. This is the risk involved when technology progresses. As a result of the introduction of these low-cost 1-chip games, the market skyrocketed and became much more sophisticated. Manufacturers must now compete not only in cost but also in the complexity and sophistication of the games they offer.

Now, new complex games are being introduced that cannot be implemented on a single chip. The successful new games again use a microprocessor system, repeating the cycle once more.

What will be the next consumer application to use microprocessors? The answer to this is simple. Any device that costs one hundred dollars or more is a likely candidate. The extra cost involved in adding a microprocessor/microcomputer to the system is small compared to the overall price of the device. As long as the extra "intelligence" introduced by the microcomputer is marketable, the application will inevitably appear on the scene.

SPECIALIZED APPLICATIONS

Specialized applications are characterized by specific constraints, such as the microminiaturization of the product. The main fields that are governed by such constraints are military, avionic, aerospace and medical applications. They are usually characterized by an absolute requirement for low volume, low power consumption, and often a disregard for software costs. In such applications, the use of a microprocessor may often not be justifiable for functional or economic reasons, but nonetheless is a necessity because of the size constraint.

"Government" applications (military, avionics, and aerospace) have, in fact, been an essential force behind the development of LSI technology. Aerospace programs provided the funding necessary for this effort. CMOS technology, with its very low power consumption and high noise immunity, was developed by RCA specifically for avionics applications. Initially, special-purpose designs were used in these aerospace and military applications. However, an interesting phenomenon occurred. When microprocessors moved into the mass market, the essential financial incentive for manufacturers was to supply this mass market with new advanced products rather than to cater to a shrinking government market. Competition led manufacturers to introduce, as quickly as possible, highly complex devices designed for general-purpose use. As a result, special-purpose designs implemented for military applications have become generally less complex than commercial designs. In fact, government studies have recommended that the military use commercial microprocessors rather than special-purpose designs. Commercial microprocessors simply provide more functions and may be more reliable than special-purpose military microprocessors. However, standardization is far from being accomplished. For example, the avionic applications in the new F16 bomber use more than 30 microprocessor systems, of which at least ten are different.

Microprocessors are used on airplanes for a variety of functions. They regulate control mechanisms, from fuel injection to the reactors to the automated flight control system. Bit-slices plus regular monolithic microprocessors are used in radar systems. Bit-slices are widely used for high-speed avionic applications. In the past, one of the main problems encountered in implementing efficient radar guidance systems in planes was, of course, the bulk and weight of such equipment. This problem has been solved by the availability of bit-slice devices. As a result, most of the algorithms used for radar processing are now programmed rather than hardwired. Another advantage of using the slices is the introduction of the flexibility of programming. These radars can be dynamically reconfigured. This is a major advantage for ECM (electronic counter measures) used in EW (electronic warfare). Bit-slices offer the capability of dynamic reconfiguration to respond to a newly identified threat. As an example, the nose radar of the F16 (which is implemented by Westinghouse, using bit-slice technology) has achieved a weight and space savings of more than 30%. The space gain has allowed the implementation of additional sophisticated ECM functions within the nose of the aircraft. In addition, the radar provides improved operational capabilities because of the sophistication of the algorithms that can be implemented and later refined.

Portable medical applications are usually motivated by similar constraints. They must be light in weight and small in volume. They should naturally be as inexpensive as possible, but this is not the significant constraint. Two main types of applications have been developed that use microprocessors:

1. systems that are implanted in humans

2. systems that are for external use.

Several applications involving the use of microprocessors that are implanted into the human anatomy have been developed recently. For example, ordinary pacemakers provide cardiac stimulation at fixed time intervals. The disadvantage of these pacemakers is that the patient cannot exert any extreme effort. When a healthy person exercises, the toxins released by muscles into the bloodstream are eliminated by a more rapid pumping of the blood. Unfortunately, a standard pacemaker does not increase blood flow. It can only continue to stimulate the heart at the same rate. Microprocessor-equipped pacemakers now provide cardiac stimulation proportional to respiratory rhythm. Simple sensors have been developed that provide this input to the "proportional" pacemaker. Other experimental devices have been developed that provide a programmed stimulus to the nervous system in response to the detection of abnormal brain activity. Such devices are now in experimental stages, but so far they have not posed any significant technical problems.

A number of other applications have been proposed and may be developed soon. One of these is a device that is similar in appearance to a watch and monitors the cardiac rhythm by sensing blood pressure at the wrist. Such a device has the capability of sounding an audible alarm whenever a cardiac malfunction is predicted. In some cardiac diseases or malformations, a heart attack can be predicted with a high level of accuracy several minutes before it actually happens. Such a device would give the bearer enough time to take preventive action whenever possible.

External systems using microprocessors in medical applications are analogous to industrial control systems. They are usually in charge of a process-monitoring function. They offer the advantages of speed, reliability, and "intelligence." For example, most of the vital functions of a patient in a hospital can be monitored directly by microprocessor-based equipment placed at the patient's bedside. This provides 24-hour monitoring of the cardiac rhythm, blood pressure, and other vital functions. Whenever an unusual phenomenon is detected, it may be possible to predict a medical problem by using the computing power of the processor. In addition, automated equipment is usually more reliable than medical personnel for monitoring such functions, especially at night.

Microprocessors can also be used for diagnostics or for automating medically-related operations whenever a clear algorithm exists. They can be used for counting blood cells and for performing other laboratory tests for which speed, accuracy and reliability are essential. Microcomputers can also be used for data collection both in a laboratory and in a business environment of a hospital. In addition, microprocessor-equipped instruments will no doubt be developed that can be used by physicians in their own offices for more sophisticated detection of an abnormal vital function.

Technically, these systems are not substantially different from industrial systems or consumer devices. They are, however, higher in cost.

SUMMARY—APPLICATION AREAS

We have now described the four main application areas of microprocessors. It is expected that the differences between these applications will wane rapidly. As the use of microprocessors becomes widespread, all types of microprocessors will be used for all kinds of applications. It is still interesting to differentiate types of applications, inasmuch as they require different components. We will see, however, that the organization of most systems is the same. We will now demonstrate the actual building of several applications, using the same architecture. We will also examine a number of actual case studies.

BUILDING A MICROPROCESSOR APPLICATION

We have shown in the previous chapters how easy it is to assemble a CPU board. The process of assembling a system for a given application is almost as simple. Two essential problems, interfacing and programming, need to be solved for each application. These two tasks will be addressed in the next two chapters. Since 1977 most of the usual interfaces required to connect standard input/output devices have been available in 1-chip form and can be easily connected to a system.

In the following sections we will use a standard microprocessor (in this case, a 4-bit device known as the 4040) to build progressively more complex applications. We will see that the architecture of the system remains the same and that additional functions are obtained by connecting additional components. Assembling systems using other microprocessors (e.g., a 6502, a Z80 or an 8080), would involve a similar process. We will begin by building a basic microcomputer board with a hexadecimal input and an LED output. Next, we will build a paper-tape reader/punch controller, and a cassette controller. Finally, we will add analog facilities for industrial control.

A SINGLE-BOARD COMPUTER

As shown in Figure 6.4, only four LSI chips are required to construct a minimal single-board computer: the 4040 MPU and its clock; the 4201; a 4002 RAM (which provides read/write and I/O capabilities); and a 4308 ROM and I/O (which provides program storage and I/O capabilities). In this basic design the number of components is minimized. Two special chips, which incorporate both memory and I/O facilities, are used to reduce the chip count. In a larger system involving more memory and I/O, the memory and I/O chips would generally be separate.

The 4002 and the 4308 both provide memory capability and I/O facilities. Each provides 16 lines of I/O. The use of these I/O lines will be illustrated in the following applications.

The single-board computer receives its input from the keyboard and displays its output on the four-digit display. It can also communicate with external devices or another computer via a 16-bit bus shown on the right of Figure 6.4. The program is contained in the 4308 ROM. The working memory, or "scratch-pad," required for storing temporary data and performing computations is supplied by the 4002 RAM. Let us now look in more detail at the input/output functions provided by the 4308, and used to connect both the keyboard and the LED display.

Four pins from the 4308 are connected to the columns of the 16-key keyboard, in order to use a scanning technique to monitor the keyboard. (This technique is described in detail in the next chapter.) Four pins are used to collect data from the four keyboard rows. Four more pins are connected to each LED display in order to select the proper

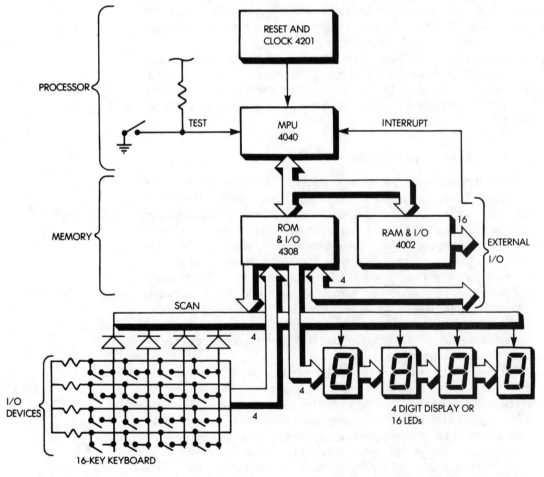

Figure 6.4: A Single-Board Computer

combination of segments. Only three lines are required for standard seven-segment LEDs. The first four (leftmost) I/O lines of the 4308 that are used to scan the keyboard are also used to scan the LED display. Note that the same four lines are also connected to the top of each LED.

Each time a keyboard column is activated, an LED is simultaneously selected. Digits are displayed on the LEDs in rapid succession. Provided the scanning is fast enough, there is no visible blinking of the LED display. This solution (the sharing of four lines between input and output) saves valuable I/O lines on the 4308 for additional functions.

The remaining four (rightmost) bits of the 4308 may be used for other purposes, such as communicating with another device or computer. Communication with a computer is accomplished by using the 16 lines coming out of the 4002 (on the right-hand side of the illustration) for data, plus the four remaining lines of the 4308 for control. The interrupt line can also be used if required.

This is a very simple application example. It is essentially analogous to a pocket calculator but it also has communication lines to the outside world. We will use this system as a base and build progressively more complex applications by adding more LSI chips to achieve the required additional functions.

A PAPER-TAPE READER/PUNCH CONTROLLER _____

We will now create a paper-tape reader/punch controller from our basic board. Such a tape controller reads seven or eight bits of ASCII data from a paper tape and punches data on a tape with its punching mechanism. In addition, it is equipped with a front panel (or "test-panel") that requires eight lines for communication. Four lines are necessary to issue commands to the mechanism, and four sense lines are necessary to get switch and status indications from it. The required functions can be supplied by merely adding three I/O chips to the previous system. The architecture of the system appears in Figure 6.5.

The 4265 GP I/O is a general-purpose interface chip providing 16 lines that are individually programmable in direction; i.e., they may be used either for input or for output.

The 4308 ROM is used to exchange control information with the paper-tape reader/punch. As indicated, eight lines interface to the mechanism proper and eight lines interface to its test panel. The data exchange with the paper-tape reader/punch transits on an 8-bit bidirectional bus (ASCII data) (appearing at the bottom center of the illustration). Finally, communication with a host computer is accomplished via a 16-bit bidirectional data bus (shown at the bottom left of the illustration).

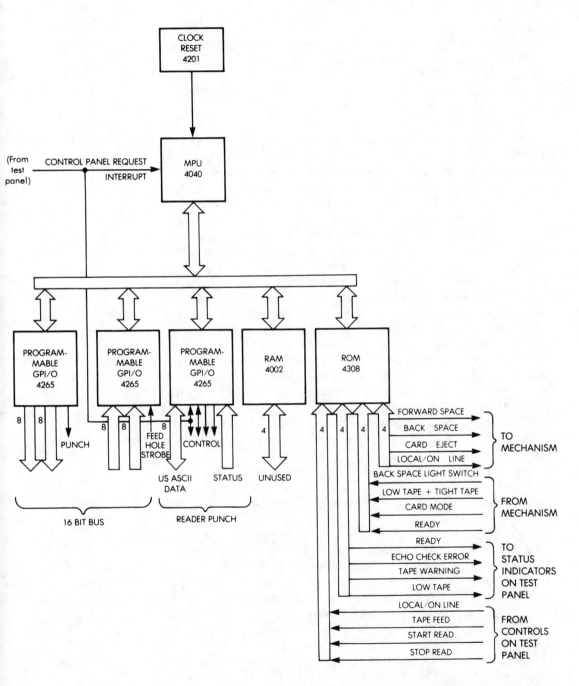

Figure 6.5: A Paper-Tape Reader/Punch Controller

The control logic required to interface to the reader/punch mechanism has been accomplished by using seven chips. Our next application will be accomplished with the same number of chips, using a different combination.

A CASSETTE-DRIVE CONTROLLER

The cassette controller uses the same number of chips as in the previous example. A 4308 ROM is used instead of a GP I/O to provide additional program memory. The GP I/O (shown in the upper right corner of Figure 6.6) provides 16 control lines to and from the tape mechanism. Data coming from or going to a tape drive is serial.

In our example this data is already converted from serial to parallel 4-bit and is gated to the 4308 (bottom right of the illustration). The serial/parallel conversion can be accomplished by an additional UART chip (not shown). Let us summarize the organization. Data coming from or going to the tape cassette arrives at the 4308 ROM (appearing on the right side of the illustration). The 4265 GP I/O (on the top right-hand side of the illustration) provides the 16 lines required by the mechanism. Each line is labeled to indicate the function provided. The remaining lines of the 4308 ROM (bottom right of the illustration) are used to provide the necessary control functions, both for data transmission purposes and for interfacing to the control panel or sensing information coming from it. The data accumulated by this cassette controller may be transmitted to or from a host computer via a 16-bit bidirectional data bus (appearing at the bottom of the illustration). The second 4308 ROM, the 4002 RAM and the second 4265 GP I/O are used for this purpose.

If additional I/O functions had been required, they could have been provided by using an extra GP I/O chip. If a longer program were to be implemented, the required storage would be provided by using additional 4308 ROM chips.

We could continue to "complicate" the examples by adding functions and by adding the required chips, but as long as the basic microprocessor unit used for computing functions is fast enough to provide the required response time for the algorithms that must be implemented, our approach is valid. If the 4040 used in this example should prove to be too slow, it would be replaced by a faster microprocessor such as an 8-bit microprocessor. The overall organization would remain the same.

One apparent conclusion that might be drawn from the examples just presented is that there is essentially no hardware design problem in assembling the basic microcomputer board. Functions are achieved by

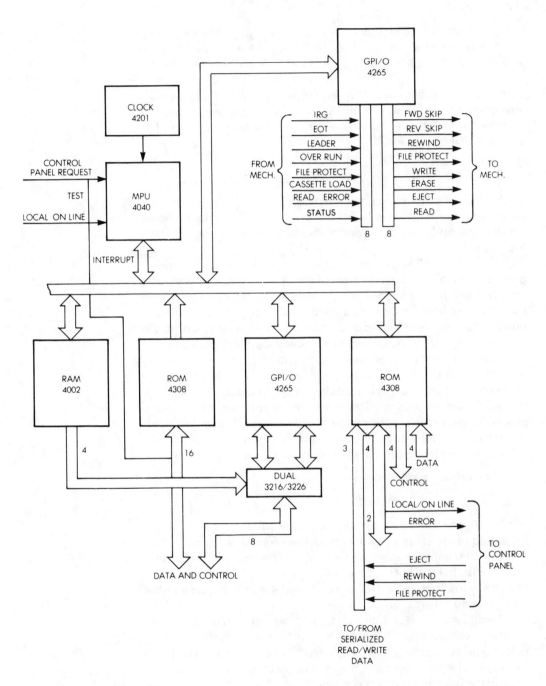

Figure 6.6: A Cassette-Drive Controller

simply connecting extra chips to the system as long as processing speed is sufficient to do the job. This is correct. We have not considered the additional complexity of writing software. This problem will be addressed later.

An important additional facility required in most industrial systems is analog input and output. This function can be easily provided and will be examined next. We will first summarize the techniques used in analog/digital conversion.

ANALOG-TO-DIGITAL CONVERSION

Most natural phenomena are analog, i.e., continuous, while their computer representation is digital (binary). In order to communicate with the real world, analog-to-digital and digital-to-analog conversions must be performed.

Until the late 1970s, analog-to-digital conversion was a significant problem. It involved a large number of components, as opposed to the small number that are needed to implement the microprocessor system itself. But this has changed. Analog-to-digital converters (ADCs) are now available on a single chip at low cost. New ADC chips incorporate tri-state drivers and the buffers required to interface directly to a standard microprocessor data bus. Building multichannel analog interfaces can be done with only a few components. In addition, a number of ready-made modules and boards are available commercially that interface directly with most existing microprocessor systems. In short, a microprocessor system can now be coupled easily to an analog-to-digital and digital-to-analog multichannel conversion assembly.

The two main techniques in the field of ADC are:

1. successive approximations

2. dual-slope integration.

In the successive-approximation technique an analog input value is compared to the value of a counter (converted to analog) and a progressively finer approximation is generated. The resulting precision is average (8 to 10 bits), but the conversion speed is high (20 µs). There are now many low cost ($10) 1-chip ADCs available that implement the successive-approximation technique.

In the dual-slope integration technique, a capacitor is connected to a reference voltage and charged during a known number of timing pulses. The capacitor is then discharged through the voltage to be measured. The time elapsed during the discharge is proportional to the value of the voltage. This is a precise technique, yielding high precision (12 or 13 bits); however, it is intrinsically slower (20 ms). Several 1-chip converters are available that implement the dual-slope integration technique but the cost is higher than the successive-approximation technique. An ADC may even be built within the microprocessor chip itself.

As an example of a direct analog microprocessor, the system used for spark timing on the Oldsmobile Toronado (General Motors) is described in the "Case Studies" section appearing later in this chapter. This system uses a custom microprocessor implemented by Rockwell. Let us now return to our 4040-based system, and equip it with analog I/O capabilities.

The task of providing analog input/output functions is accomplished just as easily as providing the digital functions in the examples just presented. An ADC is used for analog-to-digital conversion. (A DAC is used for digital-to-analog conversion.) Our simple 4040 system, configured to provide such analog facilities, appears in Figure 6.7.

An 8-bit (low precision) ADC is used to convert an external analog signal into a digitized 8-bit value. One or more DACs are connected on the right of the system in order to convert the digital output into an analog signal that is connected to monitors or relays.

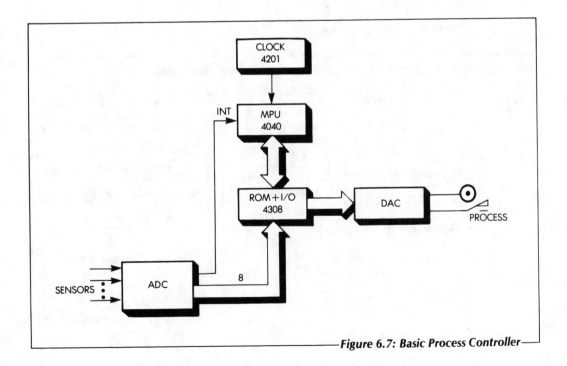

Figure 6.7: Basic Process Controller

In an actual industrial application, the ADC would normally be interfaced to the external analog signals via a *multiplexer* and one or more *sample-and-hold* circuits, which freeze the information for the ADC. The role of the multiplexer is to connect several analog signals while using only one (expensive) analog-to-digital converter, as long as the resulting conversion speed is sufficient.

A typical system capable of sensing two analog inputs, and equipped with 8 switches plus a display, is shown in Figure 6.8. A 1-chip ADC is used to convert an analog input to a digital value. A sample-and-hold circuit is used on each input line to "freeze" the value being measured during the conversion process. The two sample-and-hold circuits are connected to the ADC by a 2-to-1 multiplexer (MUX) that selects between the two inputs. The 8 switches are read via 8 dedicated lines of the second 4308 ROM.

Whenever multiple inputs must be sensed, and conversion speed is not essential, an analog multiplexer will be used in order to reduce the component count. A typical example appears in Figure 6.9. The multiplexer in the lower right corner of the illustration can select one of eight

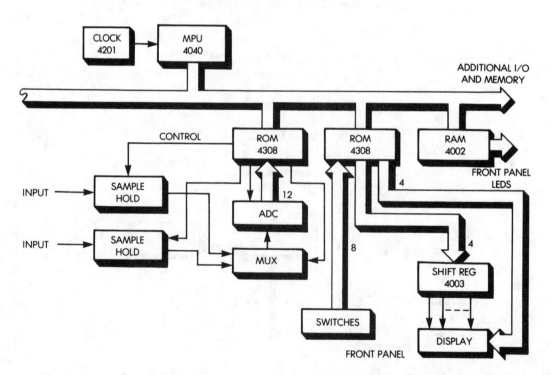

Figure 6.8: 4-Bit I/O Control with A/D

analog inputs. Selection is accomplished by specifying a 3-bit code. Three lines of the address bus, labeled A0, A1, and A2, are used to select the input signals. The analog signal selected is then gated through an amplifier to the sample-and-hold circuit, which will freeze it. One line is used from the microprocessor to the sample-and-hold circuit (abbreviated S/H), which will give the freeze signal. The ADC can then use the value frozen in the S/H and convert it to digital form. A conversion order will be given by the microprocessor on a separate line, which appears in the illustration. The ADC will then provide 8 bits or more of data to the microprocessor. A 10- or 12-bit ADC first transmits 8 bits out and then transmits the remaining bit on the microprocessor data bus.

The system just described is an 8-channel data acquisition system. Adding analog facilities to our basic system has once again been accomplished by adding a modest number of chips to the standard architecture. This suggests a general rule. Other special-purpose functions that may later be required in an application will be provided by connecting the required interface to the same basic microprocessor system. The architecture of the system is essentially constant. As a result, any standard microprocessor board can be considered for most applications. Once a basic board is available, the technical challenges in a given application may be present in the interface design area, and in the programming.

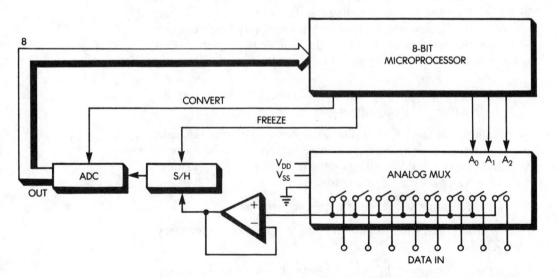

Figure 6.9: An 8-Channel Data Acquisition System

To illustrate some of the constraints and solutions used in actual applications, let us now look at three case studies.

THREE CASE STUDIES

In this section we will describe two industrial applications and a consumer application. The first industrial application is an urban traffic controller, which uses a standard microprocessor system. The second one is an automobile ignition timing system, which uses a special-purpose processor. The third application is in the consumer field: a microwave oven controller.

These three examples will serve to illustrate the concepts and techniques that were introduced previously and to explain actual motivations for specific designs.

AN URBAN TRAFFIC CONTROLLER

One of the first published descriptions of the use of microprocessors in an industrial environment was the optimal control of traffic signals in an urban environment. (The author of this book was responsible for one of the first such designs.) The regulation of traffic lights at intersections had traditionally been accomplished by using electromechanical controllers in simpler cases and "electronic" controllers in more complex cases. Algorithms for controlling the flow of traffic in an urban zone have grown progressively more sophisticated, requiring complex electronic facilities for sequencing the lights. Some of the functions that must be performed by a traffic-light controller are:

— the basic sequencing of each phase (a phase is a logical grouping of traffic lights: red-amber-green).

— timing-cycle selection. This may involve a number of different cycles such as normal sequencing, night timing, rush-hour cycle, and other cycles depending on the time of the day or the measured values of traffic parameters.

— an initialization sequence after power is applied.

— special facilities such as preemption (by police or emergency vehicles).

— an actuation facility in response to pedestrians or cars passing over loop detectors ("traffic-responsive" mode).

— modules for the computation of required traffic parameters such as "density" or "volume."

— modules for connecting transmission lines required to link the controller to a central computer or other traffic controllers in a network. Typically, a receiver, transmitter, and modem are required.

The main limitations of the traditional electronic traffic-controllers are:

— cost. Any change in the functions required is expensive in view of the extensive rewiring and redesigning involved.

— limitation in the complexity of the algorithms that can be implemented.

— adaptation required for every new intersection and for every different algorithm.

— low reliability of the system in view of high hardware complexity.

Minicomputers had been used with good results for the implementation of highly complex control procedures. However, the cost and the size of minicomputer systems made their use prohibitive in standard traffic controllers (where the cost is typically less than a few thousand dollars). The structure of a microprocessor-equipped traffic controller appears in Figure 6.10.

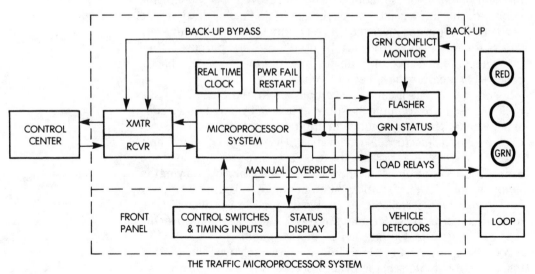

Figure 6.10: Urban Traffic Controller

The use of a microprocessor has made it possible to replace most of the traditional complex hardware modules with software equivalents. A microprocessor-equipped traffic controller simply uses a standard microprocessor board plus the required interface facilities. Most of the system-specific functions are accomplished by software.

At the center of Figure 6.10 the microprocessor module is the CPU of the system. This microprocessor-based board provides memory, I/O and processing facilities. Two special modules appear at the top of the illustration. They are the *real-time clock* necessary for precise timing of external events, and the power fail/restart (PFR) unit necessary for restarting the system after a power failure and preserving essential data when a power failure is detected.

The sensing and controlling functions are accomplished on the right of the illustration. Traffic control strategies are based on the information provided by the vehicle detectors. The most often used vehicle detector is the loop detector. A rectangle is cut in the pavement at the intersection. Two or more loops of wire are deposited inside the groove, and the extremities of the loop are connected to an LC oscillating circuit. The frequency of oscillation depends on the impedance of the loop. The presence of any large magnetic mass, such as a car, over part or all of the loop will change its inductance and oscillating frequency. This frequency shift can easily be detected and will cause activation of a switch or relay, resulting in a discrete signal that can be monitored directly by the microprocessor. A *vehicle-detector* box (appearing on the right side of the illustration) is the unit in charge of converting the frequency shift into an external discrete signal (indicating the presence of a vehicle above the loop). Loops will normally be installed in every lane of the intersection. They can be used for several purposes. They can detect the presence of a vehicle, measure the length of a line of vehicles, or measure the speed of a vehicle.

Speed measurement can be accomplished in two ways. The basic principle used is to compute the speed as $S = D/T$ where D is distance and T is time. The most accurate method of measurement consists of using two loop detectors, D meters apart. The microprocessor simply measures the time, T, separating the two successive presence pulses on each of the two loop detectors and computes the speed by applying the simple formula given above. An alternate method is used whenever only a single loop is available. Assuming the vehicle is of average size, the duration of the presence pulse triggered by a vehicle going over the loop can be used to compute the estimated speed.

Loop detectors are an essential tool for providing dynamic, optimal traffic control at intersections. The processor's role is to measure as many parameters as possible and to optimize traffic as a function of these indications. Several optimization strategies can be implemented. It may be desirable to optimize the number of vehicles that will go through any given intersection, the speed of the vehicles in a given street, or the flow of cars through several streets in an urban network. Finally, in many cases, it may be desirable to guarantee a "green wave" along a specified arterial. A green wave means that whenever a car enters the arterial it will drive along the complete length of the street without having to stop at a traffic light, as long as it maintains the recommended speed. In a given urban traffic network, a combination of these optimizing strategies might be necessary. When strategies are mutually incompatible, they will result in great complexity in optimizing the flow of traffic over the complete network.

Look again at the right half of Figure 6.10 and examine the rest of the control mechanism. The microprocessor must light each of the bulbs on the traffic light in sequence (green, amber, red). Because of the power involved, the switching is accomplished through load relays.

We have already discussed the importance of providing status feedback to verify the correct execution of an order in any industrial control system. This is implemented by the status line coming out of the load relay back into the microprocessor system. At a minimum, green status and, ideally, the status of all three lights should be monitored. Every time the microprocessor attempts to turn the green on, it will check a few milliseconds later that the load relay has indeed closed by verifying its status. If the load relay has not closed, the order will be issued again a number of times. If the failure of the load relay is permanent, an emergency mode is provided for safe system operation. Using this feedback information, it can be guaranteed that, short of a microprocessor malfunction, no gross control problem should occur. The system can be even further refined by gating the status information directly from the light bulb at the intersection. This solves the problem created by a defunct bulb.

We have also indicated that *soft-fail* facilities must be provided in case a hardware or software malfunction occurs. This is the role of the green-conflict monitor and its flasher unit, appearing at the top right of the illustration. The green-conflict monitor monitors the green status continuously for all lights at the intersection. If two conflicting greens at right angles should be turned on simultaneously, the green-conflict monitor will detect this event, and automatically disconnect the microprocessor system (assuming it has failed) and turn on the flasher unit. The flasher will flash alternate red and amber signals in all directions. This degrades the operation of the system but does not result in a potentially disastrous situation with green lights turned on in directions that would result in collisions. This device is called a soft-fail mechanism and is mandatory in California and most other states in the U.S. Should a software or hardware malfunction occur that results in a green conflict, this device will automatically detect the condition and take the actions indicated. The system is not totally disabled; only some of its functions are disabled by the malfunction. Naturally, other more refined soft-fail techniques are used within the microprocessor itself to diagnose or correct a number of possible error conditions at the input or output levels.

Note that two lines labeled "back-up bypass" appear at the very top of the illustration. They connect into the transmitter and the receiver on the left of the microprocessor system. These lines carry the loop-detectors' information and the green status, respectively. They are transmitted to a control center. In practice, a network of such traffic control processors is installed in the city. All of them communicate with a traffic control center, which may be equipped with a coordinating minicomputer. The information displayed at the control center includes the status of every intersection (green alone or green-amber-red). In addition, the density of traffic can be evaluated at the control center simply by displaying the actuations coming from loop detectors. Naturally, this information can also be measured at the control center and coded and displayed in digital form. This essential input and status feedback information can also be directed to a neighboring traffic controller for synchronization of successive controllers along an arterial. Should a malfunction occur, a second microprocessor could conceivably take over the function of the first one if it were equipped with an additional line connecting it to the load relays. In cases where a significant flow of information is transmitted between the local traffic controller and the control center, time division multiplexing (TDM) is used to encode the data onto a single communication line. A microprocessor can be used to provide TDM facilities in software, thus eliminating the need for a separate hardware TDM unit.

Finally, looking at the bottom of the illustration, the front panel provides the required on-site human interface. The front panel includes control switches and timing knobs as well as display information. Control switches are used by the traffic engineer to specify locally a number of parameters. In particular, the timing intervals for amber are normally specified on site by rotary or other switches. In addition, selection between various modes of operation can also usually be specified on site directly by switches. The status of the system, including display of the traffic lights on small LEDs, is also usually directly provided on this front panel ("status display"). In addition, the system must be equipped with manual actuation or manual preemption facilities for emergency operation. These facilities are used, for example, by police when an accident occurs. In this case, intersections can be placed into specific modes or sequenced manually through push-buttons on the front panel. The manual override line provides this facility and connects the front panel to the flasher (as seen in the illustration). This allows authorized personnel to place the intersection in alternating red and amber flashing mode manually.

We have now described all of the functional modules of the system. Let us briefly discuss their impact on cost.

Communication facilities, the green-conflict monitor and flasher, load relays and loop detectors, each cost at least several hundred dollars. The front panel facility also implies a similar cost, not to mention the metal cabinet and installation. As a result, the microprocessor board probably costs the least of any module within the system.

What are the advantages derived from the microprocessor? Because of the high cost of the various modules required in such a system, the introduction of the microprocessor instead of hardwired logic does not represent significant savings in the production of a small number of units. However, once again the savings are substantial when the items are produced in large numbers. The main nonfinancial advantage of the microprocessor is the unlimited *intelligence* capability that it brings to the implementation of the control algorithms. Its most significant value is the removal of the limitations of hardwired logic on the complexity of algorithms that might reasonably be implemented.

One important hidden cost on a traffic controller lies in the fact that each traffic controller must usually be customized for the intersection. Usual parameters for such customization are the geometry of the intersection, actual number of phases and traffic lights, and most importantly, the algorithms or combination of algorithms that must be implemented locally. Various hardware modules such as volume counters, time-of-day sequencing modules, or pedestrian-actuation modules must then be inserted into a traditional design. An important advantage of a microprocessor is that it replaces all these hardware modules with software programs or subroutines. Required combinations of software programs to accomplish the specified functions can be easily assembled manually or automatically. They will be "burned into" PROMs, then be inserted on the standard intersection control system.

Since customization occurs almost exclusively at the software level (except for the obvious choices in number of loop detectors and number of load relays), it is possible to mass-produce identical, standardized traffic controllers. All the required adaptation and custom-programming is done on a powerful development system at the software level. The economy in labor is very significant. In addition, because of the possible mass production of identical hardware units, the resulting hardware cost of the total controller decreases significantly. Another resulting advantage to the user is that, once the system is installed, its functions or algorithms can be changed by merely inserting new PROMs. Software features such as status monitoring result in greater reliability as well as the automatic detection of faulty load relays or light bulbs.

The availability of programmed logic at the intersection has allowed the implementation of a variety of novel and complex algorithms. For example, complex green waves can now be implemented. For a number of the most important arterials in the network, a car can proceed through all or most of the city without stopping. This is accomplished by transmitting information from one traffic microprocessor to the next one in the network and/or coordinating the operation of the network from a central site. In addition, a variety of alternative algorithms can be provided simultaneously on a single controller. The cost of providing additional algorithms is simply the cost of providing additional PROM chips rather than costly hardware modules.

Typically, a microprocessor-equipped traffic controller will operate in one of three modes:

— The controller always starts in mode 0 or "restart mode," where it assumes that no information is available. This is the power-up mode that has to be used until other system parameters become available. The two essential system parameters used by such a controller are: a) the time of the day, and b) the actual traffic measurements.

— The next mode of operation is "time-of-day." Depending on the value of the clock, the microprocessor will implement one of several timing programs. These "timing programs" have been developed by the local traffic engineer and are used during key segments of the day. A typical time-of-the-day operation includes special timings for rush-hour as well as night operation.

— The next mode of operation is "parameter-actuated." After the microprocessor has been in operation for some time, traffic parameters can be acquired, such as speed of vehicles, density, and the distance between vehicles. More sophisticated traffic control strategies can be implemented using these parameters. If the system is equipped with sufficient memory, it can also use the data that was acquired during previous days or weeks and compare it to the data currently being measured.

Finally, it is now possible to seriously consider dynamic, self-optimizing systems. A microprocessor will start in time-of-day mode, and then switch to parameter-actuated operation as soon as enough parameters become available. It will then possibly switch into a self-optimizing mode. Unfortunately, traffic control is very complex and the simultaneous measurement of a variety of parameters is needed. No simple mathematical formula exists that allows direct optimization of the timing of the network.

Heuristic techniques must be used. It is possible, however, to experiment with new control strategies and to implement them on the microprocessor using adequate safeguards. For example, the microprocessor will implement a new strategy and measure the resulting network or intersection performance. If this performance is seen to be an improvement over the performance obtained in similar situations during the same day or during previous days, the strategy will be repeated. If any resulting parameter shows an unusually large variation, then use of this new strategy can be automatically discontinued, thus reverting to a safer established strategy. This process permits testing strategies in real time while the safety of the network is guaranteed by reasonableness testing. Within a few days, techniques can be tested that might otherwise have been impossible to test or would have required a great amount of time as well as costly hardware.

Microprocessor-based traffic control systems have now become the rule rather than the exception for new installations within most of the United States and in some European cities. Techniques used to control the flow of vehicles in an urban environment are very close to the techniques used to control continuous or discrete flow. Modified versions of these traffic controllers are used to provide flow-metering to control water and other liquids.

The traffic-controller example illustrates the essential advantages and constraints of using a microprocessor in an industrial control environment. We will now consider another case study that requires a radically different approach, i.e., the use of a custom-designed chip.

MICROPROCESSOR CONTROLLED SPARK IGNITION SYSTEM

In 1976, Delco-Remy, a division of General Motors, introduced the first car spark-timing system controlled by a microprocessor. This system is used on the Oldsmobile. A diagram of the system appears in Figure 6.11. Sensors supply the microprocessor with the required information. Inputs to the microprocessor include the engine vacuum, the crankshaft position, reference timing, and coolant temperature.

The system produces three forms of output. The main one is the timing signal, which is gated to the spark plugs via the distributor. The other two outputs are status information: "check ignition" and "hot." A picture of the actual controller module appears in Figure 6.12. The custom microprocessor is the DIP, which appears in the center of the illustration (it has a round lid).

A special-purpose microprocessor was designed for this application by the automotive division of Rockwell. The system functions in a table-driven mode. There is no simple algorithm that determines the proper timing for the spark in function of the input conditions. Generating this timing is considered an art. Every engine, once it goes into production, is extensively tested. The manufacturer establishes tables that determine the desired timing as a function of a variety of external parameters. Delco-Remy's MISAR*system implements an automated version of this table look-up mechanism. A subset of the tables is stored in a special ROM memory. For each set of external conditions

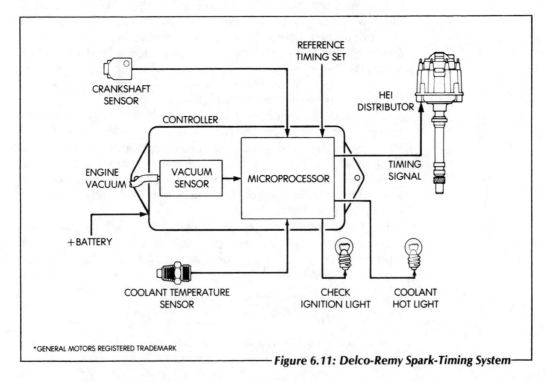

*GENERAL MOTORS REGISTERED TRADEMARK

Figure 6.11: Delco-Remy Spark-Timing System

measured by the system, the closest matching entries in the tables are found. An interpolation technique is used to compute the intermediate values. Special instructions within this custom microprocessor perform the interpolation. The microprocessor is equipped with direct input/output lines as well as direct analog facilities.

General Motors claims a number of advantages for this system. The most significant one is, without a doubt, the reduction in pollutants. Precise control of timing results in significantly improved engine combustion and much lower emission levels. It is expected that the use of this programmed spark-timing system will eliminate the need for the catalytic converter that is now found in most American cars. The catalytic converter was made necessary by tougher emission standards. It is a costly item and its elimination would result in substantial savings to the company. Other advantages claimed are small improvements in gas consumption and engine responsiveness. A significant advantage of this technique (to the manufacturer) is that through mass testing of this approach the program will continue to improve, which will eventually result in significantly better timing of the engine under

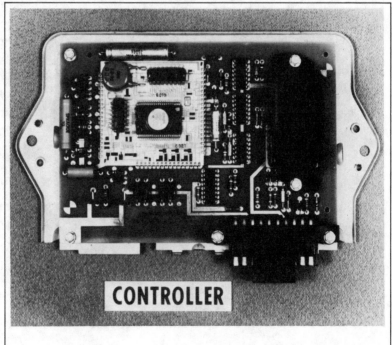

Figure 6.12: Controller (MISAR)

most conditions. This will lead to improved gas economy and still greater pollution reduction. Since General Motors' implementation of this system, other manufacturers have announced similar devices. Ford has been working with Toshiba in Japan as well as Motorola and Essex in the U.S. A photomicrograph of the custom microprocessor appears in Figure 6.13.

Figure 6.13: The Custom Microprocessor—Rockwell

Microprocessors can be used in cars for a number of additional functions. They can be used to monitor engine conditions and to display them to the driver, to supply diagnostics, to manage the display panel (from digital clock to digital speedometer), and to monitor abnormal engine conditions. The reliability and the performance of microprocessors in severe environments is adequate for such applications. The main problem is no longer the microprocessor chip but the required sensors and displays. The cost of sensors is still high and their proven reliability is sometimes not sufficient for a severe environment. As a result, automobile manufacturers still refrain from using microprocessors, since every fraction of a cent is significant in automobile cost. However, it is just a matter of time until the required sensors and displays are developed to the required specifications. In the future we can expect that cars, like other complex mechanical devices, will be equipped with a variety of microprocessors implementing a number of new functional and safety features. Once microprocessors are installed in vehicles, the "free" spare power that will then be created will provide a number of intelligence and convenience features that could never have been achieved before. However, in all likelihood we are still a few years away from such a large-scale use.

A MICROWAVE OVEN CONTROLLER

This third case-study will focus on a consumer product. A microwave oven controller (shown in Figure 6.14) is characterized by a very simple control algorithm that has traditionally been implemented in electromechanical form. The high volume production implies the lowest possible cost for the control logic. Control is accomplished with a single-chip microcomputer such as an F8, an 8048, a PPS-4/1 or a TMS-1000. Surprisingly, one of the main costs involved in using a 1-chip microprocessor may not be with the microcomputer itself or even with the display and keyboard but it may simply be with the required power-supply level. In this example, the system is equipped with a hexadecimal keyboard. In some cases the number of keys is extended to 28 or more. The keyboard is the standard input mechanism. The user will specify (through the keyboard) the time that the oven is to start cooking, the nature of the meat or vegetable being cooked, and the weight. If unreasonable data are entered (for example, "chicken" and "20 pounds"), an audible alarm is set off and a light starts flashing—the data are rejected.

This is an "intelligent" oven controller in that it uses reasonableness testing and will reject any data deemed unreasonable. There is no 20-pound chicken in the realm of the microprocessor-equipped oven controller. The user is thus advised of the mistake and can punch in new instructions. Provided that the data supplied are reasonable, the controller will automatically compute and implement the required cooking time. This results in added convenience for the user at a very small cost to the manufacturer. In quantities of tens of thousands or more (a quantity typical of microwave oven controllers), the cost of a 1-chip microcomputer is around two dollars.

In addition, the microprocessor will provide several other functions, such as a time display. Should additional control functions become necessary at a later date, they could be implemented simply by modifying the program on the microprocessor. Automating typical functions such as required cooking time is accomplished by simple table look-up operations. Thus, microprocessor-equipped appliances can automate most of the tedious procedures that were previously done by hand. Their convenience value is high and they are likely to be in high demand. In this case the microprocessor introduces no more control capability than an electromechanical implementation. Its value is simply an added convenience, but since microwave ovens are convenience-oriented, this is a significant selling point. Let us look at one

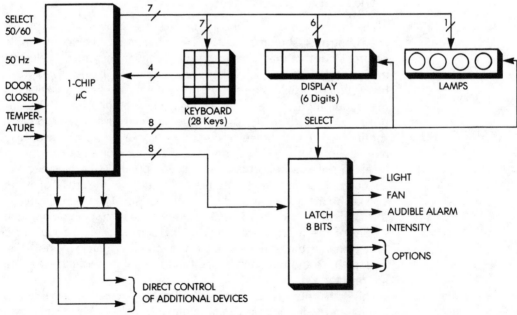

Figure 6.14: Microwave Oven Controller

final example, analogous to the previous one. We will examine the copier controller.

COPIER CONTROLLER

The structure of a copier controller appears in Figure 6.15. It has a striking resemblance to the previous system. The reason for this resemblance should be obvious: the copier controller is a 1-chip microcomputer with a keyboard input, LED and relay output. The only significant difference between the two systems lies in the role of the various input and output lines in the systems.

In the case of the copier controller, additional control functions are now possible that could not be considered previously. Whenever a mechanical malfunction, such as paper jamming, occurs, a number of control algorithms can be implemented that will solve the jamming problem (such as ejecting a sheet of paper by rotating the motor in the reverse direction). The results of adding these extra functions include improved product performance (more and better copies), improved convenience (less jamming), improved diagnostics, and improved

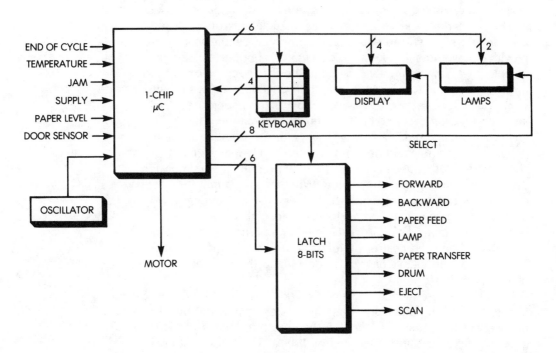

Figure 6.15: Photocopier Controller

overall reliability. Testing routines can improve reliability even more. The microprocessor can run checks on the various input and output media of the copier and verify that they are operational prior to initiating copier operation. In addition, a single board of hardware may be developed for a variety of copiers. Only the program will change from one model to the next, resulting in benefits similar to those that have been outlined in the case of the traffic controller.

At this point it would probably be repetitive to continue to look at "typical" applications. We have seen that the structure of the basic computer system remains constant. Only the interface and the software (i.e., the role played by the system) are different in each application.

One new area of microprocessor use deserves a special mention here. It is the new "personal computing" market.

THE IMPACT OF PERSONAL COMPUTERS

We have seen in the previous chapters how simple it is, with the advent of complete families of components for microprocessors, to assemble a complete system. Several manufacturers realized this fact and began marketing kits of components and diagrams for easy assembly. Once assembly instructions and the printed circuit board were provided, it would only take a novice a matter of hours to assemble a complete working computer. The computer has become one of the most sophisticated toys (or tools) ever introduced. By now, students, electronics engineers, doctors, lawyers and business people are actively involved in using small computers and in programming them. The computer can be used in a variety of ways. Business and professional people can assemble and program systems for file management, accounting, etc. Other users can build them or program them simply for their entertainment and game value. Whether they admit it or not, many users probably are attracted to personal computing largely because of its game value. The business impact of this new market will be very significant. The main obstacle when purchasing the systems has always been the cost of peripherals. In view of the new mass market, new peripherals have been developed that cost only a few hundred dollars.

A technical consequence of this new market has been the advent of new standards. In particular, a new bus system, the S-100 bus, has become a de facto standard. The S-100 bus was introduced by MITS on its Altair microcomputer, also used by IMSAI. The S-100 is strongly directed to the 8080 but is essentially compatible with the Z80 and can be adapted to the 6800. As a result of the mass market that has been created, a majority of the low-cost peripheral manufacturers today produce devices that are directly compatible to the S-100. Such devices can then be plugged directly onto the bus. The sheer number of S-100 bus users has established for the first time a real bus standard. This standard is described in Chapter 7.

Another significant phenomenon that has occurred along with the increase in the number of personal computers has been a spectacular drop in the cost of software. BASIC interpreters and utility programs are now available at a very low cost. Many early users have developed programs in their spare time. This, in turn, has caused the demise of a number of small software houses, since the time invested by these persons for programming was essentially free. However, this has opened the era of "canned software" at low cost.

Most cities now boast microcomputer stores that cater to this new market. These stores also sell "plastic software," i.e., plastic bags containing PROMs with libraries of useful programs that can be plugged onto any standard microcomputer. To that extent, software has become a plastic bag commodity.

The impact of this new market on the technical field has been significant. For the first time, a consumer-type market has been opened to semiconductor houses, forcing many of them into the systems business. In addition, the pool of ingenuity now working on original microcomputer applications is bound to generate a number of surprising and original applications. Entirely new applications will now be devised that have never been implemented before.

SUMMARY

The four main application areas for microcomputers—computer systems, industrial systems, consumer devices, and specialized applications—were presented in this chapter. Case studies were described illustrating the advantages and disadvantages of typical microprocessor applications. It was shown that building an application progressively by adding modules to it is a very simple proposition. The originality in any design lies in the interfacing and in the programming of the application—areas that we will examine in Chapters 7 and 8.

EXERCISES

6-1: Why were microprocessors first used by computer manufacturers?

6-2: What is the main characteristic of microprocessor devices used in consumer applications?

6-3: What are distributed systems?

6-4: What are the advantages and disadvantages of multimicroprocessor systems? Describe cases in which they are used to advantage.

6-5: What are the main hardware differences between a microprocessor system used for general-purpose computing and one used for industrial control?

6-6: Explain the purpose of a status feedback loop.

6-7: What is reasonableness testing?

6-8: Is programmed filtering a hardware or a software technique?

6-9: Explain the difference between the successive approximations technique and the dual-slope integration technique used in analog-to-digital conversion.

6-10: Examine Figure 6.4, showing a single-board computer. Describe the chips that would be used if this were a pocket calculator for the consumer market. (Keep in mind that the number of components has to be minimized in order to reduce cost.)

6-11: What is an advantage and a disadvantage of using an analog multiplexer, such as the one shown in Figure 6.9?

6-12: Explain the function of each module in the urban traffic controller shown in Figure 6.10.

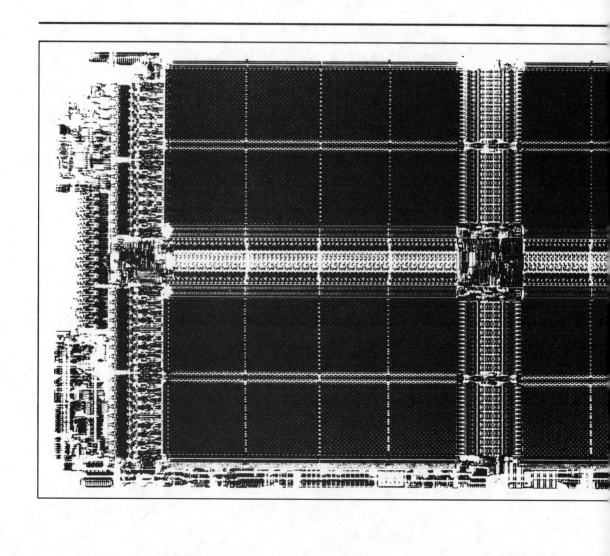

CHAPTER *7*

INTERFACING TECHNIQUES

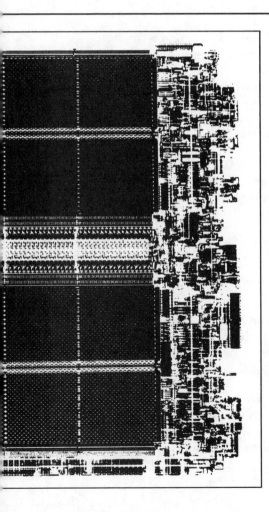

OBJECTIVE

Interfacing a microprocessor system to external devices involves both hardware and software techniques. In the design of a new system, there is always a tradeoff between hardware and software. Generally, the use of hardware components simplifies the design and provides improved performance, but it also raises the component count. Alternative software techniques can eliminate many hardware components and result in lower system cost; however, such techniques usually also result in increased software complexity and lower speed.

The main techniques and LSI components available to interface microprocessor systems to external devices are presented in this chapter. The interfaces covered here range from a simple keyboard interface to a complex floppy disk interface. This chapter focuses on the *hardware* implementation of the interfacing techniques. The user should always keep in mind that alternative software implementations can generally be used. For a more complete treatment of interfacing techniques, the reader is referred to *Microprocessor Interfacing Techniques* (see *The SYBEX Library*).

In this chapter we will interface progressively more complex devices to a standard microprocessor system. These devices include a keyboard, an LED display, a teletype, a floppy disk, and finally, a CRT display. Multimicroprocessor interfacing considerations will also be presented. Finally, important busing standards—such as the IEEE 488, IEEE 583 (CAMAC) and the S-100 bus—will be described.

We will begin by connecting a keyboard to our standard system.

KEYBOARD

There are two categories of keyboards: the fully-encoded keyboard and the non-encoded keyboard.

The *fully-encoded keyboard* automatically supplies the ASCII code corresponding to the key that has been pressed. Associated electronics must then automatically detect the key (from a selection of 64 or more keys), and supply the code corresponding to it. A strobe signal is also normally provided. Finally, two usual facilities, *debounce* and *multiple-key rollover* protection (described below), must also be supplied.

Naturally, a fully-encoded keyboard is the easiest device to use in a system since it performs all the operations that must otherwise be accomplished by software or other extra components. However, because of the cost of the associated electronics, a completely encoded keyboard is expensive. Its use is generally restricted to two areas of application:

1. It is used whenever a small number of units are built, i.e., whenever the hardware cost is not a dominant factor.

2. It is used whenever the keyboard itself is complex, i.e., whenever the keyboard involves 64 keys or more (a complete alphanumeric keyboard).

The *non-encoded keyboard*, on the other hand, is probably the least expensive medium available today for input to microprocessors. It simply provides a matrix of rows and columns. Everything is accomplished by software. We will soon see, however, that new hardware alternatives are now available.

In this section we will examine the techniques used to interface directly to a non-encoded keyboard. All the techniques we will discuss can be implemented using software, but we will see that most of these techniques can also be accomplished using new LSI interface chips.

Four tasks must be accomplished by the interface:

1. identifying the key

2. generating the corresponding code

3. debouncing

4. protecting against rollover.

Let us examine these tasks in detail.

KEY IDENTIFICATION

Two basic techniques are used to identify the key that has been pressed. The traditional method is called *row-scanning*. A more recent method, known as the *line reversal* technique, is also made possible by components such as the PIO. We will begin by looking at row-scanning.

Row-Scanning

Figure 7.1 shows the four steps involved in row-scanning a 4-by-4 keyboard. In the illustration, the black key is the key that has been

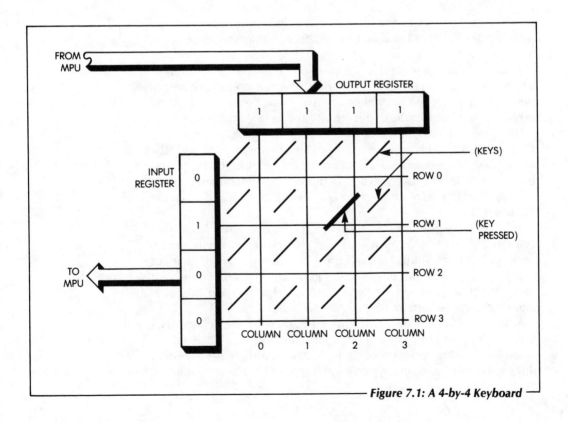

Figure 7.1: A 4-by-4 Keyboard

pressed; the key closure must be detected. The task of detecting the key that has been pressed is not as simple as it first appears.

With encoded keyboards, each key is connected to a separate wire and it is a simple task to identify each key and its corresponding wire. This is not the case, however, with a non-encoded keyboard. In order to manufacture keyboards at low cost, a 16-key non-encoded keyboard generally has only eight wires—four wires for rows and four for columns. Pushing a key merely connects a row to a column. Let's now examine how this works. Here we will use the columns as output and the rows as input to a microprocessor port.

Let us output the value 1111 on the microprocessor port. With each column line assuming the value 1, the resulting value read on input will be 0100 (as shown in Figure 7.1). A 1 is set in row 1 because of its connection to column 2, accomplished by the key closure. Unfortunately, this information does not tell us which *column* has been activated. With only one set of data (input and output values), there is simply no way to determine which column and which row are connected. To determine which column the key is on, we must output a 1 successively on each of the columns: column 0, column 1, column 2, and column 3. In other words, we must *scan* the columns. Note that even though we have used columns rather than rows in this example, the name of this technique is *row-scanning*.

Figure 7.2 shows an example of how row-scanning is used to identify the key that has been pressed. For clarity, the actual polarities have not been respected in the illustration. Actual input polarities would be reversed. (In other words, 0s become 1s and 1s become 0s.)

Let us follow through the steps of this technique in parts A, B, C, and D of Figure 7.2. In phase A we output a 1 in column 0, producing the value 1000. Since column 0 is not connected to any of the four rows, the resulting input is 0000. Similarly, in phase B the 1 in column 1 (giving an output of 0100) is not transmitted to any of the rows, and again the input is 0000.

In phase C we output a 1 in column 2, producing 0010. Recall that column 2 is connected to row 1, since this is where a key has been pressed. The 1 of column 2 is thus transmitted to row 1, giving an input of 0100. So, with the output/input configuration of 0010-0100 we have identified the key pressed in column 2, row 1. However, we must continue scanning because of the rollover problem.

A *rollover* problem occurs if a user accidentally (or deliberately) presses more than one key at a time. This situation must be detected. Scanning must therefore proceed through its fourth phase where, in this example, a 1 is output on column 3 (phase D). Since no rollover was involved in this example, the resulting input value is 0000, and the row-scanning process is finished, i.e., no other key closure has been detected.

The next task is that of generating the code that corresponds to the key, i.e., in our example, to convert 0010-0100 into a suitable 4-bit code. This is accomplished easily by using a ROM table look-up. In other words, the bits 0010-0100 will address the contents of a ''keyboard codes'' table stored in the memory and will identify the appropriate 4-bit code.

Whenever a rollover condition exists, i.e., when more than one key closure is detected, the simplest solution is to ignore the data and to continue reading until only a single signal is detected, indicating that

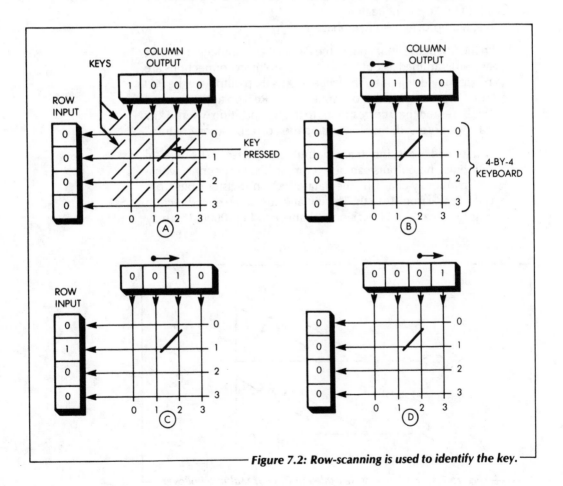

Figure 7.2: Row-scanning is used to identify the key.

only one key is left pushed down. Whenever more than two keys are pushed simultaneously, an additional electrical problem arises that requires the use of interconnection diodes (as shown in Figure 7.3). Using diodes limits the flow of current to one direction.

Line Reversal _____

The universal parallel interface, the *PIO*, has made possible a new technique for key identification. It is called line reversal. If it is possible to dedicate a complete 8-bit port of a PIO to keyboard interfacing, this method is faster and more elegant than row scanning. The essential fact to remember is that each line of a PIO port or each group of lines is programmable independently as an input or output. Figure 7.4 shows the use of a PIO for key identification.

Identification proceeds in two phases:

1. In the first phase, four lines of the PIO that are connected to rows are programmed as outputs. The four column connections are programmed as inputs. The value 0000 is then output on the PIO port. The resulting value on input is 1011. Real polarities are used this time, and the 0 corresponds to the row position where a key has been pressed, thus grounding the corresponding column.

2. In a second phase, inputs and outputs are reversed. The reversal of inputs and outputs can be accomplished very simply with a PIO by merely changing the data-direction-register's bits from 0s to 1s and from 1s to 0s. The initial value of the data direction register was 00001111; it is now changed to 11110000. This may

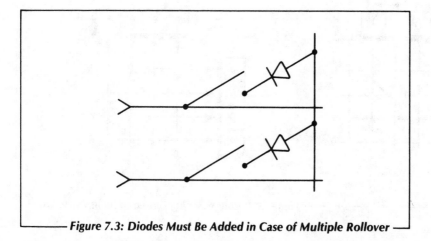

Figure 7.3: Diodes Must Be Added in Case of Multiple Rollover

be performed by a single instruction: *"complement data-direction-register"*. No change is performed on the data register itself.

The final resulting value of the data register is then read. As we can see in Figure 7.4, the input is now 1011. The 0 corresponds to the row where a key has been pressed. The complete value of the data register 10111011 (where each 0 denotes a key closure) now identifies the row and the column. The microprocessor uses this 8-bit code as a branch vector to a table in ROM that contains the 8-bit code corresponding to the keyboard. Any jump to an illegal location would be detected as a rollover or noise problem and a new reading would take place. The corresponding program is:

OUTPUT 0000 TO DATA REGISTER

COMPLEMENT DIRECTION REGISTER

READ DATA REGISTER IN INDEX REGISTER

READ TABLE ENTRY INDEXED

This method generally requires only four instructions and is thus more efficient than the row-scanning method.

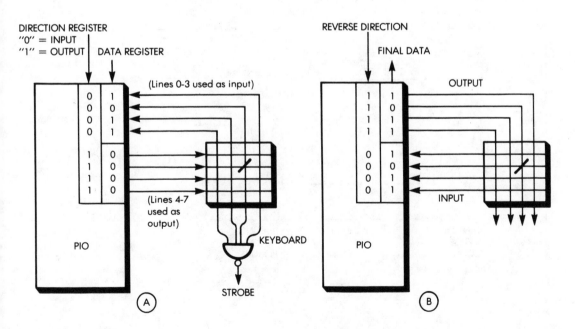

Figure 7.4: Line Reversal Requires a PIO

A disadvantage of the line reversal technique is that 8 pins of a PIO must be allocated to keyboard management. In view of the high cost of a PIO compared to the cost of a keyboard, such a solution may not be acceptable; the use of decoders might be preferred. However, when 8 pins are available, this solution is generally used.

THE DEBOUNCING PROBLEM

In any contact involving electromechanical components, true contact closure occurs only after an oscillation period of several milliseconds. Usually 10 to 20 milliseconds elapse between the time the key is first pressed and the time the contact is stabilized. The same problem occurs when the key is released. Figure 7.5 illustrates these leading-edge and trailing-edge bounces. A simple hardware solution to the problem is the use of an RC (resistor capacitor) filter. This is the solution normally used whenever a small number of keys is involved.

The software solution to this problem is to check the key closure again after n milliseconds (ms) have elapsed (where n = 5 to 20, depending on the quality of the keyboard used). The software-debouncing technique is most often used when the number of keys rises to 16 or more. It is accomplished simply by using a software delay routine. Delays are described in Chapter 8.

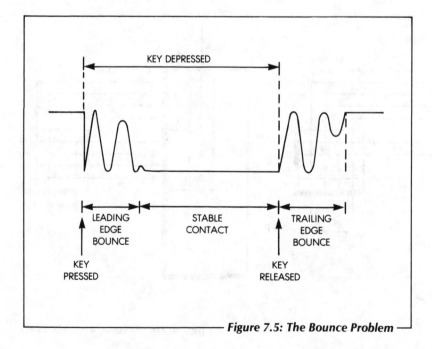

Figure 7.5: The Bounce Problem

COMPLEX KEYBOARDS

Any complex keyboard involving a large number of keys (for example, 64, as in Figure 7.6) can be decoded by one of the methods we have described. To connect a 4-bit port on the microprocessor to 16 rows, a 4- to 16-bit decoder is used on the output. This is illustrated in Figure 7.6.

A full alphanumeric keyboard is equipped with "shift" and "control" keys. These keys create four modes of operation or 4×64 possible characters. Keyboard management then becomes complex and involves sizeable and complex software routines, as well as additional hardware decoders. It then becomes advantageous to consider the new special LSI components developed specifically for keyboard and display control.

As an example, Figure 7.7 shows how the Intel 8279 keyboard/display controller interfaces directly to a 64-key keyboard and an LED display with two sets of 16 LEDs. Figure 7.8 shows the internal architecture of the device. The device provides automatic keyboard debouncing and row-scanning. It includes an internal 16×8 display RAM and an 8×8 FIFO. (A FIFO is a First-In-First-Out structure, i.e., a true waiting list of bytes that are accumulated from the keyboard.) This device does not, however, provide keyboard encoding functions, i.e., the substitution of an 8-bit code for each key that is pressed.

A *keyboard encoder,* such as the NEC-UPD 364 DO2, can be used to provide scanning, debouncing, and keyboard decoding. Using a 3600-bit internal ROM, this encoder provides a 10-bit code for up to 90

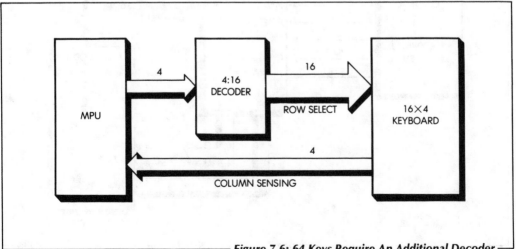

Figure 7.6: 64 Keys Require An Additional Decoder

keys in any one of four modes. It may operate in normal, shift, control, and shift-plus-control modes. Figure 7.9 displays the architecture of the NEC keyboard encoder. Other keyboard encoders are available from various manufacturers (e.g., Rockwell).

In summary, keyboards may be interfaced simply to a microprocessor system. In the case of a non-encoded keyboard with few keys, a software technique is generally used. In the case of a large keyboard, special-purpose interface chips are also used.

Let us now connect a simple output device, the LED display.

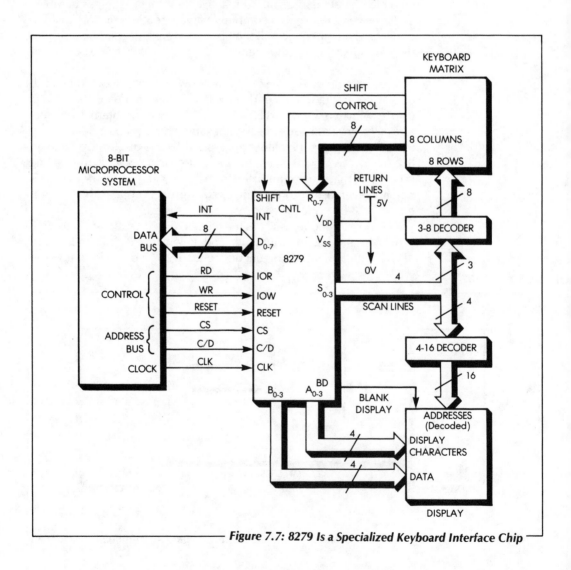

Figure 7.7: 8279 Is a Specialized Keyboard Interface Chip

LED DISPLAY

Recall that LED stands for Light-Emitting Diode. Figure 7.10 shows a 7-segment LED. Different combinations of its seven segments are illuminated to display specific digits. Each segment position is labeled by a letter from A to G. For example, to illuminate 0, segments A, B, C, D, E, F will be selected; to illuminate 1, segments B, C will be selected and so on. Displaying hexadecimal digits on a specific LED requires selecting

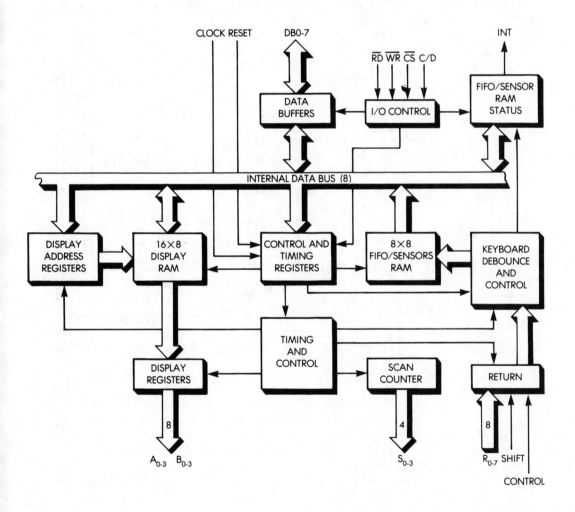

Figure 7.8: 8279 Internal Structure

the LED component and selecting the combination of segments that must be illuminated.

Another problem lies in the fact that the number to be displayed on the LED is usually encoded in the BCD (binary coded decimal) system. This number must first be converted from BCD into a seven-segment code. This decoding may be accomplished in several ways; for example, it may be handled by a ROM memory table look-up or by a BCD to seven-segment decoder. (Figure 7.11 shows an LED interface with such a decoder.) Note that each of the seven segment lines must include a driver to provide a sufficient current. A scanner-driver chip could be used to minimize the number of components.

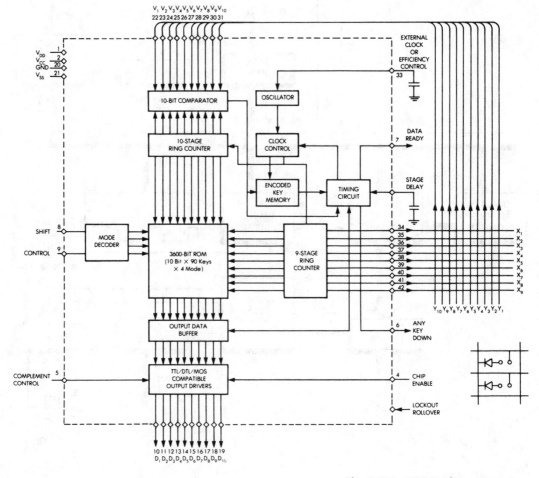

Figure 7.9: NEC Keyboard Encoder

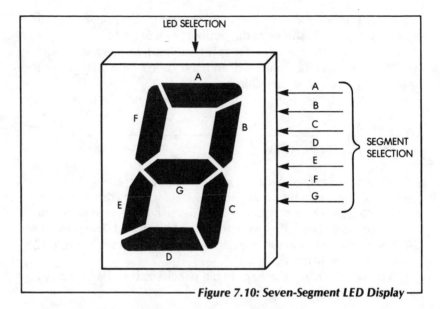

Figure 7.10: Seven-Segment LED Display

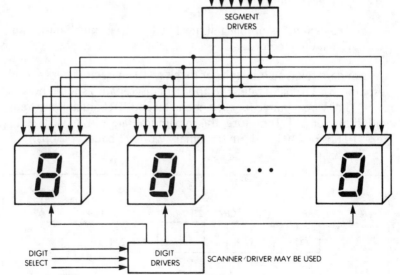

Figure 7.11: LED Interface

Using a 3-bit code we will select one of eight LEDs through an additional digit decoder, shown at the bottom of Figure 7.11.

In summary, interfacing LEDs simply requires decoders and drivers. The software may be simplified and the speed increased using a scanner-driver combination chip.

Let us now connect a simple input/output terminal, the teletype.

TELETYPE INTERFACE

The teletype is a serial device. It encodes every character into a 7-bit code plus parity, resulting in an 8-bit character code. Transmission to or from a teletype is asynchronous and special bits are used to denote the beginning and end of a character being transmitted. The standard teletype convention is to use one *start* bit and two *stop* bits. Figure 7.12 shows the shape of the signal.

In a standard teletype there are 11 bits per character, of which only 7 are used to identify the character:

— The start bit tells the TTY that a character is coming.

— The next 7 bits identify the character.

— The 8th bit of the character is an optional parity bit for verifying proper transmission.

— The next two stop bits tell the TTY to stop its mechanism, and give it time to do so.

A standard teletype transmits or receives 10 characters per second, resulting in a 110-baud rate. The apparent discrepancy should now be clear: 11 bits are required for each character and 10 characters are transmitted per second. Therefore, the maximum transfer rate is 10 × 11, i.e., 110 bps or 110 baud. (In the binary world, 1 baud = 1 bps.)

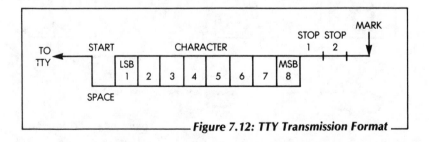

Figure 7.12: TTY Transmission Format

An interface is required for serial/parallel conversion and for the connection of the 20-milliamp teletype current loop. Some teletype models provide a direct RS-232 interface.

Teletype interfacing involves little more than a standard UART for serial-to-parallel and parallel-to-serial conversion, plus the appropriate level conversion for the required interface standard, whether current loop or RS-232. Figures 7.13 and 7.14 show two such interfaces. Figure

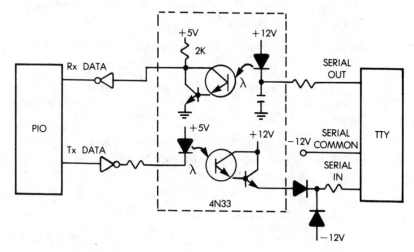

Figure 7.13: PIO-TTY Interface

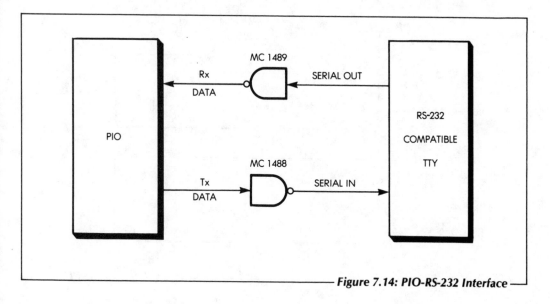

Figure 7.14: PIO-RS-232 Interface

7.15 offers a more detailed timing chart of a teletype with its tape-reader-punch.

We will now describe the receiving and transmitting sequences for the teletype.

THE TRANSMITTING SEQUENCE

The transmitting sequence for a teletype occurs in the following way:

1. The teletype keyboard is activated and the paper tape reader is blocked by a mechanical switch.

2. As long as the keyboard is inactive, it supplies a mark signal (1), a 20-milliamp current.

3. When a key is pressed, the 8-bit character code plus the stop and start bits are transmitted; i.e., the teletype transmits a start bit (0) to the UART, whose input is triggered from 1 to 0.

4. The UART now records the next 8 data bits and generates a "data-ready" signal for the microprocessor. It verifies the presence of the two stop bits, but other than that, it ignores

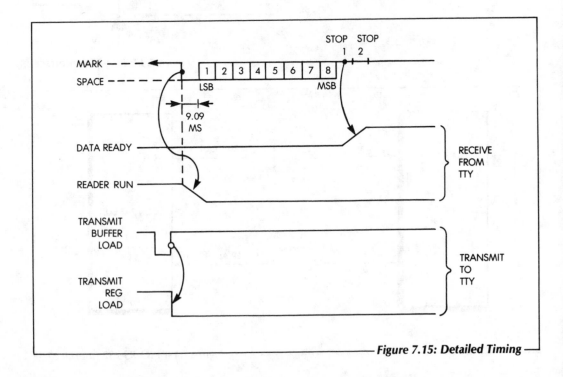

Figure 7.15: Detailed Timing

them. The UART also verifies parity if parity is used. (The eighth character bit, shown as MSB or most significant bit, is the parity bit.) The clock frequency of the UART is $16 \times 110 = 1.76$ KHz.

THE RECEIVING SEQUENCE

Let us now look at a receiving sequence:

1. If the UART output buffer is free, the microprocessor loads it.

2. The output buffer holds the data word to be serialized to the teletype. The UART automatically formats this data word, inserting the start and stop bits, and serializes it towards the teletype.

The standard UART thus completely automates the processing involved in communicating with a teletype-like device, including serial-parallel conversion, format conversion and parity verification or generation.

Naturally, it is not necessary to use a UART for serial-to-parallel conversion. This function can be performed through software. For example, Figure 7.16 shows an interface using an 8080 plus a latch without a UART. Figure 7.17 shows the corresponding functional flowchart.

Many low-speed terminals use a teletype format and connection. Interfacing them to a microprocessor system is simple, using a UART and a standard bus. RS-232 has been developed to facilitate such connections. RS-232 is described later in this chapter.

Let us now connect to a telephone line.

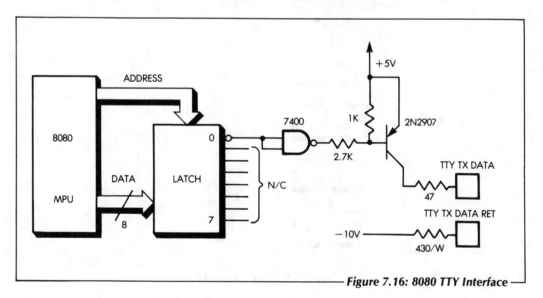

Figure 7.16: 8080 TTY Interface

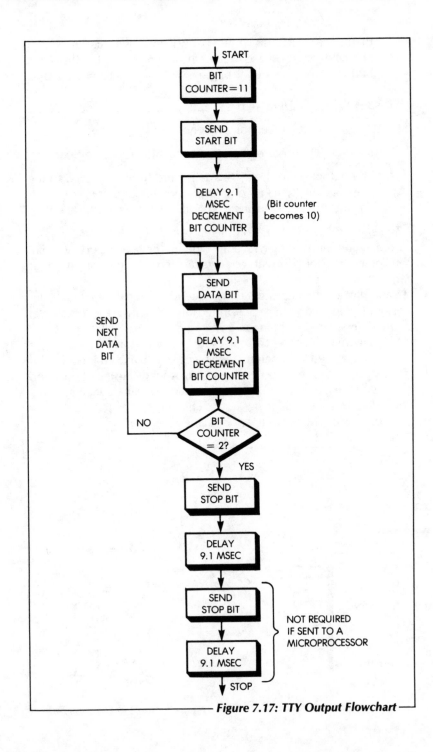

Figure 7.17: TTY Output Flowchart

Adding A Modem _____

A modem is a modulator-demodulator. It is now available in single-chip form. A modem allows the transmission of serial data in the form of audible frequencies over telephone lines. As an example, Figures 7.18

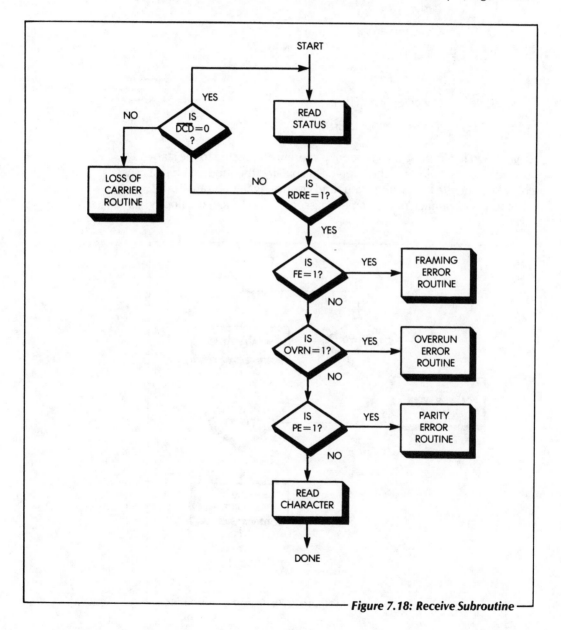

Figure 7.18: Receive Subroutine

and 7.19 present flowcharts showing the reception and transmission of data (RS-232 format). The acronyms are:

- DCD = Data Carrier Detected
- PE   = Parity Error
- OVRN = Overrun (error)
- CTS   = Clear To Send
- FE   = Framing Error
- RDRE = Receiver Data Error
- TDRE = Transmitter Data Error

As shown in Figure 7.20, a modem is merely connected to the standard RS-232 port used for the teletype. Typically, the modem chip(s) check or generate the various status and control signals automatically.

Let us now interface to a complex mass memory device, the floppy disk.

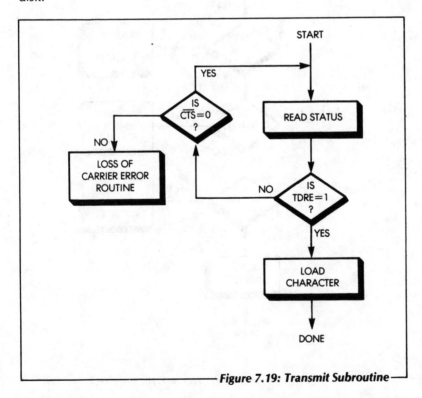

Figure 7.19: Transmit Subroutine

FLOPPY DISK

The floppy disk, or its offspring the mini- or micro-floppy, is one of the most widely used mass memories for microcomputers. A typical mini-floppy supplies 110K bytes with a transfer rate of 125K bps, using a 5.25-inch diskette, with a power consumption of 7.5 to 15 watts.

The name "floppy" disk is derived from the fact that the disk itself is made of a soft material. A floppy disk is recorded magnetically on either one or both of its sides and is permanently enclosed in a square cardboard envelope lined internally with a special low-friction material. When in use, the floppy rotates at high speed inside its cover while being applied against the read/write head. The read/write head moves horizontally along a radius of the floppy disk through a hole in the cover called the "head slot" (see Figure 7.21).

Information on the disk is structured into *tracks* and *sectors*. The disk is divided into concentric rings called *tracks*. Tracks are typically numbered from 0 to 76 (for a regular size floppy), and are divided into radial sectors like slices of a pie. Each block within a sector on a track typically has 128 bytes of useful information.

To access information within the disk, it is necessary to retrieve the sector on which information is stored and then to transfer information to or from that sector. The head must be positioned mechanically over the desired track, and when the appropriate sector comes under the head, information can be transferred serially. The *disk controller* automatically accesses a block of data on the disk. It also performs a number of other tasks, which are explained below.

A basic read sequence includes the following steps:

1. Access the desired track, i.e., position the head above the appropriate track.

2. Identify the initial sector (in a multi-sector transfer).

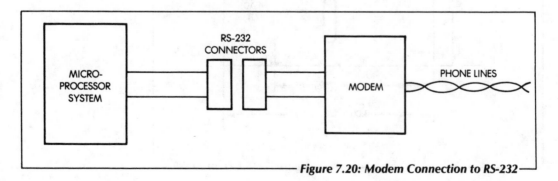

Figure 7.20: Modem Connection to RS-232

3. Transfer the requested number of sectors to the system's memory.

4. Perform CRC (cyclic-redundancy check) validation on the data. CRC is a simple algorithmic technique used to verify that information within the block is correct. The CRC word that indicates the integrity of data within the preceding words is stored at the end of every logical block. A special circuit must be available to verify the CRC by first recomputing it and then comparing that result to the CRC value that is read from the disk.

Note that the step that identifies the sector number varies according to the type of floppy disk used.

Regular floppy disks are said to be *soft-sectored*; i.e., the format on the disk can be defined by the user. Sector numbers are encoded on each sector. The position of sector zero is detected by an index hole punched in the disk. By contrast, most mini-floppies are *hard-sectored*. In a hard-sectored disk, a hole is punched in the diskette at the position

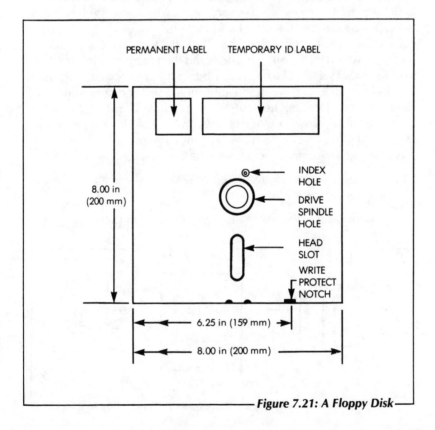

Figure 7.21: A Floppy Disk

corresponding to each successive sector. Sector detection is then done by hardware.

FLOPPY DISK CONTROLLERS

Since 1977, a floppy disk controller has been available on a single chip. All FDCs (floppy disk controllers) must provide a number of common functions, including automatic verification, format compatibility, CRC generation and verification, read or write with simple or multiple blocks, automatic sector search, complete track read or write, and simultaneous control of several disk drives. All FDCs for standard size floppies are compatible with the IBM 3740 soft-sectored standard for floppy-disk format.

It is the responsibility of the programmer to keep track of the location of information on disks. Programmable controls include track-to-track stepping time, head-settling time, head-latching time, step-motor or 3-phase motor control, and programmed DMA transfer. The use of a DMA is imperative for all standard-speed disks, as no microprocessor could keep up with the required transfer rate if transfers were completely accomplished by program.

Let us now examine an FDC.

A SINGLE-CHIP FDC

We will now examine the FD 1771B, the single-chip floppy disk controller from Western Digital. The internal architecture of this FDC appears in Figure 7.22. The four main circuits are:

1. the CRC logic (which appears in the bottom left corner of the illustration). The CRC logic automatically generates the CRC for the information coming in or going out. During a read operation, the computed CRC will be compared to the CRC read from the disk. If both agree, the data will be presumed valid.

2. the ALU (appearing on the right of the illustration), which is used to compare, increment or decrement registers. The registers are described below.

3. the disk-interface control, which manages the requisite control lines.

4. the microprocessor interface, which implements the required handshake dialogue with the system.

The disk-interface control and the microprocessor interface are detailed in Figure 7.23. They will be described later in more detail.

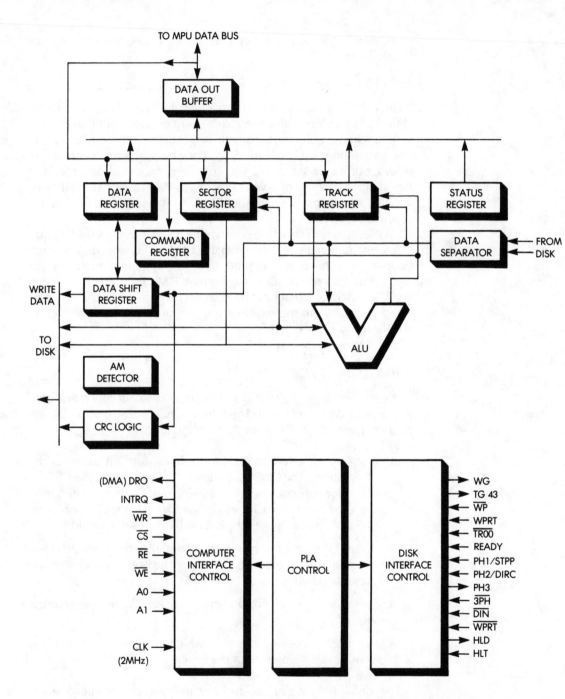

Figure 7.22: Western Digital FD 1771B

The FDC Register _____

The six FDC internal registers appear at the top of the illustration in Figure 7.22. They are:

1. the data-shift register, which accumulates 8 bits of data from the floppy disk and outputs them into the data register. Conversely, it will input 8 bits from the data register and serialize them in order to write data serially on the disk.

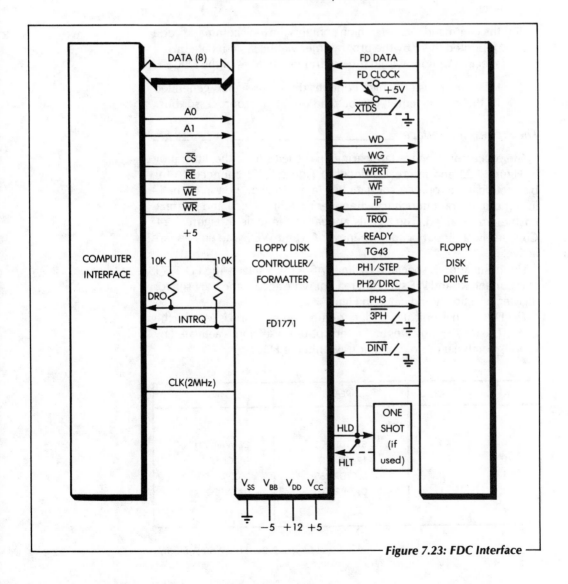

Figure 7.23: FDC Interface

2. the data register, which is simply a bidirectional 8-bit buffer register used for read or write operations on the microprocessor data bus.

3. the track register, which records the actual position of the head (from 0 to 76). It is incremented while moving toward Track 76 and decremented while moving toward Track 0.

4. the sector register, which contains the number of the required sector.

5. the command register, which contains the 8-bit command code deposited there by the programmer via the system data bus. It specifies options within the control possibilities of the FDC.

6. the status register, which contains the status signals generated by the component. It can be read on the microprocessor bus.

The Processor Interface _____

The processor interface (appearing on the left side of the illustration in Figure 7.22 and in greater detail in Figure 7.23) connects to the bidirectional microprocessor data bus (appearing at the top of the illustration). An output occurs whenever CS (chip select) and RE (read enable) are enabled. The signals appear in the table in Figure 7.24. Conversely, an input occurs whenever CS and WE (write enable) are active.

The destination is specified by lines A0-A1. CS selects the FD 1771 component. RE and WE specify a read or write access and are used for register selection as indicated in Figure 7.24.

The DRO signal indicates a "data-request-output" and is used by the DMA. The INTRQ indicates an "interrupt-request" and is activated by various combinations of conditions within the FDC.

A1	A0	READ	WRITE
0	0	STATUS REG.	COMMAND REG.
0	1	TRACK REG.	TRACK REG.
1	0	SECTOR REG.	SECTOR REG.
1	1	DATA REG.	DATA REG.

Figure 7.24: Function Selection

Floppy Disk Interface

The floppy disk interface lines appear on the right side of Figure 7.22. Three facilities are supplied:

1. position control of the head

2. write control

3. data transfer.

A square-wave clock is used with a frequency of 2MHz (divided by 4 internally). The moveable head may be programmed in three-step increments: 100, 125, and 166 steps-per-second. The stepping rate is determined by bits 0 and 1 of the command word. The length of the sector may be specified by multiples of 16.

Read Operation

A read operation is performed in five steps, including:

1. loading the track register

2. generating a "Seek"

3. waiting for proper positioning

4. transferring data towards the microprocessor under interrupt control

5. verifying that the operation has been correctly executed after the specified data transfer has occurred.

Writing On The Disk

The operation of writing on the disk is performed in seven steps:

1. loading the track register

2. generating a "Seek" order

3. waiting for proper positioning

4. giving a "Write" command

5. loading the data as soon as the data-request signal is received

6. loading the remaining data

7. verifying the status indicators "Busy" and "CRC-Error."

In summary, the FDC connects to the microprocessor system in a straightforward manner (as shown in Figure 7.23). It automates the specific tasks required for disk control. Interfacing a disk has now become a simple task with the availability of specialized controller chips.

CRT INTERFACE

A CRT (cathode-ray tube) display is a television-like tube. CRTs are convenient output devices for professional and business applications. CRTs are silent and can display pages of data quickly. The disadvantage of a CRT is that it does not produce hard copy, so a printer is still needed.

Interfacing to a CRT involves high-speed data moves and requires the use of a DMA. The basic system configuration for interfacing to a CRT is illustrated in Figure 7.25.

The microprocessor appears at the left of the illustration. The RAM memory (on the right) is used to refresh the contents of the CRT periodically. The DMA is used for automatic block transfers from the RAM to the CRT. Automatic block transfers to the CRT are buffered on a

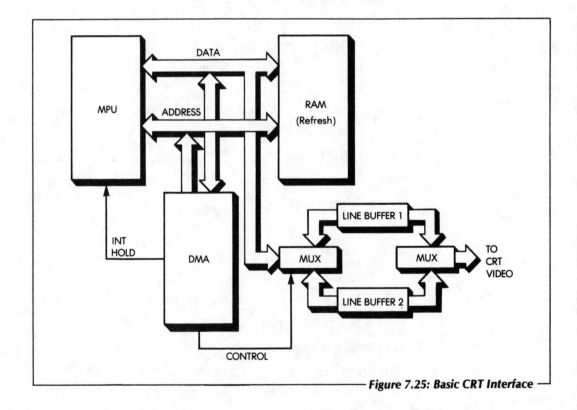

Figure 7.25: Basic CRT Interface

two-line basis. Two line buffers, labeled in this case *line buffer 1* and *line buffer 2*, are normally provided.

The normal utilization of the system is as follows. Data are transferred from the memory into line buffer 1 until it is full. During this time, line buffer 2 is presumed to be full. It will empty itself into a shifter communicating with the video output of the screen. Typically, it takes much longer to empty line buffer 2 onto the screen than it takes to load line buffer 1 from the RAM. When line buffer 2 is empty, the multiplexer (MUX) (on the right of the illustration) switches automatically to line buffer 1. The contents of line buffer 1 are then sent progressively to the screen. At the same time, the empty line buffer 2 is reloaded automatically under DMA control from the memory; and so the process continues.

Actually, the total picture is more complex than this. The bits traveling from the memory specify characters in an 8-bit code, but this code is not adequate for display of characters on a screen. The method normally used to display characters uses a *dot matrix*. The 8-bit character code must therefore be converted into a suitable dot-matrix pattern to be displayed on the screen. This conversion process is accomplished by a ROM table look-up or by a *character generator*. The process is illustrated in Figure 7.26.

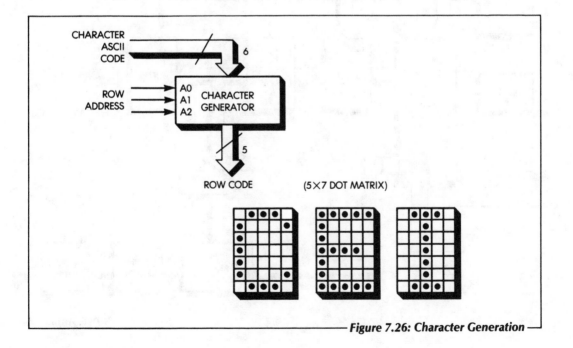

Figure 7.26: Character Generation

A CRT controller chip (CRTC) may be used to simplify the design. The connection of a CRTC (exclusive of the DMA) appears in Figure 7.27, which shows the ROM character generator required for the output into the shift register and into the video output.

Assuming the use of a a 5-by-7 dot matrix to represent characters, each 8-bit character code results in an output of 5-by-7 values (*"dot"* or *"no-dot,"* i.e., black or white). A 5-bit-wide ROM can be used as a character generator. Seven successive lines of dots must be output for every character. The first row must be output, then the next row, and then the next row. In order to specify one of seven possible rows, a 3-pin row address (labeled A0, A1, and A2 in Figure 7.26) must be provided.

As another example, the interface implemented with an 8275 CRT controller (Intel) appears in Figure 7.28. The block diagram is identical.

Many functions are required of a CRT controller. One of the main requirements is the ability to program the shape of the characters, i.e.,

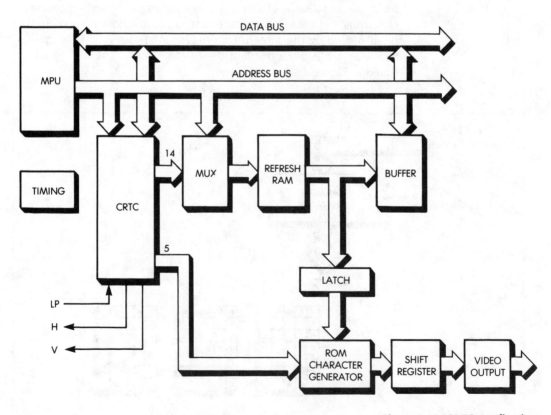

Figure 7.27: CRTC Application

the number of dots on a line for each character and the distribution of the dots. This function is accomplished by the character generator, the number of lines per sync, and the cursor (a small blinking square, triangle, or other shape). A special register keeps track of the cursor's position. An extra register may be required if a light-pen is used on the screen.

In addition, a powerful controller should incorporate as much of the external hardware as possible, including line buffers. In a complex system, the controller should also supply complex functions such as *scrolling* and *paging*. *Scrolling* refers to the vertical movement of text across the screen. *Paging* refers to the flipping from one screen-full of data to the next, every n lines.

The various CRTCs available from different manufacturers automate various combinations of these facilities, so that a complete interface still requires several chips.

We have just described the standard interface techniques for the most widely used input/output devices. Complete details cannot be provided within the scope of this book, but the techniques and devices presented here should substantially clarify interfacing techniques.

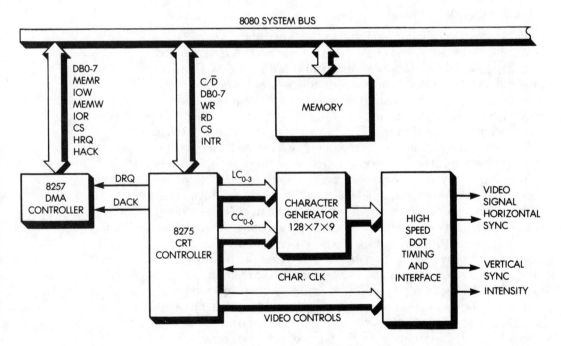

Figure 7.28: Intel 8275 CRT Interface

However, there is still one aspect of interfacing that has not yet been described. This involves the interfacing of one microprocessor system to a second microprocessor system or even several microprocessor systems, thus producing *multimicroprocessor* systems. Let us now examine the main interconnection strategies.

MULTIMICROPROCESSOR SYSTEMS

There are several techniques for interconnecting two or more monolithic microprocessors. The three most widely used techniques are:

1. memory communication

2. interregister communication

3. direct bus intercommunication.

The third technique—direct-bus intercommunications—is used only in specific cases (for reasons that will be explained later). The two most often used interconnections strategies are illustrated in Figure 7.29.

MEMORY COMMUNICATION _____

The memory communication strategy is shown at the top of Figure 7.29. This technique uses a *two-port RAM*. A two-port RAM is equipped with a special interface supplying dual connections to the data bus and the address bus (two *ports*). Access priority is resolved internally. In the case of simultaneous requests, one of the ports has a higher priority; this is determined by hardware.

This strategy is called the *mailbox* system; the system's operation is asynchronous. A specific area of the memory is reserved for interprocessor communication. Every microprocessor can then access this common memory and either deposit data into or read data from the mailbox area. One obvious problem lies in the access-control mechanism. A microprocessor must not modify the contents of a memory area while another microprocessor is reading that memory area. This problem is solved by a *lock*, which can be implemented in hardware or software. A lock is a mechanism that forbids access to a memory zone by one processor. Extra bits can also be used on the memory and one bit allocated to memory protection. Whenever such a protection bit is turned on, the memory word cannot be accessed by another processor. On the other hand, a memory word can be reserved for data access control and contain (at all times) the limits of the zones accessible to any of the two microprocessors.

This simple interconnection mechanism is used for sharing *blocks* of data. It is expensive, since it requires a special two-port interface for the memory. It is also relatively slow as it involves the testing of memory words prior to transfers.

INTERREGISTER COMMUNICATION

The process of communicating through registers is illustrated at the bottom of Figure 7.29. In the past, communication through registers involved the use of actual microprocessor registers. Nowadays, with the availability of interface chips such as the PIO, the shared register is an I/O register residing *in the PIO.* In such a case, half of a PIO is dedicated to microprocessor communication. Any of the microprocessors may then deposit a word of data within a PIO and the other microprocessor can read it. Interrupts or their equivalent may be generated by any processor. If both microprocessors are to assume equivalent roles, a cleaner communication scheme would involve the use of one PIO for each microprocessor in the system for interrupt-handling purposes. This communication scheme is most efficient for a *word-oriented* dialogue. (It would be slow in the case of block transfers.) Another

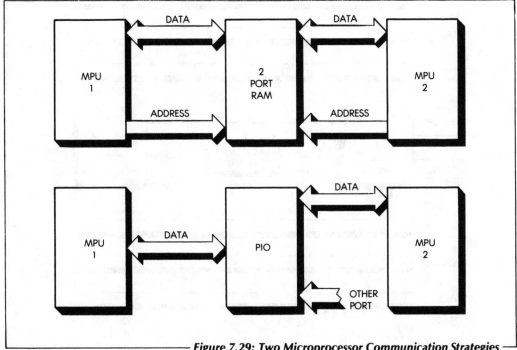

Figure 7.29: Two Microprocessor Communication Strategies

feature is the automatic generation of interrupts whenever a data word is deposited inside a PIO. Note that the two techniques just described can be used *simultaneously*.

If the highest possible communication speed is necessary, a direct bus interconnection can be used. This, however, requires independent processing (which is now possible with 1-chip microcomputers). Connecting two microprocessors on the same bus is possible, but only if one of the microprocessors is inactive (on the bus) at all times. A master/slave mode facility is then required, which is available on newer MPU's.

Multiple microprocessors can also be connected via multiple buses. A multi-bus interconnect mechanism involves a buffering between the buses, which is analogous to the interregister communication implemented with a PIO. For this reason, the old "common bus" interconnect has been superseded by the use of PIOs. For example, the actual structure of a multiprocessor system implemented by Raytheon in a radar application appears in Figure 7.30. We can see the extensive use of *dual-port RAMs*.

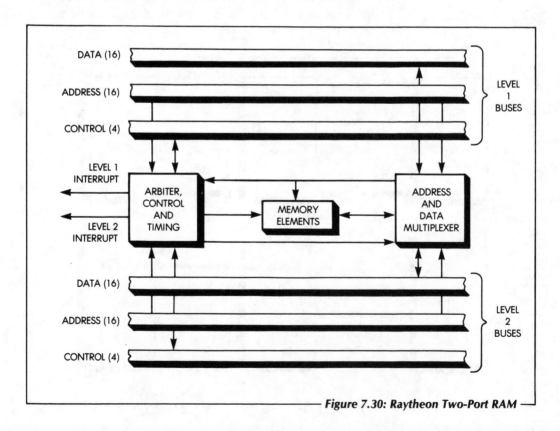

Figure 7.30: Raytheon Two-Port RAM

Microprocessors can also be interconnected using variations of the above schemes. For example, they can communicate via telephone or other communication lines using a UART and a modem. However, in concept this is essentially an interregister communication that happens to include the necessary serial transmissions.

So far we have reviewed the main techniques available for interconnecting all the important devices to a microprocessor system. Let us now connect the system to the outside world. To facilitate such connections, both within and outside the microcomputer, a number of busing standards are widely used. A user developing a system involving a large number of peripherals can simplify the design by selecting one of the existing bus standards, so that the peripherals may be connected directly to the system. It is therefore important to review here the main busing standards.

BUS STANDARDS

The four "classic" bus standards for microprocessors are: the RS-232C, the IEEE 488, the CAMAC, and the new S-100 bus. We will now discuss each of these four standards.

RS-232C

The RS-232C is the classic binary serial interface. Standard interface levels are defined. A status character is sent whenever the device is ready to accept new data. Resulting transmission speeds range from 110 to 9600 baud. The RS-232C is frequently used with CRT displays and slow printers. Figure 7.31 displays typical RS-232C signals.

IEEE 488

The IEEE standard 488 dates back to 1971, but it was not officially published by IEEE in the U.S. until 1975. The IEEE 488 is known as the "Instrument Standard;" the "General-Purpose Interface Bus" (GPIB); the "HPIB" (Hewlett-Packard Interface Bus—in view of the prominent role played by Hewlett-Packard in promoting the standard); or the ASCII bus (since data formatting on the 8-bit bidirectional data bus is not specified and it is almost always in an ASCII format). Since 1975 the bus has also been called the ANSI MC1.1-1975 Standard.

A single 24-pin connector is specified:

1. 8 ground lines

2. 16 signal lines:
    8 for data
    3 for transfer: DAV, NFRD, NDAC
    5 for bus management: IFC, ATN, REN, SRQ, EOI

Figure 7.32 presents an illustration of the standard IEEE 488 bus. Figure 7.33 shows the control signals and Figure 7.34 shows the validation process for a data transfer handshake.

During a data transfer, the ATN line becomes low and the 8-bit code is gated on DIO. Data on DIO are not formatted. They may be either data, addresses, instructions to the instruments, measurements, universal commands, or status words.

We should stress that the use of unformatted data on the 8-bit bus is both a strength and a weakness of the system. Because data are unformatted, there is great freedom in interpreting these data by instruments or other devices. However, an *intelligent* instrument is required to make sense out of a stream of 8-bit words on such a bus. It is the responsibility of the instrument connected to this bus to decode the sequence of words that is presented to it and then to implement them. A significant amount of processing is necessary to do this. Two typical interfaces to GPIB (talk and listen) are shown in block form in Figures 7.35 and 7.36.

		PIN NO.
__ GROUNDS		1, 7
__ XMIT DATA	(TO COM)	2
__ REC DATA	(FROM COM)	3
__ REQUEST TO SEND	(TO COM)	4
__ CLEAR TO SEND	(FROM COM)	5
__ DATA SET READY	(FROM COM)	6
__ DATA TERMINAL READY	(TO COM)	20
__ RING INDICATOR	(FROM COM)	22
__ RECEIVED LINE SIGNAL DETECTOR	(FROM COM)	12
__ SIGNAL QUALITY DETECTOR	(FROM COM)	21
__ DATA RATE SELECTOR	(TO COM)	23
__ DATA RATE SELECTOR	(FROM COM)	23
__ TRANSMITTER TIMING	(TO COM)	15
__ TRANSMITTER TIMING	(FROM COM)	24
__ RECEIVER TIMING	(FROM COM)	17

Figure 7.31: RS-232C Signals

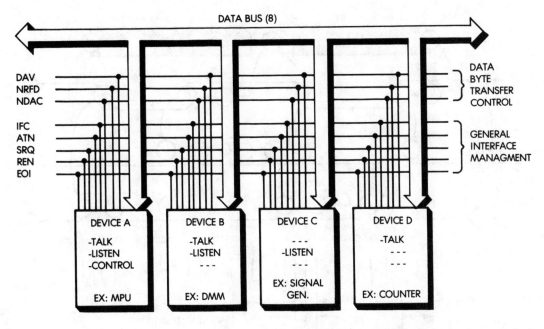

Figure 7.32: IEEE 488 Instrument Bus Standard

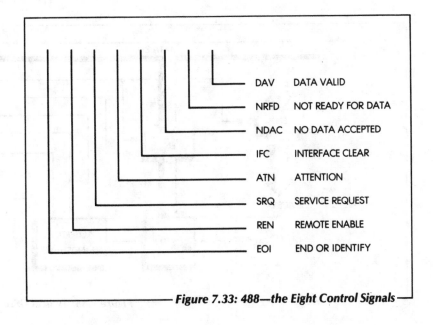

Figure 7.33: 488—the Eight Control Signals

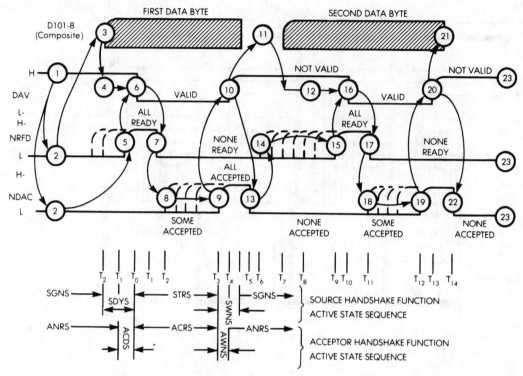

Figure 7.34: 488—Handshake

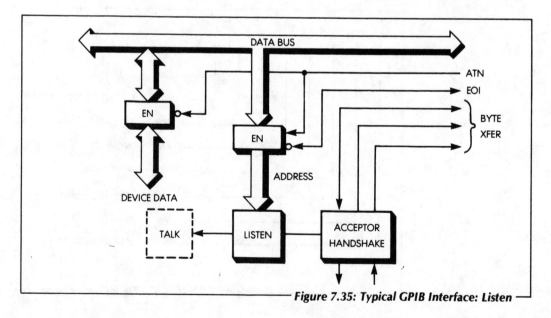

Figure 7.35: Typical GPIB Interface: Listen

The main physical limitations of GPIB are:

— a maximum transfer rate of 1M-byte-per-second.

— a word width of 8 bits (rather than 16 bits—which would be advantageous when connecting instruments to a minicomputer).

— the requirement that instruments be positioned close together (2 meters maximum).

— finally, the difficulty of understanding the standard itself.

The main advantage of GPIB is that it allows the easy interconnect of many instruments to a universal bus. The non-specific nature of the bus requires an intelligent and complex control at the levels of the instruments connected to it. This may not be an objection in the case of expensive instrumentation, but it is an objection in the case of simpler devices.

In order to facilitate interfacing to the IEEE 488, special interface chips have been introduced that greatly simplify the design. As an example, Figure 7.37 shows an interface using the Motorola GPIA chip.

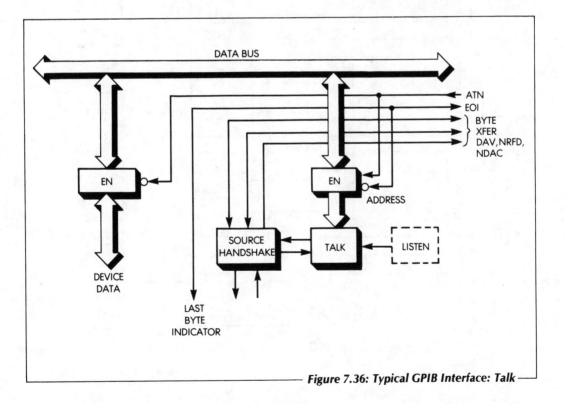

Figure 7.36: Typical GPIB Interface: Talk

CAMAC _____

CAMAC is the IEEE standard 583. IEEE 488 is a simple hardware inter-communication convention; the CAMAC standard goes well beyond this convention and specifies a parallel interface bus together with specific physical modules called *crates*. The word "crate" is closely associated with the CAMAC standard and implies strictly specified modules.

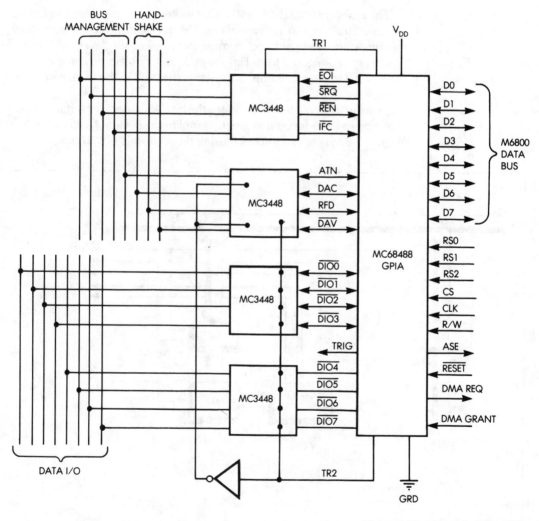

Figure 7.37: Motorola GPIA Chip

Figure 7.38 shows a simple CAMAC system. Each module is terminated with an 86-pin connector. A crate is a card rack with 25 positions. A crate controller resides at the end of every crate and almost always uses a microprocessor. The CAMAC standard has been developed for the standardization of nuclear applications and is now finding significant use in industrial process control, where modularity is essential.

A disadvantage of the CAMAC is that it is expensive, since modules are completely specified; this is often wasteful. An advantage of the CAMAC is the interchangeability of functions on a hardware module basis.

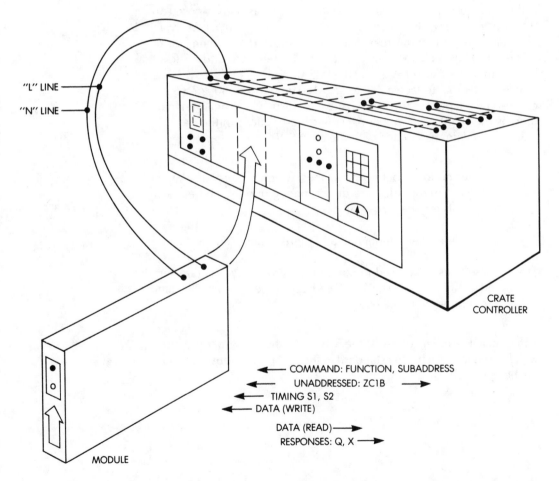

Figure 7.38: IEEE 583, CAMAC Interface Standard

THE S-100 BUS

The S-100 bus, originally called the Altair/IMSAI standard and now the IEEE 696, came into being in 1976 when the two main manufacturers of personal computers at that time—MITS and IMSAI (now defunct)—supplied a "common" hundred-line bus intended for connecting the 8080 to external devices. This bus is now widely used by manufacturers of 8080-, 8085- and Z80-based systems and allows users to exchange boards between various S-100 systems. The S-100 bus has become an important standard, and many memory and interface boards are S-100 compatible.

The emergence of the S-100 standard has probably been the first time in the history of computing that a de facto standard has been imposed on the industry by *users*. It is not a well-designed standard but it is an available standard, and for this reason it can be expected to remain in use.

The S-100 bus is characterized by a 5- or 10-inch card and a 3-level power supply: +8V, +18V (16 in the IMSAI version) and −18V. It is a simple matter to interface a Z80 to an S-100 bus; and a 6800 or a 6502 can also be adapted to the bus. Figure 7.39 displays the actual signals used by the S-100 bus. Appendix D offers descriptions of the signals.

Some problems associated with the early S-100 bus were:

— Parasitic coupling between the lines, which requires insulation of the motherboard. Note that using a ground-trace between the signals reduces cross-talk.

— Several lines were undefined and therefore not standardized.

— These lines were used in contradictory ways by several users and manufacturers. The S-100 bus has now become an IEEE standard under the name 696.

In terms of numbers of users, the S-100 is without a doubt the most widely used internal busing standard in the computer industry. It cannot be ignored.

1	+8V		51	+8V
2	+16V		52	−16V
3	XRDY		53	GND
4	VI0		54	SLAVE CLR
5	VI1		55	DMA0
6	VI2		56	DMA1
7	VI3		57	DMA2
8	VI4		58	sXTRQ
9	VI5		59	A19
10	VI6		60	SIXTN
11	VI7		61	A20
12	NMI		62	A21
13	PWRFAIL		63	A22
14	DMA3		64	A23
15	A18		65	NDEF
16	A16		66	NDEF
17	A17		67	PHANTOM
18	SDSB		68	MWRT
19	CDSB		69	RFU
20	GND		70	GND
21	NDEF		71	RFU
22	ADSB		72	RDY
23	DODSB		73	INT
24	φ		74	HOLD
25	pSTVAL		75	RESET
26	pHLDA		76	pSYNC
27	RFU		77	pWR
28	RFU		78	pDBIN
29	A5		79	A0
30	A4		80	A1
31	A3		81	A2
32	A15		82	A6
33	A12		83	A7
34	A9		84	A8
35	DO1/DATA1		85	A13
36	DO0/DATA0		86	A14
37	A10		87	A11
38	DO4/DATA4		88	DO2/DATA2
39	DO5/DATA5		89	DO3/DATA3
40	DO6/DATA6		90	DO7/DATA7
41	D12/DATA10		91	DI4/DATA12
42	D13/DATA11		92	DI5/DATA13
43	D17/DATA15		93	DI6/DATA14
44	sM1		94	DI1/DATA9
45	sOUT		95	DI0/DATA8
46	sINP		96	sINTA
47	sMEMR		97	sWO
48	sHLTA		98	ERROR
49	CLOCK		99	POC
50	GND		100	GND

Figure 7.39: S-100 Bus (IMSAI)

SUMMARY

In this chapter we examined the main interfacing techniques for usual microprocessor input/output devices. We also examined some of the software and hardware alternatives and learned about multi-microprocessor systems and bus standards. At this point, the task of assembling the hardware of a complete system should seem simple. We have seen solutions for all of the significant problems.

The problem that remains to be solved is programming. This is the subject of Chapter 8.

EXERCISES

7-1: What is the difference between a fully-encoded keyboard and a non-encoded keyboard?

7-2: Describe the debouncing problem.

7-3: Explain the multiple key roll-over problem.

7-4: Describe the row-scanning technique.

7-5: Describe the line reversal technique used with a PIO connected to a keyboard.

7-6: Looking at Figure 7.7, explain the functions of the 8279 keyboard interface chip.

7-7: Looking at Figure 7.9, explain the functions of the NEC keyboard and encoder.

7-8: The seven segments of a typical LED display are shown in Figure 7.11. Assume that segment A is connected to bit 6, segment B is connected to bit 5, etc. Show in hexadecimal form the code that must be sent to the LED in order to display the digits from 0 to 9 and A to F.

7-9: Describe the function of a modem.

7-10: What is the function of the CRC validation technique used on disk records?

7-11: What is the difference between soft-sectored and hard-sectored disks?

7-12: Explain the operation of a floppy disk controller such as the 1771B shown in Figure 7.22.

7-13: Explain the operation of the two line buffers of a basic CRT interface (shown in Figure 7.25).

7-14: What is the function of the character generator shown in Figure 7.28?

7-15: Explain what a two-port RAM is. What is its main advantage? What are its disadvantages?

7-16: Explain the various methods used to communicate between two microprocessor systems.

7-17: What is the IEEE 488 used for?

7-18: What are the advantages of the S-100 bus?

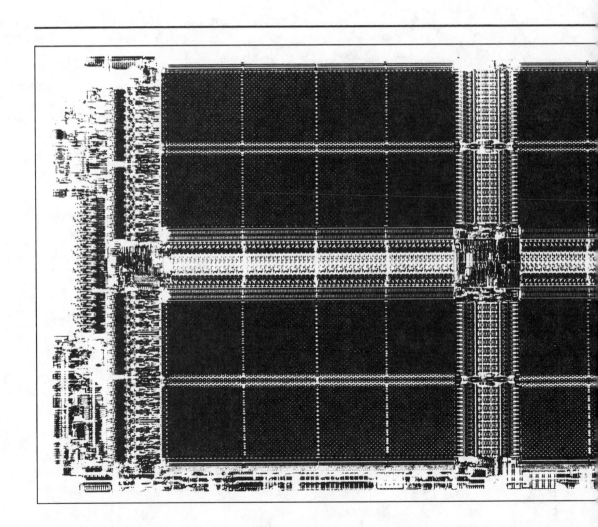

CHAPTER **8**

MICROPROCESSOR PROGRAMMING

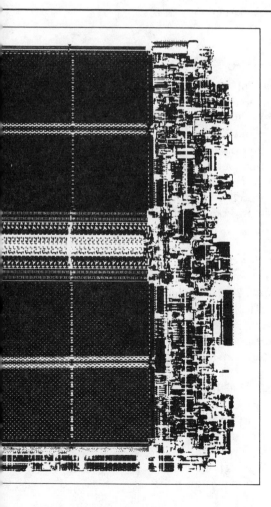

OBJECTIVE

This chapter presents a comprehensive introduction to programming. It covers the main definitions, the basic concepts, and many of the problems and essential techniques for programming. By the end of the chapter, the principles involved in programming and writing programs should be clear. However, programming cannot be taught within a single chapter of a book. Mastering the concepts, problems, and techniques of programming requires at least one other essential ingredient: actual practice.

DEFINITIONS

ALGORITHM AND PROGRAM

We will first consider how to solve a control problem. The problem's solution will be expressed as an *algorithm*. An algorithm is a step-by-step specification of a sequence of operations that will solve a problem. An algorithm can be expressed in any form and in any language. For use on a particular processor, however, we must convert the algorithm to a form that the processor can execute directly. We have already seen that a microprocessor can only execute *binary* instructions. Typically, for an 8-bit microprocessor, each binary instruction is 1, 2, 3, or 4 bytes long. (Recall that a byte is a group of 8 bits.) The set of instructions that implements the algorithm is called the *program*.

PROGRAMMING LANGUAGE

A fundamental problem is to convert the algorithm into a machine-executable *language*. A translation is required to convert the algorithm directly into binary patterns. Unfortunately, binary patterns are not particularly easy to use or memorize. Because of this inconvenience and the resulting inefficiency at the human level, a number of alternative program representations have been devised. Artificial languages, called *programming languages*, have been created, where instructions to the processor are represented in *symbolic* form. Each instruction of a programming language is translated by a special translator program into one or more binary-level instructions. There are two *levels* of programming languages: assembly and high-level.

Assembly language is a direct symbolic representation of the binary instructions that can be executed by the processor. For example, let us recall one of the 8080 instructions we studied in Chapter 2: ADD r. This instruction, known as the *mnemonic* representation of a binary instruction, adds the contents of register r to the accumulator. An *assembler* program automatically converts ADD r into the corresponding binary code. Conversely, a *disassembler* converts binary instructions into their symbolic mnemonic representation.

Using assembly language allows the representation of all binary instructions in symbolic form. Because each assembly-level instruction will normally be translated into *one* machine-level (binary) instruction, this is the most efficient programming language from the standpoint of *machine* efficiency. It allows direct manipulation of the registers and bits within the machine. Thus, assembly language is the most frequently used language for any application that requires execution efficiency.

Unfortunately, programming in assembly language is tedious and slow, since the programmer must write instructions for data transfers at the register and internal bus levels. To alleviate this inefficiency at the human level, *high-level languages* have been developed. High-level languages are closer than assembly-level languages to the functional representation of algorithms and are independent of the internal architecture of the processor.

It is not possible to communicate directly with a computer using ordinary language. Human languages have syntax ambiguities that are resolved by context or by other forms of communication not available to a computer. In view of the complexity of human languages, we must communicate with computers in artificial languages that have simpler, non-ambiguous grammars. Many high-level languages have been developed. Each one has a specific syntax that may make it more convenient for a given class of applications, such as science (FORTRAN, BASIC, Pascal), business (COBOL, PL/1), and list processing (LISP).

The translator program that converts high-level instructions into binary or *machine code* is called a *compiler* or an *interpreter*, depending on whether it translates the entire user program at once (a compiler) or one instruction at a time (an interpreter).

The two high-level languages most often used for microprocessors are PL/M and BASIC. PL/M is derived from PL/1 and was originally introduced by Intel and later by most other manufacturers. BASIC was developed as an interactive language and is now widely used, as it requires only a small interpreter.

A high-level language provides the means to specify powerful instructions such as: *"Execute the next instructions 24 times,"* or *"Perform the following instructions until the variable n reaches the value 2024."* It is no longer necessary to program at the register level. Programs are written symbolically, using variable names and other data structures.

Recall that these high-level instructions (called the *source code*), however, must still be converted into machine-executable code. Automatic translation is accomplished by a *compiler* or an *interpreter* program. A compiler translates each high-level instruction into *many* binary instructions. The resulting code is called the *object* (or binary) *code*. Because translation is automatic, many assumptions are made by the computer that are less than ideal, and the resulting object code is not in its optimal form. Depending upon the efficiency of the compiler, the resulting binary code may be two to five times bulkier than if it had been directly generated by a human programmer in assembly language. The result is wasted memory space and slower execution of the program by the processor. The overwhelming advantage of a high-level language, however, is the savings in the programmer's time; that is, it offers fast and efficient programming. We will address the problem of system efficiency in Chapter 10.

DEBUGGING

Once a program is written in a programming language, it must be *debugged*. Debugging refers to the identification and elimination of errors within the program. Debugging usually proceeds in four phases:

1. *paper checking:* the program is checked "by hand" by following the execution of instructions (on paper) and checking the results manually.

2. *program translation:* depending on the language used (assembly-level or high-level), an assembler or a compiler converts the source code into binary code. Error messages may be generated, giving the programmer clues for correcting syntax errors.

3. *debugging on the processor:* the translated object program is executed on the processor. Logical errors are identified (from the "output" results) and corrected.

4. *final execution:* the program is now considered "error-free" and is installed in the memory.

FLOWCHART

One intermediate step is often taken between developing the algorithm and writing the program. This is the preparation of a *flowchart*. A flowchart is a symbolic representation of the sequencing of operations involved in the algorithm. Two essential symbols used in a flowchart are the rectangle (used for orders, commands or instructions to be executed) and the diamond (used for logical tests). Two or more arrows lead out of a diamond, depending on the test. If the test is binary (i.e., if a "yes or no" answer is implied), two arrows will lead out of a diamond. Simple examples of the use of decision diamonds appear in Figure 8.1.

Flowcharts are the most frequently used representations of algorithms. They are language-independent, and thus, if drawn with care, can be converted easily into programs, using any programming language. Flowcharts are used throughout this book to illustrate specific algorithms.

SUMMARY—DEFINITIONS

We have presented the main definitions relating to programming concepts. We will now study the internal and external representation of data and the types of instructions available to manipulate them. In Chapter 9 we will examine the facilities and techniques of assembly language and high-level programming.

Most of the considerations presented in the rest of this section are relevant to assembly-level programming, but they are also useful to any programmer who wants to understand what happens within the system.

INTERNAL REPRESENTATION OF INFORMATION

Two kinds of information must be represented within the system: the *program* and the *data*. The instructions of a program are always

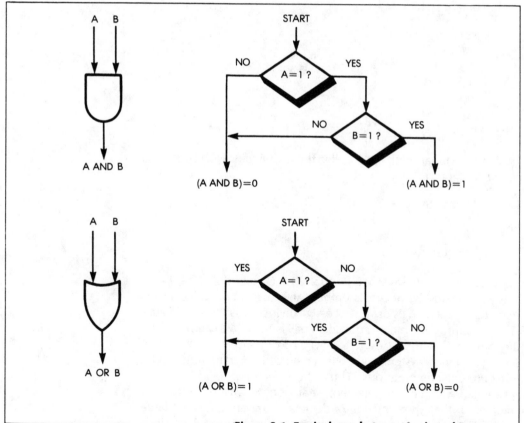

Figure 8.1: Equivalence between Logic and Program

represented in binary code. The binary encoding of the instructions is imposed by the manufacturer and cannot be modified by the user. Also, the user will generally not have to worry about the actual binary encoding of instructions unless he or she is programming directly in hexadecimal. Programs are normally written by the programmer in assembly language or in a high-level language, rather than in binary format.

A major task lies, therefore, in the binary representation of the *data* that the program will manipulate. Two kinds of data must be represented: *numeric* and *alphanumeric* (characters). We will now examine the usual techniques for encoding data.

REPRESENTATION OF NUMERIC DATA

We will first show how an ordinary decimal number is converted to binary. Then, we will see that many alternative conventions may be used to represent negative and fractional numbers.

In the binary system,

0	represents	0
1	"	1
10	"	2
11	"	3
100	"	4
101	"	5
etc.		

The rightmost binary digit (bit) is called the least significant bit (LSB) and represents 2^0 ($=1$). Thus,

$$0 \text{ represents } 0 \times 2^0 = 0$$

and

$$1 \text{ represents } 1 \times 2^0 = 1$$

Thus, 101 is interpreted as $(1 \times 2^2) + (0 \times 2^1) + (1 \times 2^0) = 4 + 0 + 1 = 5$. Conversely, a positive decimal number can be easily converted into its binary representation by using successive divisions, as shown in Figure 8.2. For example, the binary equivalent of 9 is 1001. We can verify that $1001 = (1 \times 2^3) + (0 \times 2^2) + (0 \times 2^1) + (1 \times 2^0) = 8 + 1 = 9$.

Using the binary system, eight bits can be combined to form 2^8 (i.e., 256) different combinations. Thus, the integers 0 to 255 may be represented within 8 bits. This representation, however, is often not sufficient for the representation of decimal numbers and other large numbers, so a more complex representation must be used. Two kinds of numbers must be represented: *integers* and *floating-point* (or decimal) numbers; and specific representations are used for each. We will assume for now that integers are used, and describe the floating-point representation later on in this chapter.

Also, the *sign* of a number must be indicated. The universal technique for encoding the sign of the number is to dedicate the leftmost bit (the MSB) to the sign. A 0 represents a "+" and a 1 represents a "−". The remaining bits are used to encode the value of the number. Four main representations—sign magnitude, one's-complement, two's-complement, and binary coded decimal—have evolved, which we will now describe.

Sign Magnitude

The *sign-magnitude* representation is probably the simplest and most intuitive convention. As usual, the most significant bit (MSB) represents the sign. The remaining bits represent the magnitude of the number in a straight binary representation. We have already seen that a single byte is not enough to encode large numbers with sufficient precision. A multi-byte representation is therefore normally used, and at least two bytes are necessary to represent 32K integer values. (Recall that the sign takes up one bit; i.e., there are only 15 usable bits for the magnitude in a 2-byte representation and $2^{15} = 32K$).

Let us now look at an example of the sign-magnitude representation. In this example we will see that there is a disadvantage to using this

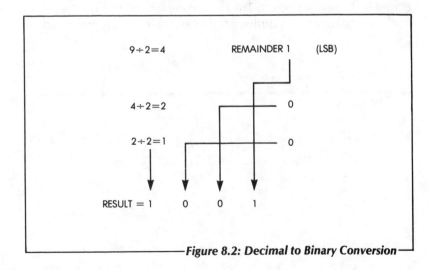

Figure 8.2: Decimal to Binary Conversion

technique. For simplicity, we will use only a single byte:

- 1 is represented by 00000001, where the leftmost 0 denotes a +.

- − 2 is represented by 10000010, where the leftmost 1 is "−", and 0000010 is 2.

We will now add these two numbers using the rules of regular binary addition (shown in Figure 8.3):

$$\begin{array}{ll} 00000001 & (1) \\ +\ 10000010 & (-2) \\ \hline =\ 10000011 & (-3) \end{array}$$

The result is − 3 in our sign-magnitude representation, rather than − 1. Thus, the rules of regular binary addition do not work with this representation. This is a disadvantage of the sign-magnitude representation.

It should be noted, however, that the method of encoding the numbers is not the most important feature of a number-representation system, since this is done automatically by the assembler or the compiler. The important feature to look for is processor efficiency in performing arithmetic operations, as this efficiency results in higher execution speeds. Let us now look at other alternatives for representing numbers.

One's-Complement

One's-complement is another technique used to represent negative numbers in such a way that arithmetic operations may be performed efficiently by digital circuits. The *one's-complement* of a number is its mathematical (binary) complement. For example, if 2 is represented by

00000010

$$\begin{array}{cccc} 0 & 0 & 1 & 1 \\ +0 & +1 & +0 & +1 \\ \hline =0 & =1 & =1 & =(1)0 \\ & & & \downarrow \\ & & & \text{CARRY} \end{array}$$

Figure 8.3: The Rules of Binary Addition

the one's-complement of 2 in this representation is

11111101 (− 2)

Each 0 is replaced by a 1 and each 1 is replaced by a 0. Note that the MSB is still the sign bit. One's-complement is often used in large central processing units, as it results in significantly improved efficiency in the design of the CPU.

Unfortunately, we still have a problem. If we add 00010110 (+ 22) and 11111101 (− 2) encoded in one's-complement, the result using the rules of binary addition is:

```
    00010110 (+ 22)
+   11111101  (− 2)
(1)00010011    (19)   (with a carry)
```

The result must be corrected by adding the carry: 19 + 1 = 20.

Thus, the rules of ordinary binary addition do not work if the signs are different. The ALU must be designed for one's-complement operations. Let us now consider a third representation.

Two's-Complement

The *two's-complement* notation is the most frequently used representation in the microprocessor world for reasons that are immediately clear. The two's-complement representation of a negative number is computed as follows:

1. The positive number is complemented to 1 (one's-complement).

2. 1 is then added, resulting in the two's-complement encoding of the number.

The rules of ordinary binary addition may then be used. Let us look at some examples:

The number + 3 is represented by: 00000011.
The one's-complement of + 3 (i.e., − 3) is: 11111100.
Its two's-complement is obtained by adding 1: 11111101.

Let us now add two numbers that have different signs:

```
    00000010 (+ 2)
+   11111101 (− 3)
=   11111111 (− 1)
```

The result is − 1 in two's-complement representation. It works!

Figure 8.4 offers a comparison between the sign magnitude, the one's-complement, and the two's-complement representations. Positive numbers have the same code in all three representations, but negative numbers differ.

The main advantage of two's-complement representation is that the programmer may use the rules of binary addition and does not have to worry about the sign bit when performing arithmetic (addition or subtraction) operations. The result is correct regardless of the signs of the numbers, as long as the number is not too large for the number of bits used (an *overflow* condition). This mathematical property of two's-complement representation can be easily proved. (The proof is left to the reader.)

Since the microprocessor does not have to test the sign of arithmetic numbers explicitly during addition or subtraction operations, efficiency is increased. Because of this advantage, two's-complement is universally adopted as the representation of signed numbers for microprocessors.

We have now described a suitable representation of positive and negative integers. We will next discuss the representation of *fractional* or decimal numbers.

DECIMAL	SIGN MAGNITUDE	ONE'S COMPLEMENT	TWO'S COMPLEMENT
−8	----	0111	1000
−7	1111	1000	1001
−6	1110	1001	1010
−5	1101	1010	1011
−4	1100	1011	1100
−3	1011	1100	1101
−2	1010	1101	1110
−1	1001	1110	1111
−0	1000	1111	0000
+0	0000	0000	0000
+1	0001	0001	0001
+2	0010	0010	0010
+3	0011	0011	0011
+4	0100	0100	0100
+5	0101	0101	0101
+6	0110	0110	0110
+7	0111	0111	0111

Figure 8.4: The Three Representations

Fractional Numbers _____

The problem with representing fractional numbers is that the arithmetic programs that perform addition, subtraction and other arithmetic operations can operate efficiently only on *fixed-length* data because of the limited width of internal high-speed registers and buses. If processing efficiency is required, numbers must be represented in the computer within a fixed number of bytes, which limits the accuracy of the representation of these numbers. Thus, there must be a trade-off between speed and accuracy. Except in cases where the absolute precision of results is indispensable, such as in accounting applications, *floating-point* is the representation universally adopted for programs requiring *execution efficiency*.

There is one representation that has been specifically devised for the business world that solves this *precision* problem. It is the BCD representation, which we will describe in the next section. But first, let us examine floating-point representation.

In floating-point representation, a fixed number of bytes are allocated to the representation of fractional numbers. As an example, we will consider a 4-byte (32-bit) representation.

The principle of floating-point representation is to encode the number in two parts: the *mantissa* and the *exponent*. The number is represented as: $N = M \times 2^E$, where M is the mantissa, E the exponent, and N the fractional number. (See Figure 8.5.) Both the mantissa and the exponent are represented in two's-complement notation, and the leftmost bit of each denotes the sign.

The mantissa is *normalized* by discarding leading 0s, in order to guarantee that the maximum number of significant digits of the number will be retained in the representation. In our example, 23 bits (plus the leftmost bit used for the sign) are available to represent the magnitude of the mantissa.

Using this technique corresponds to retaining the first k non-null

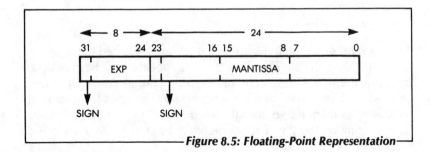

Figure 8.5: Floating-Point Representation

digits (counting from left to right) of the number expressed in the usual notation and discarding digits to the right of the kth digit (a truncation). The decimal point is moved to the left of this mantissa. For each position that the point is moved to the left, the exponent is increased by one. Or, if it is moved to the right, the exponent is decreased by one.

Here is an example in the decimal system. The number:

>1234.56

becomes

>.123456 *(mantissa)*
>$\times 10^4$ *(where 4 is the exponent)*

and

>0.00123

becomes

>.123 *(mantissa)*
>$\times 10^{-2}$ *(where −2 is the exponent)*

In reality, this process is performed on the binary representation of the number. The only difference is that the exponent then denotes a power of 2 rather than a power of 10. This representation guarantees the best possible relative precision, given the number of bits available. It also guarantees that the mantissa will not contain leading zeros.

Using the decimal notation, this encoding is characterized by:

>$10^{-1} \leqslant |M| < 1$

where $|M|$ denotes the absolute value of the mantissa (the magnitude, regardless of sign). In other words, the magnitude of M is at least 0.1 and is always less than 1.

Similarly, in binary, the mantissa is such that:

>$2^{-1} \leqslant |M| < 1$

In the representation in Figure 8.5, 8 bits are allocated to the exponent, including the sign, and 24 bits are allocated to the mantissa, including the sign. This is a common representation. More bits could be used if a higher precision were necessary. The rules for operating on floating-point numbers are naturally more complex than those used for operating on straight two's-complement numbers. Mantissas and exponents must be operated on separately. *Floating-point routines* must be written. The scope of such programs, however, is beyond this introductory book. But, briefly, numbers must be "made compatible" before addition or subtraction (i.e., they must be normalized by making their exponents equal). A multiplication can be performed by multiplying mantissas and adding exponents, then normalizing the results. Naturally, execution of floating-point routines will be very slow compared to the execution of the standard arithmetic routines.

If the execution of floating-point routines is found to be too slow for an application, newly developed chips called *floating-point processors* can be used that connect directly to standard microprocessor buses. They execute floating-point arithmetic directly.

The floating-point representation that we have just described is normally best suited to any type of problem that requires *high* precision and does not need *absolute* precision. Unfortunately, in business-type applications such as accounting, no error can be tolerated. For example, in the accounting for a company or a store, a "small" error of "only a few cents" on a total gross of several thousand dollars is clearly unacceptable. A new representation is needed that will guarantee strict accuracy of each digit in the result. As previously stated, this representation is called BCD.

Binary-Coded Decimal (BCD)

The principle of binary-coded decimal (BCD) is simple. The ten decimal digits from 0 through 9 must be encoded, which requires the use of 4 bits. (Three bits would only encode 2^3 combinations. Four bits encode 16 combinations; four bits are therefore used to encode the ten decimal digits.) For example:

> 1 is represented by 0001
> 9 is represented by 1001

(See Figure 8.6.) However, four bits generate 16 possible combinations, and the combinations from 1010 to 1111 are unused and thus *illegal* in a BCD encoding. The presence of these unused combinations complicates arithmetic operations.

We will now try to add two BCD digits, using a four-bit code:

```
      0001 (1)
  +   0011 (3)
  =   0100 (4)
```

In this case, the correct result is obtained. However, let us try some larger numbers:

$$\begin{array}{r} 1000 \ (8) \\ + \quad 1000 \ (8) \\ \hline = (1)0000 \ (?) \end{array}$$

The result, 1 followed by 0 in BCD, i.e., 10 in decimal, is *incorrect*. The problem should be obvious. When using the rules for regular binary addition, the six illegal combinations from 1010 to 1111 must be "skipped over." In other words, 6 must be added to the result whenever this result falls within the forbidden combinations.

Let us try the problem again, but this time we will add the binary representation of 6 (0110) to the result:

$$\begin{array}{r} 1000 \ (8) \\ + \quad 1000 \ (8) \\ \hline = 1\,0000 \ (\textit{uncorrected result}) \\ + \quad 0110 \ (+6) \ (\textit{correction}) \\ \hline = 1\,0110 \ (16) \ (\textit{correct result}) \end{array}$$

This result is 1 followed by 6, i.e., 16 in BCD, the correct answer. Thus, using the BCD representation, 6 must be added to the result in cases where the addition would go through the forbidden binary codes. In most microprocessors, this adjustment is automatically performed by a DAA instruction executed after an addition. In fact, virtually all microprocessors are equipped with this instruction. This is surprising

	2^3	2^2	2^1	2^0
0	0	0	0	0
1	0	0	0	1
2	0	0	1	0
3	0	0	1	1
4	0	1	0	0
5	0	1	0	1
6	0	1	1	0
7	0	1	1	1
8	1	0	0	0
9	1	0	0	1

Figure 8.6: BCD Representation

as it significantly complicates the design of the processing unit. The reason is historical. Microprocessors evolved from pocket calculators, many of which were already using the BCD notation for accounting applications. As a result, this special operation was simply carried forward into microprocessor designs.

Subtraction in BCD presents a further problem. Subtraction must be performed by adding the ten's-complement of one number to the other number. Unfortunately, many microprocessors are not equipped with a BCD subtract instruction, so the ten's-complement must be computed explicitly. Naturally, the DAA must also be used in this case at the end of the operation.

Finally, another practical problem arises. Since a BCD digit is encoded in 4 bits, a decimal number will require a number of nibbles (a nibble is 4 bits) for its representation. Typically, the first nibble of its representation will carry the sign bit and all the following nibbles will carry the BCD digits. This is called *packed BCD*, with more than one BCD digit per byte. Adding or subtracting only one nibble at a time would be highly inefficient. Therefore, operations are carried out on a full byte at a time. However, if a carry is generated within the 8-bit result (from one nibble into the one on its left), this fact must be detected to correct the result. This requires the availability of a special flag bit that detects a carry from bit 3 into bit 4. This is the *half-carry* (H or AC) introduced in Chapter 2. By testing this bit, the programmer will be able to take appropriate corrective action whenever the addition of two nibbles results in a bit added to the left nibble of a byte.

SUMMARY OF INTERNAL NUMBER REPRESENTATIONS

In most cases, two's-complement notation is used with a 16-, 24- or even 32-bit format. The programmer is then limited to integers, and cannot achieve absolute precision. However, high execution speeds can be obtained. This is the case with numbers used in assembly language and interpreters such as Integer BASIC.

In cases where fractional numbers are used, a floating-point representation is used, at the cost of a slower computation speed. In the case of accounting applications, BCD is used for strict accuracy, at the cost of serious loss of computation speed.

We have now learned to represent numbers. Let us see how to represent text.

REPRESENTATION OF ALPHANUMERIC DATA

To represent alphanumeric characters (text) or other special symbols, a method of encoding characters into a binary representation is required. At least 82 symbols are usually encoded: 52 symbols to represent the upper and lower case letters of the alphabet, 10 symbols for the 10 decimal digits, and at least 22 symbols for special characters such as +, −, , ., and ?. A 7-bit minimum binary encoding must be used. Seven bits allow 128 possible combinations, which is sufficient for virtually all character sets. In practice, since microprocessors are generally structured in 8-bit bytes, characters are encoded in an 8-bit format. The eighth bit (the MSB) is normally used to carry parity information for improved transmission reliability. In order to facilitate the exchange of information, two standards have evolved that are used universally. They are the ASCII standard (American Standard Code for Information Interchange), used for nearly all microprocessors (as well as other computers), and the EBCDIC code, used by IBM. EBCDIC is analogous to ASCII but it modifies the sequence in which characters are encoded, claiming improved efficiency during comparisons of the rank of characters in the sequence. For all practical purposes, only ASCII is of relevance here unless direct interface to IBM equipment is required. The ASCII code is shown in Appendix E.

An interesting problem now arises. An identical 8-bit code might be used to encode binary data, a character, or perhaps even an instruction. How will the processor know what the code represents? The key is that each of these representations is used in a strictly specific context. *Instructions* are used in the program area of the memory and will automatically be loaded inside the microprocessor for execution. Whenever *data* are handled by the processor, the programmer is responsible for making sure that the data are interpreted correctly. Should the programmer decide to add *characters* together, the microprocessor will execute the requested addition whether or not the result has any meaning. In an assembly or a high-level language, facilities are provided to encode the numbers and characters into their binary representations automatically. However, the programmer must still choose operations appropriate for the data being used. (This is part of the art of programming.)

We have now learned how to represent both numbers and characters internally within the memory. How will they be displayed externally?

EXTERNAL REPRESENTATION OF INFORMATION

There are three main ways to represent information externally:

1. The ideal way is to display information in the most convenient

format—using a *symbolic* representation. Thus, the letter A is displayed as an A and 12.3 is displayed as 12.3.

Indeed, a sophisticated debugging program displays results or contents of registers in symbolic form. Characters are displayed as characters, instructions as (symbolic) mnemonics, and numbers are displayed in their actual, decimal form. Unfortunately, less sophisticated programs that do not enjoy a large amount of working memory— or are not as good—use less sophisticated forms to display results or the contents of registers.

2. The second way, which is the easiest for the processor, is to use the direct binary representation of data in its "raw" form (untranslated). However, from the programmer's standpoint, this is clearly the most *inconvenient* representation to use.

3. The third way, and now the universal representation in the world of microprocessors, is called *hexadecimal*. Hexadecimal is very close to (but constitutes a significant improvement over) binary representation. In the hexadecimal representation, a nibble is encoded into one hexadecimal digit. As its name implies, hexadecimal encodes 16 combinations into unique symbols. The digits 0 through 9 are used to represent their exact binary equivalent. The remaining six combinations of four bits are named by the first six letters of the alphabet. A through F are used to represent 1010 through 1111 (see Figure 8.7). The advantage of hexadecimal is that eight binary digits can be encoded as two hexadecimal

BINARY				HEXADECIMAL
0	0	0	0	0
0	0	0	1	1
0	0	1	0	2
0	0	1	1	3
0	1	0	0	4
0	1	0	1	5
0	1	1	0	6
0	1	1	1	7
1	0	0	0	8
1	0	0	1	9
1	0	1	0	A
1	0	1	1	B
1	1	0	0	C
1	1	0	1	D
1	1	1	0	E
1	1	1	1	F

Figure 8.7: Hexadecimal Representation

symbols. The "human interface" is much simpler; it is much easier to handle two-symbol codes than 8-bit binary codes. Here are some examples:

FF represents 11111111
01 represents 00000001
1A represents 00011010

There is one more reason for the overwhelming success of hexadecimal in the microprocessor world. The hexadecimal (16-key) keyboard happens to be one of the least expensive input media for a microprocessor. Each key can be labeled with a hexadecimal symbol so that one 8-bit word can be entered into the memory or a register by pressing only two keys. A simple software routine is used to convert from hexadecimal to binary.

Conversely, 7-segment LEDs, one of the cheapest output media, can be used to display hexadecimal numbers. Thus, most single-board microprocessor systems are equipped with at least six LEDs:

— Four LEDs display the 16 bits of an address.

— Two LEDs display the 8-bit contents of registers or memory.

We have now learned to represent data, whether text or numerical, both inside and outside the microprocessor. Let us go on to examine the representation and format of program instructions.

REPRESENTATION OF INSTRUCTIONS

We saw in Chapter 2 that instructions are orders given to the microprocessor; they are decoded by the control unit. For standard 8-bit microprocessors, the format for instructions is 1, 2, 3 or 4 bytes. The shorter the instruction, the faster it executes; the longer the instruction, the more time it takes to fetch the bytes out of memory, and the more time the instruction needs for completion.

We can classify instruction types in various ways. One obvious classification is the nature of the order to be executed, i.e., *logical, arithmetic*, or *control* operations. Another possible classification is by the module that an instruction references: i.e., *register-type, memory-type*, and *input/output* instructions.

The encoding of the instruction itself into a bit pattern is irrelevant in a general discussion of programming. The codes are different for each microprocessor and are fixed once and for all by the manufacturer.

An instruction code can be broadly divided into its *opcode field* and its optional *literal field*. For example, LDA addr (an 8080 instruction) can be represented as:

> 00111010 address *(16 bits)*
> opcode literal *(address)*

For the sake of efficiency, the opcode usually occupies the first 8 bits of the instruction. Recall that this will be the byte placed in the instruction register that will be decoded by the control unit. This way, the nature of the instruction is immediately recognized by the CU. In a stricter sense, the opcode should refer only to the *operation* specified and it should not include any register specification. This is the convention in traditional minicomputers and computers. However, in the case of microprocessors, it has become common to use the name "opcode" for designating the operation as well as any register specification that might appear within the field.

The second and third bytes of an instruction are called the *literal* field. The literal field, if used, contains either an *operand* (data) or an *address* (8 or 16 bits). Sometimes a fourth byte is used either as an opcode or a literal extension. (This is the case for the Z80.)

Only 8 bits are available for the opcode of a "standard" microprocessor. As a result, at most, 256 (2^8) different instructions may be specified. However, several addressing modes must be provided (addressing modes are explained in the next chapter), and normally at least 2 bits are allocated to this function. This leaves only 6 bits for the true opcode, i.e., only 64 (2^6) possible different instructions. This is why virtually no 8-bit microprocessor has more than 64 *truly* different instructions. As we discussed in Chapter 3, manufacturers often claim a larger number of instructions by differentiating between the various addressing modes, or by individually listing identical instructions operating on separate registers. This practice is simply misleading.

SUMMARY

In this chapter we learned that programming a microprocessor first requires designing an algorithm, and then translating the algorithm into a program that can be executed on the microprocessor. We saw how information is represented inside and outside the microcomputer.

We will now go on to describe the main aspects of assembly-language programming and characteristics of the main high-level languages in Chapter 9.

EXERCISES

8-1: Define the terms *algorithm, program,* and *assembly language.*

8-2: What is the difference between the source code and the object code?

8-3: Draw a flowchart for a simple process of your choice, such as the sequence of steps involved in starting a car or in executing a cooking recipe.

8-4: What is the binary representation of: 12, 46, 125, 6?

8-5: Using the sign-magnitude representation, what are the binary representations for: 5, −3, 125, −32, 46?

8-6: Using the one's-complement representation, what are the binary representations for: 2, −2, 5, −5, 125, −32, 43?

8-7: Using the two's-complement notation, what are the binary equivalents for: 2, −3, 24, 125, −32?

8-8: Execute the two's-complement addition of 15 and 10; then the subtraction of 3 from 5.

8-9: Explain how fractional numbers can be represented using a floating-point notation.

8-10: Give the BCD representation using packed BCD, i.e., 2 BCD digits per byte, for the following numbers: 12, 5, 56, 99.

8-11: Give the hexadecimal equivalents of the following numbers: 12, 46, 78, 99, 124, 1024, 496.

8-12: Explain the opcode field of an instruction.

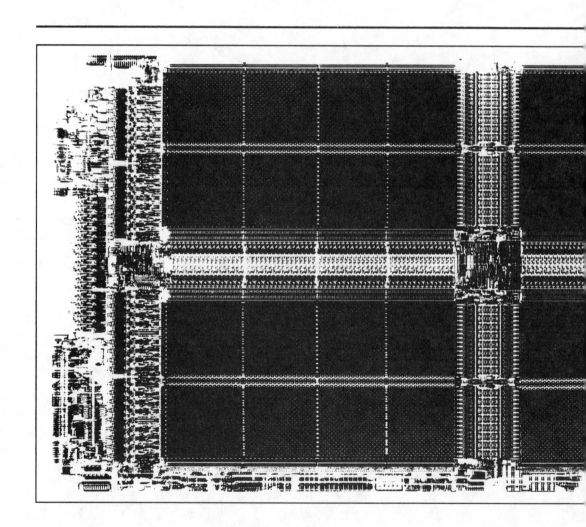

CHAPTER 9

ASSEMBLY AND HIGH-LEVEL PROGRAMMING

OBJECTIVE

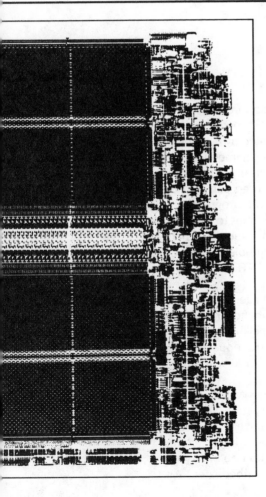

OBJECTIVE

This chapter provides a description of assembly-language facilities, including instruction types and addressing techniques. We will examine, in detail, actual program examples using the 8080 and the 6800, and we will study alternative programming approaches, using high-level languages.

ASSEMBLY LANGUAGE

Except for the simplest applications, where programming may be done directly in hexadecimal (i.e., practically in binary), microprocessors are normally programmed in either assembly or a high-level language. Programming in assembler results in shorter programs and a higher execution speed. Programming in a high-level language requires much less time of the programmer. In this section we will describe the facilities of an assembler and the types of instructions it provides. We will also present actual programs.

Recall that an assembler is a program that automatically translates the symbolic representation of instructions into their binary encoding. For example, the 8080 assembler translates:

ADI 16

into:

11000110 00010000

Thus, an assembler allows the programmer to specify instructions in a mnemonic or symbolic format. For example, *"add immediate"* is represented by ADI. The accumulator can be represented by A, or ACC, or some other symbol. Registers can generally be given names. Register 0 could be called "ALPHA," register 1, "BETA" or any other user-defined symbolic name. Similarly, the data being used can also be assigned names that facilitate writing and reading the program. The assembler provides specific commands that assign names to variables and registers, as well as memory locations. Constants, such as 3.1416 or 5, can also be given names. Most numbers and symbols can thus be given meaningful names such as PI, AGE, TABLE, POINTER, CHARACTER, or RESULT.

The assembler offers another important advantage. During the assembly process, it will generate error diagnostics whenever it detects incorrect syntax. The assembler will detect errors in spelling, addressing mode, and type of operands. It will also catch the erroneous duplication of symbolic names. However, *it will never detect logical errors.* That is the responsibility of the programmer.

Recall that a program written in assembly language is called a *source program*. Once translated by the assembler into binary code, it is called the *object code*. Programming in assembly-level language results in the same execution efficiency as programming directly in binary code. Each assembly-level instruction will be translated into one binary instruction. (One exception to that rule is macros, described later.) An assembly language provides two distinct types of statements: *declarations* and *executable instructions*.

DECLARATIONS

Declarations are special instructions designed to facilitate writing a program in symbolic form. They will generally specify the binary equivalent of symbols used by the programmer for convenience. Declarations can also be used to assign a value to constants or addresses.

For example, the following declaration:

ORG $1000

specifies that the program will reside at address 1000 hexadecimal (origin) in memory. Whenever such an origin specification is used, the program will reside at a fixed address within the memory. This is called *absolute programming*. Conversely, a program that can be loaded anywhere in the memory is called a *relocatable program*.

In order to place a relocatable program in the memory, the symbolic addresses used in the program must be converted into actual addresses. This task is accomplished by the loader program. In the case of microprocessors used in control applications, most programs are loaded only once into a ROM memory that cannot be changed. Programs are therefore loaded at absolute addresses. In most other cases, however, programs may have to reside anywhere in the memory. Further, even in the case of ROM-based programs, the facility to reload a program is much used during the development phase, since there is no way of knowing in advance how long each program segment will be, and, therefore, where each one will reside. Once a program is completely written and checked out, its addresses can be converted to absolute locations.

An important word of caution: the *debugger* (usually supplied by the manufacturer), which will be used to test the correct execution of the program, must allow the specification of addresses *relative to the beginning* of the program. Otherwise, the benefit of relocatable programs is lost. The user would have to compute the address of every instruction within the program manually.

Assigning a symbolic label to an address is typically accomplished by a declaration such as:

ADR1 EQU $1000

This statement assigns the absolute address 1000 hexadecimal to the symbol ADR1 used in the program.

Assigning a symbolic name to *data* requires two separate facilities. Data must be specified as to *format* and *content*. Here is an example of such a double specification:

DATA RMB 1

This declaration reserves 1 byte for the data structure called RMB (in the 6800 assembly language). Similarly,

TABLE RMB 50

allocates 50 bytes to the data structure called TABLE.

Here are additional examples. The statements:

VAL1 FCB $10

CAR1 FCC "A"

assign actual values to the data. The first instruction assigns the value 10 hexadecimal to the symbol VAL1. The second instruction assigns the 8-bit ASCII code corresponding to "A" to the variable CAR1. The assembler automatically converts the symbol "A" into the corresponding binary code. The last C in FCC tells the assembler that the symbol is an ASCII character. Facilities also exist for using other types of data such as octal or decimal.

In summary, declarations are mostly used to assign a name to data, addresses or registers. In addition, every assembly-level program must be terminated by a special declaration instruction such as "END".

EXECUTABLE INSTRUCTIONS

We examined several executable instructions in Chapter 2 when we studied the internal operation of the 8080. These instructions specify operations to be performed with the 8080. They are merely translated by the assembler into binary and are intended to be executed by the microprocessor.

Recall also from the previous chapter that the binary instruction has only two fields: opcode and operand (or literal). The assembler associates two more fields to each instruction: an optional address label, and an optional comment field.

In assembly level, the four fields are:

1. symbolic address

2. mnemonic instruction (opcode)

3. operand or literal

4. comment.

The following example illustrates these fields:

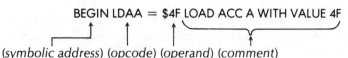

BEGIN LDAA = $4F LOAD ACC A WITH VALUE 4F

(*symbolic address*) (*opcode*) (*operand*) (*comment*)

We will now examine each field in turn.

The *address* field, also called the *label* field, is of major importance. This field allows any instruction to be referenced using a symbolic label rather than an absolute address. Naturally, not every instruction needs to be labeled. However, labeling is a convenient facility for referring to instructions or for specifying branch operations. Through symbolic labeling it becomes possible, for example, to insert an additional instruction easily within the program without having to rewrite any of the other branch instructions. (A branch operation specifies, for example: *"execute the instruction at address TEST next"*). Branch addresses, if expressed in absolute form (as numbers), would have to be modified, since all instructions would be "pushed-down" in the memory by the added instructions. During the assembly phase, the assembler will automatically substitute the appropriate numeric address for the symbolic one.

Labels make it possible to refer to instructions or groups of instructions within a program. They improve the readability and clarity of the program. Labels and other names in assembly language are usually limited in length, as well as in the kinds of symbols that can be used to form them (usually letters and digits only). Usually they are limited to six characters in length, and must start with a letter.

The second field, the *mnemonic* (also called the symbolic opcode), must always be specified. It symbolically represents the instruction to be executed. In the above example, LDAA is the mnemonic field; it specifies that the accumulator A must be loaded from the contents of a memory location. The memory location must still be specified.

The third field, the *operand*, is the most complex. Its syntax varies according to the instruction. It may contain a symbolic address (8 or 16 bits), immediate data (8 or 16 bits), or even simple arithmetic expressions (such as P + 1). In addition, a number of special symbols may be used within that field, such as =, $, and '.

The equal sign (=) is typically used for immediate addressing. The dollar sign ($) is used to indicate a hexadecimal value. Single or double quotes (',") are used to denote an alphanumeric symbol.

The assembler also allows the use of the symbols plus and minus (+, −) to specify simple address computations such as:

ADR + 2

This specification references the address computed as: (the value of ADR) + 2.

In the case of *indexed* addressing (explained below), the index register will be specified in this field, unless it was specified as part of the mnemonic field. The specification could be:

    ADR,X

where X is the name of an index register, and ADR is a memory address. This indicates that the effective address is to be obtained by adding the value of ADR to the contents of index register X.

Indirect addressing is usually specified by a special character such as an asterisk (*). For example:

    ADR*

indicates that ADR is to be interpreted as an indirect address (the final address is the one stored at location ADR).

Finally, the operand field may contain symbolic register names for register-type instructions, such as:

    ADD B,D

which specifies an addition of registers B and D.

The operand field may be empty whenever an instruction does not require an operand: 8-bit instructions have an empty operand field.

The fourth field is the *comment* field. It is optional and is provided for the convenience of the programmer, to improve program readability. The programmer is encouraged to write comments within the program that clarify the execution of the instruction or the program segment. Most comment fields may be of arbitrary length; some are restricted as to the number of characters that may be used. Comments help to produce a self-documented program. This is another important advantage of assembly language. No such facility exists when programming at the hexadecimal or binary levels. The comment field is completely ignored by the assembler at assembly time. It is only used by the assembler when listing the program.

Syntax conventions may differ from one assembler to the next. For example, either $12 or 12H may be used to specify 12 hexadecimal. However, all assemblers are generally alike. Any user who has mastered the use of one assembler will usually find it very simple to switch over to another one.

MACROS

Another special facility is provided by good assemblers: *macros*. Macro is simply a name given to a group of instructions. A macro represents several instructions rather than just one. Macros save time when writing programs. They also improve the readability of programs and reduce the risk of error. Good assemblers are even equipped with a *conditional* macro facility, thus permitting the conditional assembly of macros at assembly time, depending on computed values. This is an efficient method for building different programs from predefined modules in function of parameters known at assembly time.

We have now described the format, or the appearance, of assembler instructions. Let us now examine what they can do, i.e., the types of instructions available to program a microprocessor.

TYPES OF INSTRUCTIONS

In the previous chapter we discussed ways of classifying instruction types and indicated that several methods could be used. The most straightforward classification is by the opcode, i.e., the type of operation being performed. We will discuss six categories of instructions here:

1.   transfer instructions involving external devices (memory or I/O)

2.   transfer instructions between registers (internal to the MPU)

3.   arithmetic instructions (such as ADD and SUB)

4.   logical instructions (such as OR and AND)

5.   skew instructions (such as ROT and SHIFT)

6.   control instructions (branch and test).

Addressing modes will be discussed separately; each instruction type may use a variety of addressing modes.

It is usual in the world of standard computers to distinguish I/O instructions from other instructions. Usually this distinction cannot be made with microprocessors, since I/O addressing is normally performed in exactly the same way as memory addressing. Therefore, we do not distinguish I/O instructions, but simply merge them within the transfer instructions.

Let us now review the six instruction types in more detail.

Transfer Instructions To And From External Devices _____

These instructions are responsible for moving information between one of the microprocessor's registers and the specified external location, such as memory or a device register (see Figure 9.1). Such information may be either 8 bits or 16 bits in length. Let us consider some examples from the instruction set of the 6800:

> LDAA ADR1
>
> LDAB ADR2

The above instructions load the contents of the addresses ADR1 and ADR2 in registers A and B, respectively. (A and B are the two internal accumulators of the 6800.) ADR1 may refer to a memory location or an I/O chip register. The reverse instructions are:

> STAA ADMEM1
>
> STAB ADMEM2

The above two instructions store the contents of A and B in memory addresses ADMEM1 and ADMEM2, respectively.

Let us now look at two similar instructions from the instruction set of the 8080:

> MOV r,M
>
> MOV M,r

The first instruction moves the contents of a memory location into

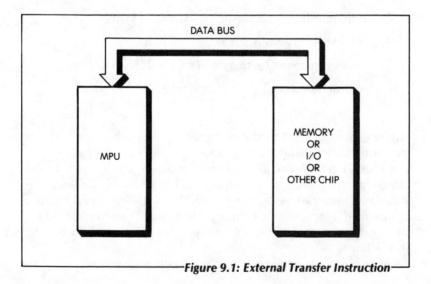

Figure 9.1: External Transfer Instruction

register r and the second instruction moves the contents of register r into the memory location. In the case of these specific instructions, the memory address M is contained in registers H and L. The 8080 provides another instruction for the immediate specification of the address field; however, it is restricted exclusively to referencing accumulator A.

Any instruction referencing the memory address may be used in any one of the addressing modes provided on the microprocessor. For example, with the 6800:

    LDAA = 44

loads the accumulator with the immediate value 44. The operand is loaded ''as is'' into the accumulator rather than interpreted as a memory address, as in the previous case.

Similarly:

    LDAA ADR, X

first computes an effective address by adding ADDR to the contents of index register X and then loads the contents of this address into the accumulator. This is called indexed addressing.

Other special instructions may be provided: the Z80 is equipped with several special instructions, which can do block-transfers or even search for a specified binary pattern within a memory block. The 8085 is also equipped with similar special instructions.

Interregister Transfers

Interregister transfer instructions manipulate data internal to the MPU without referencing any external device (see Figure 9.2). They are

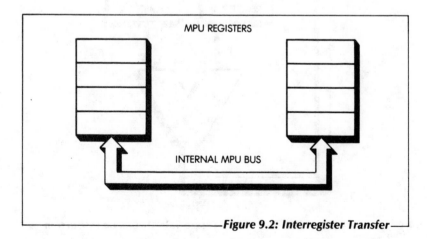

Figure 9.2: Interregister Transfer

executed much faster than instructions referencing external devices since they operate internally within the MPU.

On the 6800, instructions TAB and TBA transfer data between registers A and B. On the 8080, the instruction MOV r1, r2 performs any possible transfer between any two registers. Special instructions may also be available to facilitate special types of transfers: on the Z80, the instruction:

EX DE, HL

automatically exchanges the contents of registers DE with the contents of registers H and L (16 bits wide).

Arithmetic Instructions

Because of the limited area available on the microprocessor chip to implement CPU functions, arithmetic instructions are generally limited to add, subtract, increment and decrement, plus some support instructions, such as DAA and carry manipulation (see Figure 9.3). Ideally, arithmetic instructions should include all the usual arithmetic instructions plus at least multiply and divide. Multiply and divide functions are provided only on the newer, more powerful 16-bit microprocessors.

We can further subdivide arithmetic instructions into instructions involving transfers between registers only, and instructions involving

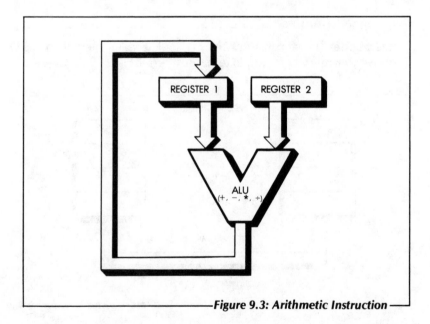

Figure 9.3: Arithmetic Instruction

transfers between registers and external devices. For example, in the case of the 8080 the instruction:

ADD r

specifies the addition of register r to the accumulator. The instruction:

ADD M

specifies the addition of a memory word to the accumulator. In this example, the memory address is assumed to be in registers H and L. In both of these cases, the result is left in the accumulator.

With the 6800, the instruction:

ADD A MEM

adds the value contained in memory location MEM to accumulator A.

The 8080, the Z80, the 8085, and the 6809 all provide special instructions that operate on 16 bits even though all three are 8-bit microprocessors. This results in improved efficiency in manipulating 16-bit data. For example, on the Z80, the instruction ADD HL,BC results in adding the contents of registers H and L to registers B and C (16 bits wide). The same instruction exists on the 8080 and the 8085.

All microprocessors are equipped with instructions for incrementing or decrementing the contents of specified registers. This is indispensable for any counting operation.

With the 6800, the instructions INC MEM, A or B, and DEC increment or decrement a memory location (or the contents of accumulators A or B). Special instructions INX and DEX are provided to increment or decrement the 16-bit index register. Similarly, the 8080, the 8085 and the Z80 are equipped with INC and DEC instructions that operate on 16-bit registers.

We have seen in the previous chapter that, in order to perform BCD operations efficiently, the decimal-adjust (DAA) operation must also be available. This instruction is provided on virtually all microprocessors. Depending on the microprocessor, DAA executes more efficiently while performing an addition, rather than a subtraction operation, or vice-versa. Two types of DAA instructions are usually not provided for both operations.

The arithmetic instructions most notably lacking in 8-bit microprocessors are multiply and divide. Floating-point operations are never available. (They are seldom available even on minicomputers, in view of the amount of logic necessary to implement them.) However, since multiply and divide instructions are not available on 8-bit microprocessors, the *multiply step* and *divide step* instructions can be of special value. A multiply step is a conditional ADD based on the value of the carry bit. A divide step is a conditional subtraction. In addition, a *sign extend* facility must be available. A sign extend consists of duplicating the sign bit during a right shift. This is necessary for handling two's-complement numbers. Unfortunately, few 8-bit microprocessors provide these instructions, although the newer ones do, thus resulting in improved arithmetic speeds. Special chips, such as floating-point processors, may also be used to improve arithmetic speed.

Logical Instructions

Logical instructions perform a logical operation using the ALU (see Figure 9.4). A minimum of four logical operations must be provided: OR, AND, exclusive OR (abbreviated XOR or EOR), and NOT (complement). The result of logical operations is traditionally shown by *truth tables*. The truth tables for each of these operations appear in Figure 9.5. Within the truth table, a 0 represents "false" and a 1 represents "true."

An OR statement is true whenever *either* or *both* of the inputs are true. Thus,

>0 **OR** 0 = 0
>0 **OR** 1 = 1
>1 **OR** 0 = 1
>1 **OR** 1 = 1

as shown on the truth table in Figure 9.5.

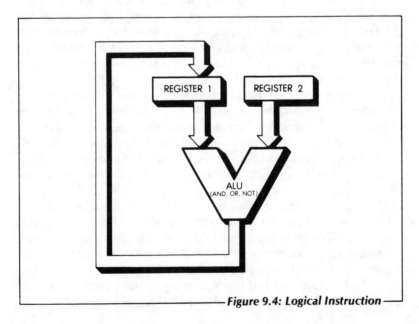

Figure 9.4: Logical Instruction

An XOR statement is true whenever *one and only one* of the inputs is true. An AND statement is true only when *both* inputs are true:

1 **AND** 1 = 1

A NOT statement simply complements the input, turning a 0 into a 1 and a 1 into a 0.

NOT 0 = 1

NOT 1 = 0

Logical instructions are often used for input/output operations. They are also used to force specific values into a location, as the following examples demonstrate.

A logical OR is used to force a 1 into a given bit position, for example:

10000000 **OR** 00001100 = 10001100

    ↑   ↑   ↑

(register)   *(pattern)*   *(result in register)*

The inclusive OR forced the value 11 into bit positions 2 and 3 of the original word. The instruction guarantees that the 1s contained in the second word will be imprinted in the first one, or vice-versa.

OR				AND		
A	B	A ∨ B		A	B	A ∧ B
0	0	0		0	0	0
0	1	1		0	1	0
1	0	1		1	0	0
1	1	1		1	1	1

XOR				NOT	
A	B	A XOR B		A	Ā
0	0	0		0	1
0	1	1			
1	0	1			
1	1	0		1	0

Figure 9.5: Logical Truth Tables

The XOR can be used to test whether or not two words are identical. If the contents are identical, the result will be 0. If any two bits are different (i.e., one bit contains a 1 and the other a 0), the XOR forces a 1 into that bit position. We see on the truth table for XOR that the result is 0 only if all bits are identical in A and B.

XOR can thus be used to test whether a value has changed in an input register. A previous value of the input register is simply XORed with a new value of the input register. If the result is 0, no change has occurred. If the result is 1, at least one bit position has been modified. In fact, the bit positions that have been modified are identified by 1s in the corresponding bit position of the result.

Logical AND is used to mask a specified bit position within the register, i.e., to force a 0 into it. We see on the truth table for AND that whenever one of the operands is a 0, the result is always 0. The result is 1 only if both inputs are 1. For example:

11111110 **AND** 11101111 = 11101110

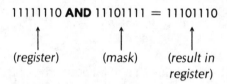

(register)   (mask)   (result in
                                register)

Only bit 5 was *masked* by the 0 contained in the second byte. It was forced to the value 0 in the result.

All four of these logical operations are available on all microprocessors, though mnemonics may differ. COMP, for example, is often used for the NOT operation. EOR may be used instead of XOR. We will demonstrate these instructions later on in this chapter in the program examples.

Skew Operations

Skew operations refer to *shift, rotate,* and similar operations that change the order of bits within a register (see Figure 9.6). Shift operations are necessary both for executing multiplication and division instructions, and for testing the contents of any bit within a register. In the case of 8-bit microprocessors, these instructions will generally operate exclusively on the accumulator (or accumulators), although it is highly desirable to have them operate on any register. Variations may be provided; for example, the *nibble exchange* exchanges the left 4 bits with the right 4 bits.

As we will see in a later program example, a 1-bit left shift is equivalent to a multiplication by two in the binary system. Similarly, a right shift is equivalent to a division by two.

The three types of shifts are:

1. logical shift, right or left
2. arithmetic shift, right or left
3. rotation, right or left.

We will now examine them.

Logical Shift.   A logical shift is a "pure" shift. In a left-shift operation, the contents of the left-most bit will be shifted out of the register and fall into the carry bit. Conversely, the contents of the right-most bit will be zero (see Figure 9.7).

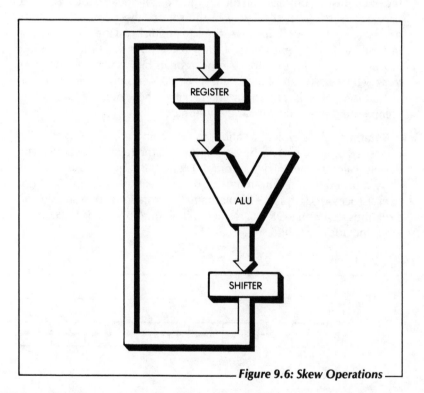

Figure 9.6: Skew Operations

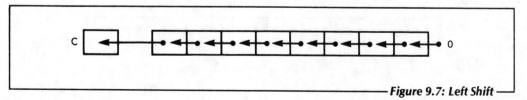

Figure 9.7: Left Shift

For example, on the 6800, the instruction LSR (logical shift right) results in a right shift: bit 0 will be deposited into the carry bit and bit 7 will be shifted by one position to the right. A left shift operates in exactly the same way, only in the reverse direction.

One word of caution: on most microprocessors, the usual convention is to label the right-most bit as bit 0 and the left-most bit as bit 7, so that the bit position corresponds to the binary weight. However, a few manufacturers, mostly minicomputer manufacturers, reverse this convention.

Arithmetic Shift.   Arithmetic shifts are used for handling two's-complement numbers. When shifting a two's-complement number to the right, the bit coming in on the left must be identical to the sign bit to prevent an inadvertent change in the sign of the number. In other words, if the number is negative, the bit coming in on the left must be 1 rather than 0. A *"sign-extend"* facility carries out this task. The 6800 instruction, ASR, for example, simply repeats bit 7 whenever the contents of the register are shifted right. The Z80 is equipped with a similar instruction. This is an important facility when performing two's-complement multiplication and division.

Rotation.   In a typical rotation, the bit going out of the register is deposited into the carry. The bit coming into the register is taken from the old value of the carry (bottom of Figure 9.8). This means that the carry must contain an input and an output section. Rotation in most microprocessors is thus a *9-bit* mathematical rotation. For example, instructions ROL and ROR will result in a 9-bit rotation on the 6800. (The 9 bits include the C bit.)

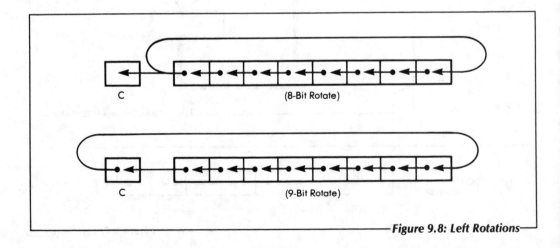

C   (8-Bit Rotate)

C   (9-Bit Rotate)

Figure 9.8: Left Rotations

The 8080, the Z80, and the 8085 are equipped with an additional rotation instruction that rotates only the accumulator, i.e., only 8 bits: RLC, RRC (see top of Figure 9.8). In addition, bit C is set to the value of the bit falling out. The 8080, however, does not have a "true" shift as defined above.

Control Instructions

Control instructions change the order in which a program is executed, either unconditionally or in a way that depends on the value of status indicators. Control instructions provide the so-called "intelligence" capabilities of a computer. These instructions differentiate a *computer* from a *calculator*. They give the computer the capability to implement different decisions (different programs) depending on the values of measured or computed parameters. There are three kinds of control instructions. They include:

1. unconditional branch

2. conditional jumps

3. special instructions.

We will now examine each type.

1 . Unconditional Branch: An unconditional branch or jump instruction is simply: GOTO addr. This instruction forces a branch to a specified memory location addr. In the normal execution mode of a program, instructions are executed sequentially. When a

    GOTO addr

is encountered, the next instruction to be executed is the one at address addr. This is called a branch or a jump. In the case of the 8080, such a branch is carried out by the instruction: JMP addr.

The next instruction executed after the JMP will be the instruction at address addr. The literal address *addr* will actually be forced into the program counter inside the MPU (see Figure 9.9). This results automatically in the fetching of the next instruction from address addr.

The 6800 provides two branch instructions: BRA and JMP. JMP is the general jump instruction, whereas BRA is used to make a short-distance jump within an 8-bit field. The availability of a short jump (BRA) allows the use of faster 16-bit instructions (8-bit opcode and 8-bit short address), versus the long jump that requires 24 bits. The 8080, on the other hand, is equipped with a very short jump, the RST instruction, which specifies a 3-bit jump address within an 8-bit code. RST is restricted to jumps in multiples of eight bytes within the first 256 memory locations. This instruction is very fast and is used primarily for interrupts.

2. Conditional Jumps: Conditional branch instructions are used when a condition must be tested in a program. The instruction normally tests the condition of one of the bits within the status register. If the condition is met (the bit is 1), the branch will occur. If the condition is not met (the bit is 0), the branch will not occur, and the program will continue in its normal sequence.

The bits within the status register are normally set automatically by most instructions. Each manufacturer supplies a list of the status flags that are affected by each of the instructions. It is sometimes possible to set specific bits explicitly through specialized instructions.

Usually each bit of the status flags can be tested independently for the value 0 or for the value 1 and can result in a branch. The corresponding branch instructions will bear a different name depending on the manufacturer. Sometimes more sophisticated instructions are available that will test combinations of bits or combinations of conditions, such as a bit being "greater than or equal to," or "less than or equal to" another bit.

As an example of a simple conditional branch, in the case of the 6800, the instruction BEQ will result in a branch if $Z = 1$. BPL will result in a branch if $N = 0$.

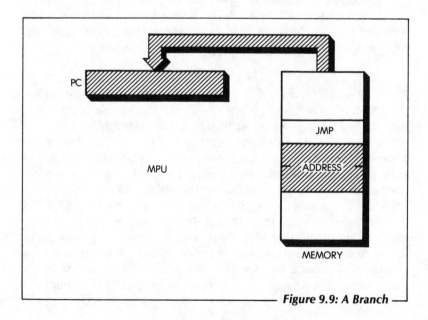

Figure 9.9: A Branch

Each test condition in a flowchart will be implemented by one or more conventional branches in the program. These branches represent the equivalent of an "IF...THEN...ELSE..." statement in a high-level language.

Naturally, they implement only binary choices, i.e., "yes or no" decisions. Whenever a more complex decision must be made in assembly-language programming, a *sequence* of binary tests is used.

One special case of a multi-branch decision is an 8-direction branch, which depends on the value of a bit within the accumulator or a register. Unfortunately, such a facility has been provided on few 8-bit microprocessors. It is especially efficient for implementing one of eight possible decisions, depending on which of eight conditions is true. It is equivalent to "ON...GOTO..." in a high-level language.

3. Special Instructions: Special control instructions that do not fit into the above two categories include:

— halt and suspension instructions

— subroutine calls

— interrupt management

— management of other facilities that might be included on the microprocessor chip, such as a programmable timer.

Whenever specific input and output instructions are available, they may also be classified here. Finally, stack manipulation instructions are actually a special case of implicit addressing. However, they also change the contents of the stack pointer automatically, and therefore should be considered as special instructions.

With two exceptions, the miscellaneous special instructions that we have listed do not require any special explanation. The exceptions are subroutine calls and stack handling. We will now describe these two categories of instructions.

SUBROUTINES

A *user program* is the sequence of instructions that will be placed inside the microprocessor's memory for execution. A *subroutine* is a group of instructions (a subprogram within the main user program) that has a specific name and is delimited by two specialized instructions: SUB at the beginning and RETURN at the end. A subroutine is written once and used many times within the program through a special CALL mechanism.

The use of subroutines is illustrated in Figure 9.10. Usually, subroutines are listed by the assembler at the end of the main program. However, they can reside anywhere within the memory, just like any segment of a program.

The mechanism for using subroutines is the following. In the course of the main program, a special instruction is encountered: CALL SUB1 (as we see in the program box on the left of the illustration in Figure 9.10). This subroutine call causes a jump to the starting address of subroutine SUB1. Control is "transferred" to the subroutine. This is not the only effect of the CALL instruction; but let us defer this point temporarily. Subroutine SUB1 is then executed. (For the time being, we will ignore SUB2, which appears in the box at the right of the illustration.) SUB1 is executed until the instruction RETURN is encountered. The RETURN instruction causes a return to the main program. The next instruction following the CALL SUB1 in the main program is then executed, as shown in Figure 9.10.

Conceptually, the effect is analogous to inserting SUB1 at the location where the CALL instruction resides. Internally, to return from SUB1 to the main program, it is necessary to keep track of the return address in the main program. At the time that the subroutine call is encountered, the program counter has already been incremented and contains the

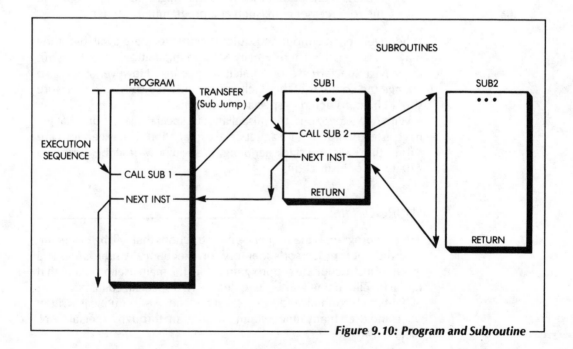

Figure 9.10: Program and Subroutine

address of the next executable instruction, i.e., the address of "NEXT INST". This address must be preserved, and doing so is the second effect of the CALL instruction. The return address will be preserved in the *stack*.

Successive subroutine calls can be made any number of times. Let us refer again to Figure 9.10. In the course of executing SUB1, another subroutine call is encountered: CALL SUB2. This second call results in the transfer of control to subroutine SUB2 (the box on the right in Figure 9.10). Rather than continuing execution within SUB1, the next instruction executed is the first executable instruction of SUB2.

Let us say SUB2 contains no further subroutine calls. SUB2 then normally executes until the special instruction RETURN is encountered. The RETURN causes a return to the next instruction within SUB1 following the call to SUB2. Execution then proceeds within SUB1 until RETURN is encountered. This finally causes a return to the calling program and execution of NEXT INST.

Normally, nothing prevents one subroutine from calling itself. This is called a *recursive* subroutine call. In such a case, it is assumed that some mechanism (such as a counter) is used within the program so that execution will eventually terminate.

The Subroutine Mechanism

The internal mechanism for implementing the subroutine calls is quite simple. When a CALL is encountered, the program counter must be saved in the stack. Every CALL instruction preserves PC, then loads the address of the beginning of the subroutine into PC. Conversely, the RETURN instruction restores PC. It simply pops the top two bytes of the stack into the PC register. Execution then proceeds normally.

Each successive subroutine "level" results in a new entry in the stack. In addition, each subroutine normally needs "working registers" for its own use. The programmer must save in the stack the contents of registers needed within the subroutine, and must restore these registers when leaving the subroutine. An example of this procedure appears later in this section when we discuss the 8080 interrupt handler.

Each new subroutine call encountered within a subroutine is said to create a new "subroutine level"; the new call creates a new entry or "level" in the stack. At least two bytes per level are necessary for storing the PCs, and usually more bytes are needed for preserving registers that the subroutine should not erase. Thus, the programmer must always reserve a sufficient stack area in the memory.

The main advantage of a subroutine is that it need be written only once, yet it can be executed any number of times by various programs. It represents a significant savings in the *amount of memory* that has to be provided.

Subroutines offer several other advantages:

- They substantially clarify the readability of a program.

- Once written, they can be shared by a number of users. (One can build a library of subroutines.)

- They can be debugged individually, a significant advantage.

A disadvantage of subroutine use is the *overhead* involved in switching to and from the subroutine. Extra instructions, the CALL and the RETURN instructions, must be executed in order to branch to the subroutine and come back from it. If a routine is very short and if efficient performance is essential, as in the case of multiply and divide routines, it is preferable simply to repeat the group of two or three instructions several times throughout the program rather than use a subroutine. In this case, the incentive is to maintain efficiency at the expense of increased memory usage.

A programmer must bear in mind that a subroutine needs registers to operate. It may require some registers that were already used by the main program. Any user must be aware of which registers the subroutine will write into. Should a subroutine require the use of registers that are not available because they are already being used by the main program, the programmer will have to preserve these registers in the stack or in the memory at the beginning of the subroutine, then restore them at the end of the subroutine.

The RETURN operation is not a mere branch operation. It must restore the status of the program counter, using a "pop" operation from the stack. The value of the program counter (which has been preserved on top of the stack) is transferred back into the PC, causing an automatic transfer to the next instruction following the subroutine call. This mechanism can be repeated to any depth, as long as sufficient stack space exists.

As an example, let us examine the subroutine mechanism in the 8080. A subroutine call is implemented by CALL SUBAD, where SUBAD is the starting address of the subroutine. Execution of the call results in automatically saving the current value of PC on top of the stack (see Figure 9.11). Since the first available word on top of the stack is pointed to by the stack pointer, the SP register is decremented by two, and execution is transferred to address SUBAD. The stack pointer must be decremented by *two* locations because we are saving the contents of a

16-bit register (PC). In the 8080, addresses *decrease* when going *up*, by convention. A stack *growth* is characterized by a *decrementation* of the stack pointer.

Conversely, the return is implemented by RET. Execution of RET results in an automatic pop of the top two words of the stack into the SP. At the same time SP is automatically incremented by two. Equivalent instructions in the 6800 are JSR (Jump to Subroutine) and RTS (Return from Subroutine).

STACK INSTRUCTIONS

In Chapter 3 we discussed the role of the stack in interrupts. We have now seen how the stack is used for subroutines to preserve the value of the PC register. The maximum number of subroutine calls that can be implemented is determined by the available length of the stack.

The stack can also be used to advantage during ordinary processing. In particular, the stack is often used to transfer incoming data quickly to the memory while capturing a block of data. A single PUSH instruction will result in data being transferred to a memory address. The need for additional instructions to set and increment the memory address is removed.

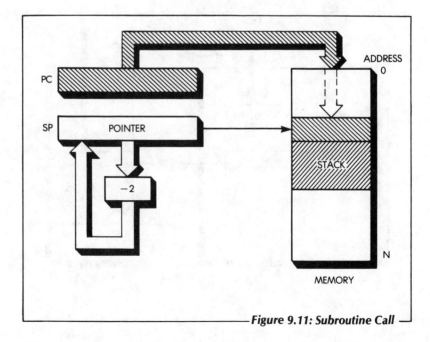

Figure 9.11: Subroutine Call

We have seen that the stack will also be used whenever the need arises for preserving internal registers within any given subroutine. The programmer can then explicitly copy any needed machine registers into the stack, use them and then restore them from the stack. This is specifically what occurs in the case of interrupt handlers. Let us look at an actual example of an 8080 interrupt handler.

An 8080 Interrupt Handler Program

In the 8080, each interrupt handler routine must preserve registers at the beginning and restore them at the end. The following instructions are used to preserve the registers (see Figure 9.12):

        PUSH PSW
        PUSH H
        PUSH D
        PUSH B

Note that each PUSH saves two registers: PUSH PSW saves PSW (flags) and A. PUSH H saves H and L, etc.

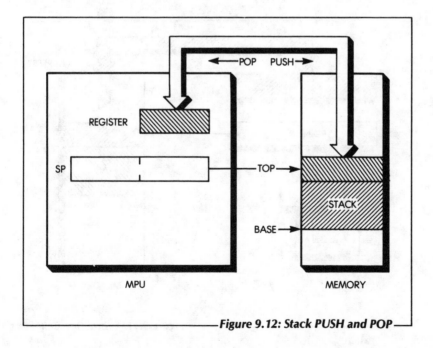

Figure 9.12: Stack PUSH and POP

Conversely, the following instructions will restore the registers at the end:

    POP B
    POP D
    POP H
    POP PSW

Naturally, registers must be restored in the reverse of the order they were pushed.

Stack instructions in the 6800 are PSHA and PSHB. They will deposit the contents of accumulator A or accumulator B on top of the stack. Conversely, PULA or PULB will remove the top word of the stack and transfer it into either A or B. The SP register will be automatically incremented or decremented by the operation on the stack.

The 8080 and the Z80 push or pop elements from the stack in similar ways. In addition, they are equipped with an automatic incrementer/decrementer that may operate on any register pair. Using this facility, any register pair can be used as a pseudo-stack pointer.

We have now described the various types of instructions. In addition, each type of instruction may use a variety of addressing modes to retrieve the final data. The availability and nature of addressing modes provided with a given microprocessor are crucial to its efficiency.

Let us now define and explain these addressing modes.

ADDRESSING TECHNIQUES

Addressing refers to the method of accessing a value, whether data or address in the memory or in a register. For efficiency in handling various data structures, such as lists and tables, several addressing modes must be provided. However, providing several modes complicates the CPU design, and many microprocessors will only provide a subset of the facilities that we will describe here. If fewer addressing modes are available, then accessing structured data may involve a large number of operations.

The main addressing modes are illustrated in Figures 9.13 through 9.21. We will describe seven addressing techniques. Combinations of these techniques may also be used.

IMPLICIT ADDRESSING

Implicit addressing indicates that the code of the register(s) addressed by the instruction does not appear as a separate field within the opcode (see Figure 9.13). Implicit addressing is normally used for addressing the accumulator or other special-purpose registers, such as PC or SP. One example is the instruction "ADD r", which was described in Chapter 2. It means *"ADD register r to the accumulator and leave the results in the accumulator."* The accumulator is not explicitly referenced by this instruction. Naturally, the reference to the accumulator is *contained* within the operation code of the instruction. The point is that this referencing does not require an explicit 3-bit code (there are 8 internal registers) but is implicitly contained in the opcode itself, resulting in improved efficiency in the allocation of opcodes. If the accumulator were explicitly specified along with register r, 6 bits would be used (3 per register), leaving only 2 bits to the opcode.

Thus, implicit addressing results in a shorter instruction, making it possible to use an 8-bit format, which is the most efficient one to execute on an 8-bit microprocessor. Why, then, do we not use implicit addressing for referencing any register within the machine? This would result in two problems. First, if the number of registers is large, too many bits would be required. Second, this would result in a more complex internal decoder. This increased complexity is unacceptable. Thus, a compromise must then be found between *implicit* and *explicit* addressing. Recall that explicit addressing, using 3-bit codes to address eight registers, is easily decoded within the microprocessor and can be gated directly to the register multiplexer.

IMMEDIATE ADDRESSING

Immediate addressing refers to the fact that the operand (or literal) immediately follows the opcode. The operand may be one or two words. The total instruction may, therefore, use either two or three words. (This is illustrated in Figure 9.14.) The literal operand that appears in the second and possibly the third byte may be either data or address. For example, an immediate instruction will load a literal value in an internal register or add it to the contents of an internal register.

Specific addressing modes are used with branch instructions. Let us examine them.

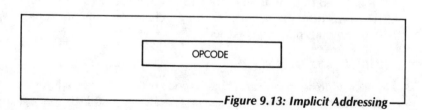

OPCODE

Figure 9.13: Implicit Addressing

DIRECT ADDRESSING

Direct addressing is the simplest type of addressing used by a branch instruction, where an 8-bit (short) branch address is specified after the branch opcode (see Figure 9.15).

A *branch* instruction, which is a jump to a specified location in the memory, normally requires three bytes in the case of an 8-bit microprocessor: one byte for the opcode and two bytes for a 16-bit address. Executing such a branch is slow, as it requires three memory accesses. In order to improve the speed of branch operations, especially in cases where response time is critical (such as responding to an interrupt), a *direct addressing* mechanism is usually provided. Direct addressing is characterized by an 8-bit address that permits branching to locations 0 through 255 in the memory. These first 256 locations can be encoded by an 8-bit code. Using direct addressing, a 2-byte instruction can then be used to branch to any one of those locations. This addressing mode is provided in the case of the 8080 but with some restrictions: one can only jump to locations in multiples of 64. In addition, remember that the 8080's RST instruction is implemented within a single byte, for an even faster response to interrupt.

However, branching should not be restricted to such a short displacement. Normal addressing must also be provided.

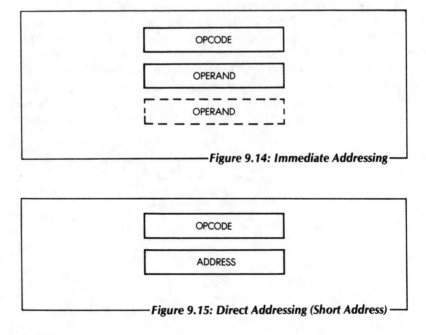

Figure 9.14: Immediate Addressing

Figure 9.15: Direct Addressing (Short Address)

EXTENDED OR NORMAL ADDRESSING

Extended, or normal, addressing is simply a normal memory addressing, using a three-word format. The first word contains the opcode and the next two words contain the 16-bit address. (See Figure 9.16.) Extended addressing is used for any type of normal branch or jump operation. The term "extended" is used by some manufacturers simply to differentiate it from "direct" addressing, in which only an 8-bit jump address is permissible.

A more complex addressing mode is also usually provided to improve efficiency when accessing tables. This is indexed addressing.

INDEXED ADDRESSING

Most programs refer repeatedly to the contents of one or more tables of values stored in the memory. A table is simply a group of words stored in sequence. It is often necessary to refer repeatedly to entries within the table (for example, *"read the 3rd entry"* and then *"read the 72nd entry"*). Indexed addressing facilitates such table accesses. (See Figure 9.17.)

The register called IX, or index register, is used to hold the start address of the table in the memory. The indexed addressing instruction contains a displacement field (BASE in Figure 9.18) that is automatically added to the contents of the specified index register. Often the displacement field is limited to eight bits so that the indexed addressing instruction can be specified in just two bytes. This limits the maximum length of the table to 256 words. An alternative is to specify the starting address of the table within the first 256 locations and consider the contents of the index register as a displacement field. This is an advantage if the index register is 16 bits wide. Ideally, the displacement field should also be 16 bits so that it can be interchanged with the index register. In the case of ROM-based programs, the significant difference between memory and registers is

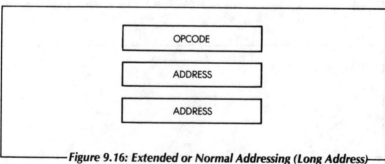

Figure 9.16: Extended or Normal Addressing (Long Address)

that once instructions are deposited into ROM, they cannot be changed. Often, the starting address of the table will be fixed, whereas a displacement will change dynamically. Thus, in microprocessors, the starting address of the table should be placed in the instruction field whereas the displacement will have to reside in the index register. An index address facility should be evaluated in that light.

The mechanism we have just described is called "preindexing." A variation of this mode is "postindexing," which is illustrated in Figure 9.19.

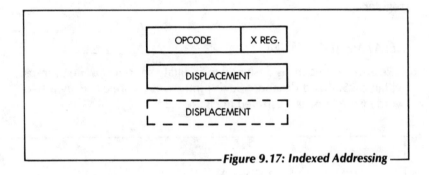

Figure 9.17: Indexed Addressing

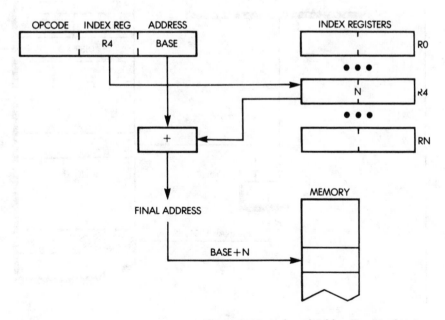

Figure 9.18: Indexed Addressing Mechanism

In postindexing, the contents of a short displacement field D are interpreted as the *address* of the final displacement N in the memory. This
should be considered as "indexed-indirect" addressing. (Indirect addressing is explained below). In postindexing, the contents of IX are
added to N, not to D.

Several index registers are often available in the processor, and indexing is indeed a valuable facility for accessing multiple tables. When
more than one index register is provided, the instruction must contain
a pointer to the index register being used. This is illustrated in Figure
9.18, where the index register field selects one of the indexable
registers.

RELATIVE ADDRESSING

Relative addressing is designed to facilitate short loops, i.e., jumps,
within a 256-word distance. Such jumps can be specified by a two-
word instruction, as illustrated in Figure 9.20.

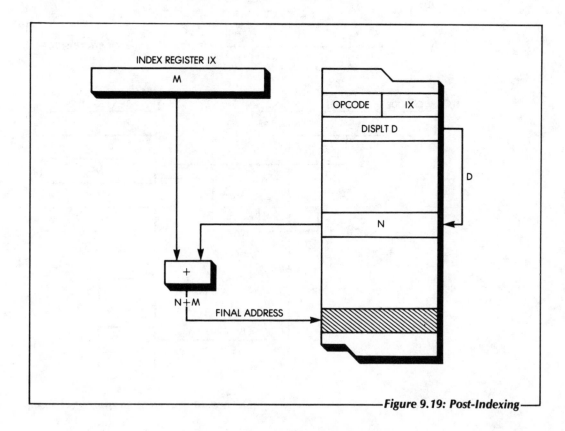

Figure 9.19: Post-Indexing

Relative addressing allows the use of a fast jump in two bytes. (A generalized jump with a full 16-bit displacement requires three bytes.) It is called "relative" because it specifies a jump relative to the current address plus the specified displacement. This displacement can be either positive or negative. Using two's-complement notation, 8 bits may be used to specify a forward jump of up to +126 locations or a backward jump of up to −127 locations. The relative address generated by this instruction is equal to PC plus the signed displacement. One bit (the MSB) is used for the sign, leaving 7 bits for the displacement, hence the +127 displacement limitation.

The availability of relative addressing may be of critical importance to the efficiency of routines that require a short loop to be executed a large number of times, such as arithmetic routines or block transfers.

INDIRECT ADDRESSING

Indirect addressing is illustrated in Figure 9.21. In assembly language the indirect mode is usually indicated symbolically by a "*" appended to the instruction.

Indirect addressing means: *"Go to the memory address specified by A1 and fetch its contents (A2). Then use A2 as the final destination address."* This implies, in turn, that the "contents" of A1 will be a 16-bit word, requiring two bytes in the memory.

Indirect addressing is universally used to share information among several users or several programs. This technique is analogous to hiding a key under the mat. The key's location is known; it is memory location A1. Each program that wishes to access the data residing at location A2 (which may be moved around frequently in the memory) will always look at the fixed memory location A1 and find the actual data's address (its key) there.

Typically, when different programs are executed, data will reside at unpredictable locations within the RAM. Whenever variable-length data are used, tables will be kept at an agreed location in the RAM with pointers to these data structures. Any routine or program that needs to

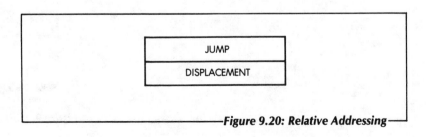

Figure 9.20: Relative Addressing

access a given data structure will look up the actual address of the structure in this pointer table. Data can then be accessed efficiently using indirect addressing; the data whose address appears at the specified entry in the table will automatically be fetched.

Because shared data is usually stored in the form of tables rather than isolated memory locations, indirect addressing is most efficient when coupled with indexed addressing. It then becomes possible to address a specific entry in the table in a single instruction, using the indexed specification while specifying an indirect fetch to obtain the final data. In a powerful processor, indexed and indirect addressing should both be provided.

Unfortunately, indirect addressing is available on few 8-bit microprocessors. It can be implemented to a limited extent through the H and L registers on both the 8080 and the Z80. The Signetics 2650 provides true indirect addressing.

Auto-indexing refers to indexing followed by an automatic increment/decrement of the associated pointer. Whenever auto-indexing is supplied, any register pair can potentially be used as a stack pointer, even if explicit stack management facilities are not provided. For example, the SCMP from National is equipped with three pointer registers, P1, P2, P3, which serve very effectively as stack pointers, using the auto-indexing facility.

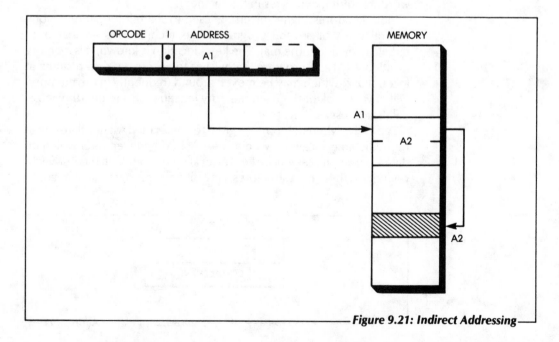

Figure 9.21: Indirect Addressing

In summary, the availability of multiple addressing modes reduces the number of words required to perform a jump or retrieve a word of data, thereby increasing the processing speed of the microprocessor. While some microprocessors may have a similar arithmetic performance, the availability of sophisticated addressing capabilities usually has a major impact on text processing and data-base management. In order to achieve efficient programming, a good understanding of addressing modes is required.

PROGRAMMING EXAMPLES

We will now present several actual program examples for the 8080 and 6800. The instruction sets for these two microprocessors appear at the end of this book.

We will first study an arithmetic example which will illustrate the manipulation of internal registers and data transfers within the MPU. Then, we will present several examples of input/output programming, including a program for microprocessor-generated music. These programs will illustrate the concepts that have been presented so far and show some of the problems involved in developing actual programs. They are intended as examples only; and actual practice is strongly recommended for a true understanding of programming.

AN ARITHMETIC PROGRAM: MULTIPLICATION

In this example we will perform an 8-bit by 8-bit integer multiplication using the Intel 8080. Since this operation is not available as an instruction, we must first design a multiplication algorithm. To understand the algorithm that will implement a solution to the multiplication problem, let us consider the usual multiplication technique in decimal, in the example 13 × 12:

$$
\begin{array}{rl}
13 & \textit{(multiplicand)} \\
\times\ 12 & \textit{(multiplier)} \\
\hline
26 & \\
13 & \\
\hline
156 & \textit{(result)}
\end{array}
$$

The multiplication algorithm used in a computer is quite similar to the steps presented above. The main difference is that the partial multiplications are immediately added together, resulting in a partial product. The algorithm is the following. Examine the multiplier. Test its rightmost digit (i.e., the LSB). If it is not 0, multiply the multiplicand by this digit and add it to the current partial product. If the digit is 0, do nothing. The next entry to be added to the partial product will be offset to the left by one position (i.e., it will be shifted left by 1).

In any case, whether the multiplier digit is 0 or not, the next number to be added will be shifted left. However, if the digit is 0, nothing will have to be added. If the digit is not 0, then an addition will occur. This technique implements a solution to the multiplication problem by performing a sequence of additions since there is no multiplication instruction. A left-shift in the case of a decimal number is equivalent to a multiplication by 10.

The algorithm used for binary numbers is identical. Let us now multiply 3 by 5 in binary:

Multiplicand:	011	(3)
Multiplier:	× 101	(5)
Testing the rightmost "1" of 101:	011	(The partial product is 011)
Testing the "0" of 101:	+ 000	(The partial product is 011)
Testing the leftmost "1" of 101:	+ 011	(The partial product is 01111)
Result:	= 01111	(15)

As in the previous example, the rightmost bit of the multiplier, i.e., its LSB, is tested. If it is 1, the multiplicand is added. If it is 0, no addition occurs. In either case, the next addition of the multiplicand to the partial product will be performed after moving positions left by 1 bit in the multiplicand.

Since it is more practical in a processor to accumulate a partial sum than to memorize a sequence of additions to be performed at the end (the opposite of which is true on paper), the computer algorithm differs slightly from the hand multiplication technique. When a multiplicand value must be added, it is immediately added to the *partial product*. Only the partial product need be remembered. In order to add the multiplicand to the partial product, we can use one of two methods equivalently. We can either shift the multiplicand to the left or shift the partial product to the right. The result is identical. They are moved with respect to each other by one bit position. The corresponding flowchart is shown in Figure 9.22.

Multiplication is normally accomplished in binary by the above sequence of adds and shifts. In order to demonstrate the relationship between hardware limitations and software techniques, we will use a standard programming trick to minimize the number of internal registers required by the program. Every time the least significant bit of the multiplier is tested, it is no longer needed. In order to test this bit, it is necessary to shift right the bits of the multiplier one after the other. Therefore, bit positions will become available on the left of the register containing the multiplier each time it is shifted to the right. Recall that, concurrently, we will compute a partial product at each step. The partial product will grow by one bit at each step. It will initially be contained in an 8-bit register, then it will require an additional bit, and so on. Instead of using an additional register to store the expanding partial product,

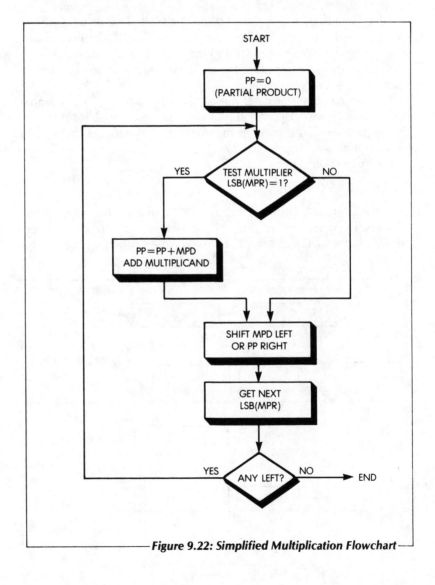

Figure 9.22: Simplified Multiplication Flowchart

we will use the left part of the multiplier register and progressively shift bits of the partial product into the left part of the multiplier register (see Figure 9.23). This "trick" saves time and increases efficiency.

At any point during multiplication, the register initially allocated to the multiplier will contain part of the multiplier on the right and the least significant part of the partial product on the left (see Figure 9.24). In order to end the multiplication we must keep track of the remaining number of bits in the multiplier. This problem will be solved by the use of a bit counter. We will use register E of the 8080 to store the bit count. It will be initialized with the value 9, and the multiplication will be complete when this counter has been decremented to 0. Registers C and D will initially hold the multiplier and the multiplicand, respectively. At the end of the multiplication, the result will be contained in B and C (see Figure 9.25).

The program that translates this algorithm into the 8080's assembly language is shown in Figure 9.26. We will now describe each instruction in the program and explain its meaning. (See Appendix C for a summary of 8080 instructions.)

The instruction

MVI B,0

means *Move immediate* the value 0 into B. We must define a zero initial value of the partial product, i.e., *initialize* it to the value 0. This is an example of an *immediate* instruction in which the data word to be loaded

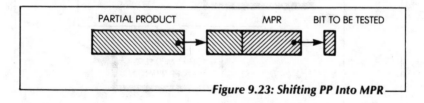

Figure 9.23: Shifting PP Into MPR

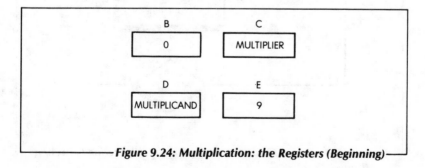

Figure 9.24: Multiplication: the Registers (Beginning)

into the register appears in the second byte of the instruction (here 00000000).

MVI E,9

Similarly, the value 9 is loaded into the counter E. The reader should be certain, by the end of this example, that the value 9, not 8, is indeed correct. We will now deposit the least significant bit of the multiplier in the carry bit, where it can be tested:

MOV A,C

This instruction merely moves the contents of register C into the accumulator. We now have the following problem. We want to test the least significant bit (LSB) of the multiplier, which is contained in C. However, the 8080 does not allow us to test the bit of an arbitrary register—only the accumulator. In order to test the LSB, it must be

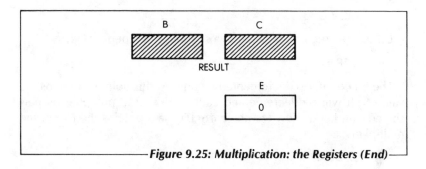

Figure 9.25: Multiplication: the Registers (End)

```
MULT      MVI     B,0      INITIALIZE MSBYTE OF PARTIAL PRODUCT TO ZERO
          MVI     E,9      BIT COUNTER SET TO 9
MULT0     MOV     A,C      ROTATE LSB (MPR) TO CARRY AND SHIFT RIGHT
          RAR
          MOV     C,A      LSBYTE OF PARTIAL PRODUCT
          DCR     E        DECREMENT COUNTER
          JZ      DONE     EXIT IF COMPLETE
          MOV     A,B
          JNC     MULT1    TEST VALUE OF CARRY BIT
          ADD     D        ADD MULTIPLICAND IF BIT = 1
MULT1     RAR              CARRY WAS ZERO. SHIFT MSBYTE OF PARTIAL PRODUCT
          MOV     B,A
          JMP     MULT0    DO IT AGAIN
DONE      ...              NEXT INSTRUCTION
```

Figure 9.26: 8 × 8 Multiplication Program

shifted out into the carry bit where it can be tested by a specialized branch instruction. Here, we must copy the contents of register C into the accumulator, shift it, and finally, copy the contents of the accumulator back into register C. This is accomplished by the third, fourth and fifth instructions:

RAR

Rotate accumulator right. This statement is illustrated in Figure 9.27. The contents of the accumulator (which have been set from the contents of register C, i.e., the multiplier) are rotated right by one position. The rightmost bit of the multiplier falls into the carry bit C, where it will be tested. Note what happens to the bit coming in from the carry into the accumulator. We will see that this is the mechanism that is used to transmit the partial product automatically into the left part of register C.

The rotation has been accomplished by RAR; the contents of the accumulator can be copied back into C. The contents of the carry bit C will not be affected by the move operation:

MOV C,A

Let us now record the fact that a shift has been performed:

DCR E

The bit counter is decremented by one. At this point it contains the value 8. It will be decremented each time that a multiplier bit gets shifted out. Let us now test the carry bit that contains the LSB of the multiplier:

JZ DONE

JZ stands for jump on zero. This instruction tests the value of the carry bit. If the counter has decremented to the value 0, we are finished, and we jump to the label "DONE" shown at the bottom of the program in

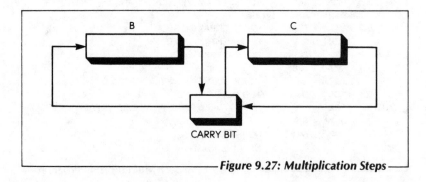

Figure 9.27: Multiplication Steps

Figure 9.26. The next executable instruction of the program resides there.

Note that the counter is decremented and tested for zero *before* any addition to the partial product. We will have to test and add eight times since there are eight bits in the multiplier. The first time that we get to this segment of the program, the counter has the value 8. The last time that we go through the following instructions, it will have the value 1. This is why we had to start with the value 9 rather than 8 in the bit counter. We will verify this point again later. Let us go back to the program. We must get ready to add the multiplicand to the partial product:

    MOV A,B

B contains the partial product. It was initialized to the value 0 at the beginning of the program but it will soon have non-zero contents, since we will add the multiplicand to the partial product. In the case of the 8080 this addition requires that the partial product be contained in the accumulator. Again, we need to move the contents of a register in the accumulator in order to execute a subsequent instruction: B is moved into A by MOV A,B. Let us now test the carry bit:

    JNC MULT1

None of the previous instructions have modified the value of the C bit, and C contains the LSB of the multiplier. JNC is "Jump on No Carry." JNC results in a jump if there is no carry. If the carry is 0, we do not add the multiplicand to the partial product, and we jump to the label MULT1 which appears two lines below. However, if the carry is equal to 1, i.e., if the right-most bit of the multiplier was equal to 1 (it has been preserved in C), then we must add the multiplicand and execute the next instruction:

    ADD D

This instruction simply adds the contents of register D, i.e., the multiplicand, to the accumulator, which contains the partial product. The addition will modify the value of the C bit; provided that we multiply positive numbers, the ADD instruction will result in a 0 carry. Let us now save the value of the new partial product:

    RAR

The contents of the accumulator are rotated right by one position. The old value of the carry (0) is input on the left of the accumulator. The rightmost bit of the partial product is deposited as the new value of the carry. This is illustrated in Figure 9.27 as a rotation performed on register B, since the accumulator temporarily holds the contents of B.

We simply need to copy back the contents of the accumulator into register B:

>   MOV B,A

The contents of the accumulator are moved back into register B. The loop is now completed by coming back to the first instruction of the loop:

>   JMP MULT0

This is an unconditional jump, forcing a return to the address MULT0, the third line of our program. Again, the contents of C will be rotated right in order to be tested, and so on.

In order to verify that this program does indeed perform the multiplication of two 8-bit numbers, the reader should check the program by hand using the table in Figure 9.28. Complete the table as follows. On the left, write the instruction being executed. Then, in each of the six columns, write the value of the C-bit and the values of the other five registers at the time the instruction is executed. Do this for each instruction. Start by multiplying 5 (in C) by 3 (in D). You should obtain the binary value of 15 as a result. Be very careful to check what happens to the C bit every time that an instruction is executed. Some instructions will modify the C bit, while others will leave it intact. For convenience, this table can be extended on ordinary sheets of paper.

SUMMARY OF THE MULTIPLICATION PROGRAM _____

This multiplication program illustrates the use of the basic instruction types that we have described. It shows how information is transferred

INSTRUCTION	REGISTER	A	B	C	D	E	C BIT
MVI	B,0	00000000	00000000	00000101	00000011	--------	-
MVI	E,9	00000000	00000000	00000101	00000011	00001001	-
MOV	A,C	00000101	00000000	00000101	00000011	00001001	-
RAR		00000010	00000000	00000101	00000011	00001001	1
•••							

Figure 9.28: Multiplication Exercise

between the various registers in the machine. It also shows inadequacies of this early microprocessor; because a bit cannot be tested directly on any register, registers need to be copied into the accumulator before their contents can be tested. This results in "needless" transfers between registers and the accumulator, which reduce the efficiency of the program.

For comparison, here is the same program for a Z80, including the four instructions required to load the multiplier from memory address MPRAD into register H and the multiplicand from address MPDAD into register E:

```
MUL 88   LD    HL,(MPRAD-1)   (Load instruction)
         LD    L,0            (Only register H is used)
         LD    DE,(MPDAD)     (Multiplicand in E)
         LD    D,0
         LD    B,8            (B is counter)
MULT     ADD   HL,HL          (Double H and L
                              = Shift left)
         JR    NC,NOADD       (Test carry bit)
         ADD   HL,DE          (Add MPD if required)
NOADD    DJNZ  MULT           (Decrement counter
                              and jump back until zero)
         LD    (RESAD),HL     (Save result in memory)
         RET
```

The program proper uses only five instructions. This gain in efficiency is possible because of a more powerful instruction set.

We have seen how a program is executed inside the MPU, using only internal registers; we will now connect the microprocessor to the external world and execute input and output operations.

SIMULATING DIGITAL LOGIC BY PROGRAM

Every microprocessor is equipped with a basic set of logical instructions such as AND, OR, and NOT. It is therefore capable of implementing by software the equivalent of any logic function normally implemented in hardware with AND, OR and NOT gates. Since all logic functions can be accomplished with these three primitives, the process should be able to accomplish any logic function normally done by hardware. Indeed, sequential or combinatorial logic *can* be replaced by a program equivalent. However, we must stress that this concept, although correct, is misleading. Gates can be replaced by programs on a one-to-one level, but this would be the worst possible kind of programming and would lead to gross inefficiency. Programming must be approached in a completely different way. Programming aims at replacing complete functional modules with programmed solutions. A program does not have to copy the hardware solution.

For example, a control unit implemented by a microprogram is an example of direct replacement of random logic by software. The microprogram is a direct replacement of a random logic implementation. However, the microprogram does not necessarily implement the same sequencing or the same techniques as random logic implementation. The two are equivalent at the *functional* level.

A programmed implementation of logic functions has several advantages: lower cost, speed of implementation, ease in debugging, and flexibility whenever changes are required. Special hardware devices such as buffers and drivers are often eliminated in the case of a programmed implementation. In addition, the fan-in and fan-out limitations are eliminated, as well as the other electrical constraints.

We will now present four simple examples of hardware replacement by program: an inverter, AND/OR gates, a flip-flop, and a delay.

PROGRAMMED INVERTER

An *inverter* implements a NOT function. A high signal on input is converted into low output and vice-versa. The symbolic representation of the circuit is shown in Figure 9.29.

A high signal will be encoded as a logical 1. A low signal will be encoded as a logical 0. In a program, the inversion function will be accomplished by complementing the value of a bit. The following example will be programmed in the 6800 assembly language. (A listing of 6800 instructions and their functions appears in Appendix B.)

```
LDA A    SIGNAL    (Load value of signal)
COM A              (Complement A)
STA A    SIGNAL    (Store complemented value
                    into variable signal)
```

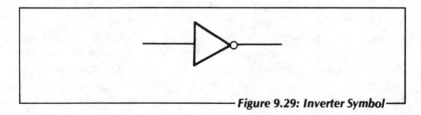

Figure 9.29: Inverter Symbol

The symbolic variable "SIGNAL" in the above program references a memory cell or an input/output register. The first instruction of the program loads the value of the memory cell at address SIGNAL in accumulator A. It is assumed that the value of the input signal is in the cell called "SIGNAL". In a standard 6800 system, this would be implemented by using a PIA input register at this location. Address SIGNAL would therefore refer to a PIA port.

As a result of this 3-instruction program, the values of the 8 bits of the signal are complemented simultaneously. This may not be the desired result, however. To complement only one particular bit, a *mask* would be used. We will now see how to use a logical AND to implement a mask.

Let us assume we wish to invert the signal connected to bit 1 of a PIA port. The actual signal inversion will be performed by the following sequence:

```
LDA      SIGNAL      (Transfer input to A)
TAB                  (Save A in B)
COMA                 (Complement A)
ANDA     #02         (Mask out bit 2 in A)
ANDB     #$FD        (Zero bit 2 in B)
ABA                  (Add A + B)
STA A    SIGNAL
```

The symbol "#" in the above program indicates immediate addressing. The "$" indicates a hexadecimal value (FD = 11111101).

The "AND" operation on the fourth line of this program is used to mask out all bits except bit 1, which can then be added into accumulator B where all of the other bits have been set to 0. Let us examine this program in detail.

LDA   SIGNAL

The value of the input signal is loaded in accumulator A.

TAB

The value is preserved in accumulator B in order to remember the original value of bit 1 later on.

COMA

The contents of A are complemented.

ANDA   #02

The effect of this instruction is to zero all bits in A, except bit 2. The value 02 is called the mask. Recall that ANDing a zero into any bit position zeroes that bit. Bit 1 has now been complemented and isolated. It must be written back into the output register.

        ANDB   #$FD

Clear bit 1 in register B. FD in hexadecimal is 11111101 in binary. This mask affects only bit 1. Now B contains the original value read as input, and a zero in bit position 1. Let us copy the correct value of bit 1 into that position by adding it from register A:

        ABA

A and B are added. The result is in A:

        STA   SIGNAL

The result is sent as the new output signal.

One more improvement is needed to use this sample program effectively in the general case. In practice, a single port on a PIA may not be used for both input and output. For example, we might use port A of the PIA as input and port B as output. The program then becomes:

```
        LDAA    SIGNALA     (Input signal on A)
        LDAB    SIGNALB     (Output signal on B)
        COMA
        ANDA    #02
        ANDB    #$FD
        ABA
        STAA    SIGNALB
```

SIGNALA and SIGNALB represent the addresses of port A and port B of the PIA, respectively. The signal is received into port A of the PIA, inverted by the program, and output in port B. Since the signals of port B other than bit 1 should not be modified, all other signals are masked. This is performed by the ANDB instruction and the ABA, which restores the original value of the other signals.

If we had wanted to invert all the lines of port B, the program would have been simpler since no masking would have been required. In general, whenever operations are performed on 8 bits simultaneously, program efficiency is improved. The length of a program is not necessarily related to the function to be performed.

PROGRAMMED AND-OR FUNCTIONS

The symbol for an AND gate is shown in Figure 9.30. The output is 1 only when both inputs are 1, otherwise it is 0.

A two-input AND gate can be simulated by program as follows:

```
LDAA    SIGNALA
ANDA    SIGNALB
STAA    SIGNALC
```

Let us assume for the sake of simplicity that signals A and B both refer to eight bits. The resulting output is SIGNALC, (eight bits). If only one bit is to be selected on A and B, they must be in corresponding bit positions, or else additional shifts will be required.

Similarly, the OR function is performed as follows:

```
LDAA    SIGNALA
ORAA    SIGNALB
STAA    SIGNALC
```

The program is straightforward. Let us examine a slightly more complex circuit.

FLIP-FLOP SIMULATION

The flip-flop symbol is shown in Figure 9.31. A flip-flop is characterized by three inputs and two outputs, Q and $\overline{Q}$. From a logical standpoint, a flip-flop may be represented by a single bit, which may be stored in a memory location. A reset will force the value 0 in the bit, whereas a set will store the value 1 in it. A corresponding program is:

```
RESET    LDAA    0
         STAA    BASCUL
SET      LDAA    1
         STAA    BASCUL
```

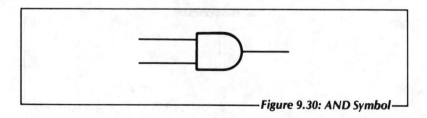

Figure 9.30: AND Symbol

The program will operate simultaneously on eight bits. A memory word will store eight flip-flops. (Indeed, a memory word is *implemented* by eight flip-flops.)

We will now examine another common problem, the generation of a delay.

IMPLEMENTING A DELAY

A programmed delay can be simply implemented by a program loop. The execution time for each instruction is known. If T is the delay to be implemented, and D is the duration of the instructions contained in the loop, the loop will have to be executed T/D times. However, the result of T/D may not be an integer. Since every loop must be executed an integer number of times, the actual resulting delay will be true within some approximation. Here is a programmed delay for the 6800. The delay is achieved by decrementing a counter register for a specified number of times:

```
        LDAB    TIMES
LOOP    DECB
        BNE     LOOP
```

The number of times that the loop must be executed is contained in

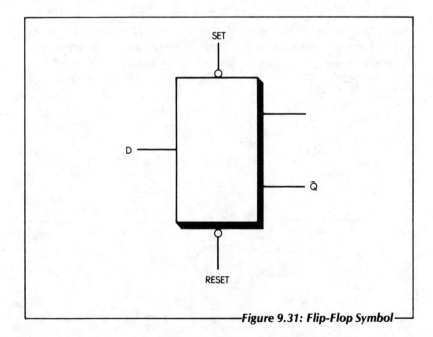

Figure 9.31: Flip-Flop Symbol

the location TIMES. It is loaded into accumulator B. This register is then decremented with the DEC instruction until it reaches the value 0. BNE (branch if not equal to zero) tests whether or not the result of the decrementation is 0. BNE performs this function by testing the Z bit, which is conditioned by the previous DEC. As long as the result is not 0, the program will branch back to the beginning of the loop. Whenever the value 0 is reached, it will not branch anymore and the next instruction in the program is executed. The resulting delay is equal to TIMES multiplied by the sum of the duration of DEC and the duration of BNE. The DEC instruction requires two cycles or two microseconds. BNE requires four microseconds. The total duration of one iteration through the loop is therefore six microseconds. Using this programmed delay, no delay of less than six microseconds can be implemented and only multiples of six microseconds can be achieved. In addition, since our counter is 8 bits wide, the maximum delay that can be achieved with this program is $256 \times 6 = 1536$ microseconds.

If the delay must be longer, several solutions are possible. The simplest is to add instructions between DECB and BNE. Each typical instruction, such as an NOP (no operation), will add a two-cycle delay to the loop. Another method of providing longer delays would be to use a 16-bit register, such as register X, as a counter.

LIMITATIONS OF PROGRAMMED LOGIC

It has been shown how simple logic functions can be achieved by software. Any combination of those functions can also be achieved. However, since a program is executed sequentially, it is not possible to execute tasks simultaneously (at the microsecond level). For example, delays cannot usually be implemented in parallel (however, some tricks exist that may make it possible). In a real-time environment, this creates the need for introducing additional components to implement these delays. This is, in particular, a role of the *programmable-interval timer* (PIT) (described in Chapter 3).

Programmed logic is not intended to replace components at the gate level. Programmed logic is to be used to replace components at the *functional* level. In particular, the availability of many other instructions within the microprocessor makes it possible to implement sophisticated algorithms to perform the same functions as random logic in a different way. The only significant drawback is that programmed logic is slower than a hardware implementation. Whenever speed is a crucial factor, the fastest possible way to execute programmed instructions must be used; thus, microprogramming is necessary. This applies in particular to bit-slice systems.

Let's now examine a more complex program—one that generates sound.

MICROPROCESSOR-CONTROLLED MUSIC _____

This program will generate notes that are played by an external loudspeaker. We will use a 6800 microprocessor equipped with a PIA. The PIA is connected to an external speaker via a resistor (an amplifying transistor may be used for a louder output).

We will not address the details of programming a PIA here. The structure of the PIA appears in Figure 9.32. We will assume that bits 4 and 5 of the control register (CRA) within the PIA have been set to the value 1. Bit 3 of the control register (CRA) will then be used to set the output signal CA2 to the value 1 or 0. The CA2 line will be connected to the

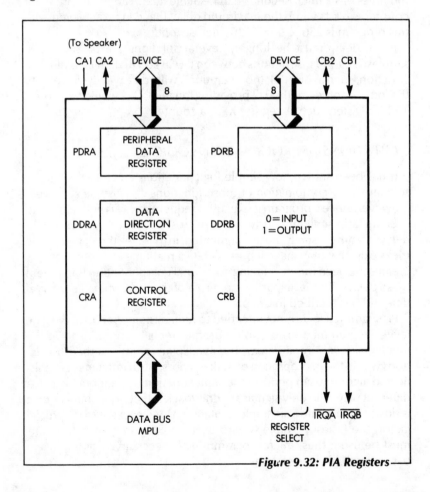

Figure 9.32: PIA Registers

loudspeaker. A sound of given frequency will be generated by alternately switching this bit from 0 to 1 and 1 to 0 at the required frequency.

We will connect the PIA to the address bus in such a way that addresses 4004 to 4007 correspond to the PIA's internal registers. The PIA requires four memory locations, two per channel. The address of the control register for port A (CRA) is 4005. The address for the data direction register (DDRA) is 4004. Thus, address PIADRA will be 4004 and address PIACRA will be 4005.

To modify the value of the output bit on CA2, a value will be stored at address PIACRA. We will set the remaining bits of the PIA control register as follows: bits 0, 1, 2 are set to 1; bits 6 and 7 are set to 0. The details of PIA control are not relevant here.

To set CA2 to 1, we write the following into CRA: 00111111. To write a 0 into CA2, we write: 00110111. In hexadecimal, these values are represented respectively by ''3F'' and ''37''. Thus, to cause a high-to-low transition of the output signal, we change the value in PIACRA from 3F to 37, and vice-versa. The details of register addressing for the PIA are shown in Figure 9.33.

In this program we use programmed delays. The actual program appears below:

```
            ORG    $200      (Origin of program in memory)
PIADRA      EQU    $4004     (Address of PIA output
                             register)
PIACRA      EQU    $4005     (Address of PIA control
                             register)
            LDAA   #$3F      (Value for turning speaker ON)
            LDAB   #$37      (Value for turning speaker
                             OFF)
PLAY        STAA   PIACRA    (Turn speaker ON)
            LDX    DELAY     (Read delay)
DURAON      DEX              (Decrement)
            BNE    DURAON    (Loop until delay elapses)
            STAB   PIACRA    (Turn speaker OFF)
            LDX    DELAY     (Read same delay)
DURAOF      DEX              (Decrement)
            BNE    DURAOF    (Loop until delay elapses)
            BRA    PLAY      (Go back to turn speaker ON)
DELAY       FCB    $80       (1 ms delay)
```

This program generates a sound of frequency N by turning the speaker alternately on and off, thus simulating a sine wave. The speaker is turned on for t milliseconds, then off for t milliseconds, as shown in Figure 9.34.

RS1	RS0	CRA 2	CRB 2	REGISTER SELECTED
0	0	1	—	PERIPHERAL REGISTER A
0	0	0	—	DATA DIRECTION REGISTER A
0	1	—	—	CONTROL REGISTER A
1	0	—	1	PERIPHERAL REGISTER B
1	0	—	0	DATA DIRECTION REGISTER B
1	1	—	—	CONTROL REGISTER B

Figure 9.33: Addressing PIA Registers

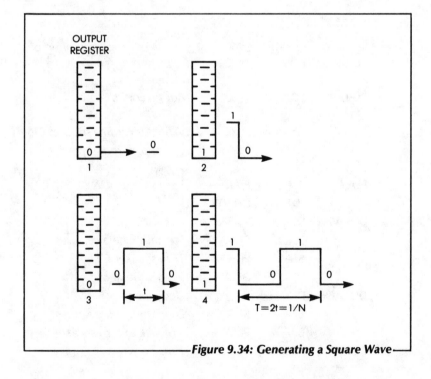

Figure 9.34: Generating a Square Wave

Let us now look at this program in detail. The first three statements are assembler declarations. The first declaration of the program sets the starting memory address to hexadecimal 200. The next two declarations assign the hexadecimal values 4004 and 4005, respectively, to the symbols PIADRA and PIACRA. In the next two instructions, the program loads the hexadecimal values 3F and 37, respectively, in A and B. Then the speaker is turned on (PLAY) for a duration DELAY. The value of the symbol DELAY, which appears in the seventh instruction, is defined at the very end of the program as hexadecimal 80. We will see that this results in a delay of 1 millisecond. As a result, a 500 Hz frequency will be generated by the speaker.

Let us look at label DURAON. This is the beginning of the delay loop. In the next instruction, a test is performed to determine whether or not the delay has been decremented to 0. As long as the counter is not zero, the program loops back to DURAON. Whenever the counter is decremented to 0, the next instruction is executed:

```
        STAB            PIACRA
```

The value stored in B (37 hexadecimal) is transferred into the control register CRA of the PIA, turning the speaker bit off. In order to simulate a sine wave, an equal delay must be generated while the speaker is off, and it is implemented by the next three instructions:

```
                LDX       DELAY
        DURAOF  DEX                 (Decrement
                                    Counter)
                BNE       DURAOF    (Loop until delay
                                    elapses)
```

At the expiration of this second delay, a branch back to the beginning of the main loop occurs:

```
        BRA PLAY
```

The square wave will be generated again.

Computing The Frequency

The loops used to keep the bit at the value 1 or 0 each last for eight cycles: four cycles for DEX and four cycles for BNE, i.e., eight microseconds for one iteration through the loop. The variable DELAY is set to 80 hexadecimal or 128 decimal. The resulting actual delay is $128 \times 8 =$ 1024 microseconds. This is approximately 1 millisecond. The resulting period is 2 milliseconds and the frequency is the inverse of the period, or 500 Hz. For any desired tone frequency F, the necessary value of DELAY will thus be computed by the formula: DELAY = F/4. By modifying the value of DELAY, the resulting frequency can be changed at will. It then becomes an easy matter to implement an electronic piano. This is left as an exercise for the reader.

Hint: at the end of the program, where the BRA PLAY instruction appears, we could branch to a routine that reads the keyboard. If a new key is pressed on the keyboard, this will be interpreted as a request for the generation of a new tone. The delay will be recomputed, i.e., reset, according to the key, and the program will then jump back to PLAY to generate the requested frequency. This requires few additional instructions. (Techniques for reading a keyboard were presented in Chapter 7.)

We have now described the facilities of an assembler and presented several program examples. We will now go on to examine high-level languages.

HIGH-LEVEL LANGUAGES

High-level languages permit the user to specify instructions in a language that is "close" to the English language (or close to formulas expressed in the English language); they are therefore much easier to use than assembly language. With high-level languages, the programmer no longer needs to worry explicitly about registers and buses. Many powerful operators, such as multiplication, division, exponentiation and other mathematical operators, are provided as part of the language. In addition, high-level programming languages typically provide parameters for operating on data structures, such as blocks, arrays and files. Depending on the language used, the facilities offered by the language may favor the mathematical user, the business user, or other programmers with a specific competence. There is no best programming language; there are simply those programming languages best-suited for the programmer's training and purpose.

High-level programming languages, like any programming language, follow a strict syntax, and consist of a sequence of instructions forming a program. For example, the following is a sequence of instructions in the BASIC language that will compute the product of two numbers, A and B, and print the result:

```
10 LET A = 5
20 LET B = 12
30 LET P = A*B
40 PRINT A, "*", B, "=", P
50 END
```

A high-level language must be translated by a compiler or an interpreter into an object code that a microprocessor can execute. Each instruction in a high-level language is typically translated into many binary instructions. Thus, a program written in a high-level language is usually much shorter than a program written in assembly-level language and is much easier to design and read.

Writing in a high-level language saves time. However, programs written in a high-level language are translated by automatic translator programs (compilers and interpreters) and the resulting binary code is not optimal, resulting, for example, in many unnecessary transfers between machine registers. The binary code created by such translators is normally much less efficient than code written directly in assembly-level language. Thus, whenever the speed of execution and the program size must be optimized, assembly language is normally used. Whenever programming time must be minimized at the expense of speed and size, a high-level language is used.

Typically, when a product must be introduced on the market quickly, a high-level language is used to implement and test the required algorithms, thus insuring that the programs are debugged quickly. Then the programs are tested in actual prototypes and the code is refined, by being recoded by hand in assembly-level language (in order to optimize it). Then the resulting optimized program is installed on the production models in order to improve performance and reduce the amount of memory.

THE MAIN LANGUAGES

The main high-level languages used in the world of microprocessors are PL/M, BASIC and Pascal. PL/M was the first high-level language compiler available for microprocessors. Developed by Intel, and inspired by PL/I, PL/M is available from most microprocessor manufacturers and has been designed for control applications.

Here are some simple PL/M statements:

```
IF A > 41 THEN X = 2;
ELSE X = 9;
Y = 4 + X;
```

Here is a more complex example of PL/M, defining a procedure that can then be used repeatedly:

—Definition: SUM$SQUARE : PROCEDURE(A,B) ADDRESS;
                DECLARE (A,B) ADDRESS;
                RETURN A*A + B*B;
                END

—Call: X = 3;
                Y = 5 + SUM$SQUARE (X,4)

BASIC was developed at Dartmouth College for its educational value. This language is normally interpreted, i.e., executed on a statement-by-statement basis, in an interactive manner, thereby facilitating debugging. The language has been designed for ease in learning and can be mastered in a short time. An example of a BASIC program has already been provided at the beginning of this section. Because of the ease in implementing interpreters for simple versions of BASIC, BASIC has become the most widely-used language on microcomputers. Large numbers of programs are available that are written in BASIC and are ready to use. However, BASIC, like any programming language, suffers from a number of limitations, depending on the version used.

Still other languages are used for their specific merits. For example, Pascal has gained increasing acceptance in educational and engineering circles. Pascal is a *structured* language that encourages good programming habits. It is therefore used extensively in educational institutions. In addition, extended versions of Pascal allow simultaneous processing, and facilitate the writing of long and complex programs, an advantage for complex control applications.

SELECTING A LANGUAGE

The respective merits of languages will be studied in the next section. The main advantage of BASIC is the ease with which the language can be learned. However, the capabilities of BASIC are limited and the user will find that some applications are impractical or even impossible when using BASIC.

PL/M allows the user to work close to the level of the microprocessor hardware, permitting the specification of data length and allowing the user to include assembly-level routines within a PL/M program. PL/M is therefore generally used for control applications where machine-level efficiency is required.

Pascal tends to be used for large and complex programs as it facilitates program writing and documentation.

New languages are constantly being introduced in the computer world, and a programmer will tend to choose the language that he or she is most familiar with, since proficiency results in shorter programming time. Provided that no additional requirements are imposed upon the programmer, this is normally the best decision. However, it is often necessary to share programs with others so that they can be modified at a later time. If this is the case, then standardization around one programming language offers a significant advantage.

Learning a high-level programming language requires much less time than learning how to program an assembly-level language. Further, because of reduced programming time, the cost of programming is lower when using a high-level language. As a result, a high-level language is generally preferred in all applications that involve small numbers of units, or that are highly complex. Whenever a large number of units must be produced, the economics of reduced memory size come into play and programs must generally be written in assembly-level language in order to attain that efficiency.

ADVANTAGES OF PROGRAMMING

The three main advantages of programming are:

1. Flexibility.   Changes in a program are simple, compared to hardware changes. They are facilitated by powerful programming tools that will be described in the next chapter. Finding errors in a complex program usually takes much less time than finding errors in an equivalent hardware system. Similarly, once a program has been developed, it can easily be changed or improved.

We have also seen that program segments can be structured as subroutines. Libraries of subroutines can be built to supply new functions and they can be conveniently added to the program. Examples of these are data collection or optimization algorithms that are often installed at a later date.

Debugging normally occurs via the keyboard, with the assistance of a *debugger* program (versus an oscilloscope and a soldering iron in the case of hardware). During debugging, the program and the data can also be displayed symbolically, thus further facilitating the process. (The steps and tools involved in program development are presented in the next chapter.)

2. Development Speed.   Speed here refers to human efficiency in programming and developing solutions to a problem. (The *execution* of a program is usually slower than specific hardware designed to accomplish the same task.) Development is particularly efficient when a high-level language is used. High-level languages get new microprocessor-based products to the market faster. They also allow efficient testing of new algorithms.

Once a basic level of competence in programming is acquired, new applications can generally be developed in a short time with a high probability of success.

3. Cost-effectiveness.   The major cost advantage of programming is experienced on repetitive systems where the programs run on *minimal and standardized hardware modules*. The same module can be used for a variety of applications and it can be manufactured in large quantities. Generally, few, if any, components must be added or removed to tailor the board to specific new applications. Instead, the software is changed. The mass-production of such standardized modules makes it possible to achieve very low costs for the hardware portion of a system. This standardization also results in lower documentation costs and reduced hardware debugging time.

SUMMARY

In this chapter we described assembly-language programming and high-level languages. We also presented actual programs, and discussed the advantages of programming over hardware design. Let us now go on to examine the problems involved in writing and developing programs. Hardware and software aids have been developed to solve these problems. These topics will be addressed in Chapter 10.

EXERCISES

9-1: Explain the purpose of declarations in the assembler.

9-2: What is absolute programming?

9-3: What is a relocatable program?

9-4: What is the purpose of symbolic labels?

9-5: What is an executable instruction?

9-6: What is the purpose of the operand or literal field within an instruction?

9-7: What is the purpose of a comment within an instruction?

9-8: Explain the purpose of macros.

9-9: Explain the possible classifications for instruction types.

9-10: Give an example of a logical OR being used to force a 1 into bit position 3.

9-11: Give an example of a logical AND being used to mask out bit positions 0 through 4, inclusive.

9-12: What is the difference between a shift and a rotate?

9-13: What is the difference between an 8-bit rotation and a 9-bit rotation?

9-14: What is the purpose of the branch instruction?

9-15: What is the use of conditional jumps?

9-16: Explain the use and purpose of subroutines.

9-17: Is the number of subroutines unlimited? If not, explain the limiting factor(s).

9-18: Explain the operation of the stack pointer when the subroutine mechanism is used.

9-19: What is an interrupt handler?

9-20: Why must registers be preserved in the stack when an interrupt routine starts execution? How are they restored?

9-21: Explain the difference between implicit addressing and immediate addressing.

9-22: Explain indexed addressing.

9-23: Explain indirect addressing.

9-24: Review the various types of addressing and explain when each type is used to advantage.

9-25: Write the detailed multiplication flowchart that corresponds to the program of Figure 9.26.

9-26: Complete the multiplication exercise by filling out the table shown in Figure 9.28.

9-27: Write a program in the assembly-level language of the Motorola 6800 that inverts the signal connected to bit 3 of the PIA port.

9-28: Write a delay program in the assembly-level language of the M6800 that achieves a delay of approximately 500 microseconds.

9-29: Describe the relative merits of PL/M, BASIC and Pascal.

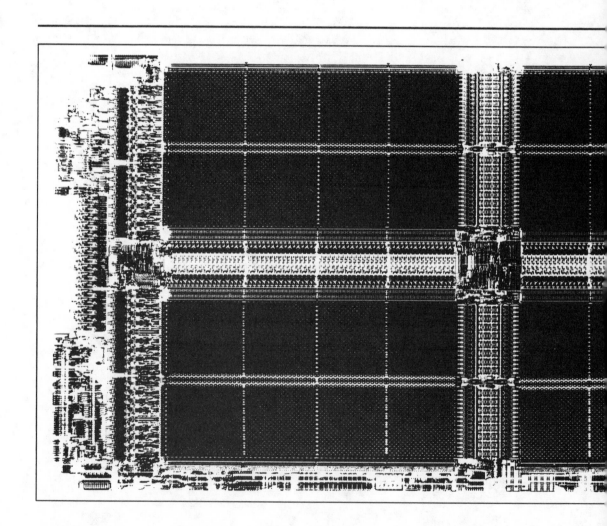

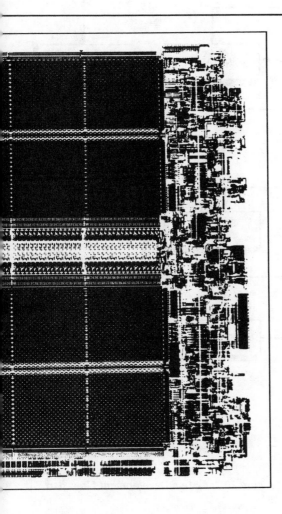

CHAPTER **10**

SYSTEM DEVELOPMENT

OBJECTIVE

In the previous chapters we learned how to assemble and design the hardware part of a microprocessor-based system. We also examined the main software tools and the choices available. In this chapter we will consider the sequence of steps involved in developing a microprocessor system. We will look at the problems involved with each of these steps and we will present solutions. Finally, we will describe the hardware and software tools that have been developed to facilitate these solutions.

THE STEPS OF SYSTEM DEVELOPMENT

Figure 10.1 is a basic flowchart showing the sequence of steps involved in the development of a system. We will examine this flowchart from top to bottom and distinguish seven successive phases.

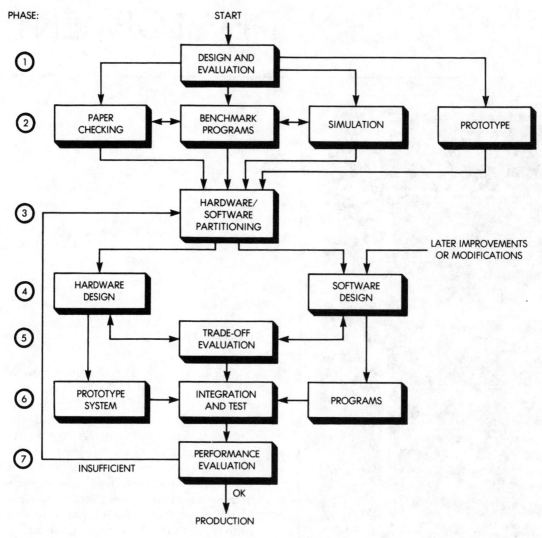

Figure 10.1: System Development Flowchart

PHASE 1: DESIGN AND EVALUATION

The initial phase of any development is design and evaluation. In this phase, a solution to a specific problem is designed. This involves both the selection, or design, of a suitable microprocessor system and the design of the software functions to be implemented on it. The primary technical consideration at this point is whether or not the performance level of the resulting hardware/software system will be adequate to meet the given specifications. At this stage designs are often represented by flowcharts and block diagrams.

PHASE 2: DESIGN VERIFICATION

Four techniques—paper-checking, benchmark programs, simulation, and prototyping—may be used (either separately or together) to verify the design hypotheses and techniques. (This phase is shown in the second row of the flowchart in Figure 10.1.) Let us now examine each of these techniques.

Paper-checking

Paper-checking refers to the checkout of the design on paper. This technique may be used either for logic design or for programs. The exercise that was recommended at the end of the multiplication routine in Chapter 9 (Figure 9.28) is an example of a paper-checking technique. In this exercise the reader executes the program by hand, by filling in entries in a table corresponding to the values of the registers. By completing this paper-checking exercise, the designer can be assured that the results of the program at least appear to be correct.

This method is clearly the least expensive one to use, but it is also the longest and most tedious. Paper-checking is normally accomplished at the flowchart level to verify the overall correctness of the design.

This technique is not very useful for evaluating performance. The execution speed of a program segment may be computed by hand, but, in general, an actual computer run is necessary to form a realistic estimate of the system's performance.

Benchmark Programs

Benchmark programs are specific programs written and implemented *by the user* to test the performance of a given system. To supply a true measure of the efficiency of the programs, a valid benchmark must be written *by the user* and be representative of the user's programming skill. The advantage of benchmarks is the following. When the application is clearly defined (such as in a block-transfer program) it is possible to run it on several different processors (such as an 8080, a 6800, and a Z80) and then decide which processor will be best for that type of application. Unfortunately, such a clear definition is infrequent. Except in the simplest cases, there are few "typical" programs that determine the performance of a system.

Often, manufacturers will supply so-called "benchmark" programs. These are indeed programs that will, for example, accomplish a block transfer or a bit serialization. They were, however, written *by the manufacturer* and are very carefully optimized; therefore, *they are not valid benchmarks.*

Simulation

A third technique used to verify a design hypothesis is *simulation.* Simulation refers to the replacement of one device (such as a hardware module) by another one (such as a software module) whose performance can be measured more easily. Simulation may be accomplished in a number of ways. For example, programs that will be written in assembly language can be initially written in a high-level language and run in simulated mode on a large computer. This method is costly and involves additional programming time, but it gives very precise results—more precise, in fact, than the results of either of the first two methods. The speed of the final assembly-level program will always be superior.

Prototyping

In cases where novel hardware designs are created, or where an exact measure of performance is required, both hardware and software prototypes may be built to provide a more accurate measurement of performance. This is rarely the case, however, for microprocessor-based systems, since hardware design is essentially standardized.

Design Experience

An essential ingredient to the evaluation process has not been mentioned yet. This is design experience. *Design experience* is an important criterion used by system designers in deciding whether or not a design will meet the required specifications. The four techniques just described can be used as tools to aid in this decision. Design experience takes into consideration additional parameters, such as the level of competence of the designer, parts performance and reliability, time constraints, cost and personnel.

We will now examine the third phase of system development in Figure 10.1: hardware/software partitioning.

PHASE 3: HARDWARE/SOFTWARE PARTITIONING _____

One of the critical decisions to be made by the designer is how much of the system should be implemented in the form of chips and how much should be implemented in the form of programs. This is called "hardware/software partitioning."

The essential criterion in making this decision is the *number* of systems to be produced. If the quantity is large, then the number of hardware components must be carefully minimized and as much as possible should be accomplished in software. On the other hand, if a small number of systems are going to be produced, it is usually advantageous to use more hardware chips if this method results in a decrease in the complexity of programming or in the use of a standard board. This becomes a matter of estimating the complexity of the software and the resulting time and cost involved. If the decrease in software cost and required time is significant, then it is worth adding an additional ten- or fifteen-dollar chip. This, in fact, is usually the case.

Also, it is often possible to use a standard (existing) microprocessor board equipped with "too many" components. Such a board is usually cheaper and more reliable than a special purpose design that optimizes the number of components.

Hardware/software partitioning is one of the most delicate tasks performed by the system designer. The chosen allocation should be continually criticized and re-evaluated throughout the design process, and trade-offs should be carefully considered as they evolve in time. Partitioning has a major impact on the software design.

PHASE 4: PARALLEL DESIGN OF HARDWARE AND SOFTWARE _____

Once the hardware and software designs have been partitioned, these two tasks can be accomplished in *parallel*. This is a major difference between microprocessor development and pure hardware development. The hardware design can be accomplished independently of the software development. The hardware design is usually simple when it involves a standard microprocessor system; it may occasionally be more complex when it involves unusual interfaces. Typically, the most significant task is the software design. In this chapter we will present a number of development tools that have been introduced to design software efficiently and independently of the hardware.

PHASE 5: TRADE-OFF EVALUATION

Throughout the design process, a trade-off evaluation should be pursued in order to reconsider the hardware/software partitions that were made. (See Figure 10.1.) It may become necessary to switch from a polling to an interrupt technique in order to improve performance, for example, or to add hardware decoders on the board, in order to simplify the software design or to improve performance.

Once these trade-offs have been evaluated, and improved designs have been completed, a hardware prototype system and a set of prototype programs are ready.

PHASE 6: INTEGRATION AND TESTING

The next phase (the sixth level of the flowchart) is integration and testing. *Integration* consists of connecting the modules together, i.e., installing the programs onto the prototype system and debugging the resulting hardware/software system. This is often the most complex and time-consuming task of any system development. It is often called the "pointed-index" phase, in which both the hardware designer and the software designer point an index finger at each other saying, "It is your fault." This phase also stresses the importance of having a single project leader who is familiar with both the hardware and the software designs and can resolve such disputes.

One essential tool, in-circuit emulation, has been designed to facilitate the final integration and testing of actual systems. It is described at the end of this chapter.

PHASE 7: PERFORMANCE EVALUATION

Finally, a complete system is assembled and built with debugged hardware and software. At this point, the system must undergo a performance evaluation. If its performance meets the specifications, then it can go into production. If it does not, then it must go back to the design or hardware/software partitioning phase. Typically, it is possible to identify one or more functions that do not provide the required performance. At this point, it may be necessary to recode software programs using different techniques, or even to replace them with additional hardware modules that provide improved speed.

It must be stressed that, on a good design, there will no longer be any hardware changes at this stage. Any later improvements or modifications will be accomplished by adding new *software* functions. This is the reason for the arrow appearing on the right of Figure 10.1, labeled "later improvements or modifications."

SOFTWARE DEVELOPMENT

Developing a program involves coding the algorithm into a programming language. We addressed this topic in Chapters 8 and 9. Generally, the most difficult and time-consuming task is *debugging* the program, i.e., making it operate correctly. Let us consider the steps involved and the support required. Let's look at Figure 10.2. We see that the devices appear on the left of the illustration and the programs appear on the

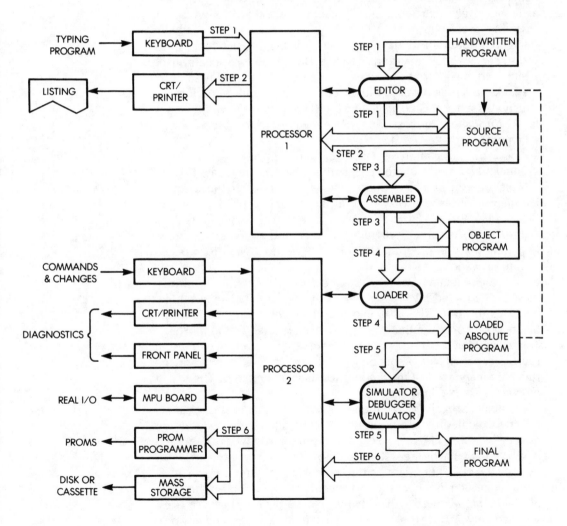

Figure 10.2: Software Facilities

right. The central column is used to represent the processor or processors necessary for translating and debugging the program. Let's now examine each step.

The user must first enter the handwritten program into the memory of the system. This is step 1, when the user types the program at a keyboard. The program is then stored in the memory of the system. In the illustration in Figure 10.2, the program appears on the right as a *source program*, written in symbolic form and stored in binary ASCII code. The source program could be written in high-level language or in assembly-level language. We will assume here that it is written in assembly-level language.

It is highly desirable to have an *editor* available to facilitate the entry of the program into the system. In Figure 10.2, the *editor* appears on the right side of the illustration. An editor is a program that allows convenient manipulation of text. With the editor, it is possible to perform instructions such as: *"Go back to line 3 and insert the following"*; *"Look for R2 throughout the text and replace it with R3"*; or *"Add the next statement typed after line 42."*

A powerful editor improves efficiency for entering a program into the system and for modifying the program once errors are located.

Next, once the user has typed a complete program into the system, it is usually desirable to display it or print it in order to verify that it is complete and "correct." To do this we use a printer, as shown in step 2 of Figure 10.2. The source program is printed and appears as a *listing*. Assuming that the program is "correct," we now want to proceed toward execution.

Since the program is written in source code, i.e., in symbolic form, it must be translated into machine-executable format. The *assembler* performs this task. The assembler translates the source code into a binary object program that can be directly executed by the machine. The assembler substitutes actual addresses for symbolic ones. It substitutes actual binary encoding of data for symbolic names and the suitable binary code of instructions for their mnemonics. The *object program* is created in step 3 of our illustration.

The object program is a sequence of binary instructions that can be directly executed by the processor. It generally resides as a *file* on diskette or tape. A file is a collection of information that has a name and is handled as a unit by the system. At this point, it becomes necessary to execute the object program on the processor. This brings up an interesting point. It is not necessary to execute the program on the same processor that was used to develop the object program. The first processor need only provide the editing and assembly facilities, and any processor can be used to do this. In fact, using a larger computer system for editing and assembly offers many benefits, including powerful peripherals, speed in processing, and sophisticated software facilities.

A *cross program* is a program for machine A that resides on machine B. For example, a *cross assembler* for a Motorola 6800 is an assembler that will produce 6800 code but which executes on a Digital Equipment PDP-11.

We will now proceed toward the actual execution of the program. Processor 1 may indeed be the microprocessor that will execute the program. However, if *another* computer has been used so far, we will now switch to the final processor that will execute the program. Later we will see that another alternative is possible: we can stay with one processor throughout, if there is a *simulator* available.

The object program must now be placed in the memory of the system in which it will execute. This is the *loading* phase, or step 4 of Figure 10.2. The loading is accomplished by a *loader* program. The result is a loaded, or *absolute*, program residing in the memory. It can then be executed.

Step 5 is real execution. Execution proceeds under the control of a *debugger*. A debugger is a program designed to facilitate the final debugging of a user program. The debugger offers facilities such as: *"Stop at instruction x"*; *"Execute instructions one at a time"*; *"Display the contents of registers"*; *"Display the contents of memory (in binary, hexadecimal, or even in symbolic form)."* Using a debugger, the contents of the registers can be changed and the program can be restarted with new data.

The advantages of the debugger may not be obvious at first. But consider the following. On a hardware microprocessor, how do you examine the contents of registers once execution is stopped? This is impossible. The only way to examine them would be to connect microprobes to the actual flip-flops of the registers *inside the chip*. Once the microprocessor is sealed, only the contents of its buses are visible. An essential feature of a debugger is that it allows examination of the contents of registers and changes to the contents. This is accomplished by the debugger, either by executing display instructions on the microprocessor or by executing under the control of a simulator or an emulator, which stores a copy of the value of the registers in the memory. One of the classic debuggers was developed by Digital Equipment for its PDP line; it is called "DDT," "the bug killer."

An essential facility of a debugger is that it provides *breakpoints*. Breakpoints are addresses, specified by the user, at which the program will stop automatically. Using breakpoints, the user can examine the value of variables in the memory, or the contents of registers. The program execution is said to be suspended.

While the user program is being debugged under the control of the debugger, diagnostics are generated. They will normally be printed on the printer or displayed on a front panel or some other display. Limited corrections are then possible if the user is willing to modify memory locations directly. Otherwise, the user must go back to the beginning of the process, type in corrections, reassemble, and go through the complete sequence again. (This step is shown by the dashed line on the right of Figure 10.2.)

Rather than execute the program directly on the real microprocessor, an *emulator* or *simulator* can be used. A *simulator* is a program that runs on another machine, say an IBM 370, and executes 8080 code; it simulates an 8080. Naturally, a simulator cannot operate in real-time because of the slowness of the software interpretation involved.

An emulator is a simulator that runs in real-time. *Emulation* implies that the behavior is identical to the target. Examples will be presented later in the chapter.

After the program is completely debugged, i.e., after its execution is presumed to be correct, the object code must be stored away on a disk or cassette, or implanted in real PROMs. During debugging, the program was residing in a RAM. Once corrected, however, it is implanted in the PROMs. A PROM programmer will be connected to the development system (step 6 in Figure 10.2), and the binary form of the program will be transferred onto PROM chips. PROM chips can then be inserted in the production system. Stand-alone PROM programmers are also available. (They are discussed at the end of the chapter. They also appear in Figure 3.14).

SOFTWARE DEVELOPMENT TOOLS

We will now examine the facilities necessary for efficient program development. All the software facilities we have discussed should be available for the convenient development of any program involving more than a very few instructions. In fact, they are an absolute necessity for any program involving hundreds or thousands of instructions. Here is a quick summary:

- *editor* for typing in the program
- *assembler* for translation to binary form
- *loader* for conversion of addresses to absolute values
- *simulator, debugger, emulator* for debugging
- *operating system* for using the computer
- *file system* for storing the program modules.

It may be difficult to use these support programs unless additional facilities are also available. In particular, the support programs must be stored on a convenient medium easily accessible to the processor. This implies the need for a general *file system*. The medium used for a file system may be tape cassettes or floppy disks.

Tape cassettes are advantageous because they are low in cost, but they are relatively slow. It may often take more than a minute to access the desired information. Access to information on a cassette is sequential and, if data must be successively accessed at several points on a tape, extensive winding and rewinding will be involved, with the corresponding delays. Therefore, this solution is seldom used, except to save a finished program.

The alternative to tape cassettes is a *disk*. This is definitely the best storage medium available but it is higher in cost. A disk allows fast access (within milliseconds) to any portion of the disk. We should stress that, without such devices, development can be quite unpleasant. Assuming that a 2K program is being developed and that a file system is not available, the user program as well as the support programs will be stored on paper-tape. Punching out a program on a teletype may then require 20 minutes or more. The other support programs necessary for debugging will then have to be loaded into the system's memory, one at a time—a task requiring 10 or 20 minutes every time it is performed. This would clearly be an irritating obstacle in any development process. Disks may be hard or floppy. Floppy disks are generally used because of low cost and sufficient speed and capacity.

A MEMORY MAP

Let us examine the way the memory of a microprocessor system looks in a "typical" case. Figure 10.3 shows the memory *map*, displaying the main modules. We will now describe them.

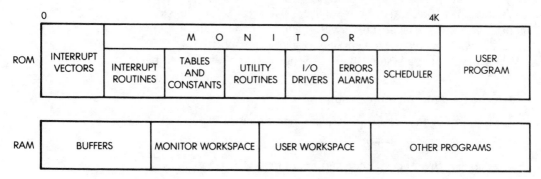

Figure 10.3: Typical Memory Map

- *The ROM* almost always contains a basic monitor program that continually examines input lines, such as a keyboard or other sensors, and allows the external user to communicate with the system.
- *Interrupt routines* are present when interrupts are used.
- *Tables and constants* contain fixed values.
- *Utility routines* perform special functions such as multiply, divide, enter in a list, convert into a code.
- *I/O drivers* are routines that communicate with the input/output devices connected to the system.
- *Errors/alarms* are routines that tell the external world about an erroneous or exceptional condition.
- *The scheduler* determines the order in which devices are sensed and controlled.
- *The user program* is the user's application program, debugged, and presumed correct, now placed in ROM. Or, often, the user program will reside in RAM.
- *The RAM* generally contains workspace and other programs. It generally contains the operating system, if one is used, as well as other user programs.

We will now examine the basic choices.

BASIC CHOICES

THE FOUR CHOICES

We have now presented the techniques used for system development at the hardware level, the software level, and finally at the systems level. We will now review the choices available at each step.

When developing a system, there are four essential choices to be made:

1. choosing the microprocessor
2. performing the hardware/software partitioning
3. choosing the programming language
4. choosing the necessary development tools.

Let's examine them.

Choosing The Microprocessor

In Chapter 4 we addressed the process of *selecting a microprocessor*. Recall that two essential criteria to consider when selecting a microprocessor are the quantity of units to be produced, and an adequate performance level for the application considered. Another consideration is the availability of various components and development support.

Hardware/Software Partitioning

For *hardware/software partitioning*, the designer must evaluate the cost and performance merits of each technique under consideration. Throughout this book we have presented the various techniques that can be used to assemble a microprocessor system, as well as the essential software techniques that can be used in the implementation, and we have evaluated their advantages and disadvantages. These evaluations should facilitate the hardware/software partitioning process.

We will now briefly discuss two other important decisions—the *choice of a programming language*, and the *choice of suitable development tools*. Let us now consider them.

Programming Languages

The three choices for selecting a *programming language* or level are:

1. direct binary or hexadecimal

2. assembly language

3. high-level language.

Let us now examine each method in turn.

Binary or Hexadecimal Coding. Programming in binary, or equivalently in hexadecimal, could be called the "poor man's choice." Clearly, it does not require any support in terms of hardware or software. This method is used on the simplest systems, such as single boards or educational kits. The user communicates with the system via a hexadecimal keyboard and four to six LEDs. Instructions and data can then be input to the system via the keyboard in hexadecimal form. This is cost-efficient in terms of hardware. It is also slow and aggravating from the point of view of the programmer. It is indeed possible to design short programs and enter them into the machine using this method. It is by no means advisable for longer programs, in view of the alternatives available.

Binary programming is also used during the final debugging stage, i.e., when the user wants to change only one, or just a few, instructions within the memory while in debugging mode. This eliminates the tasks of having to go back to the editor to enter the changes, then reassemble, reload, and go back once again into execution mode. Binary programming is therefore a common and legitimate method that gains time.

In general, programming in binary or in hexadecimal is used only for short programs when there are no other alternatives available. It has been the constant and deliberate trend of computer evolution to make more powerful and sophisticated programming aids available to the user. It would be unreasonable for a programmer to ignore these aids unless the cost is prohibitive.

Assembly Language. Assembly-level language is simply a mnemonic or symbolic representation of the binary code. In terms of the execution speed of the user program, programming in assembly-level language is the most efficient method, and the one most frequently used for control applications.

Unfortunately, programming at the assembly level requires manipulating registers and buses, and testing bits. It demands a good understanding of the hardware structure of the system in order to optimize system resources.

The assembler automatically converts symbolic programs into the executable binary format. In addition, the assembler detects any gross syntactical errors and flags them to the user before execution. (However, *the assembler will never detect logical errors.*) The disadvantage of programming in assembly-level language is the tediousness of the task and the resulting time required.

In summary, whenever efficient software performance is sought at the cost of programming difficulty, programming in assembly-level language is the most highly desirable technique.

High-Level Languages. Some high-level languages were described in Chapter 9. These languages, including PL/M, Pascal, and BASIC, allow the programmer to use powerful instructions to specify an algorithm. A high-level programming language often comes close to matching the conventions that would be used in the actual specification of the algorithm (mathematical, business, etc.). Because of this similarity it is possible to code (i.e., to program) an entire algorithm in a short period of time. Programming in a high-level language is generally at least ten times faster than programming in assembly-level language, especially for long programs.

The disadvantage of a high-level language is that the compiler (or the interpreter), which produces the object code, is inefficient. It compiles one high-level instruction into a number of machine-level binary instructions. Because it does not optimize the use of registers, it causes many unnecessary register transfers. Typically, a compiler generates two to five times as many instructions as would be generated by a skilled assembly-level programmer. This results in a waste of memory and in an execution time that is two to five times slower than with an assembly-level program. This objection, however, may be much less important than other considerations.

Two main points should be kept in mind:

1. If the program is very complex, or seems complex to the programmer, then the program might never work correctly if it has to be programmed in assembly-level language. In contrast, the use of a high-level language would most likely permit quick writing and debugging. (Later, it might be possible to hand-produce an optimized version of the program in assembly language.) High-level languages make possible the fast implementation of correct programs by non-expert programmers. High-level languages are generally used by all those who want to implement a program quickly and correctly and do not particularly care about the efficiency of the program.

2. The difficulty of coding a complex program in assembly-level language may make this type of programming grossly inefficient and perhaps totally unreasonable. Although it is possible to achieve register-level efficiency, the overall program may not be structured and designed optimally simply because of length. The only reasonable solution then may be to use a high-level language.

Let us elaborate on this point. It is possible to code the solution of a problem in a high-level language quickly and efficiently, especially if an *interactive* interpreter such as BASIC is used. An interactive interpreter can execute instructions one at a time and verify immediately whether or not the syntax is correct or if an error has been committed. An interpreter translates each instruction into binary immediately so that any part of a program may be executed as soon as it is typed in. It provides immediate diagnostics, which lead to much easier and faster debugging.

In addition, most compilers allow the user to develop a program in a high-level language first and then to substitute assembly-language modules within the high-level program. The advantage of this is clear. If performance is not at a sufficiently high level, or if the memory waste is too significant, the user can then recode, section by section, the high-level modules into assembly language and substitute them progressively into the program.

Thus, it is possible to code a program quickly in a high-level language and to get it to run correctly. Once this is done, the prototype is completed, and the software that verifies the system's design and performance is immediately available. Then, while production plans are being readied, the person who wrote the high-level program can directly recode as many modules as necessary into assembly-level language. Since it has already been proven that the overall algorithm and structure of the program are correct, all that remains is a simple recoding task. The efficiency of the program will then be improved by a factor of several times and the memory use by the program will be reduced accordingly. This results in a faster, better, and less expensive product. Another advantage of this strategy is that the product can be introduced into the field early, thus beating the competition. The product can then be optimized before entering mass production.

The best method for deciding whether to use a high-level language or an assembly-level language is to first evaluate the complexity of the program and the level of programmer expertise available, and then to estimate the resulting software cost.

If only a few units are to be produced, the software cost will be dominant. The cost of software will be diminished by going to a high-level language. While this will result in some added memory cost per system, the additional hardware cost will be very small compared to the savings in programming time. On the other hand, if the system is to be produced in large quantities, the quantity of memory used is most significant. The programming costs will be distributed over a large number of units. The idea, therefore, is to evaluate the programming cost and to divide it by the intended number of units. This results in the software cost per unit, which can then be compared to the hardware savings per unit realized by using an assembly-level language.

SYSTEM DEVELOPMENT TOOLS

Only one of the program development techniques we have described does not require any significant tools: hand programming. All that is required to develop a program directly in binary or hexadecimal is a hexadecimal keyboard and LEDs to display the output. The only other tools needed are paper and a pencil.

On the other hand, the more frequently used programming techniques require suitable tools if programming is to be accomplished easily. In this section we will present and evaluate the respective merits of the four main tools: a time-sharing system, an in-house computer, a personal computer, and a development system.

THE TIME-SHARING SYSTEM

A time-sharing system is a general-purpose computer used in *time-sharing* mode. In time-sharing mode, a number of users use the computer at the same time in interactive mode (i.e., the system responds immediately, on-line). The service offered by a time-sharing system is one of the best that can be obtained. The dialogue with the machine is instantaneous, i.e., there is no waiting time (at least in theory). In addition, time-sharing systems are usually equipped with highly sophisticated peripherals and software support. They generally have powerful file systems, editors, and other software facilities, as well as high-speed printers, large disks and plotters.

A microprocessor program can be almost completely developed and debugged on a time-sharing system. Most commercial time-sharing systems today provide the cross programs (assemblers or compilers) necessary to generate code for virtually any existing microprocessor, as well as simulators for program testing. User programs can then be generated and debugged efficiently on the system.

One drawback of time-sharing systems is that a simulator must be used to execute programs, rather than the actual microprocessor. When programs are executed by a simulator, performance testing is incomplete when it is not impossible. While it is possible to debug the logic of the program, it is not possible to check input/output performance and to measure its speed. (While it is indeed possible to count the simulated duration of the instructions that will be executed within the MPU, it is very difficult to simulate the architecture of the system, and in particular, the input/output functions that will be performed.)

In addition, as we have seen, the sophisticated input/output chips are becoming processor-equipped; i.e., they are also programmable. But in order to verify the complete results of program execution, it is also necessary to simulate their behavior. This is so complex as to be impracticable.

Another advantage of a time-sharing system is to allow several users to use the system at the same time on several terminals. However, this facility must be used cautiously as it is generally undesirable to have several people working simultaneously on the same program.

In summary, a time-sharing system is a convenient facility available for the fast development of a program. However, a time-sharing system does not allow complete program debugging from the point of view of timing and verification of input/output functions. Also, such a system is usually quite expensive. Let us now examine some alternatives.

THE IN-HOUSE COMPUTER

Here we will distinguish the in-house computer, typically a mini- or a large computer, from a personal computer. An in-house computer can be used to execute the cross assembler, cross compiler, and other programs, just like a time-sharing system. However, the service provided will be only as good as the quality of service of the in-house system. If the computer is used in batch mode, i.e., if the program is submitted on cards, paper tape, or another batch medium, and the results are returned hours or days later, such a delay is generally a major obstacle to program development. Usually, developing a program for a microprocessor involves changes at the bit level. It is intolerable to have to put up with delays of hours or even days to make such changes. However, if an in-house system provides time-sharing capabilities, or if it is fully accessible to the designer without delay, its advantages are the same as those presented above, and what is more, its use is usually free.

An in-house system, like a time-sharing system, does not offer any hardware checking capability or system integration. We will now consider a special case of the in-house system, the personal computer.

THE PERSONAL COMPUTER

The personal computer is a microcomputer system. At a minimum, it must be equipped with a keyboard, CRT, disks and a printer. As long as the personal computer uses the same microprocessor as the system under development, it can be used to develop software. An assembler is almost always available, and programs can execute on the real microprocessor. Further, if it is possible to insert the board under development in a slot of the motherboard inside the personal computer, real-time testing can be performed on the actual hardware.

However, in general, development software on personal computers is poor, usually offering a minimal assembler (no macros or other facilities), a minimal debugger, no linking loader, and poor diagnostics. In such a case, the personal computer can still be used as a convenient tool for the preliminary stages of program development. However, the final stages of integration and debugging must be performed on a full development system.

The only tool that allows complete and convenient software and hardware testing is the development system. We will now examine it.

THE DEVELOPMENT SYSTEM

A development system is a microcomputer system equipped with all the facilities required for complete and convenient system development. Physically, it looks like any traditional minicomputer or microcomputer system (see Figure 10.4). Sometimes it is equipped with a simple front panel to facilitate debugging, but this feature is disappearing, as CRTs have replaced front panels.

When a development system is sold by a microprocessor manufacturer, it uses the manufacturer's microprocessor; however, this is not a technical requirement. Many development systems are now available that use one microprocessor to produce and test code for a variety of other manufacturers' microprocessors.

The development system offers all the facilities that we have described, plus additional ones such as in-circuit emulation and PROM programming. It provides a file system capable of handling a variety of peripherals (for example, disk use requires a Disk-Operating System or DOS). From a software standpoint, it should be equipped with all the

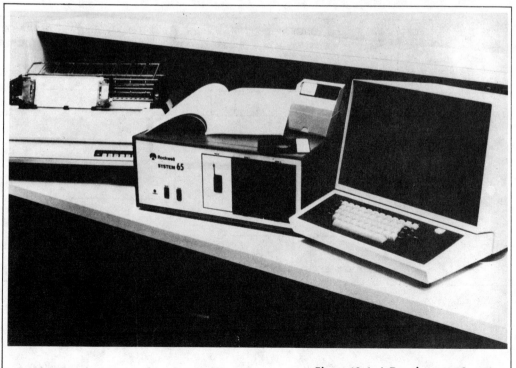

Figure 10.4: A Development System

required programs (see Figure 10.5): editor, assembler, and debugger, as well as other support programs, such as front-panel interpreter and utility routines for symbolic debugging. In addition, if high-level programming is planned, it must provide a resident compiler (such as PL/M) or interpreter (such as BASIC). These compilers require large amounts of memory and are sometimes not resident on the development system itself.

All development systems should provide common hardware facilities, including:

— a microcomputer with 64K of RAM memory and interface boards for all common peripherals, plus free slots. The serial interface board has an adjustable speed from 110 to 9600 or 19200 baud for connecting the CRT, modem, printer, or PROM programmer

— a CRT terminal (for user interaction)

— a printer (for listings)

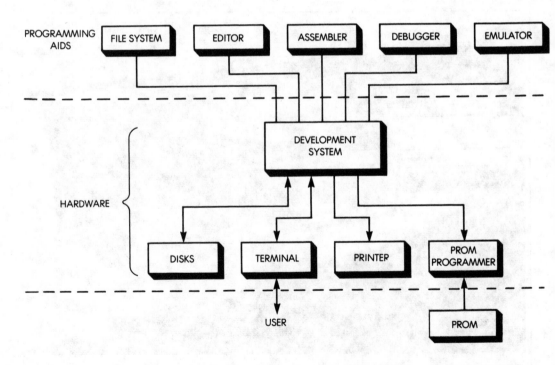

Figure 10.5: Development System Modules

- two or more floppy disks (for file storage)
- a paper tape reader (less common)
- a PROM programmer (for burning PROMs)
- an in-circuit emulator.

They should also provide the following software facilities:

- disk operating system
- editor
- assembler
- loader
- debugger
- emulator
- compiler and interpreters (PL/M, BASIC, and Pascal).

When purchasing a system, remember that the cost of all of these facilities must be added to the "basic unit."

Any savings in the peripheral area will be accompanied by an inconvenience in programming, and will usually result in a much larger financial loss in programming time (not to mention the added aggravation).

As an example, Figure 10.6 shows an Intel Intellec development system. Enclosed in a single enclosure, the basic unit is essentially a microcomputer unit with special interfaces and software. The unit incorporates a single board with CPU, 32K RAM and 4K ROM. It also provides interfaces for a high speed paper tape reader/punch, a printer and a universal PROM programmer. The keyboard, CRT, and a 250K-byte floppy disk are integrated into the cabinet. This system supports the 8048, 8080 and 8085 microprocessor families.

When evaluating development systems, we should keep in mind that most of these systems have the basic facilities, including an editor, an assembler, and a debugger. The essential differences among these systems are usually in terms of convenience at the software level. For example, a resident compiler and an assembler with *conditional macros* are both significant software facilities that may or may not be available on a given development system. The evaluation should therefore be made not in terms of the overall system cost but in terms of its software resources.

The In-Circuit Emulator

We will now describe one of the most significant hardware/software tools, the in-circuit emulator, which is used for debugging systems.

An *in-circuit emulator* is a program plus a board that simulates (or, in fact, emulates) the execution of the microprocessor in "almost" real-time. As an example, Figure 10.7 shows Intel's in-circuit emulator (called ICE). The in-circuit emulator executes within the system development cabinet and requires an additional board plus external cable. The cable coming out of the back of the MDS is called the "umbilical cord." It is terminated by a 40-pin connector identical to an 8086 pin-out.

On the user system under development, the actual 8086 has been removed, and the 40-pin connector at the end of the umbilical cord has been plugged in. The in-circuit emulator behaves exactly as an 8086 does. It generates the same signals on the same pins.

What is the advantage of using an in-circuit emulator? A real 8086 cannot be suspended easily. There is no way to examine its registers or to change them without adding external hardware. By substituting a

Figure 10.6: Intel's Intellec System

software program for the real 8086, it is possible to use all the features of a powerful debugger and other utility programs to control execution of the system under development. *Breakpoints* can be set. The program can be executed on the *real* system on the right and then stopped at a specified breakpoint. It is then possible to examine registers *symbolically*, to examine the memory, or even to try alternatives. Commands can be implemented by hitting keys at the keyboard rather than by inserting a new PROM. From the keyboard, it is possible to close valves and verify the values of actual sensors connected to a real application. In addition, part of the program may be stored in the RAM of the development system. When sections of the program are correctly debugged, they can be progressively burned into PROM and then inserted into the real system.

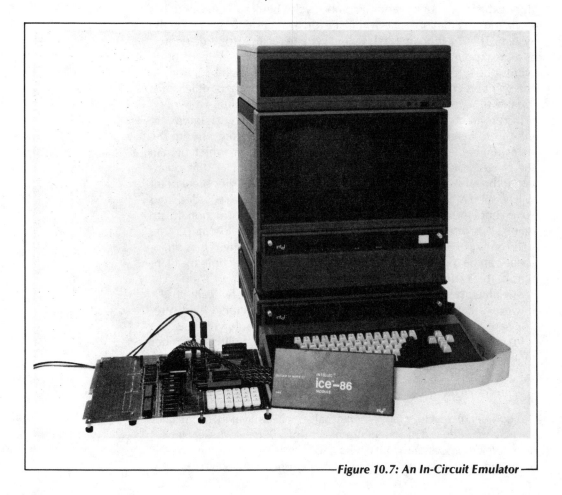

Figure 10.7: An In-Circuit Emulator

For the first time in the history of software development, the in-circuit emulator offers the capability of conveniently testing and debugging an actual system connected to its actual input/output devices in real-time. This is one of the most powerful facilities that has been devised for the true debugging of a complete hardware/software system. It is indispensable for efficient debugging on any real-time system. In the case of the MDS80 system, the emulator executes only 10% slower than a standard 8080. (This is accomplished by using a faster version of the 8080, the 8080-2, which operates with a 3MHz clock on the ICE board.)

One of the important facilities of an in-circuit emulator is the trace capability, which we will now describe.

The Trace Capability   ICE, like most similar systems, offers a "recording" capability called the *trace*. It will automatically record events during the forty-four previous machine cycles before it is stopped. It is analogous to a film of events within the forty-four previous cycles of the system. This is a fundamental facility. Whenever an error is diagnosed at a breakpoint, it is usually too late to identify the problem. In other words, the error has usually been caused by a *previous* instruction. At the point where the bug has been diagnosed, the programmer must identify the instruction that has resulted in a wrong value.

In a program containing a number of branching points, it is often very difficult to determine which branch was being executed prior to the detection of the error. It is therefore essential to record which path in the program has been followed up to the breakpoint. At this point, either the faulty instruction can be identified or an earlier breakpoint will be set. Forty-four new machine cycles will then be recorded, and so on, until the error can be traced to the erroneous instruction. In addition, it is often possible to trigger an external oscilloscope if fine debugging is needed for complex hardware interfacing. The oscilloscope can be triggered by execution of a specific instruction, by an interrupt, or by detection of a specified pattern.

Manufacturers' versions of an in-circuit emulator are typically costly; however, they require only a small amount of additional hardware. They are also available from independent vendors at lower costs.

In summary, an in-circuit emulator is an essential facility to consider for integrating hardware/software debugging in a short time.

ALTERNATIVES TO MANUFACTURERS' SYSTEMS _____

A number of development systems that supply equivalent capabilities have been produced by independent vendors. Because these vendors are not microprocessor manufacturers, such systems are *microprocessor-independent*. The same system can then be used for an 8080, a 6800, a

6502, a Z80 and others. An example is shown in Figure 10.8. Note the in-circuit emulator at the front. Development systems supplied by independent vendors are truly general-purpose development systems and are not limited to a given microprocessor. As such, they may be particularly attractive to a user who is reluctant to invest too much money in a system before committing to a chip. Once the commitment to a chip has been made, however, development systems supplied by the manufacturers usually provide better software capabilities for the chosen microprocessor, as well as the prospect of continued improvements.

OTHER DEVELOPMENT TOOLS

There are several tools, such as signature analyzers, now available that are useful for *troubleshooting*, but they are beyond the scope of this book. A number of *diagnostic aids* are available from a variety of vendors. In particular, a new breed of instruments has been developed, the *microprocessor analyzer*, which evolved from the digital analyzer. They are available from Hewlett-Packard, Tektronix, Fluke, Biomation, and others. They are indispensable to the fine tuning and debugging of complex hardware interfaces.

The main remaining tool that we have not yet described is the PROM

Figure 10.8: An Independent Development System

programmer. The purpose of the PROM programmer is to program the EPROMs or the PROMs on which the programs will reside. As an example, a PROM programmer appears in Figure 10.9. These programmers are used to load programs into PROMs and UV-erasable PROMs. They are equipped with a hexadecimal keyboard, which allows the manual input of data. In addition, they have a paper-tape reader or a connection to a serial post so that the program, once punched on paper-tape or stored on disk, can be read directly by the device. Usually they include additional interfaces, such as an RS-232 connector, so that they can be connected to a microcomputer system on which the program is resident. A number of additional features may be offered, such as automatic duplication, personality modules for various memory devices, contents verification, and more.

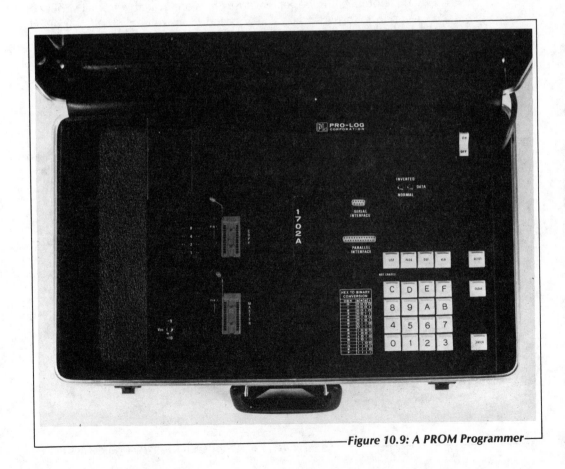

Figure 10.9: A PROM Programmer

SINGLE-BOARD MICROCOMPUTERS

What about *kits* and single-board microcomputers? For efficient software development, there are not many alternatives to the development tools that we have presented. However, if goals are more limited, alternatives exist. In particular, kits or assembled boards are a good tool for gaining familiarity with simple programming at the machine-language level. Typically, they are not even equipped with an assembler, so that programming must be performed directly in hexadecimal, thus limiting the length of programs that can be reasonably developed on them to a few hundred instructions. The most frequently used mass memory for such a board is the cassette recorder, which can easily be interfaced to the board. Programs can then be saved with reasonable ease. Though such boards are valuable educational tools, they cannot be used alone as a true development facility for any "real" program.

SUMMARY

Developing a microprocessor system involves hardware and software tools and techniques. Basic hardware and software techniques were presented in the preceding chapters. In this chapter we described specific tools and techniques for developing a system. The main problem in development is usually the software debugging phase. We have addressed this problem and described the tools available to solve it. We have seen that the most efficient tool for both hardware and software development is system development. Alternatives are time-sharing systems, in-house computers, and personal computers. An essential facility for debugging complex systems, especially real-time systems, is in-circuit emulation. The substantial investment required for a complete development system pays off rapidly in terms of reduced programming time and faster completion of a project. Thus, such a complete system should be appropriately budgeted.

EXERCISES

10-1: Describe the four basic techniques used in the design verification stage of a system.

10-2: Describe the role and merits of benchmark programs.

10-3: Provide an example of software/hardware partitioning alternatives for the design of your choice.

10-4: Define the following terms: editor, assembler, object program, file, cross-program, loader, simulator, absolute code, debugger, breakpoint.

10-5: What are the basic software development tools required for efficient program development?

10-6: What is the role of the file system? What are some desirable characteristics?

10-7: Explain the basic rules for selecting the proper microprocessor.

10-8: Describe the main alternatives for selecting a programming language indicating the advantages and disadvantages.

10-9: In terms of program speed, is it always more efficient to code in assembly-level language?

10-10: Can you define characteristics for a high-level language suited to your needs?

10-11: What is the advantage of an interactive system?

10-12: What is a time-sharing system?

10-13: Can a personal computer be used for complete system development? What are its limitations?

10-14: What is the difference between a development system and a general-purpose personal computer?

10-15: How does an in-circuit emulator work?

10-16: Explain the trace capability and its role in debugging a program.

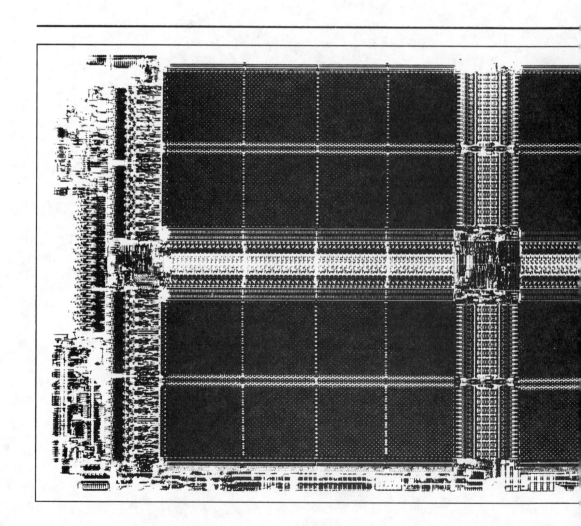

CHAPTER **11**

THE FUTURE

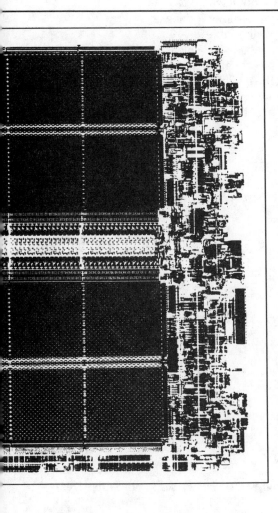

INTRODUCTION

Throughout this book, we have made a number of statements regarding the evolution of components, systems, and techniques in the future. We will now present guidelines for evaluating future trends.

Predicting the future is a difficult proposition in a domain where the technological evolution has taken place so quickly. Indeed, most technological predictions are generally proved false, although we will see here that a number of reasonably safe ones are possible. In this chapter, a discussion of the evolution of microprocessor technology will lead us to some obvious conclusions and to a number of short- and long-term predictions.

One of the main technical factors that will bear on our discussion is the yield, as it is the main factor influencing the pricing of LSI chips. In the following section, we will, therefore, consider the parameters influencing the yield.

THE YIELD

The *yield* is the percentage of good chips in a production batch. Yield problems are caused by physical and process factors. Chips are normally defective because of difficulties encountered during production. Problems can be caused by contamination, microcracks, insufficiently precise handling or process control, fit or mask defects, inadequate mask alignment and processing variations. If any of these conditions exists, then a few chips (or even all the chips) can end up being defective. In fact, at the start of production of a new component, it is not uncommon for all the chips produced to be defective. If this happens, the process is then improved until the yield increases to a point where production becomes profitable. This is why the availability of a few working chips does not mean that a new design is economically viable.

As illustrated in Figure 11.1, the main parameter affecting the yield is the surface area of the chip. The yield decreases exponentially as the area of the chip increases. At any given time during the evolution of the technology, each manufacturer knows how to implement a chip of given area. An increase in area leads to an exponential increase in the probability of failure.

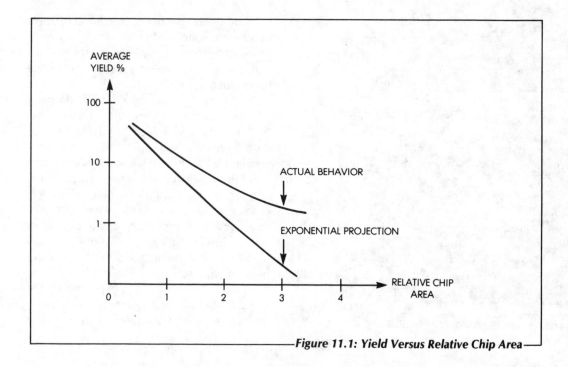

Figure 11.1: Yield Versus Relative Chip Area

Conversely, once a manufacturer has produced a sufficient quantity of chips, it is usually possible to achieve a greater yield and reduce the area of the chip. This phenomenon is illustrated by the *learning curve* shown in Figure 11.2. (This is the most important curve in Silicon Valley.) The rule of the learning curve states that: "The price of a semiconductor circuit decreases by 30% every time the industry-wide production doubles." The more components produced, the better the process can be controlled and improved. As a result, the yield increases. The learning curve implies that whenever more devices are produced, the yield is increased and the cost is decreased. This was the original cause of the fast decrease in the cost of LSI components. The second cause, which has now become dominant, is competition, and in particular, the competition of *second sourcing*. Second sourcing has led some semiconductor manufacturers to announce prices that are in no way connected to their yield.

Aggressive companies wishing to introduce a new chip on the market will be satisfied with an initial yield of 10%, which proves they can manufacture the chip. They hope that the manufacturing process will improve quickly to the point where yield will reach from 50% to 90%, thus resulting in high profits. This is why the price of components is so closely related to volume, and why single-chip microcomputers can be sold in large quantities for less than two dollars.

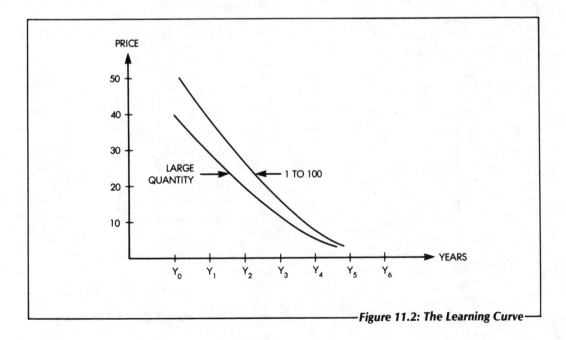

Figure 11.2: The Learning Curve

TECHNOLOGICAL EVOLUTION

The technological evolution of LSI products is proceeding in two directions: toward greater speeds and toward greater component densities.

The *evolution toward higher speeds* has temporarily reached a limit. The physical restrictions of the photolithographic process used today limit the precision with which gates can be defined on the silicon. This in turn limits switching efficiency. As a result, the current limitation on the execution time of a typical instruction is on the order of 1 microsecond, as shown in Figure 11.3. However, a new process, the electron beam process, has been developed which results in greater speed by providing finer resolution. Whenever this process becomes widely used, or whenever some other process is sufficiently refined, the search toward higher speed will resume.

The *evolution toward higher densities* or toward the implementation of more components on a single chip can be achieved either by shrinking the design into a smaller chip area, or by increasing the size of the chip. Both methods are currently being pursued. The component dimensions in a chip today are on the order of 5 microns and will progressively decrease toward 1 micron, the actual limit of the photolithographic

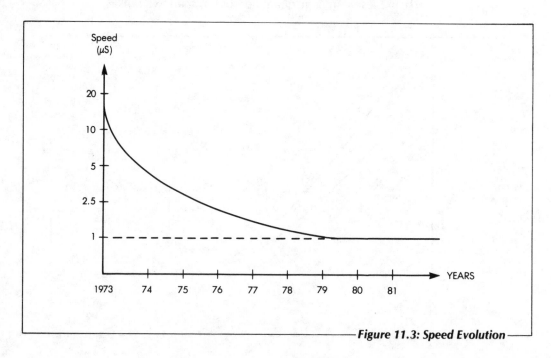

Figure 11.3: Speed Evolution

process. In addition, as processes are becoming better known, the yield and the area of the chip are increasing regularly. There is no theoretical limitation to the maximum area that can be used, and, therefore, for the time being, there is no limitation to the maximum number of components per chip.

Figure 11.4 shows the evolution of density, measured by the number of components per chip. This method is called the "Moore Curve" (Dr. Gordon Moore from Intel was the first to present this prediction in this form to the public).

Simply stated, this method states that the densities of dynamic RAMs quadruple every two years, i.e., the densities double every year. This pattern has been verified for ten years, but the growth has started to slow down. One can reasonably predict that component densities per chip will still continue doubling every few years for several years to come. It is already possible to implement 50,000 to 100,000 transistors on a single chip.

We are progressing into SLSI (Super-Large-Scale-Integration), with up to several hundred thousand transistors on a single chip. At that point it will be possible to implement a complete contemporary computer on a single chip. Each chip might then sell for only a few dollars. The impact of this statement is this: the capability that was available on a large-scale computer selling for a million dollars or more several years ago will be available in the near future as a component of minimal

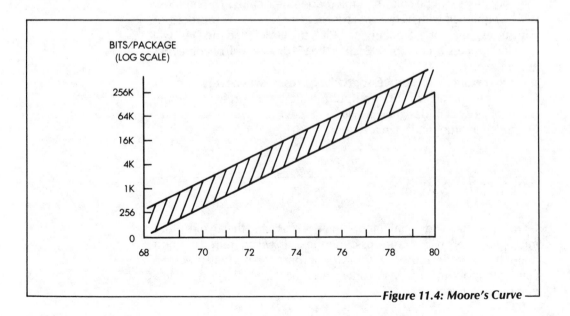

Figure 11.4: Moore's Curve

volume costing only one dollar. The true impact of this phenomenon cannot yet be measured.

For the first time in the history of our industrial age, a true form of "intelligence"—automated intelligence—will be available at minimal cost within a minute volume. It will be possible to associate this intelligence with virtually any man-made device. The consequences of this phenomenon cannot yet be estimated. This is one of the reasons why the emergence of microprocessors has been called the "second industrial revolution."

COMPONENT EVOLUTION

Throughout this book we have made predictions about component evolution. We will summarize these predictions here. Essentially, with the present technology, processing power has become one of the least expensive resources in a system. As a result, it is possible to dedicate processors to virtually any application. Consequently, the structures of the systems themselves will be changed. This intelligent processing capability will eventually be used on virtually every task of a system.

We are entering an era of *distributed processing*. Within the microprocessor system itself, each of the input/output and peripheral chips will become processor-equipped. In fact, we can predict that fewer memory chips will be sold than microcomputer chips. The memory will be equipped with its own microprocessor (or the microprocessor with its own memory). Similarly, the PIO, the UART, and the DAC will be microprocessor-equipped. Each of the LSI devices will become *programmable*.

In other words, microprocessors will be present whenever any other functions (in particular, input/output functions) are present. For any engineer or system designer, it will be necessary to understand programming in order to design a system.

SOCIAL IMPACT

From a human and social standpoint, it is predicted that in the future microprocessors will become as common as (or even more common than) the electric motor is today. Microprocessors will become commmonplace in home and work environments, which will result in a number of conveniences.

More significantly, microprocessors are likely to displace a significant segment of the work force. By automating most of the processes that require simple control algorithms, they will eliminate a large number of jobs. As a result, new and probably more challenging job opportunities will evolve. Education will be the key to successful change. This book has been written as a step in that direction.

ELECTRONIC SYMBOLS
EQUIVALENCES
BASIC SYMBOLS
NEGATIONS

GATES

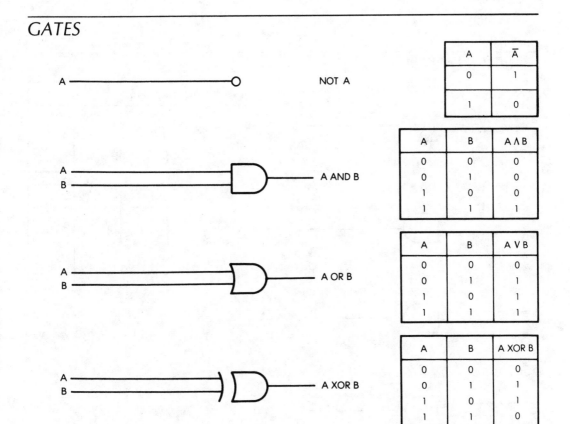

NOT A

A	$\overline{A}$
0	1
1	0

A AND B

A	B	A ∧ B
0	0	0
0	1	0
1	0	0
1	1	1

A OR B

A	B	A ∨ B
0	0	0
0	1	1
1	0	1
1	1	1

A XOR B

A	B	A XOR B
0	0	0
0	1	1
1	0	1
1	1	0

NEGATIONS

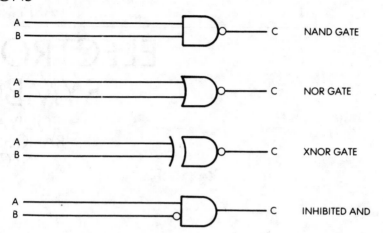

EQUIVALENCES

NAND

A	B	C
0	0	1
0	1	1
1	0	1
1	1	0

NOR

A	B	C
0	0	1
0	1	0
1	0	0
1	1	0

OR

AND

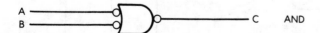

OTHER SYMBOLS

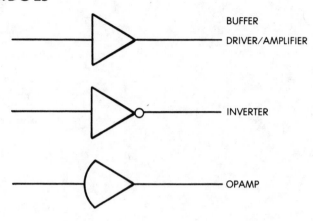

BUFFER
DRIVER/AMPLIFIER

INVERTER

OPAMP

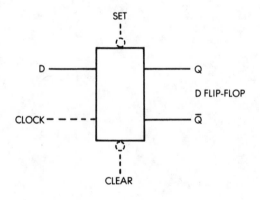

D FLIP-FLOP

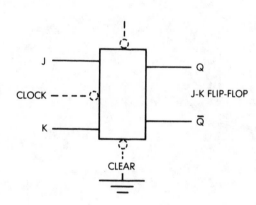

J-K FLIP-FLOP

3-STATE BUFFER

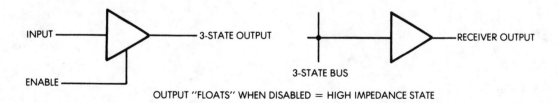

OUTPUT "FLOATS" WHEN DISABLED = HIGH IMPEDANCE STATE

MOTOROLA 6800 INSTRUCTION SET

ABA	Add accumulator B to accumulator A
ADC	Add with carry
ADD	Add without carry
AND	Logical AND
ASL	Arithmetic Shift Left
ASR	Arithmetic Shift Right
BCC	Branch if carry clear
BCS	Branch if carry set
BEQ	Branch if equal
BGE	Branch if greater than or equal to zero
BGT	Branch if greater than zero
BHI	Branch if higher
BIT	Bit test (ACCX), (M)
BLE	Branch if less than or equal to zero
BLS	Branch if lower or same
BLT	Branch if less than zero
BMI	Branch if minus
BNE	Branch if not equal
BPL	Branch if plus
BRA	Branch always (unconditional)
BSR	Branch to subroutine
BVC	Branch if overflow clear
BVS	Branch if overflow set
CBA	Compare accumulators A and B
CLC	Clear carry: C bit = 0
CLI	Clear interrupt mask: I bit = 0
CLR	Clear: ACCX or M = 00
CLV	Clear two's-complement overflow bit: V bit = 0

CMP	Compare: (ACCX), (M)
COM	Complement
CPX	Compare index register: (IX), (M)
DDA	Decimal adjust ACCA
DEC	Decrement
DES	Decrement stack pointer: SP ← (SP) − 1
DEX	Decrement index register: IX ← (IX) − 1
EOR	Exclusive OR: ACCX ← (ACCX) EOR (M)
INC	Increment
INS	Increment stack pointer: SP ← (SP) + 1
INX	Increment index register: IX ← (IX) + 1
JMP	Jump
JSR	Jump to subroutine
LDA	Load accumulator
LDS	Load stack pointer: SP ← (M)
LDX	Load index register: IX ← (M)
LSR	Logical Shift Right
NEG	Negate: ACCX or M ← ($\overline{ACCX \text{ or } M}$)
NOP	No operation
ORA	Inclusive OR
PSH	Push data onto stack
PUL	Pull data from stack
ROL	Rotate left
ROR	Rotate right
RTI	Return from interrupt
RTS	Return from subroutine
SBA	Subtract accumulator: ACCA ← (ACCA) − (ACCB)
SBC	Subtract with carry: ACCX ← (ACCX) − M − C
SEC	Set carry: C bit = 1
SEI	Set interrupt mask: I bit = 1
SEV	Set two's-complement overflow bit: V bit = 1
STA	Store accumulator: M ← (ACCX)

STS	*Store stack pointer*
STX	*Store index register*
SUB	*Subtract: ACCX ← (ACCX) − (M)*
SWI	*Software interrupt: stacks PC, IX, ACCA, ACCB, CC*
TAB	*Transfer from accumulator B to accumulator A:* *ACCA ← (ACCB)*
TAP	*Transfer from ACCA to CC (condition codes register):* *CC ← (ACCA)*
TBA	*Transfer from B to A: ACCA ← (ACCB)*
TPA	*Transfer from processor CC to ACCA: ACCA ← (CC)*
TST	*Test*
TSX	*Transfer from stack pointer to index register:* *IX ← (SP) + 0001*
TXS	*Transfer from index register to stack pointer:* *SP ← (IX) − 0001*
WAI	*Wait for interrupt: PC ← (PC) + 00001*

Symbols:

ACCA	*Accumulator A*
ACCB	*Accumulator B*
ACCX	*Accumulator A or B*
PC	*Program Counter*
SP	*Stack Pointer*
IX	*Index Register*
CC	*Condition Codes Register*
M	*Memory Address*

INTEL 8080 INSTRUCTION SET

( ) = contents; r = register; M = memory address defined by H and L

ACI	Add immediate to A with carry
ADC M	Add memory to A with carry
ADC r	Add register to A with carry: A ← (A) + (r) + C
ADD M	Add memory to A
ADD r	Add register to A: A ← (A) + (r)
ADI	Add immediate to A
ANA M	AND memory with A
ANA r	AND register with A: A ← (A) AND (r)
ANI	AND immediate with A
CALL	Call unconditional
CC	Call on carry
CM	Call on minus
CMA	Complement A
CMC	Complement carry
CMP M	Compare memory with A
CMP r	Compare register with A
CNC	Call on no carry
CNZ	Call on no zero
CP	Call on positive
CPE	Call on parity even
CPI	Compare immediate with A
CPO	Call on parity odd
CZ	Call on zero
DAA	Decimal adjust A
DAD B	Add B & C to H & L
DAD D	Add D & E to H & L
DAD H	Add H & L to H & L

DAD SP	*Add stack pointer to H & L*
DCR M	*Decrement memory*
DCR r	*Decrement register r: r ← (r) − 1*
DCX B	*Decrement B & C*
DCX D	*Decrement D & E*
DCX H	*Decrement H & L*
DCX SP	*Decrement stack pointer*
DI	*Disable interrupt*
EI	*Enable interrupt*
HLT	*Halt*
IN	*Input*
INR M	*Increment memory*
INR r	*Increment register r: r ← (r) + 1*
INX B	*Increment B & C registers*
INX D	*Increment D & E registers*
INX H	*Increment H & L registers*
INX SP	*Increment stack pointer*
JC	*Jump on carry*
JM	*Jump on minus*
JMP	*Jump unconditional*
JNC	*Jump on no carry*
JNZ	*Jump on no zero*
JP	*Jump on positive*
JPE	*Jump on parity even*
JPO	*Jump on parity odd*
JZ	*Jump on zero*
LDA	*Load A direct*
LDAX B	*Load A indirect B*
LDAX D	*Load A indirect D*
LHLD	*Load H & L direct*
LXI B	*Load immediate register pair B & C*
LXI D	*Load immediate register pair D & E*
LXI H	*Load immediate register pair H & L*
LXI SP	*Load immediate stack pointer*
MOV M,r	*Move register to memory*
MOV r,M	*Move memory to register r*

MOV r1, r2	*Move r2 to register r1: r1 ← (r2)*
MVI M	*Move immediate memory*
MVI r	*Move immediate register r*
NOP	*No operation*
ORA M	*OR memory with A*
ORA r	*OR register with A: A ← (A) OR (r)*
ORI	*OR immediate with A*
OUT	*Output*
PCHL	*H & L to program counter*
POP B	*Pop register pair B & C off stack*
POP D	*Pop register pair D & E off stack*
POP H	*Pop register pair H & L off stack*
POP PSW	*POP A and flags off stack*
PUSH B	*Push register pair B & C on stack*
PUSH D	*Push register pair D & E on stack*
PUSH H	*Push register pair H & L on stack*
PUSH PSW	*Push A and flags on stack*
RAL	*Rotate A left through carry*
RAR	*Rotate A right through carry*
RC	*Return on carry*
RET	*Return*
RLC	*Rotate A left*
RM	*Return on minus*
RNC	*Return on no carry*
RNZ	*Return on no zero*
RP	*Return on positive*
RPE	*Return on parity even*
RPO	*Return on parity odd*
RRC	*Rotate A right*
RST	*Restart*
RZ	*Return on zero*
SBB M	*Subtract memory from A with borrow*
SBB r	*Subtract register from A with borrow*
SBI	*Subtract immediate from A with borrow*
SHLD	*Store H & L direct*
SPHL	*H & L to stack pointer*
STA	*Store A direct*

STAX B	*Store A indirect B*
STAX D	*Store A indirect D*
STC	*Set carry*
SUB M	*Subtract memory from A*
SUB r	*Subtract register from A: A ← (A) − (r)*
SUI	*Subtract immediate from A*
XCHG	*Exchange D & E, H & L registers*
XRA M	*Exclusive OR memory with A*
XRA r	*Exclusive OR register with A: A ← (A) XOR (r)*
XRI	*Exclusive OR immediate with A*
XTHL	*Exchange top of stack, H & L*

APPENDIX D

IEEE 696 S-100 BUS SIGNALS

CONTACT#	SYMBOL*	ACTIVE LEVEL High/Low	DESCRIPTION
1	+8V		Positive 8 volts, unregulated.
2	+16V		Positive 16 volts, unregulated.
3	XRDY	H	External ready input to bus master. Bus is ready when both XRDY and RDY are true.
4	VI0	L	Vectored interrupt line 0.
5	VI1	L	Vectored interrupt line 1.
6	VI2	L	Vectored interrupt line 2.
7	VI3	L	Vectored interrupt line 3.
8	VI4	L	Vectored interrupt line 4.
9	VI5	L	Vectored interrupt line 5.
10	VI6	L	Vectored interrupt line 6.
11	VI7	L	Vectored interrupt line 7.
12	NMI	L	Non-maskable interrupt.
13	PWRFAIL	L	Power fail bus signal.
14	DMA3	L	Temporary master priority bit 3.
15	A18	H	Extended address bit 18.
16	A16	H	Extended address bit 16.
17	A17	H	Extended address bit 17.
18	SDSB	L	Status Disable. Disables line drivers for the 8 status signals.
19	CDSB	L	Control Disable. Disables line drivers for the 5 control output signals.
20	GND		System ground, common with pin 100.

*Note: Control output bus signal names are prefixed with a 'p'.

Status signal names are prefixed with an 's'.

CONTACT#	SYMBOL*	ACTIVE LEVEL High/Low	DESCRIPTION
21	NDEF		*Not to be defined.*
22	ADSB	L	*Address Disable. Disables the line drivers for the 16 address signals.*
23	DODSB	L	*Data Out Disable. Disables the line drivers for the 8 data output signals.*
24	φ	H	*Master timing signal for the bus.*
25	pSTVAL	L	*Status valid strobe.*
26	pHLDA	H	*Hold Acknowledge. Used by a permanent bus master to acknowledge a hold request for bus master transfer.*
27	RFU		*Reserved for future use.*
28	RFU		*Reserved for future use.*
29	A5	H	*Address bit 5.*
30	A4	H	*Address bit 4.*
31	A3	H	*Address bit 3.*
32	A15	H	*Address bit 15. (Most significant for non-extended addressing.)*
33	A12	H	*Address bit 12.*
34	A9	H	*Address bit 9.*
35	DO1/DATA1	H	*Data out bit 1, bidirectional data bit 1.*
36	DO0/DATA0	H	*Data out bit 0, bidirectional data bit 0.*
37	A10	H	*Address bit 10.*
38	DO4/DATA4	H	*Data out bit 4, bidirectional data bit 4.*
39	DO5/DATA5	H	*Data out bit 5, bidirectional data bit 5.*
40	DO6/DATA6	H	*Data out bit 6, bidirectional data bit 6.*
41	D12/DATA10	H	*Data in bit 2, bidirectional data bit 10.*
42	D13/DATA11	H	*Data in bit 3, bidirectional data bit 11.*
43	D17/DATA15	H	*Data in bit 7, bidirectional data bit 15.*
44	sM1	H	*Status signal indicating that the current cycle is an opcode fetch.*
45	sOUT	H	*Status signal identifying bus cycles transferring data to an output device.*
46	sINP	H	*Status signal identifying bus cycles transferring data from an input device.*

CONTACT#	SYMBOL*	ACTIVE LEVEL High/Low	DESCRIPTION
47	sMEMR	H	*Memory Read. Status signal identifying bus cycles which transfer data from memory to a bus master and are not interrupt acknowledge instruction fetch cycles.*
48	sHLTA	H	*Status signal acknowledging execution of an HLT (halt) instruction.*
49	CLOCK		*2 MHz 40% to 60% duty cycle clock.*
50	GND		*System ground, common with pin 100.*
51	+8V		*Positive 8 volts, unregulated. Common with pin 1.*
52	−16V		*Negative 16 volts, unregulated.*
53	GND		*System ground, common with pin 100.*
54	SLAVE CLR	L	*A signal to reset bus slaves. Must be active with POC, can be generated externally.*
55	DMA0	L	*Temporary master priority bit 0.*
56	DMA1	L	*Temporary master priority bit 1.*
57	DMA2	L	*Temporary master priority bit 2.*
58	sXTRQ	L	*Sixteen-bit Request. Status signal requesting 16-bit slaves to assert SIXTN.*
59	A19	H	*Extended address bit 19.*
60	SIXTN	L	*Signal generated by 16-bit slaves in response to the sixteen-bit request signal sXTRQ, indicating that a 16-bit transfer is possible.*
61	A20	H	*Extended address bit 20.*
62	A21	H	*Extended address bit 21.*
63	A22	H	*Extended address bit 22.*
64	A23	H	*Extended address bit 23.*
65	NDEF		*Not to be defined.*
66	NDEF		*Not to be defined.*
67	PHANTOM	L	*A bus signal which disables normal slave devices and enables phantom slaves. Used primarily for bootstrapping systems without front panels.*

CONTACT#	SYMBOL*	ACTIVE LEVEL High/Low	DESCRIPTION
68	MWRT	H	Memory write strobe. Indicates memory write bus cycles. MWRT is generated as follows: MWRT = (pWR AND NOT (sOUT)).
69	RFU		Reserved for future use.
70	GND		System ground, common with pin 100.
71	RFU		Reserved for future use.
72	RDY	H	One of two ready inputs to bus master.
73	INT	L	Primary interrupt request signal.
74	HOLD	L	Hold Request. Used by a temporary master to request control of the bus.
75	RESET	L	Resets bus master devices. Must be active with POC, and may be generated externally.
76	pSYNC	H	Control signal identifying start of bus cycle.
77	pWR	L	Write. Control signal indicating valid data on DO bus or data bus.
78	pDBIN	H	Data Bus In. Control signal requesting data on the DI bus or data bus from the currently addressed slave.
79	A0	H	Address bit 0 (least significant).
80	A1	H	Address bit 1.
81	A2	H	Address bit 2.
82	A6	H	Address bit 6.
83	A7	H	Address bit 7.
84	A8	H	Address bit 8.
85	A13	H	Address bit 13.
86	A14	H	Address bit 14.
87	A11	H	Address bit 11.
88	DO2/DATA2	H	Data out bit 2, bidirectional data bit 2.
89	DO3/DATA3	H	Data out bit 3, bidirectional data bit 3.
90	DO7/DATA7	H	Data out bit 7, bidirectional data bit 7.
91	DI4/DATA12	H	Data in bit 4, bidirectional data bit 12.
92	DI5/DATA13	H	Data in bit 5, bidirectional data bit 13.
93	DI6/DATA14	H	Data in bit 6, bidirectional data bit 14.

CONTACT#	SYMBOL*	ACTIVE LEVEL High/Low	DESCRIPTION
94	DI1/DATA9	H	*Data in bit 1, bidirectional data bit 9.*
95	DI0/DATA8	H	*Data in bit 0, bidirectional data bit 8.*
96	sINTA	H	*Interrupt Acknowledge. Status signal identifying bus cycles following an accepted interrupt request presented on INT.*
97	sWO	L	*Write Out. Status signal identifying a bus cycle transferring data from a bus master to a slave.*
98	ERROR	L	*Bus status signal indicating an error condition during current bus cycle.*
99	POC	L	*Power-On Clear. Resets all bus devices on power-up.*
100	GND		*System ground.*

APPENDIX E

ASCII CODE

THE ASCII SYMBOLS

NUL	*Null*
SOH	*Start of Heading*
STX	*Start of Text*
ETX	*End of Text*
EOT	*End of Transmission*
ENQ	*Enquiry*
ACK	*Acknowledge*
BEL	*Bell*
BS	*Backspace*
HT	*Horizontal Tabulation*
LF	*Line Feed*
VT	*Vertical Tabulation*
FF	*Form Feed*
CR	*Carriage Return*
SO	*Shift Out*
SI	*Shift In*
DLE	*Data Link Escape*
DC	*Device Control*
NAK	*Negative Acknowledge*
SYN	*Synchronous Idle*
ETB	*End of Transmission Block*
CAN	*Cancel*
EM	*End of Medium*
SUB	*Substitute*
ESC	*Escape*
FS	*File Separator*
GS	*Group Separator*
RS	*Record Separator*
US	*Unit Separator*
SP	*Space (Blank)*
DEL	*Delete*

ASCII IN DECIMAL, OCTAL, HEXADECIMAL

#	OCTAL	HEX	CHAR	#	OCTAL	HEX	CHAR	#	OCTAL	HEX	CHAR	#	OCTAL	HEX	CHAR
0	000	00	NUL	32	040	20	SP	64	100	40	@	96	140	60	
1	001	01	SOH	33	041	21	!	65	101	41	A	97	141	61	a
2	002	02	STX	34	042	22	''	66	102	42	B	98	142	62	b
3	003	03	ETX	35	043	23	#	67	103	43	C	99	143	63	c
4	004	04	EOT	36	044	24	$	68	104	44	D	100	144	64	d
5	005	05	ENQ	37	045	25	%	69	105	45	E	101	145	65	e
6	006	06	ACK	38	046	26	&	70	106	46	F	102	146	66	f
7	007	07	BEL	39	047	27	'	71	107	47	G	103	147	67	g
8	010	08	BS	40	050	28	(	72	110	48	H	104	150	68	h
9	011	09	HT	41	051	29	)	73	111	49	I	105	151	69	i
10	012	0A	LF	42	052	2A	*	74	112	4A	J	106	152	6A	j
11	013	0B	VT	43	053	2B	+	75	113	4B	K	107	153	6B	k
12	014	0C	FF	44	054	2C	,	76	114	4C	L	108	154	6C	l
13	015	0D	CR	45	055	2D	-	77	115	4D	M	109	155	6D	m
14	016	0E	SO	46	056	2E	.	78	116	4E	N	110	156	6E	n
15	017	0F	SI	47	057	2F	/	79	117	4F	O	111	157	6F	o
16	020	10	DLE	48	060	30	0	80	120	50	P	112	160	70	p
17	021	11	DC1	49	061	31	1	81	121	51	Q	113	161	71	q
18	022	12	DC2	50	062	32	2	82	122	52	R	114	162	72	r
19	023	13	DC3	51	063	33	3	83	123	53	S	115	163	73	s
20	024	14	DC4	52	064	34	4	84	124	54	T	116	164	74	t
21	025	15	NAK	53	065	35	5	85	125	55	U	117	165	75	u
22	026	16	SYN	54	066	36	6	86	126	56	V	118	166	76	v
23	027	17	ETB	55	067	37	7	87	127	57	W	119	167	77	w
24	030	18	CAN	56	070	38	8	88	130	58	X	120	170	78	x
25	031	19	EM	57	071	39	9	89	131	59	Y	121	171	79	y
26	032	1A	SUB	58	072	3A	:	90	132	5A	Z	122	172	7A	z
27	033	1B	ESC	59	073	3B	;	91	133	5B	[	123	173	7B	{
28	034	1C	FS	60	074	3C	<	92	134	5C	\	124	174	7C	¦
29	035	1D	GS	61	075	3D	=	93	135	5D	]	125	175	7D	}
30	036	1E	RS	62	076	3E	>	94	136	5E	↑	126	176	7E	~
31	037	1F	US	63	077	3F	?	95	137	5F	_	127	177	7F	DEL

Note: bit 7 (parity bit) is set to zero in this table.

MICROPROCESSOR MANUFACTURERS

AMD (Advanced Micro Devices)
901 Thompson Place
Sunnyvale, CA 94086
(408) 732-2400
Telex: 346306

AMI (American Microsystems)
3800 Homestead Road
Santa Clara, CA 95051
(408) 246-0330

DATA GENERAL
Route 9
Southborough, MA 01772
(617) 485-9100
Telex: 48460

ELECTRONIC ARRAYS
550 East Middlefield Road
Mountain View, CA 94043
(415) 964-4321

FAIRCHILD SEMICONDUCTOR
1725 Technology Drive
San Jose, CA 95110
(408) 998-0123

GI (General Instrument)
600 West John Street
Hicksville, NY 11802
(516) 733-3107
TWX: (510) 221-1666

HARRIS SEMICONDUCTOR
Box 883
Melbourne, FL 32901
(305) 724-7430
TWX: (510) 959-6259

HITACHI America
1800 Bering Drive
San Jose, CA 95112
(408) 292-6404
Telex: 17-1581

HUGHES Solid State Products
500 Superior Avenue
Newport Beach, CA 92663
(714) 759-2411
TWX: (910) 596-1374

INTEL
3065 Bowers Avenue
Santa Clara, CA 95051
(408) 987-8080
Telex: 346372

INTERSIL
10710 Tantau Avenue
Cupertino, CA 95014
(408) 996-5000
TWX: (916) 338-0228

ITT Semiconductor
175C New Boston Street
Woburn, MA 01801
(617) 935-6750

MMI (Monolithic Memories)
1165 East Arques Avenue
Sunnyvale, CA 94086
(408) 739-3535

MOS TECHNOLOGY
950 Rittenhouse Road
Norristown, PA 19401
(215) 666-7950
TWX: (510) 660-4033

MOSTEK
1215 West Crosby Road
Carrollton, TX 75006
(214) 323-6000
Telex: 30423

MOTOROLA SEMICONDUCTOR
Box 20912
Phoenix, AZ 85036
(602) 244-6900
Telex: 67325

NEC Information Systems
36 Washington Street
Wellesley Hills, MA 02181
(617) 431-1140

NS (National Semiconductor)
2900 Semiconductor Drive
Santa Clara, CA 95051
(408) 732-5000
TWX: (910) 339-9240

OKI Semiconductor
Suite 405,
1333 Lawrence Expressway
Santa Clara, CA 95051
(408) 984-4840

RAYTHEON Semiconductor
350 Ellis Street
Mountain View, CA 94042
(415) 968-9211
TWX: (910) 379-6481

RCA Solid State
Box 591
Somerville, NJ 08876
(201) 685-6000
TWX: (710) 480-9333

ROCKWELL INTERNATIONAL
3310 Miraloma Avenue
Box 3669
Anaheim, CA 92803
(714) 632-3698

SGS ATES
240 Bear Hill Road
Waltham, MA 02154
(617) 890-6688
Telex: 923495

SIGNETICS
811 East Arques Avenue
Sunnyvale, CA 94086
(408) 739-7700

SYNERTEK
3001 Stender Way
Santa Clara, CA 95051
(408) 988-5611

TI (Texas Instruments)
MOS Microcomputers
P.O. Box 1443
Houston, TX 77001
(713) 490-2000

TOSHIBA America
2151 Michelson Drive,
Suite 190
Irvine, CA 92715
(714) 955-1155
TWX: (910) 595-1127

TRW LSI Products
P.O. Box 2472
La Jolla, CA 92038
(714) 578-5990

WESTERN DIGITAL
3128 Redhill Avenue
Newport Beach, CA 92663
(714) 557-3550
TWX: (910) 595-1139

ZILOG
10340 Bubb Road
Cupertino, CA 95014
(408) 446-4666

APPENDIX **G**

ACRONYMS

AC	*Alternating Current*
ACC	*Accumulator*
ACK	*Acknowledge*
A/D	*Analog to Digital*
ADCCP	*Advanced Data Communication Control Procedure*
ALU	*Arithmetic Logic Unit*
ANSI	*American National Standards Institute*
ASCII	*American Standard Code for Information Interchange*
ASR	*Automatic Send and Receive*
BCD	*Binary Coded Decimal*
BCR	*Byte Count Register*
BPS	*Bits Per Second*
BRA	*Branch, (Go To)*
BSC	*Binary Synchronous Communication*
C	*Carry*
CAD	*Computer Aided Design*
CAM	*Contents-Addressable Memory*
CCD	*Charge-Coupled Device*
CE	*Chip Enable*
CLK	*Clock*
CML	*Current Mode Logic*
CMOS	*Complementary MOS*
CPG	*Clock Pulse Generator*
CPS	*Characters Per Second*
CPU	*Central Processor Unit*
CR	*Card Reader; Carriage Return*
CRC	*Cyclic Redundancy Check*
CROM	*Control ROM*
CRT	*Cathode Ray Tube*
CRTC	*CRT Controller*
CS	*Chip Select*

CTS	*Clear To Send*
CU	*Control Unit*
CY	*Carry*
D	*Data*
D/A	*Digital to Analog*
DC	*Direct Current*
DC	*Don't Care*
DCD	*Data Carrier Detect*
DIP	*Dual In-Line Package*
DMA	*Direct Memory Access*
DMAC	*DMA Controller*
DMOS	*Double-Diffused MOS*
DNC	*Direct Numerical Control*
DOS	*Disk Operating System*
DPM	*Digital Panel Meter*
DTL	*Diode Transistor Logic*
DTR	*Data Terminal Ready*
D0-7	*Data Lines 0 Through 7*
E	*Empty; Enable (Clock)*
EAROM	*Electrically Alterable ROM*
EBCDIC	*Extended Binary-Coded-Decimal Information Code*
ECL	*Emitter Coupled Logic*
EDP	*Electronic Data Processing*
EFL	*Emitter Follower Logic*
EMI	*Electromagnetic Interference*
EOC	*End of Conversion*
EOF	*End of File*
EOR	*Exclusive OR*
EOT	*End of Text, Tape*
EPROM	*Erasable PROM*
FAMOS	*Floating Gate Avalanche MOS*
FDC	*Floppy Disk Controller*
FDM	*Frequency-Division Multiplexing*
FET	*Field-Effect Transistor*
FF	*Flip-Flop*
FIFO	*First-In-First-Out*
FPLA	*Field PLA*
FSK	*Frequency Shift Keying*
G (carry)	*Generate*

GP	*General Purpose*
GPIB	*General Purpose Interface Bus*
HDLC	*High-Level Data Link Control*
HEX	*Hexadecimal*
HPIB	*Hewlett-Packard Interface Bus*
I	*Interrupt;Interrupt Mask*
IC	*Integrated Circuit*
INT	*Interrupt*
I/O	*Input/Output*
IOCS	*I/O Control System*
IRQ	*Interrupt Request*
I²L	*Integrated Injection Logic*
JAN	*Joint Army-Navy*
JP	*Jump*
K (1024)	*Kilo*
KSR	*Keyboard Send Receive*
LCD	*Liquid Crystal Display*
LED	*Light-Emitting Diode*
LIFO	*Last-In-First-Out*
LOC	*Loop On-Line Control*
LP	*Line Printer*
LPM	*Lines Per Minute*
LPS	*Low-Power Schottky*
LRC	*Longitudinal Redundancy Check*
LSB	*Least Significant Bit*
LSI	*Large Scale Integration*
MNOS	*Metal Nitride Oxide Semiconductor*
MOS	*Metal Oxide Semiconductor*
MPU	*Microprocessor Unit*
MSB	*Most Significant Bit*
MSI	*Medium Scale Integration*
MTBF	*Mean Time Between Failures*
MUX	*Multiplexer*
N	*Negative (Sign Bit)*
NDRO	*Non-Destructive Read Out*

NMOS	N-Channel MOS
NVM	Non-Volatile Memory
OCR	Optical Character Reader
OEM	Original Equipment Manufacturer
OP	Operation
OV	Overflow
P	Parity; (Carry) Progagate
PABX	Private Automatic Branch Exchange
PBX	Private Branch Exchange
PC	Printed Circuit; Program Counter
PCI/O	Program Controlled I/O
PCM	Pulse Code Modulation
PFR	Power-Fail Restart
PIC	Priority Interrupt Control
PIO	Programmable I/O Chip (Interface)
PIT	Programmable Interval-Timer
PLA	Programmable Logic-Array
PLL	Phase-Locked Loop
PMOS	P-Channel MOS
POS	Point-of-Sale Terminal
PROM	(Field) Programmable ROM
PSW	Program Status Word
PTP	Paper Tape Punch
PTR	Paper Tape Reader
Q	AC extension
QPL	Qualified Products List
R	Read
RALU	Register Arithmetic Logic Unit
RAM	Random Access Memory
RDSR	Receiver Data Service Request
RDY	Ready
RES	Reset
RF	Radio Frequency
RMS	Root Mean Square
ROM	Read Only Memory
RPROM	Reprogrammable PROM
RPT	Repeat
RS	Register Select
RST	Restart

RTC	*Real-Time Clock*
RTS	*Request To Send*
R/W	*Read/Write Memory*
Rx	*Receiver*
SAR	*Successive Approximation Register*
SDLC	*Synchronous Data Link Control*
SEC	*Scanning Electron Microscope*
SEM	*Standard Electronic Module*
S/H	*Sample and Hold*
S/N	*Signal to Noise*
SOS	*Silicon-On-Sapphire*
SR	*Service Request*
SSI	*Small Scale Integration*
STB	*Strobe*
SUB	*Subroutine*
TDM	*Time Division Multiplexing*
TDSR	*Transmitter Data Service Request*
TSS	*Time-Sharing System*
TTL	*Transistor-Transistor Logic*
TTY	*Teletypewriter*
Tx	*Transmitter*
UART	*Universal Asynchronous Receiver Transmitter*
USRT	*Universal Synchronous Receiver Transmitter*
UV	*Ultraviolet*
VMOS	*Vertical MOS*
Vss	*Ground*
W	*Write*
WPM	*Words Per Minute*
X	*Index*
XOR	*Exclusive OR*
Z	*Zero Bit*
ϕ	*(Clock) Phase*
μC	*Microcomputer*
μP	*Microprocessor*

Index

Selections from The SYBEX Library

Special Interest

COMPUTER POWER FOR YOUR LAW OFFICE
by Daniel Remer
142 pp., Ref. 0-109
How to use computers to reach peak productivity in your law office, simply and inexpensively.

THE COLLEGE STUDENT'S PERSONAL COMPUTER HANDBOOK
by Bryan Pfaffenberger
210 pp., illustr., Ref. 0-170
This friendly guide will aid students in selecting a computer system for college study, managing information in a college course, and writing research papers.

CELESTIAL BASIC
by Eric Burgess
300 pp., 65 illustr., Ref. 0-087
A collection of BASIC programs that rapidly complete the chores of typical astronomical computations. It's like having a planetarium in your own home! Displays apparent movement of stars, planets and meteor showers.

COMPUTER POWER FOR YOUR ACCOUNTING FIRM
by James Morgan, C.P.A.
250 pp., illustr., Ref. 0-164
This book is a convenient source of information about computerizing your accounting office, with an emphasis on hardware and software options.

ESPIONAGE IN THE SILICON VALLEY
by John D. Halamka
200 pp., illustr., Ref. 0-225
Discover the behind-the-scenes stories of famous high-tech spy cases you've seen in the headlines.

PERSONAL COMPUTERS AND SPECIAL NEEDS
by Frank G. Bowe
175 pp., illustr., Ref. 0-193
Learn how people are overcoming problems with hearing, vision, mobility, and learning, through the use of computer technology.

ASTROLOGY ON YOUR PERSONAL COMPUTER
by Hank Friedman
225 pp., illustr., Ref. 0-226
An invaluable aid for astrologers who want to streamline their calculation and data management chores with the right combination of hardware and software.

Computer Specific

Apple II—Macintosh

THE PRO-DOS HANDBOOK
by Timothy Rice/Karen Rice
225 pp., illustr., Ref. 0-230
All Pro-DOS users, from beginning to advanced, will find this book packed with vital information. The book covers the basics, and then addresses itself to the Apple II user who needs to interface with Pro-DOS when programming in BASIC. Learn how Pro-DOS uses memory, and how it handles text files, binary files, graphics, and sound. Includes a chapter on machine language programming.

THE MACINTOSH™ TOOLBOX
**by Huxham, Burnard,
and Takatsuka**

300 pp., illustr., Ref. 0-249
This tutorial on the advanced features
of the Macintosh toolbox is an ideal
companion to The Macintosh BASIC
Handbook.

Commodore 64/VIC-20

THE BEST OF COMMODORE
64™ SOFTWARE
by Thomas Blackadar

150 pp., illustr., Ref. 0-194
Save yourself time and frustration with this
buyer's guide to Commodore 64 software. Find the best game, music, education, and home management programs
on the market today.

YOUR FIRST COMMODORE 64™
PROGRAM
by Rodnay Zaks

182 pp., illustr., Ref. 0-172
You can learn to write simple programs
without any prior knowledge of mathe-
matics or computers! Guided by colorful
illustrations and step-by-step instructions,
you'll be constructing programs within an
hour or two.

COMMODORE 64™ BASIC
PROGRAMS IN MINUTES
by Stanley R. Trost

170 pp., illustr., Ref. 0-154
Here is a practical set of programs for
business, finance, real estate, data an-
alysis, record keeping, and educational
applications.

PARENTS, KIDS, AND THE
COMMODORE 64™
by Lynne Alper and Meg Holmberg

110 pp., illustr., Ref. 0-234
This book answers parents' questions
about the educational possibilities of the
Commodore 64.

CP/M Systems

THE CP/M® HANDBOOK
by Rodnay Zaks

320 pp., 100 illustr., Ref 0-048
An indispensable reference and guide to
CP/M—the most widely-used operating
system for small computers.

MASTERING CP/M®
by Alan R. Miller

398 pp., illustr., Ref. 0-068
For advanced CP/M users or systems
programmers who want maximum use of
the CP/M operating system . . . takes up
where our *CP/M Handbook* leaves off.

THE BEST OF
CP/M® SOFTWARE
by John D. Halamka

250 pp., Ref. 0-100
This book reviews tried-and-tested, com-
mercially available software for your
CP/M system.

THE CP/M PLUS™ HANDBOOK
by Alan R. Miller

250 pp., illustr., Ref. 0-158
This guide is easy for beginners to
understand, yet contains valuable information for advanced users of CP/M Plus
(Version 3).

IBM PC and
Compatibles

THE ABC'S OF THE IBM® PC
by Joan Lasselle and Carol Ramsay

143 pp., illustr., Ref. 0-102
This book will take you through the first
crucial steps in learning to use the IBM PC.

THE BEST OF IBM® PC
SOFTWARE
by Stanley R. Trost

351 pp., Ref. 0-104
Separates the wheat from the chaff in the
world of IBM PC software. Tells you what
to expect from the best available IBM PC
programs.

Software Specific

Spreadsheets

VISICALC® FOR SCIENCE AND ENGINEERING
by Stanley R. Trost and Charles Pomernacki
203 pp., illustr., Ref. 0-096
More than 50 programs for solving technical problems in science and engineering. Applications range from math and statistics to electrical and electronic engineering.

DOING BUSINESS WITH MULTIPLAN™
by Richard Allen King and Stanley R. Trost
250 pp., illustr., Ref. 0-148
This book will show you how using Multiplan can be nearly as easy as learning to use a pocket calculator. It presents a collection of templates for business applications.

MASTERING VISICALC®
by Douglas Hergert
217 pp., 140 illustr., Ref. 0-090
Explains how to use the VisiCalc "electronic spreadsheet" functions and provides examples of each. Makes using this powerful program simple.

DOING BUSINESS WITH VISICALC®
by Stanley R. Trost
260 pp., illustr., Ref. 0-086
Presents accounting and management planning applications—from financial statements to master budgets; from pricing models to investment strategies.

DOING BUSINESS WITH SUPERCALC™
by Stanley R. Trost
248 pp., illustr., Ref. 0-095
Presents accounting and management planning applications—from financial statements to master budgets; from pricing models to investment strategies.

MULTIPLAN™ ON THE COMMODORE 64™
by Richard Allen King
260 pp., illustr., Ref. 0-231
This clear, straighforward guide will give you a firm grasp on Multiplan's functions, as well as provide a collection of useful template programs.

Word Processing

INTRODUCTION TO WORDSTAR®
by Arthur Naiman
202 pp., 30 illustr., Ref. 0-134
Makes it easy to learn WordStar, a powerful word processing program for personal computers.

PRACTICAL WORDSTAR® USES
by Julie Anne Arca
303 pp., illustr., Ref. 0-107
Pick your most time-consuming office tasks and this book will show you how to streamline them with WordStar.

THE COMPLETE GUIDE TO MULTIMATE™
by Carol Holcomb Dreger
250 pp., illustr., Ref. 0-229
A concise introduction to the many practical applications of this powerful word processing program.

THE THINKTANK™ BOOK
by Jonathan Kamin
200 pp., illustr., Ref. 0-224
Learn how the ThinkTank program can help you organize your thoughts, plans, and activities.

Data Base Management Systems

UNDERSTANDING dBASE III™
by Alan Simpson
250 pp., illustr., Ref. 0-267
For experienced dBASE II programmers, data base and program design are covered in detail; with many examples and illustrations.

UNDERSTANDING dBASE II™
by Alan Simpson
260 pp., illustr., Ref. 0-147
Learn programming techniques for mailing label systems, bookkeeping, and data management, as well as ways to interface dBASE II with other software systems.

ADVANCED TECHNIQUES in dBASE II™
by Alan Simpson
250 pp., illustr., Ref. 0-228
If you are an experienced dBASE II programmer and would like to begin customizing your own programs, this book is for you. It is a well-structured tutorial that offers programming techniques applicable to a wide variety of situations. Data base and program design are covered in detail, and the many examples and illustrations clarify the text.

Integrated Software

MASTERING SYMPHONY™
by Douglas Cobb
763 pp., illustr., Ref. 0-244
This bestselling book provides all the information you will need to put Symphony to work for you right away. Packed with practical models for the business user.

SYMPHONY™ ENCORE: PROGRAM NOTES
by Dick Andersen
325 pp., illustr., Ref. 0-247
Organized as a reference tool, this book gives shortcuts for using Symphony commands and functions, with troubleshooting advice.

JAZZ ON THE MACINTOSH™
by Joseph Caggiano and Michael McCarthy
400 pp., illustr., Ref. 0-265
The complete tutorial on the ins and outs of the season's hottest software, with tips on integrating its functions into efficient business projects.

MASTERING FRAMEWORK™
by Doug Hergert
450 pp., illustr., Ref. 0-248
This tutorial guides the beginning user through all the functions and features of this integrated software package, geared to the business environment.

ADVANCED TECHNIQUES IN FRAMEWORK™
by Alan Simpson
250 pp., illustr., Ref. 0-267
In order to begin customizing your own models with Framework, you'll need a thorough knowledge of Fred programming languages, and this book provides this information in a complete, well-organized form.

ADVANCED BUSINESS MODELS WITH 1-2-3™
by Stanley R. Trost
250 pp., illustr., Ref. 0-159
If you are a business professional using the 1-2-3 software package, you will find the spreadsheet and graphics models provided in this book easy to use "as is" in everyday business situations.

THE ABC'S OF 1-2-3™
by Chris Gilbert and Laurie Williams
225 pp., illustr., Ref. 0-168
For those new to the LOTUS 1-2-3 program, this book offers step-by-step instructions in mastering its spreadsheet, data base, and graphing capabilities.

MASTERING APPLEWORKS™
by Elna Tymes
250 pp., illustr., Ref. 0-240
Here is a business-oriented introduction to AppleWorks, the new integrated software package from Apple. No experience with computers is assumed.

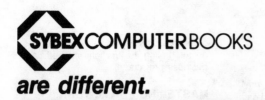

SYBEX COMPUTER BOOKS

are different.

Here is why . . .

At SYBEX, each book is designed with you in mind. Every manuscript is carefully selected and supervised by our editors, who are themselves computer experts. We publish the best authors, whose technical expertise is matched by an ability to write clearly and to communicate effectively. Programs are thoroughly tested for accuracy by our technical staff. Our computerized production department goes to great lengths to make sure that each book is well-designed.

In the pursuit of timeliness, SYBEX has achieved many publishing firsts. SYBEX was among the first to integrate personal computers used by authors and staff into the publishing process. SYBEX was the first to publish books on the CP/M operating system, microprocessor interfacing techniques, word processing, and many more topics.

Expertise in computers and dedication to the highest quality product have made SYBEX a world leader in computer book publishing. Translated into fourteen languages, SYBEX books have helped millions of people around the world to get the most from their computers. We hope we have helped you, too.

For a complete catalog of our publications:

SYBEX, Inc. 2344 Sixth Street, Berkeley, California 94710
Tel: (415) 848-8233   Telex: 336311